THACKRAY'S

2018

INVESTOR'S
GUIDE

Brooke Thackray MBA, CIM, CFP

Published in 2017 by: MountAlpha Media:

alphamountain.com

ISBN13: 978-0-9918735-8-6

Printed and Bound in Canada by Webcom Ltd.

10 9 8 7 6 5 4 3 2 1

Thackray's 2018 Investor's Guide

To my wife Jane

Acknowledgments

This book is the product of many years of research and could not have been written without the help of many people. I would like to thank my wife, Jane Steer-Thackray, and my children Justin, Megan, Carly and Madeleine, for the help they have given me and their patience during the many hours that I have devoted to writing this book. Jordan Dearsley created the algorithms necessary to analyse the data and develop new seasonal strategies. Thanks must be given to Austin Ip for helping me source and filter a lot of the data in this book. Special mention goes to Jane Stiegler, my proofreader and editor, for the countless hours she spent helping with formatting and editing this book.

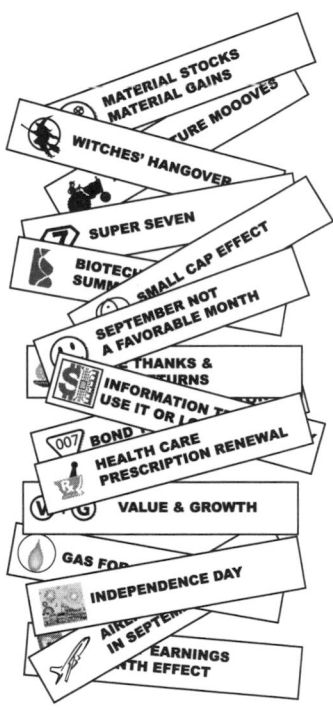

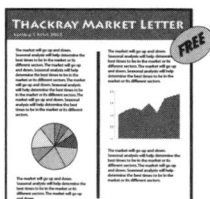

INTRODUCTION

2018 THACKRAY'S INVESTOR'S GUIDE
Technical Commentary

The seasonal strategies that I have included in my previous books have proven to be very successful. The buy and sell dates are based upon iterative comparisons of different time periods measured by gain and frequency of success. Although the buy and sell dates are the optimal dates on which seasonal investors should focus on making their investment decisions, the markets have different dynamics from year to year, shifting the optimal buy and sell dates. Combining technical analysis with seasonal trends helps to adjust the decision process, allowing seasonal investors to enter and exit trades early or late, depending on market conditions.

The universe of technical indicators and techniques is huge. It is impossible to use all of the indicators. Only a small number of indicators and techniques that suit an investment style should be used. In the case of seasonal investing, a lot of long-term indicators provide little benefit. For example, the standard Moving Average Convergence Divergence (MACD), is too slow to be of use in shorter term seasonal strategies. In this book I have chosen to illustrate the use of three technical indicators that have provided a lot of value in fine-tuning the dates for seasonal investing: Full Stochastic Oscillator (FSO), Relative Strength Index (RSI) and Relative Strength. The indicators are used in conjunction with the price pattern and moving averages of the security being considered. Investors must remember that technical analysis is not absolute and there will be exceptions when utilizing indicators and price patterns.

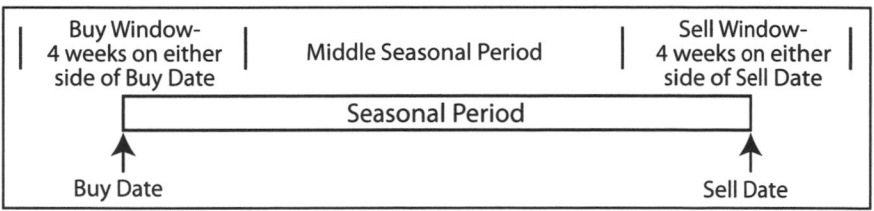

To combine technical indicators with seasonal trends, the indicators should only be used within the windows of the buy and sell dates. The indicators should be ignored outside the seasonal buy/sell windows. The only exception to this occurs when an indicator gives a signal during its middle seasonal period, which is in the seasonal period, but after the buy window and before the sell window. In this case a technical signal can support selling a full position based upon a fundamental breakdown in the price action of a security. By itself, a FSO or RSI indicator showing weakness in a security during its middle seasonal period, does not warrant action, it can only be used to support a decision being made in conjunction with underperformance relative to the broad market, or a major price action break.

Below are short descriptions of the three technical indicators that are used in this book and the metrics of how they are used with seasonal analysis. Full evaluation of the indicators and their uses with seasonal analysis is beyond the scope of this book.

Full Stochastic Oscillator (FSO)

A stochastic oscillator is a range bound momentum indicator that tracks the location of the close price relative to the high-low range, over a set number of periods. It tracks the momentum of price change and helps to indicate the strength and direction of price movement.

I have found that generally the best method to combine the FSO with seasonal trends is to buy an early partial position when the FSO turns up above 20 within four weeks of the seasonal buy date. Additionally, the best time to sell an early partial position occurs when the FSO turns below 80, within four weeks of the seasonal exit date.

For practical purposes in this book, %D, a 3 period smoothed %K, has been omitted. The standard variables are used in the FSO calculation (14 day look back period, and a 3 day simple moving average smoothing constant).

Relative Strength Index (RSI)

The RSI is a momentum oscillator that measures the speed and change of price movements. I have found that the best method to combine the RSI with seasonal trends is to buy an early partial position when the RSI turns up above 30 within four weeks of the seasonal buy date. The best time to sell an early partial position occurs when the RSI turns below 70, within four weeks of the seasonal exit date. Compared with the FSO, the RSI is less useful as it is slower and gives too few signals in the buy/sell windows.

Relative Strength

Relative strength calculates the performance of one security versus another security. When the relative strength is increasing, it indicates the seasonal security is outperforming. When the relative strength is declining, the seasonal security is underperforming. When a downward trend line is broken to the upside by the performance of the seasonal security, relative to the benchmark, this is a positive signal. This action carries a lot of weight and can justify a full early entry into a position if other technical evidence is positive. Likewise, if an upward trend line is broken to the downside, a negative technical signal is given and can justify a full early exit from a position if other technical evidence is negative.

THACKRAY'S 2018 INVESTOR'S GUIDE

You can choose great companies to invest in and still underperform the market. Unless you are in the market at the right time and in the best sectors, your investment expertise can be all for naught.

Successful investors know when they should be in the market. Very successful investors know when they should be in the market, and the best sectors in which to invest. *Thackray's 2018 Investor's Guide* is designed to provide investors with the knowledge of when and what to buy, and when to sell.

The goal of this book is to help investors capture extra profits by taking advantage of the seasonal trends in the markets. This book is straightforward. There are no complicated rules and there are no complex algorithms. The strategies put forward are intuitive and easy to understand.

It does not matter if you are a short-term or long-term investor, this book can be used to help establish entry and exit points. For the short-term investor, specific periods are identified that can provide profitable opportunities. For the long-term investor best buy dates are identified to launch new investments on a sound footing.

The stock market has its seasonal rhythms. Historically, the broad markets, such as the S&P 500, have a seasonal trend of outperforming during certain times of the year. Likewise, different sectors of the market have their own seasonal trends of outperformance. When oil stocks tend to do well in the springtime before "driving season," health care stocks tend to underperform the market. When utilities do well in the summertime, industrials do not. With different markets and different sectors having a tendency to outperform at different times of the year, there is always a place to invest.

Until recently, investors did not have access to the information necessary to analyse and create sector strategies. In recent years there have been a great number of sector Exchange Traded Funds (ETFs) and sector indexes introduced into the market. For the first time, investors are now able to easily implement a sector rotation strategy. This book provides a seasonal road map of what sectors tend to do well at different times of the year. It is a first of its kind, revealing new sector-based strategies that have never before been published.

In terms of market timing there are ample strategies in this book to help determine the times when equities should be over or underweight. During a favorable time for the market, investments can be purchased to overweight equities relative to their target weight in a portfolio (staying within risk tolerances). During an unfavorable time, investments can be sold to underweight equities relative to their target.

A large part of the book is devoted to sector seasonality – the underpinnings for a sector rotation strategy. The most practical rotation strategy is to create a core part of a portfolio that represents the broad market and then set aside an allocation to be rotated between favored sectors from one time period to the next.

It does not makes sense to apply any investment strategy only once with a large investment. Seasonal strategies are no exception. The best way to apply an investment strategy is to use a disciplined methodology that allows for diversification and a large enough number of investments to help remove the anomalies of the market. This reduces risk and increases the probability of a long term gain.

Following the specific buy and sell dates put forth in this book would have netted an investor large, above market returns. To "turbo-charge" gains, an investor can combine seasonality with technical analysis. As the seasonal periods are never exactly the same, technical analysis can help investors capture the extra gains when a sector turns up early, or momentum extends the trend.

IMPORTANT: Strategy Buy and Sell Dates
The beginning date of every strategy period in this book represents a full day in the market; therefore, investors should buy at the end of the preceding market day. For example the *Biotech Summer Solstice* seasonal period of strength is from June 23rd to September 13th. To be in the sector for the full seasonal period, an investor would enter the market before the closing bell on June 22nd. If the buy date landed on a weekend or holiday, then the buy would occur at the end of the preceding trading day.

The last day of a trading strategy is the sell date. For example, the Biotech sector investment would be sold at the end of the day on September 13th. If the sell date is a holiday or weekend, then the investment would be sold at the close on the preceding trading day.

What is Seasonal Investing?

In order to properly understand seasonal investing in the stock market, it is important to look briefly at its evolution. It may surprise investors to know that seasonal investing at the broad market level, i.e. Dow Jones or S&P 500, has been around for a long time. The initial seasonal strategies were written by Fields (1931, 1934) and Watchel (1942), who focused on the *January Effect*. Coincidentally, this strategy is still bantered about in the press every year.

Yale Yirsch Senior has been largely responsible for the next stage in the evolution, producing the *Stock Trader's Almanac* for more than forty years. This publication focuses on broad market trends such as the best six months of the year and tendencies of the market to do well depending on the political party in power and holiday trades.

In 2000, Brooke Thackray and Bruce Lindsay wrote, *Time In Time Out: Outsmart the Market Using Calendar Investment Strategies*. This work focused on a comprehensive analysis of the six month seasonal cycle and other shorter seasonal cycles in the broad markets such as the S&P 500.

Seasonal investing has changed over time. The focus has shifted from broad market strategies to taking advantage of sector rotation opportunities – investing in different sectors at different times of the year, depending on their seasonal strength. This has created a whole new set of investment opportunities. Rather than just being "in or out" of the market, investors can now always be invested by shifting between different sectors and asset classes, taking advantage of both up and down markets.

Definition – Seasonal investing is a method of investing in the market at the time of the year when it typically does well, or investing in a sector of the market when it typically outperforms the broad market such as the S&P 500.

The term seasonal investing is somewhat of a misnomer, and it is easy to see why some investors might believe that the discipline relates to investing based upon the seasons of the year – winter, spring, summer and autumn. Other than some agricultural commodities where the price is often correlated to growing seasons, generally seasonal investment strategies use the calendar as a reference for buy and sell dates. It is usually a specific event, i.e. Christmas sales, that occurs on a recurring annual basis that creates the seasonal opportunity.

The discipline of seasonal investing is not restricted to the stock market. It has been used successfully for a number of years in the commodities market. The opportunities in this market tend to be based upon changes in supply and/or demand that occur on a yearly basis. Most commodities, especially the agricultural commodities, tend to have cyclical supply cycles, i.e., crops are harvested only at certain times of the year. The supply bulge that occurs at the same time every year provides seasonal investors with profit opportunities. Recurring increased seasonal demand for commodities also plays a major part in providing opportunities for seasonal investors. This applies to most metals and many other commodities, whether the end-product is industrial or consumer based.

Seasonal investment strategies can be used with a lot of different types of investments. The premise is the same, outperformance during a certain period of the year based upon a repeating event in the markets or economy. In my past writings I have developed seasonal strategies that have been used successfully in the stock, commodity, bond and foreign exchange markets. Seasonal investing is still relatively new for most markets with a lot of new opportunities waiting to be discovered.

How Does Seasonal Investing Work?

Most stock market sector seasonal trends are the result of a recurring annual catalyst: an event that affects the sector positively. These events can range from a seasonal spike in demand, seasonal inventory lows, weather effects, conferences and other events. Mainstream investors very often anticipate a move in a sector and incorrectly try to take a position just before an event takes place that is supposed to drive a sector higher. A good example of this would be investors buying oil just before the cold weather sets in. Unfortunately, their efforts are usually unsuccessful as they are too late to the party and the opportunity has already passed.

By the time the anticipated event occurs, a substantial amount of investors have bought into the sector – fully pricing in the expected benefit. At this time there is little potential left in the short-term. Unless there is a strong positive surprise, the sector's outperformance tends to slowly roll over. If the event produces less than its desired result, the sector can be severely punished.

So how does the seasonal investor take advantage of this opportunity? "Be there" before the mainstream investors, and get out before they do. Seasonal investors usually enter a sector two or three months before an event is anticipated to have a positive effect on a sector and get out before the actual event takes place. In essence, seasonal investors are benefiting from the mainstream investor's tendency to "buy in" too late.

Seasonality in the markets occurs because of three major reasons: money flow, changing market analyst expectations and the *Anticipation-Realization Cycle*. First, money flows vary throughout the year and at different times of the month. Generally, money flows increase at the end of the year and into the start of the next year. This is a result of year end bonuses and tax related investments. In addition, money flows increase at month end from money managers "window dressing" their portfolios. As a result of these money flows, the months around the end of the year and the days around the end of the month, tend to have a stronger performance than the other times of the year.

Second, the analyst expectations cycle tends to push markets up at the end of the year and the beginning of the next year. Stock market analysts tend to be a positive bunch – the large investment houses pay them to be positive. They start the year with aggressive earnings for all of their favorite companies. As the year progresses, they generally back off their earnings forecast, which decreases their support for the market. After a lull in the summer and early autumn months, they start to focus on the next year with another rosy forecast. As a result, the stock market tends to rise once again at the end of the year.

Third, at the sector level, sectors of the market tend to be greatly influenced by the *Anticipation-Realization Cycle*. Although some investors may not be familiar with the term "anticipation-realization," they probably are familiar with the concept of "buy the rumor – sell the fact," or in the famous words of Lord Rothschild "Buy on the sound of the war-cannons; sell on the sound of the victory trumpets."

The *Anticipation-Realization Cycle* as it applies to human behavior has been much studied in psychology journals. In the investment world, the premise of this cycle rests on investors anticipating a positive event in the market to drive prices higher and buying in ahead of the event. When the event takes place, or is realized, upward pressure on prices decreases as there is very little impetus for further outperformance.

A good example of the *Anticipation-Realization Cycle* takes place with the "conference effect." Very often large industries have major conferences that occur at approximately the same time every year. Major companies in the industry often hold back positive announce- 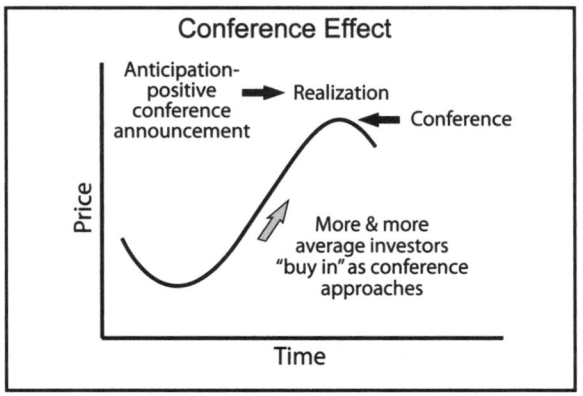 ments and product introductions to be released during the conference.

Two to three months prior to the conference, seasonal investors tend to buy into the sector. Shortly afterwards, the mainstream investors anticipate "good news" from the conference and start to buy in. As a result, prices are pushed up. Just before the conference starts, seasonal investors capture their profits by exiting their positions. As the conference unfolds, company announcements are made (realized), but as the potential good news has already been priced into the sector, there is little to push prices higher and the sector typically starts to rolls over.

The same *Anticipation-Realization Cycle* takes place with increased demand for oil to meet the "summer driving season", increased sales of goods at Christmas time, increased demand for gold jewellery to meet the autumn and winter demand, and many other events that tend to drive the outperformance of different sectors.

Does Seasonal Investing ALWAYS Work?

The simple answer to the above question is "No." There is not any investment system in the world that works all of the time. When following any investment system, it is probability of success that counts. It has often been said that "being correct in the markets 60% of the time will make you rich." Investors tend to forget this and become too emotionally attached to their losses. Just about every investment trading book states that investors typically fail to let their profits run and cut their losses quickly. I concur. In my many years in the investment industry, the biggest mistake that I have found with investors is not being able to cut their losses. Everyone wants to be right, that is how we have been raised. Investors feel that if they sell at a loss they have failed, and as a result, often suffer bigger losses by waiting for their position to trade at profit.

With any investment system, investors should let probability work for them. This means that investors should be able to enter and exit positions capturing both gains and losses without becoming emotionally attached to any positions. Emotional attachment clouds judgement, which leads to errors. When all of the trades are put together, the goal is for profits to be larger than losses in a way that minimizes risks and beats the market.

If we examine the winter oil stock trade, we can see how probability has worked in an investor's favor. This trade is based upon the premise that at the tail end of winter, the refineries drive up demand for oil in order to produce enough gas for the approaching "driving season" that starts in the spring. As a result, oil stocks tend to increase and outperform the market (from February 25th to May 9th). The oil stock sector, represented by the NYSE Arca Oil Index (XOI), has been very successful at this time of year, producing an average return of 6.9% and beating the S&P 500 by 3.8%, from 1984 to 2017.

XOI vs S&P 500 1984 to 2017		
Feb 25	positive	
to May 9 S&P 500	XOI	Diff
1984 1.7 %	5.6 %	3.9 %
1985 1.4	4.9	3.5
1986 6.0	7.7	1.7
1987 3.7	25.5	21.8
1988 -3.0	5.6	8.6
1989 6.3	8.1	1.8
1990 5.8	-0.6	-6.3
1991 4.8	6.8	2.0
1992 0.9	5.8	4.9
1993 0.3	6.3	6.0
1994 -4.7	3.2	7.9
1995 7.3	10.3	3.1
1996 -2.1	2.2	4.3
1997 1.8	4.7	2.9
1998 7.5	9.8	2.3
1999 7.3	35.4	28.1
2000 4.3	22.2	17.9
2001 0.8	10.2	9.4
2002 -1.5	5.3	6.9
2003 12.1	5.7	-6.4
2004 -3.5	4.0	7.5
2005 -1.8	-1.0	0.8
2006 2.8	9.4	6.6
2007 4.2	10.1	5.8
2008 2.6	7.6	5.0
2009 20.2	15.8	-4.4
2010 0.5	-2.3	-2.8
2011 3.1	-0.6	-3.7
2012 -0.8	-13.4	-12.5
2013 7.3	3.8	-3.5
2014 1.7	9.1	7.4
2015 0.3	1.2	1.1
2016 6.7	11.1	4.4
2017 1.3	-4.0	-5.2
Avg 3.1 %	6.9 %	3.8 %
Fq > 0 79 %	82 %	76 %

In addition it has been positive 28 out of 34 times. Investors should always evaluate the strength of seasonal trades before applying them to their own portfolios.

If an investor started using the seasonal investment discipline in 1984 and chose to invest in the winter-oil trade, they would have been very happy with the results. Over the last few years, the fact that the trade did not produce a gain in 2010, 2011 and 2012, does not mean that the seasonal trade no longer works. All seasonal trades go through periods, sometimes multiple years where they do not work. An investor can start any methodology of trading at the "wrong time," and be unsuccessful in a particular trade. In fact, if an investor started the oil-winter trade in 1990 and had given up in the same year, they would have missed the following successful twelve years. Investors have to remember that it is the final score that counts, after all of the gains have been weighed against the losses.

In practical terms, investors should not put all of their investment strategies in one basket. If one or two large investments were made based upon seasonal strategies, it is possible that the seasonal methodology might be inappropriately evaluated and its use discontinued. A much more prudent strategy is to use a larger number of strategic seasonal investments with smaller investments. The end result will be to put the seasonal probability to work with a much greater chance of success.

Measuring Seasonal Performance

How do you determine if a seasonal strategy has been successful? Many people feel that ten years of data is a good sample size, others feel that fifteen years is better, and yet others feel that the more data the better. I tend to fall into the camp that, if possible, it is best to use fifteen or twenty years of data for sectors and more data for the broad markets, such as the S&P 500. Although the most recent data in almost any analytical framework is the most relevant, it is important to get enough data to reflect a sector's performance across different economic conditions. Given that historically the economy has performed on an eight year cycle, four years of expansion and then four years of contraction, using a short data set does not provide for enough exposure to different economic conditions.

A data set that is too long can run into the problem of older data having too much of an influence on the numbers when fundamental factors affecting a sector have changed. It is important to look at trends over time and assess if there has been a change that should be considered in determining the dates for a seasonal cycle. Each sector should be judged on its own merit. The analysis tables in this book illustrate the performance level for each year in order to provide the opportunity for readers to determine any relevant changes.

In order to determine if a seasonal strategy is effective there are two possible benchmarks, absolute and relative performance. Absolute performance measures if a profit is made and relative performance measures the performance of a sector in relationship to a major market. Both measurements have their merits and depending on your investment style, one measurement may be more valuable than another. This book provides both sets of measurement in tables and graphs.

It is not just the average percent gain of a sector over a certain time period that determines success. It is possible that one or two spectacular years of performance skew the results substantially (particularly with a small data set). The frequency of success is also very important: the higher the percentage of success the better. Also, the fewer large drawdowns the better. There is no magic number (percent success rate) per se of what constitutes a successful strategy. The success rate should be above fifty percent, otherwise it would be better to just invest in the broad market. Ideally speaking a strategy should have a high percentage success rate on both an absolute and relative basis. Some strategies are stronger than others, but that does not mean that the weaker strategies should not be used. Prudence should be used in determining the ideal portfolio allocation.

Illustrating the strength of a sector's seasonal performance can be accomplished through either an absolute yearly average performance graph, or a relative yearly average performance graph. The absolute graph shows the average yearly cumulative gain for a set number of years. It lets a reader visually identify the strong periods during the year. The relative graph shows the average yearly cumulative gain for the sector relative to the benchmark index.

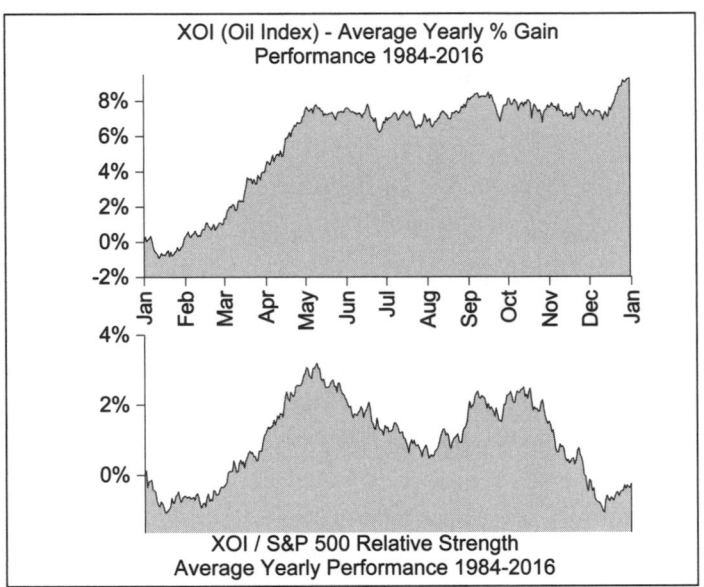

Both graphs are useful in determining the strength of a particular seasonal strategy. In the above diagram, the top graph illustrates the average year for the NYSE Arca Oil Index (XOI) from 1984 to 2016. Essentially it illustrates the cumulative average gain if an investment were made in the index. The steep rising line starting in January/February shows the overall price rise that typically occurs in this sector at this time of year. In May the line flattens out and then rises very modestly starting in July.

The bottom graph is a ratio graph, illustrating the strength of the XOI Index relative to the S&P 500. It is derived by dividing the average year of the XOI by the average year of the S&P 500. When the line in the graph is rising, the XOI is outperforming the S&P 500, and vise versa when it is declining. This is an important graph and should be used in considering seasonal investments because the S&P 500 is a viable alternative to the energy sector. If both markets are increasing, but the S&P 500 is increasing at a faster rate, the S&P 500 represents a more attractive opportunity. This is particularly true when measuring the risk of a volatile sector relative to the broad market. If both investments were expected to produce the same rate of return, generally the broad market is a better investment because of its diversification.

Who Can Use Seasonal Investing?

Any investor from novice to expert, from short-term trader to long-term investor can benefit from using seasonal analysis. Seasonal investing is unique because it is an easy to understand system that can be used by itself or as a complement to another investment discipline. For the novice it provides an easy to follow strategy that makes intuitive sense. For the expert it can be used as a stand-alone system or as a complement to an existing system.

Seasonal investing is easily understood by all levels of investors, which allows investors to make rational decisions. This may seem obvious, but it is very common for investors to listen to a "guru of the market", be impressed and blindly follow his advice. When the advice works there is no problem. When the advice does not work investors wonder why they made the investment in the first place. When investors do not understand their investments it causes stress, bad decisions and a lack of "stick-to-it ness" with any investment discipline. Even expert investors realize the importance of understanding your investments. Peter Lynch of Fidelity Investments used to say "Never invest in any idea that you can't illustrate with a crayon." Investors do not need to go that far, but they should understand their investments.

Novice investors find seasonal strategies very easy to understand because they are intuitive. They do not have to be investing for years to understand why seasonal strategies work. They understand that an increase in demand for gold every year at the same time causes a ripple effect in the stock market pushing up gold stocks at the same time every year.

Most expert investors use information from a variety of sources in making their decisions. Even experts that primarily use fundamental analysis can benefit from using seasonal trends to get an edge in the market. Fundamental analysis is a very crude tool and provides very little in the way of timing an investment. Using seasonal trends can help with the timing of the buy and sell decisions and produce extra profit.

Seasonal investing can be used by both short-term and long-term investors, but in different ways. For short-term investors it provides a complete trade – buy and sell dates. For long-term investors it can provide a buy date for a sector of interest.

Combining Seasonal Analysis with other Investment Disciplines

Seasonal investing used by itself has historically produced above average market returns. Depending on an investor's particular style, it can be combined with one of the other three investment disciplines: fundamental, quantitative and technical analysis. There are two basic ways to combine seasonal analysis with other investment methodologies – as the primary or secondary method. If it is used as a primary method, seasonally strong time periods are established for a number of sectors and then appropriate sectors are chosen based upon fundamental, quantitative or technical screens. If it is used as a secondary method, sector selections are first made based upon one of three methods and then final sectors are chosen based upon which ones are in their seasonally strong period.

Technical analysis is an ideal mate for seasonal analysis. Unlike fundamental and quantitative analysis, which are very blunt timing tools at best, seasonal and technical analysis can provide specific trigger points to buy and sell. The combination can turbo-charge investment strategies, adding extra profits by fine-tuning entry and exit dates.

Seasonal analysis provides both buy and sell dates. Although a sector in the market can sometimes bottom on the exact seasonal buy date, it more often bottoms a bit early or a bit late. After all, the seasonal buy date is based upon an average of historical performance. Depending on the sector, buying opportunities start to develop approximately one month before and after the seasonal buy date. Using technical analysis gives an investor the advantage of buying into a sector when it turns up early or waiting when it turns up late. Likewise, technical analysis can be used to trigger a sell signal when the market turns down before or after the sell date.

The sell decision can be extended with the help of a trailing stop-loss order. If a sector has strong momentum and the technical tools do not provide a sell signal, it is possible to let the sector "run." When a trailing stop-loss is used, a profitable sell point is established. If the price continues to run, then the selling point is raised. If, on the other hand, the price falls through the stop-loss point, the position is sold.

Sectors of the Market

Standard & Poor's has done an excellent job in categorizing the U.S. stock market into its different parts. Although the demand for this service initially came from institutional investors, many individual investors now seek the same information. Knowing the sector breakdown in the market allows investors to see how different their portfolio is relative to the market. As a result, they are able to make conscious decisions on what parts of the stock market to overweight based upon their beliefs of which sectors will outperform. It also helps control the amount of desired risk.

Standard & Poor's uses four levels of detail in its Global Industry Classification Standard (GICS©) to categorize stock markets around the world. From the most specific, it classifies companies into sub-industries, industries, industry groups and finally economic sectors. All companies in the Standard & Poor's global family of indices are classified according to the GICS structure.

This book focuses on the U.S. market, analysing the trends of the venerable S&P 500 index and its economic sectors and industry groups. The following diagram illustrates the index classified according to its economic sectors.

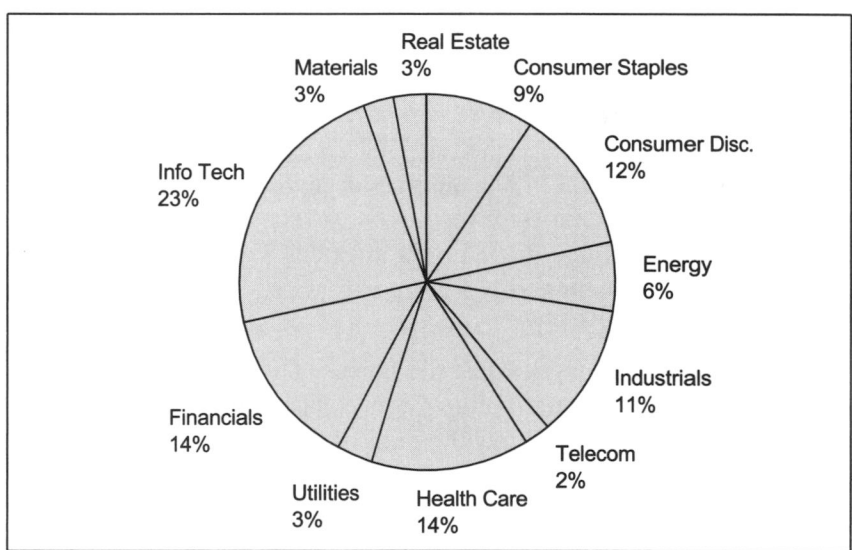

Standard and Poor's, Understanding Sectors, June 30, 2017

For more information on Standard and Poor's Global Industry Classification Standard (GICS©), refer to www.standardandpoors.com

Investment Products – Which One Is The Right One?

There are many ways to take advantage of the seasonal trends at the broad stock market and sector levels. Regardless of the investment products that you currently use, whether exchange traded funds, mutual funds, stocks or options, all can be used with the strategies in this book. Different investments offer different risk-reward relationships and return potential.

Exchange Traded Funds (ETFs)

Exchange Traded Funds (ETFs) offer the purest method of seasonal investment. The broad market ETFs are designed to track the major indices and the sector ETFs are designed to track specific sectors without using active management. Relatively new, ETFs are a great way to capture both market and sector trends. They were originally introduced into the Canadian market in 1993 to represent the Toronto stock market index. Shortly afterward they were introduced to the U.S. market and there are now hundreds of ETFs to represent almost every market, sector, style of investing and company capitalization. Originally ETFs were mainly of interest to institutional investors, but individual investors have fast realized the merits of ETF investing and have made some of the broad market ETFs the most heavily traded securities in the world.

An ETF is a single security that represents a market, such as the S&P 500; a sector of the market, such as the financial sector; or a commodity, such as gold. In the case of the S&P 500, an investor buying one security is buying all 500 stocks in the index. By investing into a financial ETF, an investor is buying the companies that make up the financial sector of the market. By investing into a gold commodity ETF, an investor is buying a security that represents the price of gold.

ETFs trade on the open market just like stocks. They have a bid and an ask, can be shorted and many are option eligible. They are a very low cost, tax efficient method of targeting specific parts of the market.

Mutual Funds

Mutual funds are a good way to combine market or sector investing with active management. In recent years, many mutual fund companies have added sector funds to accommodate an increasing appetite in this area.

As the seasonal strategies put forward in this book have a short-term nature, it is important to make sure that there are no fees (or a nominal charge) for getting into and out of a position in the market.

Stocks

Stocks provide an opportunity to make better returns than the market or sector. If the market increases during its seasonal period, some stocks will increase dramatically more than the index. Choosing one of the outperforming stocks will greatly enhance returns; choosing one of the underperforming stocks can create substantial loses. Using stocks requires increased attention to diversification and security selection.

Options

Disclaimer: Options involve risk and are not suitable for every investor. Because they are cash-settled, investors should be aware of the special risks associated with index options and should consult a tax advisor. Prior to buying or selling options, a person must receive a copy of Characteristics and Risks of Standardized Options and should thoroughly understand the risks involved in any use of options. Copies may be obtained from The Options Clearing Corporation, 440 S. LaSalle Street, Chicago, IL 60605.

Options, for more sophisticated investors, are a good tool to take advantage of both market and sector opportunities. An option position can be established with either stocks or ETFs. There are many different ways to use options for seasonal trends: establish a long position on the market during its seasonally strong period, establish a short position during its seasonally weak period, or create a spread trade to capture the superior gains of a sector over the market.

THACKRAY'S 2018 INVESTOR'S GUIDE

CONTENTS

JANUARY

	MONDAY	TUESDAY	WEDNESDAY

WEEK 01	**1** 30
	
	CAN Market Closed -
	       New Year's Day
	
	USA Market Closed -
	       New Year's Day
		2 29	**3** 28

WEEK 02	**8** 23	**9** 22	**10** 21
WEEK 03	**15** 16 USA Market Closed- Martin Luther King Jr. Day	**16** 15	**17** 14
WEEK 04	**22** 9	**23** 8	**24** 7
WEEK 05	**29** 2	**30** 1	**31**

JANUARY

THURSDAY		FRIDAY	
4	27	**5**	26
11	20	**12**	19
18	13	**19**	12
25	6	**26**	5
1		2	

FEBRUARY

M	T	W	T	F	S	S
			1	2	3	4
5	6	7	8	9	10	11
12	13	14	15	16	17	18
19	20	21	22	23	24	24
26	27	28				

MARCH

M	T	W	T	F	S	S
			1	2	3	4
5	6	7	8	9	10	11
12	13	14	15	16	17	18
19	20	21	22	23	24	25
26	27	28	29	30	31	

APRIL

M	T	W	T	F	S	S
						1
2	3	4	5	6	7	8
9	10	11	12	13	14	15
16	17	18	19	20	21	22
23	24	25	26	27	28	29
30						

MAY

M	T	W	T	F	S	S
	1	2	3	4	5	6
7	8	9	10	11	12	13
14	15	16	17	18	19	20
21	22	23	24	25	26	27
28	29	30	31			

JANUARY SUMMARY

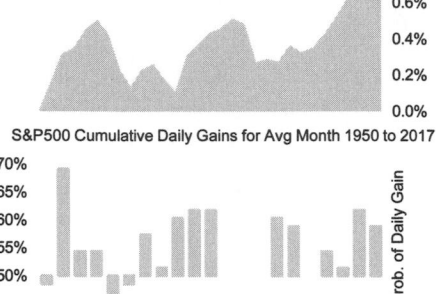

S&P500 Cumulative Daily Gains for Avg Month 1950 to 2017

	Dow Jones	S&P 500	Nasdaq	TSX Comp
Month Rank	6	6	1	5
# Up	42	40	28	20
# Down	25	27	17	12
% Pos	63	60	62	63
% Avg. Gain	0.9	0.9	2.4	1.0

Dow & S&P 1950-2016, Nasdaq 1972-2016, TSX 1985-2016

♦ Over the last ten years, January has not lived up to its long-term reputation of being one of the better months of the year, and has on average produced losses for most major stock markets. ♦ In January there is typically a lot of sector rotation. ♦ Small caps tend to perform well. ♦ The technology sector finishes its seasonal period. ♦ The industrials, materials, metals and mining sectors start the second part of their seasonal periods. ♦ Silver starts its seasonal period. ♦ The retail sector starts its strongest seasonal period.

BEST / WORST JANUARY BROAD MKTS. 2008-2017

BEST JANUARY MARKETS
- Nasdaq (2012) 8.0%
- Nikkei 225 (2013) 7.2%
- Russell 2000 (2012) 7.0%

WORST JANUARY MARKETS
- Nikkei (2008) -11.2%
- Russell 2000 (2009) -11.2%
- Nasdaq (2008) -9.9%

Index Values End of Month

	2008	2009	2010	2011	2012	2013	2014	2015	2016	2017
Dow	12,650	8,001	10,067	11,892	12,633	13,861	15,699	17,165	16,466	19,864
S&P 500	1,379	826	1,074	1,286	1,312	1,498	1,783	1,995	1,940	2,279
Nasdaq	2,390	1,476	2,147	2,700	2,814	3,142	4,104	4,635	4,614	5,615
TSX Comp.	13,155	8,695	11,094	13,552	12,452	12,685	13,695	14,674	12,822	15,386
Russell 1000	751	447	589	713	726	832	996	1,112	1,070	1,265
Russell 2000	713	444	602	781	793	902	1,131	1,165	1,035	1,362
FTSE 100	5,880	4,150	5,189	5,863	5,682	6,277	6,510	6,749	6,084	7,099
Nikkei 225	13,592	7,994	10,198	10,238	8,803	11,139	14,915	17,674	17,518	19,041

Percent Gain for January

	2008	2009	2010	2011	2012	2013	2014	2015	2016	2017
Dow	-4.6	-8.8	-3.5	2.7	3.4	5.8	-5.3	-3.7	-5.5	0.5
S&P 500	-6.1	-8.6	-3.7	2.3	4.4	5.0	-3.6	-3.1	-5.1	1.8
Nasdaq	-9.9	-6.4	-5.4	1.8	8.0	4.1	-1.7	-2.1	-7.9	4.3
TSX Comp.	-4.9	-3.3	-5.5	0.8	4.2	2.0	0.5	0.3	-1.4	0.6
Russell 1000	-6.1	-8.3	-3.7	2.3	4.8	5.3	-3.3	-2.8	-5.5	1.9
Russell 2000	-6.9	-11.2	-3.7	-0.3	7.0	6.2	-2.8	-3.3	-8.8	0.3
FTSE 100	-8.9	-6.4	-4.1	-0.6	2.0	6.4	-3.5	2.8	-2.5	-0.6
Nikkei 225	-11.2	-9.8	-3.3	0.1	4.1	7.2	-8.5	1.3	-8.0	-0.4

January Market Avg. Performance 2008 to 2017[1]

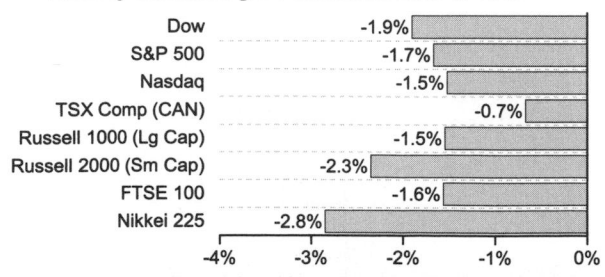

	Dow	-1.9%
S&P 500	-1.7%
Nasdaq	-1.5%
TSX Comp (CAN)	-0.7%
Russell 1000 (Lg Cap)	-1.5%
Russell 2000 (Sm Cap)	-2.3%
FTSE 100	-1.6%
Nikkei 225	-2.8%

Interest Corner Jan[2]

	Fed Funds % [3]	3 Mo. T-Bill % [4]	10 Yr % [5]	20 Yr % [6]
2017	0.75	0.52	2.45	2.78
2016	0.50	0.33	1.94	2.36
2015	0.25	0.02	1.68	2.04
2014	0.25	0.02	2.67	3.35
2013	0.25	0.07	2.02	2.79

(1) Russell Data provided by Russell (2) Federal Reserve Bank of St. Louis- end of month values (3) Target rate set by FOMC (4)(5)(6) Constant yield maturities.

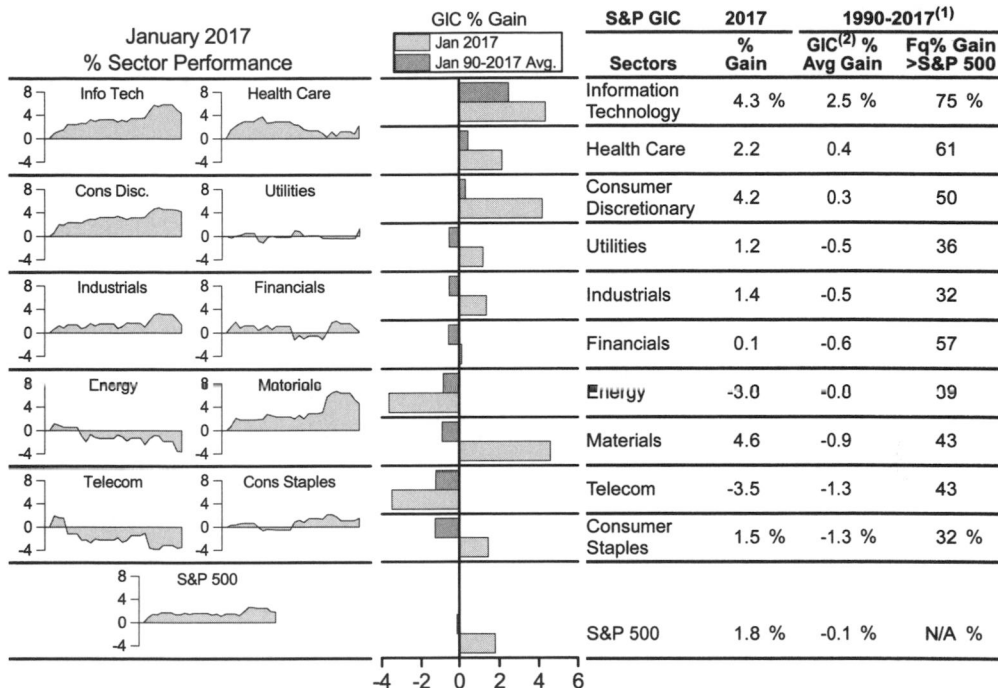

S&P GIC Sectors	2017 % Gain	1990-2017[1] GIC[2] % Avg Gain	1990-2017[1] Fq% Gain >S&P 500
Information Technology	4.3 %	2.5 %	75 %
Health Care	2.2	0.4	61
Consumer Discretionary	4.2	0.3	50
Utilities	1.2	-0.5	36
Industrials	1.4	-0.5	32
Financials	0.1	-0.6	57
Energy	-3.0	-0.0	39
Materials	4.6	-0.9	43
Telecom	-3.5	-1.3	43
Consumer Staples	1.5 %	-1.3 %	32 %
S&P 500	1.8 %	-0.1 %	N/A %

Sector Commentary

♦ In January 2017, the S&P 500 was positive as investors pushed the stock market higher based upon expectations that Trump would be able to introduce pro-business legislation. ♦ The financial sector, one of the expected main beneficiaries of Trump's proposed policies took a "breather," producing only a nominal gain in January after a strong performance since the U.S. election. ♦ The information technology sector lived up to its seasonal expectations and was one of the better performing sectors for January. ♦ The energy sector was the worst performing major sector.

Sub-Sector Commentary

♦ In January 2017, the cyclical sub-sectors gained a lot of ground. ♦ The metals and mining sub-sector, assisted by its gold mining component, gained 9.4%. ♦ Gold and silver performed well, after correcting in December. ♦ Homebuilders, in the middle of its seasonal period, produced a gain of 9.3%. ♦ The railroads sub-sector produced a strong gain of 9.4%.

SELECTED SUB-SECTORS[3]			
SOX (1995-2017)	4.2 %	3.3 %	57 %
Silver	6.5	3.1	71
Homebuilders	9.3	2.7	61
Biotech (1993-2017)	1.8	1.7	56
Gold	5.8	1.7	61
Railroads	9.4	1.1	57
Automotive & Components	3.4	0.6	50
Steel	-2.4	0.3	50
Pharma	-1.2	-0.2	57
Transportation	2.6	-0.2	50
Retail	3.6	-0.2	54
Banks	-0.1	-0.5	46
Agriculture (1994-2017)	-3.0	-0.8	38
Chemicals	4.0	-0.9	43
Metals & Mining	9.4	-1.1	43

(1) Sector data provided by Standard and Poors (2) GIC is short form for Global Industry Classification (3) Sub Sector data provided by Standard and Poors, except where marked by symbol.

U.S. Dollar vs. Euro – "V" Trade
①SELL SHORT (Nov17-Dec31)
②LONG (Jan1-Feb7)

The U.S. dollar tends to underperform the euro from November 17th to December 31st, and then outperform from January 1st to February 7th.

This down-and-up pattern, creates an opportunistic double-trade strategy. The first leg is a short sell trade for USD/EUR and the second leg is a long position. Both trades are contiguous and create a combination "V" shaped trade.

Most times, the transition between the trades will not take place precisely at the end of the year and technical analysis should be used to help with the appropriate timing.

78% of the time positive

What makes the "V" trade a success is that the sum of its parts is greater than the individual pieces. The first leg of the "V," represents U.S. dollar weakness. In its short sell seasonal period from November 17th to December 31st, during the period 1999 to 2016, the U.S. dollar has produced an average loss of 1.5% and has only been positive 39% of the time. The second leg, from January 1st to February 7th, has produced an average gain of 1.2% with a 56% success rate. Combining both legs of the trade has produced an average gain of 2.7%, with a 78% success rate, which is better than the success rate of each leg separately.

In the first part of the "V" trade, the U.S. dollar tends to weaken at the tail end of the year as U.S. dollars flow to foreign countries at this time. The year-end outward flow is the result of two factors.

First, foreign companies repatriate their profits back to their home countries in order to settle their books.

(i) *Source data: Federal Reserve Bank of St. Louis. Noon buying rates in New York City for cable transfers payable in foreign currencies.*

USD/EUR vs S&P500 1999/00 to 2016/17*

Negative Short [ ]   Positive Long [ ]

Year	Nov 17 to Dec 31 S&P 500	Nov 17 to Dec 31 USD/EUR	Jan 1 Feb 7 S&P 500	Jan 1 Feb 7 USD/EUR	Compound Growth USD/EUR
1999/00	3.5 %	2.4 %	-3.1	2.9 %	0.5 %
2000/01	-3.8	-9.1	1.6	0.6	9.8
2001/02	0.8	-0.6	-5.9	2.4	3.0
2002/03	-3.3	-3.8	-5.7	-2.9	0.8
2003/04	5.9	-6.8	2.8	-0.8	6.0
2004/05	3.1	-4.1	-0.8	6.0	10.4
2005/06	1.4	-1.4	0.5	-1.1	0.3
2006/07	1.3	-3.0	2.2	1.4	4.4
2007/08	0.7	0.3	-9.0	0.8	0.4
2008/09	3.4	-8.5	-3.8	8.1	17.4
2009/10	0.5	4.5	-4.4	5.3	0.6
2010/11	6.7	1.9	4.9	-2.1	-4.0
2011/12	1.7	4.1	7.1	-2.1	-6.1
2012/13	4.9	-3.6	5.8	-1.5	2.1
2013/14	2.8	-2.2	-2.8	1.2	3.4
2014/15	0.9	3.3	-0.2	6.8	3.3
2015/16	-0.5	-1.4	-8.0	-2.4	-1.1
2016/17	2.8	1.4	2.4	-1.3	-2.7
Avg.	1.8 %	-1.5 %	-0.9 %	1.2 %	2.7 %
Fq>0	83 %	39 %	44 %	56 %	78 %

Second, migrants remit funds back to their home countries, an activity that happens mainly at year-end. In 2016, U.S. migrants remitted $63 billion back to their home countries versus the U.S. citizens receiving $7 billion (World Bank 2016 Annual Remittance Data). The U.S. is by far the largest net remitter compared to all other countries. Although this does not have a large impact boosting the euro, the large remittances are a factor in exerting downward pressure on the U.S. dollar.

The second part of the "V" trade, the upwards leg of the U.S. dollar outperforming the euro, occurs in the New Year as foreign companies demand U.S. dollars to enact their transactions at the start of the year.

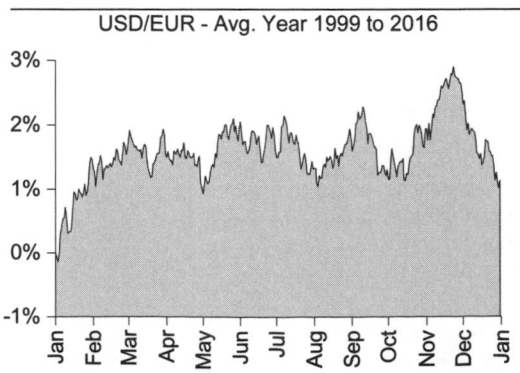

USD/EUR - Avg. Year 1999 to 2016

USD/EUR Performance

USD/EUR Monthly Performance (1999-2016)

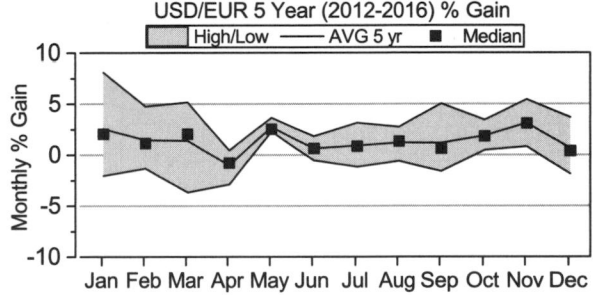

	Jan	Feb	Mar	Apr	May	Jun	Jul	Aug	Sep	Oct	Nov	Dec
Avg. % Gain	1.5	0.2	-0.1	-0.5	0.9	-0.3	-0.2	0.5	-0.4	0.6	0.5	-1.3
Med. % Gain	1.3	-0.1	0.2	-0.6	1.5	-0.2	0.4	0.0	-0.7	0.2	-0.1	-0.8
Fq %>0	67	50	56	44	67	44	56	50	39	50	44	44
Fq %>S&P 500	50	61	44	28	50	44	44	44	44	39	33	28

USD/EUR 5 Year (2012-2016) % Gain

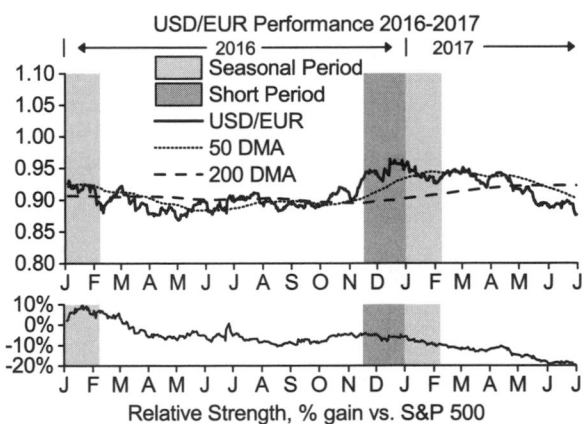

USD/EUR Performance 2016-2017

Relative Strength, % gain vs. S&P 500

Market Indices & Rates
Weekly Values**

Stock Markets	2016	2017
Dow	16,815	19,922
S&P500	1,977	2,269
Nasdaq	4,793	5,479
TSX	12,694	15,501
FTSE	6,034	7,193
DAX	10,127	11,590
Nikkei	18,096	19,523
Hang Seng	20,857	22,311
Commodities	**2016**	**2017**
Oil	34.63	53.34
Gold	1091.8	1167.0
Bond Yields	**2016**	**2017**
USA 5 Yr Treasury	1.66	1.92
USA 10 Yr T	2.19	2.43
USA 20 Yr T	2.60	2.75
Moody's Aaa	3.98	3.91
Moody's Baa	5.46	4.68
CAN 5 Yr T	0.68	1.11
CAN 10 Yr T	1.34	1.71
Money Market	**2016**	**2017**
USA Fed Funds	0.50	0.75
USA 3 Mo T-B	0.21	0.53
CAN tgt overnight rate	0.50	0.50
CAN 3 Mo T-B	0.46	0.45
Foreign Exchange	**2016**	**2017**
EUR/USD	1.08	1.05
GBP/USD	1.46	1.23
USD/CAD	1.41	1.33
USD/JPY	118.38	116.98

JANUARY

M	T	W	T	F	S	S
1	2	3	4	5	6	7
8	9	10	11	12	13	14
15	16	17	18	19	20	21
22	23	24	25	26	27	28
29	30	31				

FEBRUARY

M	T	W	T	F	S	S
			1	2	3	4
5	6	7	8	9	10	11
12	13	14	15	16	17	18
19	20	21	22	23	24	24
26	27	28				

MARCH

M	T	W	T	F	S	S
			1	2	3	4
5	6	7	8	9	10	11
12	13	14	15	16	17	18
19	20	21	22	23	24	25
26	27	28	29	30	31	

The USD/EUR tends to perform poorly in the second half of November, into the end of the year and then rebound at the start of the year. From 1999 to 2016, on average, the USD/EUR declined in December and then rebounded in January. On average, over the last five years, the seasonal trend of USD/EUR performing well in May (the second strongest month over the long-term) remained intact, as well as the seasonal trend of January being a stronger month than December.

In 2016, the gain on the short sell USD/EUR position at the end of the year and the gain on the long USD/EUR position at the beginning of 2017 produced a combined loss.

HASBRO— Play for Gains

HAS ①LONG (Jan21-Apr12) ②SHORT (Jun1-Jul21)
③LONG (Oct10-Nov26) ④SHORT(Nov27-Dec22)

Hasbro tends to perform well in the same time period as the retail sector from January 21st to April 12th, as it also benefits from a bounce off the weakest month of the year for retail sales, January.

Hasbro typically performs poorly from June 1st to July 21st as it suffers from a lack of mid-year sales. At this time of the year, investors have little interest in Hasbro as there is a lack of a strong catalyst to move the price upwards.

In autumn, Hasbro once again tends to have a strong period (October 10th to November 26th), heading into the holiday shopping season.

The busiest day of the year for Christmas holiday shopping is Black Friday in November. Average investors look to profit from the holiday shopping season by being in the retail sector, including Hasbro, in the time period leading up to Black Friday. Seasonal investors seek to enter the retail sector before the average investor, and exit around Black Friday. As a result, Hasbro has a strong seasonal period form October 10th to November 26th, and then performs poorly from November 27th to December 22nd.

(i) *HAS - stock symbol for Hasbro which trades on the NYSE, adjusted for splits.*

Gain % & Fq % Positive Hasbro vs. S&P 500 1990 to 2016
Negative Short [ ]   Positive Long [ ]

Year	Jan 21 to Apr 12 S&P 500	HAS	Jun 1 Jul 21 S&P 500	HAS	Oct 10 Nov 26 S&P 500	HAS	Nov 27 Dec 22 S&P 500	HAS	Compound Growth S&P 500	HAS
1990	1.5	-3.8	0.1	-21.2	3.7	17.8	4.8	3.4	10.5	32.8
1991	14.5	37.3	-1.4	-5.3	0.3	22.6	2.4	1.7	15.9	74.0
1992	-2.9	-5.5	-0.4	-3.4	6.6	10.7	2.6	-6.8	5.8	15.5
1993	3.5	-4.7	-0.7	-1.4	0.6	-5.4	0.9	-4.3	4.3	-4.6
1994	-5.8	3.6	-0.9	-10.2	-0.6	5.7	1.6	-5.4	-5.6	27.2
1995	9.1	14.5	3.8	-12.8	3.7	1.2	2.0	-1.2	19.8	32.3
1996	4.1	22.1	-4.5	-7.3	8.5	7.5	-0.9	-7.0	6.8	50.6
1997	-5.0	-2.6	7.6	0.0	-2.0	9.0	0.2	10.7	0.4	-5.1
1998	13.5	4.1	6.8	4.4	20.6	16.3	1.4	-9.7	48.2	26.9
1999	8.1	27.4	6.0	-5.4	6.0	13.6	1.4	-25.1	23.1	90.8
2000	1.5	7.3	4.2	-32.8	-4.3	-3.2	-2.7	-14.7	-1.5	58.2
2001	-11.9	-3.1	-3.6	0.0	9.5	15.6	-1.1	-5.1	-7.9	17.7
2002	-1.5	0.3	-20.6	-23.6	17.6	18.9	-1.9	-10.3	-9.7	62.6
2003	-3.7	22.6	1.6	11.1	1.9	6.2	3.3	-5.7	2.9	22.2
2004	0.6	6.4	-2.4	-6.9	5.4	1.2	2.3	-0.1	5.8	15.2
2005	1.1	5.4	3.0	5.8	6.1	6.8	0.0	-0.5	10.3	6.6
2006	2.1	-0.5	-2.4	-5.7	3.7	19.3	0.7	-0.1	4.1	25.5
2007	1.2	6.6	0.2	1.3	-10.1	-7.3	5.5	-4.4	-3.8	1.9
2008	0.6	30.1	-10.0	3.1	-2.4	-5.1	-1.8	5.6	-13.3	13.0
2009	6.4	4.0	3.9	3.8	3.7	5.0	0.7	7.8	15.3	-3.2
2010	5.1	21.2	-1.8	-2.0	2.1	4.6	5.8	4.0	11.5	24.1
2011	2.7	2.3	-0.1	-13.7	0.3	2.7	8.2	-5.8	11.3	26.4
2012	5.5	10.7	4.0	-4.5	-2.4	2.0	1.7	-6.0	8.8	25.0
2013	6.9	15.1	3.8	2.0	8.8	16.9	0.9	-2.3	21.8	34.9
2014	-1.3	3.1	2.6	-3.6	7.5	6.0	0.3	-6.6	9.2	20.6
2015	3.9	23.3	0.6	11.5	3.7	2.8	-2.4	-12.7	5.8	26.5
2016	10.9	16.1	3.3	7.3	2.8	10.9	2.2	-10.5	20.2	52.6
Avg.	2.6	9.7	0.1	-4.6	3.7	7.5	1.4	-4.1	8.2	28.5
Fq%>0	74	78	56	30	78	85	74	22	78	89

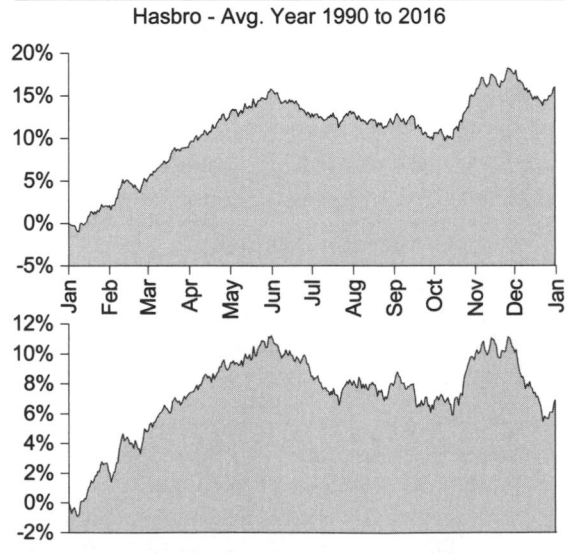

Hasbro - Avg. Year 1990 to 2016

Hasbro / S&P 500 Rel. Strength- Avg Yr. 1990-2016

Hasbro Performance

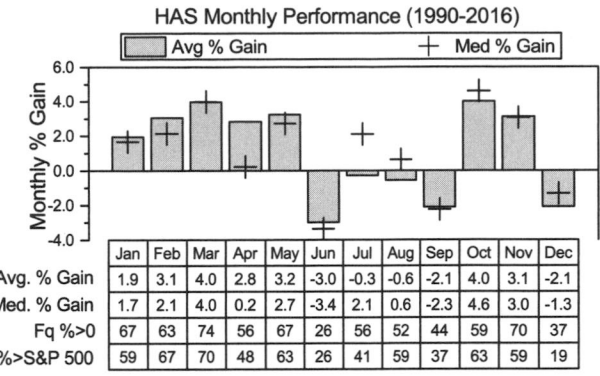

HAS Monthly Performance (1990-2016)

	Jan	Feb	Mar	Apr	May	Jun	Jul	Aug	Sep	Oct	Nov	Dec
Avg. % Gain	1.9	3.1	4.0	2.8	3.2	-3.0	-0.3	-0.6	-2.1	4.0	3.1	-2.1
Med. % Gain	1.7	2.1	4.0	0.2	2.7	-3.4	2.1	0.6	-2.3	4.6	3.0	-1.3
Fq %>0	67	63	74	56	67	26	56	52	44	59	70	37
Fq %>S&P 500	59	67	70	48	63	26	41	59	37	63	59	19

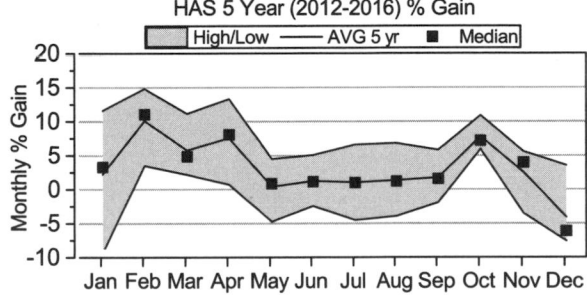

HAS 5 Year (2012-2016) % Gain

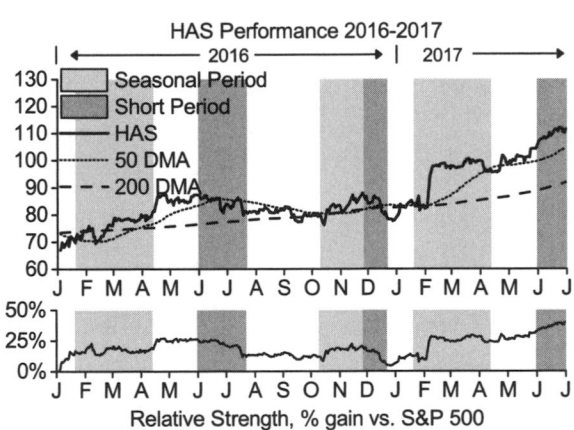

HAS Performance 2016-2017

Relative Strength, % gain vs. S&P 500

Market Indices & Rates
Weekly Values**

Stock Markets	2016	2017
Dow	16,287	19,895
S&P500	1,911	2,272
Nasdaq	4,591	5,554
TSX	12,255	15,444
FTSE	5,897	7,287
DAX	9,822	11,589
Nikkei	17,331	19,272
Hang Seng	19,775	22,801
Commodities	**2016**	**2017**
Oil	30.59	52.08
Gold	1091.3	1188.4
Bond Yields	**2016**	**2017**
USA 5 Yr Treasury	1.52	1.89
USA 10 Yr T	2.10	2.38
USA 20 Yr T	2.50	2.69
Moody's Aaa	3.95	3.87
Moody's Baa	5.42	4.62
CAN 5 Yr T	0.59	1.10
CAN 10 Yr T	1.24	1.69
Money Market	**2016**	**2017**
USA Fed Funds	0.50	0.75
USA 3 Mo T-B	0.23	0.52
CAN tgt overnight rate	0.50	0.50
CAN 3 Mo T-B	0.38	0.45
Foreign Exchange	**2016**	**2017**
EUR/USD	1.09	1.06
GBP/USD	1.44	1.22
USD/CAD	1.43	1.32
USD/JPY	117.63	115.28

JANUARY

M	T	W	T	F	S	S
1	2	3	4	5	6	7
8	9	10	11	12	13	14
15	16	17	18	19	20	21
22	23	24	25	26	27	28
29	30	31				

FEBRUARY

M	T	W	T	F	S	S
			1	2	3	4
5	6	7	8	9	10	11
12	13	14	15	16	17	18
19	20	21	22	23	24	24
26	27	28				

MARCH

M	T	W	T	F	S	S
			1	2	3	4
5	6	7	8	9	10	11
12	13	14	15	16	17	18
19	20	21	22	23	24	25
26	27	28	29	30	31	

From 1990 to 2016, March and October were on average the best months of the year for Hasbro. June, September and December were the worst months. Over the last five years, Hasbro has generally followed its long-term seasonal pattern.

In 2016 and 2017, three out of four of the seasonal periods were successful. In the June 1st to July 21st seasonal period, the Hasbro seasonal trade was not successful. Nevertheless, compound growth for the 2016/17 seasonal trades was 52.6%, versus the S&P 500 which had a return of 20.2%.

Silver— Shines at the Start of the Year
January 1st - March 31st

Silver is often thought of as the poor man's gold. Silver has a lot of similar properties to gold as it is a store of value and is used for jewelery and industrial purposes.

One of the major differences between silver and gold is the proportion of production that is used for industrial purposes. A very small amount of gold is used in industrial products due to its price. In comparison, a large portion of silver's production is used for industrial products because of its relatively low price, giving it properties of a base metal in addition to precious metal properties.

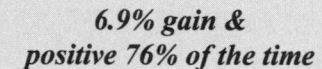

6.9% gain &
positive 76% of the time

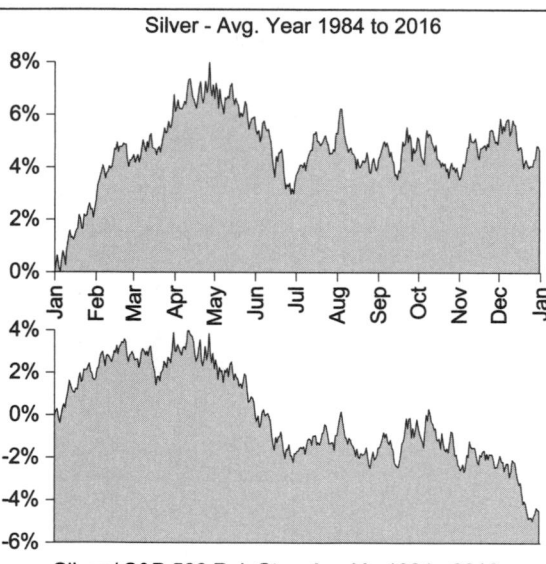

Silver - Avg. Year 1984 to 2016

Silver / S&P 500 Rel. Str. - Avg Yr. 1984 - 2016

Gold and silver have a high degree of price correlation, with silver typically mirroring the direction of gold's price changes. When gold increases in price, silver typically increases in price and vice versa. Despite this relationship, the seasonal profiles for gold and silver are different.

Base metals tend to perform well from late January into May, which helps to drive up the price of silver because of its industrial properties. The period of seasonal strength for silver does not last as long as the

Jan 1 to Mar 31	S&P 500	Silver	Positive Diff
1984	-3.5%	8.3%	11.8%
1985	8.0	5.9	-2.1
1986	13.1	-3.2	-16.2
1987	20.5	19.4	-1.1
1988	4.8	0.8	-4.0
1989	6.2	-4.7	-10.9
1990	-3.8	-4.8	-1.0
1991	13.6	-8.5	-22.1
1992	-3.2	6.7	10.0
1993	3.7	6.0	2.4
1994	-4.4	12.1	16.6
1995	9.0	6.4	-2.6
1996	4.8	7.3	2.5
1997	2.2	6.9	4.7
1998	13.5	5.8	-7.7
1999	4.7	0.4	-4.3
2000	2.0	-7.4	-9.4
2001	-12.1	-5.4	6.8
2002	-0.1	3.4	3.5
2003	-3.6	-4.4	-0.8
2004	1.3	31.2	29.9
2005	-2.6	5.5	8.1
2006	3.7	33.1	29.4
2007	0.2	3.5	3.3
2008	-9.9	21.9	31.8
2009	-11.7	21.5	33.2
2010	4.9	3.0	-1.9
2011	5.4	23.6	18.2
2012	12.0	15.1	3.1
2013	10.0	-4.4	-14.4
2014	1.3	2.4	1.1
2015	0.4	3.9	3.5
2016	0.8	11.3	10.5
2017	5.5	11.2	5.7
Avg	2.8%	6.9%	4.0%
Fq > 0	71%	76%	59%

Silver* vs. S&P 500 1984 to 2016

period of seasonal strength for base metals, as precious metals tend not to perform well in spring.

Historically, when silver has corrected sharply in December, it has often rallied strongly at the beginning of its seasonal period. This phenomenon has taken place over the last five years, including 2016.

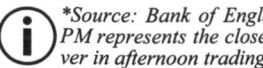

Source: Bank of England- London PM represents the close value of silver in afternoon trading in London.

Silver Performance

Silver Monthly Performance (1984-2016)

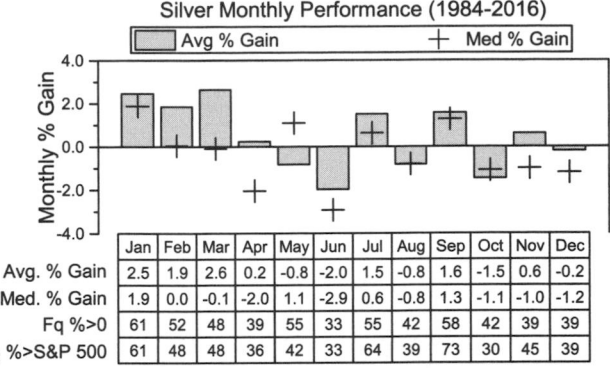

	Jan	Feb	Mar	Apr	May	Jun	Jul	Aug	Sep	Oct	Nov	Dec
Avg. % Gain	2.5	1.9	2.6	0.2	-0.8	-2.0	1.5	-0.8	1.6	-1.5	0.6	-0.2
Med. % Gain	1.9	0.0	-0.1	-2.0	1.1	-2.9	0.6	-0.8	1.3	-1.1	-1.0	-1.2
Fq %>0	61	52	48	39	55	33	55	42	58	42	39	39
Fq %>S&P 500	61	48	48	36	42	33	64	39	73	30	45	39

Silver 5 Year (2012-2016) % Gain

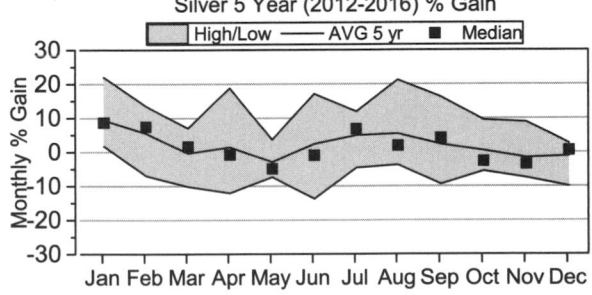

Silver Performance 2016-2017

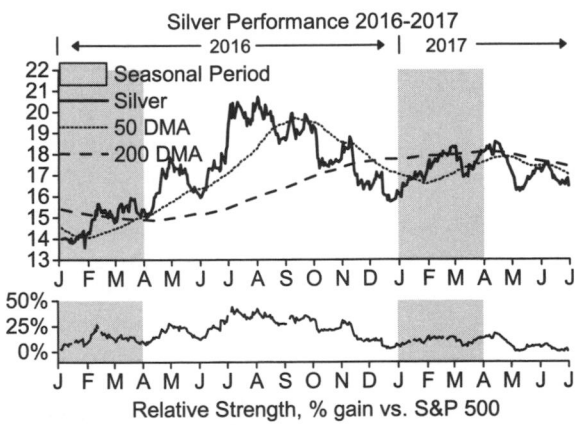

Relative Strength, % gain vs. S&P 500

Market Indices & Rates Weekly Values**

Stock Markets	2016	2017
Dow	15,940	19,798
S&P500	1,879	2,269
Nasdaq	4,503	5,547
TSX	12,043	15,455
FTSE	5,801	7,240
DAX	9,583	11,584
Nikkei	16,679	19,003
Hang Seng	19,076	22,919

Commodities	2016	2017
Oil	28.57	51.84
Gold	1094.0	1206.1

Bond Yields	2016	2017
USA 5 Yr Treasury	1.47	1.92
USA 10 Yr T	2.04	2.43
USA 20 Yr T	2.44	2.74
Moody's Aaa	4.03	3.92
Moody's Baa	5.45	4.65
CAN 5 Yr T	0.66	1.12
CAN 10 Yr T	1.22	1.72

Money Market	2016	2017
USA Fed Funds	0.50	0.75
USA 3 Mo T-B	0.28	0.53
CAN tgt overnight rate	0.50	0.50
CAN 3 Mo T-B	0.38	0.44

Foreign Exchange	2016	2017
EUR/USD	1.09	1.07
GBP/USD	1.42	1.23
USD/CAD	1.44	1.32
USD/JPY	117.68	114.19

JANUARY

M	T	W	T	F	S	S
1	2	3	4	5	6	7
8	9	10	11	12	13	14
15	16	17	18	19	20	21
22	23	24	25	26	27	28
29	30	31				

FEBRUARY

M	T	W	T	F	S	S
			1	2	3	4
5	6	7	8	9	10	11
12	13	14	15	16	17	18
19	20	21	22	23	24	24
26	27	28				

MARCH

M	T	W	T	F	S	S
			1	2	3	4
5	6	7	8	9	10	11
12	13	14	15	16	17	18
19	20	21	22	23	24	25
26	27	28	29	30	31	

From 1984 to 2016, January, February and March have on average been the strongest months of the year for silver. However, only January is a top ranked month on a median basis. The medians for February and March are "flat" and negative, respectively. In other words, some large returns have skewed the average upwards in February and March. Over the same time period, the weakest month of the year has been June.

From 2012 to 2016 the general seasonal trend has held up, as January and February have been the strongest months for silver. In both 2016 and 2017, silver was positive in its seasonal periods, with the 2017 rally extending out into July.

TJX COMPANIES INC.
January 22nd to March 30th

In 2017, TJX during its seasonally strong period, outperformed the retail sector and outperformed the S&P 500. Over the long-term, TJX has typically outperformed the retail sector when the sector has been positive, making it an excellent complement to a retail sector investment during the retail seasonal period.

TJX is an off-price apparel and home fashion retailer that typically reports its fourth quarter earnings in approximately the third week of February. The company, like the retail sector, benefits from investors expecting positive results from the Christmas season.

TJX's period of seasonal strength is similar to the seasonal period for the retail sector. The best time to invest in TJX has been from January 22nd to March 30th. From 1990 to 2017, investing in this period has produced an average gain of 12.4%, which is substantially better than the average 2.2% performance of the S&P 500. It is also important to note that the TJX has been positive 75% of the time during this period.

12.4% gain & positive 75% of the time

Equally impressive is the amount of times TJX has produced a large gain, versus a large loss in its seasonal period. In the last twenty-eight years, TJX has only had one loss of 10% or greater. In the same time period, TJX has had thirteen gains of 10% or greater.

Jan 22 to Mar 30	S&P 500	Retail	TJX
1990	0.2%	6.3%	6.7%
1991	13.3	21.7	61.9
1992	-2.3	1.7	17.0
1993	3.8	3.0	21.7
1994	-6.1	-0.1	-2.8
1995	8.1	9.7	-6.9
1996	5.5	19.7	43.6
1997	-1.1	10.4	-0.3
1998	12.6	19.7	25.4
1999	5.3	16.5	18.9
2000	3.2	5.1	35.4
2001	-13.6	1.7	16.4
2002	1.8	4.7	2.9
2003	-2.7	6.6	-6.7
2004	-1.8	5.4	3.5
2005	1.2	-0.6	-1.6
2006	3.1	4.5	3.8
2007	-0.7	-2.7	-10.2
2008	-0.8	1.4	13.1
2009	-6.3	8.1	29.0
2010	5.1	12.5	17.2
2011	3.5	3.5	6.1
2012	7.1	12.9	19.3
2013	5.6	6.2	4.5
2014	0.8	-2.7	-0.2
2015	2.7	12.5	6.8
2016	10.4	10.2	16.0
2017	4.3	5.4	5.7
Avg	2.2%	7.3%	12.4%
Fq > 0	68%	86%	75%

TJX* vs. Retail vs. S&P 500 1990 to 2017 — Positive

It is interesting to note that the seasonally strong period for TJX ends before April, one of the strongest months of the year for the stock market. It is possible that by the end of March, after a typically strong run for TJX, the full value of TJX's first quarter earnings report has already been priced into the stock and investors look to other companies in which to invest. This is particularly true if the economy and the stock market are in good shape.

On the other hand, in a soft economy, consumers favor off-price apparel companies such as TJX. In this scenario, TJX is more likely to perform strongly past the end of its seasonal period in March, allowing seasonal investors to continue holding TJX until it starts to show signs of weakness.

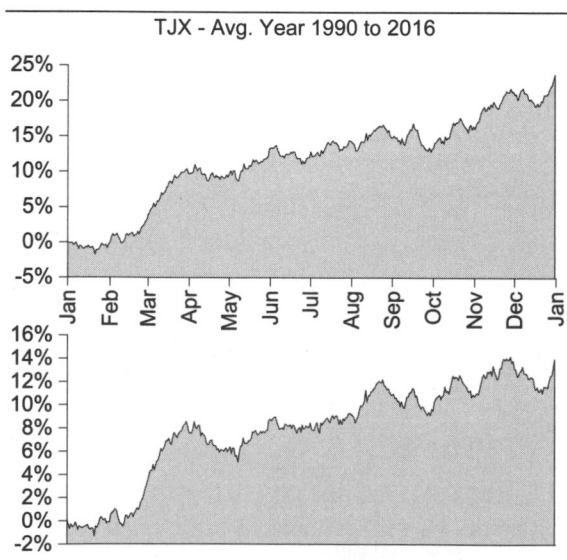

TJX - Avg. Year 1990 to 2016

TJX / S&P 500 Relative Strength - Avg Yr. 1990 - 2016

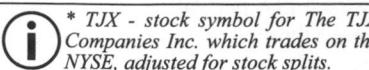

* TJX - stock symbol for The TJX Companies Inc. which trades on the NYSE, adjusted for stock splits.

TJX Performance

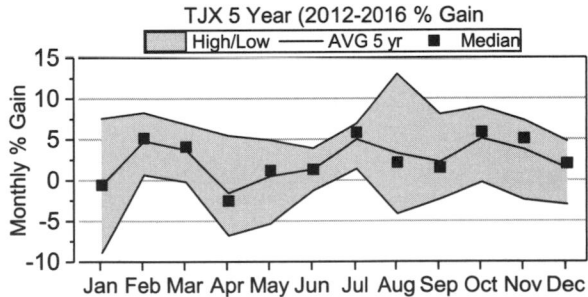

TJX Monthly Performance (1990-2016)

Legend: Avg % Gain | Med % Gain

Monthly % Gain

	Jan	Feb	Mar	Apr	May	Jun	Jul	Aug	Sep	Oct	Nov	Dec
Avg. % Gain	-0.3	3.4	6.6	-0.9	3.4	-0.9	1.9	0.8	-1.2	2.4	4.0	1.5
Med. % Gain	0.5	2.6	4.3	-2.1	1.4	-1.1	3.2	1.3	-2.1	2.8	3.4	1.4
Fq %>0	52	63	78	44	67	41	63	56	44	67	59	59
Fq %>S&P 500	59	59	78	37	59	52	67	70	48	59	59	59

TJX 5 Year (2012-2016 % Gain

Legend: High/Low — AVG 5 yr ■ Median

Monthly % Gain

Jan Feb Mar Apr May Jun Jul Aug Sep Oct Nov Dec

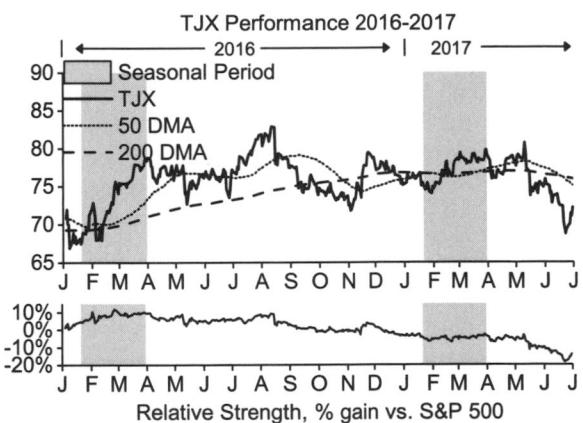

TJX Performance 2016-2017

2016 | 2017

Legend: Seasonal Period, TJX, 50 DMA, 200 DMA

J F M A M J J A S O N D J F M A M J J

Relative Strength, % gain vs. S&P 500

Market Indices & Rates
Weekly Values**

Stock Markets	2016	2017
Dow	16,107	19,995
S&P500	1,899	2,287
Nasdaq	4,535	5,625
TSX	12,453	15,585
FTSE	5,959	7,162
DAX	9,775	11,722
Nikkei	17,109	19,121
Hang Seng	19,226	23,126

Commodities	2016	2017
Oil	31.80	52.74
Gold	1112.5	1199.8

Bond Yields	2016	2017
USA 5 Yr Treasury	1.42	1.94
USA 10 Yr T	2.00	2.48
USA 20 Yr T	2.40	2.79
Moody's Aaa	4.05	3.97
Moody's Baa	5.46	4.69
CAN 5 Yr T	0.69	1.14
CAN 10 Yr T	1.24	1.77

Money Market	2016	2017
USA Fed Funds	0.50	0.75
USA 3 Mo T-B	0.32	0.51
CAN tgt overnight rate	0.50	0.50
CAN 3 Mo T-B	0.47	0.44

Foreign Exchange	2016	2017
EUR/USD	1.09	1.07
GBP/USD	1.43	1.26
USD/CAD	1.41	1.31
USD/JPY	119.07	113.88

JANUARY

M	T	W	T	F	S	S
1	2	3	4	5	6	7
8	9	10	11	12	13	14
15	16	17	18	19	20	21
22	23	24	25	26	27	28
29	30	31				

FEBRUARY

M	T	W	T	F	S	S
			1	2	3	4
5	6	7	8	9	10	11
12	13	14	15	16	17	18
19	20	21	22	23	24	24
26	27	28				

MARCH

M	T	W	T	F	S	S
		1	2	3	4	
5	6	7	8	9	10	11
12	13	14	15	16	17	18
19	20	21	22	23	24	25
26	27	28	29	30	31	

From 1990 to 2016, March has been the best month for TJX on an average, median and frequency basis. March is the core part of the seasonal period for TJX, which lasts from January 22nd to March 30th. The seasonal trade falls off sharply in April and investors should consider exiting early if weakness is evident. Over the last five years, March has been one of the better performing months.

In 2017, TJX performed well in its seasonal period, but corrected sharply, just after its seasonal period ended.

CVX CHEVRON
February 1st to May 5th

Chevron is one of the world's largest integrated energy companies with upstream and downstream operations. The company benefits from the seasonality of the energy sector, which tends to perform better in the time period from late February into early May. This energy seasonal period tends to be driven by the increased demand for oil in late spring, which is driven by the "driving season" that starts in late May on Memorial Day.

7.9% gain & positive 86% of the time

Chevron has a seasonal period that starts earlier than the energy sector, with its period starting February 1st and ending May 5th. In this period, from 1990 to 2017, Chevron produced an average gain of 7.9% and was positive 86% of the time. It outperformed the S&P 500, 64% of the time.

CVX* vs. S&P 500 1990 to 2017

Feb 1 to May 5	S&P 500	CVX	Diff
			Positive
1990	2.8%	0.4%	-2.5%
1991	10.7	8.4	-2.3
1992	2.0	7.5	5.5
1993	1.3	19.2	17.9
1994	-6.3	-6.8	-0.6
1995	10.6	9.2	-1.3
1996	0.9	9.2	8.3
1997	5.6	5.7	0.0
1998	13.8	15.3	1.5
1999	5.3	34.3	29.0
2000	2.7	8.5	5.8
2001	-7.3	12.1	19.4
2002	-5.0	6.8	11.8
2003	8.3	4.3	-4.0
2004	-0.9	9.3	10.2
2005	-0.7	-2.0	-1.3
2006	3.6	5.0	1.4
2007	4.7	8.8	4.1
2008	2.1	14.9	12.8
2009	9.4	-6.8	-16.2
2010	8.6	11.2	2.6
2011	3.8	8.1	4.3
2012	4.3	0.6	-3.7
2013	7.8	7.2	-0.5
2014	5.7	12.3	6.6
2015	4.7	5.3	0.6
2016	5.7	17.3	11.6
2017	5.3	-5.0	-10.3
Avg	3.9%	7.9%	4.0%
Fq > 0	82%	86%	64%

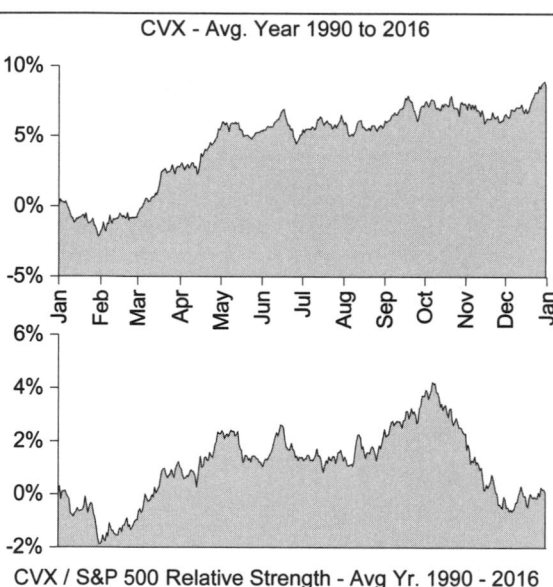

CVX - Avg. Year 1990 to 2016

CVX / S&P 500 Relative Strength - Avg Yr. 1990 - 2016

Chevron also benefits from investors rotating out of higher beta energy companies into more defensive integrated energy companies, which often occurs towards the end of the seasonal period for the energy sector.

Although Chevron has a similar seasonal period as the energy sector, it can provide value at the beginning and end parts of the energy seasonal trade by generally having more stability than most other companies in the energy sector.

Chevron is an integrated oil company with a diversified portfolio of assets. As a result, it tends to be more secure compared to many highly leveraged exploration and production oil companies. If the energy sector declines late in a year and continues into the next year, when it starts to show initial signs of strength, investors are often first attracted to integrated energy companies. Chevron is one of the companies that benefits from early interest in the energy sector.

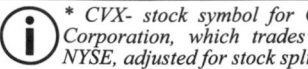

(i) ** CVX- stock symbol for Chevron Corporation, which trades on the NYSE, adjusted for stock splits.*

Chevron Performance

CVX Monthly Performance (1990-2016)

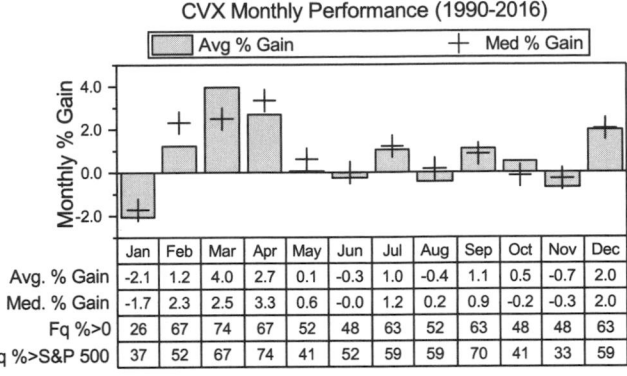

	Jan	Feb	Mar	Apr	May	Jun	Jul	Aug	Sep	Oct	Nov	Dec
Avg. % Gain	-2.1	1.2	4.0	2.7	0.1	-0.3	1.0	-0.4	1.1	0.5	-0.7	2.0
Med. % Gain	-1.7	2.3	2.5	3.3	0.6	-0.0	1.2	0.2	0.9	-0.2	-0.3	2.0
Fq %>0	26	67	74	67	52	48	63	52	63	48	48	63
Fq %>S&P 500	37	52	67	74	41	52	59	59	70	41	33	59

CVX 5 Year (2012-2016) % Gain

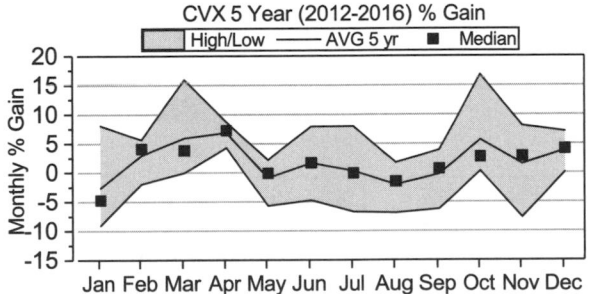

CVX Performance 2016-2017

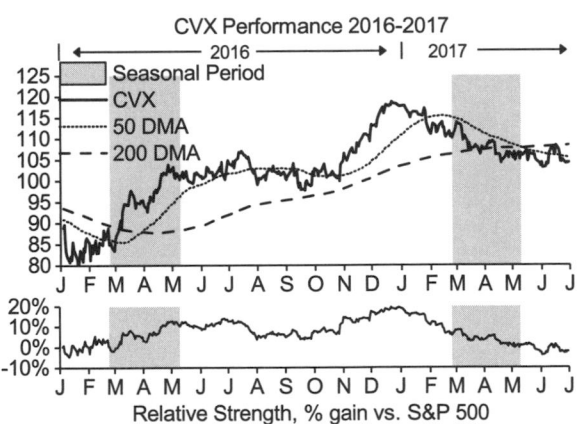

Relative Strength, % gain vs. S&P 500

From 1990 to 2016, February, March and April was the best three month contiguous period on an average, median and frequency basis. January was the weakest month of the year. With the worst month of the year being juxtaposed with the start of the strong seasonal period in the following month, selecting the best entry point with technical analysis is important. Over the last five years, Chevron has followed its overall seasonal period with the strongest months being February, March and April, and weakest month being January.

In 2016, Chevron was positive in its seasonal period. In 2017, Chevron was negative in its seasonal period.

Market Indices & Rates
Weekly Values**

Stock Markets	2016	2017
Dow	16,312	19,937
S&P500	1,910	2,284
Nasdaq	4,503	5,635
TSX	12,650	15,414
FTSE	5,913	7,131
DAX	9,491	11,631
Nikkei	17,334	19,078
Hang Seng	19,301	23,211

Commodities	2016	2017
Oil	31.28	53.34
Gold	1138.7	1209.3

Bond Yields	2016	2017
USA 5 Yr Treasury	1.29	1.92
USA 10 Yr T	1.89	2.48
USA 20 Yr T	2.30	2.80
Moody's Aaa	4.03	4.00
Moody's Baa	5.40	4.71
CAN 5 Yr T	0.61	1.12
CAN 10 Yr T	1.16	1.77

Money Market	2016	2017
USA Fed Funds	0.50	0.75
USA 3 Mo T-B	0.33	0.51
CAN tgt overnight rate	0.50	0.50
CAN 3 Mo T-B	0.45	0.46

Foreign Exchange	2016	2017
EUR/USD	1.11	1.08
GBP/USD	1.45	1.25
USD/CAD	1.39	1.30
USD/JPY	118.50	113.05

JANUARY

M	T	W	T	F	S	S
1	2	3	4	5	6	7
8	9	10	11	12	13	14
15	16	17	18	19	20	21
22	23	24	25	26	27	28
29	30	31				

FEBRUARY

M	T	W	T	F	S	S
			1	2	3	4
5	6	7	8	9	10	11
12	13	14	15	16	17	18
19	20	21	22	23	24	25
26	27	28				

MARCH

M	T	W	T	F	S	S
			1	2	3	4
5	6	7	8	9	10	11
12	13	14	15	16	17	18
19	20	21	22	23	24	25
26	27	28	29	30	31	

FEBRUARY

	MONDAY	TUESDAY	WEDNESDAY
WEEK 05	29	30	31
WEEK 06	**5** 23	**6** 22	**7** 21
WEEK 07	**12** 16	**13** 15	**14** 14
WEEK 08	**19** 9 CAN Market Closed - Family Day USA Market Closed - Presidents' Day	**20** 8	**21** 7
WEEK 09	**26** 2	**27** 1	**28**

THURSDAY		FRIDAY	
1	27	**2**	26
8	20	**9**	19
15	13	**16**	12
22	6	**23**	5
1		2	

MARCH

M	T	W	T	F	S	S
		1	2	3	4	
5	6	7	8	9	10	11
12	13	14	15	16	17	18
19	20	21	22	23	24	25
26	27	28	29	30	31	

APRIL

M	T	W	T	F	S	S
						1
2	3	4	5	6	7	8
9	10	11	12	13	14	15
16	17	18	19	20	21	22
23	24	25	26	27	28	29
30						

MAY

M	T	W	T	F	S	S
	1	2	3	4	5	6
7	8	9	10	11	12	13
14	15	16	17	18	19	20
21	22	23	24	25	26	27
28	29	30	31			

JUNE

M	T	W	T	F	S	S
				1	2	3
4	5	6	7	8	9	10
11	12	13	14	15	16	17
18	19	20	21	22	23	24
25	26	27	28	29	30	

FEBRUARY
SUMMARY

	Dow Jones	S&P 500	Nasdaq	TSX Comp
Month Rank	8	9	9	4
# Up	39	37	24	20
# Down	28	30	21	12
% Pos	58	55	53	63
% Avg. Gain	0.3	0.0	0.6	1.1

Dow & S&P 1950-2016, Nasdaq 1972-2016, TSX 1985-2016

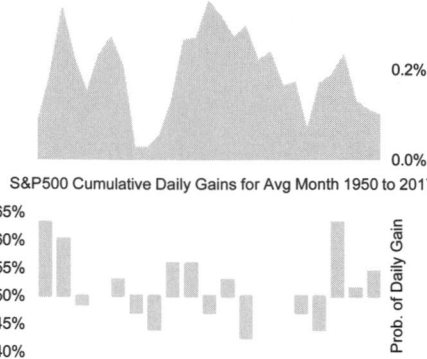

S&P500 Cumulative Daily Gains for Avg Month 1950 to 2017

♦ Historically, over the long-term, February has been one of the weaker months of the year for the S&P 500; but in recent years, February has "bucked" this trend. In 2017, the Trump rally continued into the month of February, with the S&P 500 producing an above average gain of 3.7%. ♦ Small caps tend to outperform in February. ♦ The energy sector typically starts to outperform in late February, which helps to boost the S&P/TSX Composite. ♦ The consumer discretionary sector tends to be one of the better performing sectors.

BEST / WORST FEBRUARY BROAD MKTS. 2008-2017

BEST FEBRUARY MARKETS
- ♦ Nikkei 225 (2012) 10.5%
- ♦ Nasdaq (2015) 7.1%
- ♦ Nikkei (2015) 6.4%

WORST FEBRUARY MARKETS
- ♦ Russell 2000 (2009) -12.3%
- ♦ Dow (2009) -11.7%
- ♦ S&P 500 (2009) -11.0%

Index Values End of Month

	2008	2009	2010	2011	2012	2013	2014	2015	2016	2017
Dow	12,266	7,063	10,325	12,226	12,952	14,054	16,322	18,133	16,517	20,812
S&P 500	1,331	735	1,104	1,327	1,366	1,515	1,859	2,105	1,932	2,364
Nasdaq	2,271	1,378	2,238	2,782	2,967	3,160	4,308	4,964	4,558	5,825
TSX Comp.	13,583	8,123	11,630	14,137	12,644	12,822	14,210	15,234	12,860	15,399
Russell 1000	726	400	607	736	756	841	1,041	1,173	1,067	1,311
Russell 2000	686	389	629	823	811	911	1,183	1,233	1,034	1,387
FTSE 100	5,884	3,830	5,355	5,994	5,872	6,361	6,810	6,947	6,097	7,263
Nikkei 225	13,603	7,568	10,126	10,624	9,723	11,559	14,841	18,798	16,027	19,119

Percent Gain for February

	2008	2009	2010	2011	2012	2013	2014	2015	2016	2017
Dow	-3.0	-11.7	2.6	2.8	2.5	1.4	4.0	5.6	0.3	4.8
S&P 500	-3.5	-11.0	2.9	3.2	4.1	1.1	4.3	5.5	-0.4	3.7
Nasdaq	-5.0	-6.7	4.2	3.0	5.4	0.6	5.0	7.1	-1.2	3.8
TSX Comp.	3.3	-6.6	4.8	4.3	1.5	1.1	3.8	3.8	0.3	0.1
Russell 1000	-3.3	-10.7	3.1	3.3	4.1	1.1	4.5	5.5	-0.3	3.6
Russell 2000	-3.8	-12.3	4.4	5.4	2.3	1.0	4.6	5.8	-0.1	1.8
FTSE 100	0.1	-7.7	3.2	2.2	3.3	1.3	4.6	2.9	0.2	2.3
Nikkei 225	0.1	-5.3	-0.7	3.8	10.5	3.8	-0.5	6.4	-8.5	0.4

February Market Avg. Performance 2008 to 2017[1]

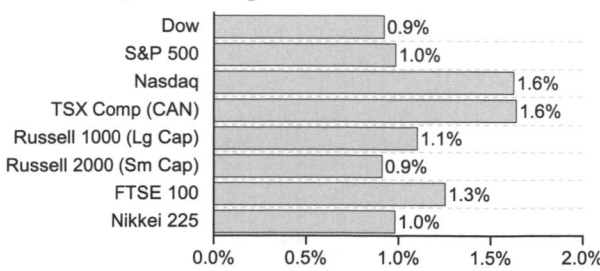

	Dow	0.9%
	S&P 500	1.0%
	Nasdaq	1.6%
	TSX Comp (CAN)	1.6%
	Russell 1000 (Lg Cap)	1.1%
	Russell 2000 (Sm Cap)	0.9%
	FTSE 100	1.3%
	Nikkei 225	1.0%

Interest Corner Feb[2]

	Fed Funds % [3]	3 Mo. T-Bill % [4]	10 Yr % [5]	20 Yr % [6]
2017	0.75	0.53	2.36	2.70
2016	0.50	0.33	1.74	2.19
2015	0.25	0.02	2.00	2.38
2014	0.25	0.05	2.66	3.31
2013	0.25	0.11	1.89	2.71

(1) Russell Data provided by Russell (2) Federal Reserve Bank of St. Louis- end of month values (3) Target rate set by FOMC (4)(5)(6) Constant yield maturities.

February 2017 % Sector Performance

S&P GIC	2017	1990-2017[1]	
Sectors	**% Gain**	**GIC[2] % Avg Gain**	**Fq% Gain >S&P 500**
Materials	0.5 %	1.6 %	61 %
Consumer Discretionary	1.8	1.3	71
Energy	-2.7	1.2	46
Consumer Staples	4.9	1.1	50
Industrials	3.4	0.7	50
Information Technology	4.9	0.3	54
Financials	5.0	0.2	61
Health Care	6.2	-0.2	39
Telecom	-0.4	-0.8	39
Utilities	4.7 %	-0.9 %	28 %
S&P 500	3.7 %	0.4 %	N/A %

Sector Commentary

♦ In February 2017, the defensive sectors of the stock market (consumer staples, utilities and health care) were strong performers, indicating that investors were starting to get nervous that the stock market rally may not continue. ♦ The energy sector continued to perform poorly as North American energy companies increased their oil production in reaction to OPEC quotas. ♦ The financial sector produced a solid gain of 5.0%, as investors were lured into the sector based on the prospect of higher interest rates increasing the net interest margin for banks.

Sub-Sector Commentary

♦ In February 2017, the metals and mining sub-sector corrected sharply after a strong rally in January. ♦ Homebuilders continued their strong January rally. ♦ Pharma performed well as investors perceived that Trump's proposed actions in the health care industry would not have a detrimental impact on drug pricing. ♦ Gold and silver continued their rally from the previous month. ♦ The retail sector was positive, but underperformed the stock market as investors were concerned about the "Amazon effect," (online sales replacing "bricks and mortar" retail sales).

SELECTED SUB-SECTORS[3]			
SOX (1995-2017)	2.7 %	2.9 %	61 %
Silver	5.7	2.7	54
Retail	2.4	2.0	71
Metals & Mining	-6.6	1.9	54
Chemicals	2.5	1.9	71
Gold	3.5	1.3	46
Steel	7.7	0.9	54
Agriculture (1994-2017)	6.1	0.9	50
Automotive & Components	2.4	0.8	46
Transportation	2.7	0.7	54
Railroads	2.6	0.5	46
Homebuilders	6.6	0.4	61
Banks	5.9	0.3	57
Pharma	8.1	-0.3	39
Biotech (1993-2017)	5.3	-0.7	52

RETAIL – POST HOLIDAY BARGAIN
SHOP Jan 21st and RETURN Your Investment Apr 12th

Historically, the retail sector has outperformed from January 21st until April 12th. From 1990 to 2017, during its seasonally strong period, the retail sector produced an average gain of 8.4%, compared with the S&P 500's average gain of 2.6%. Not only has the retail sector had greater gains than the broad market, but it has also outperformed it on a fairly regular basis: 79% of the time.

5.7% extra & 79% of the time
better than the S&P 500

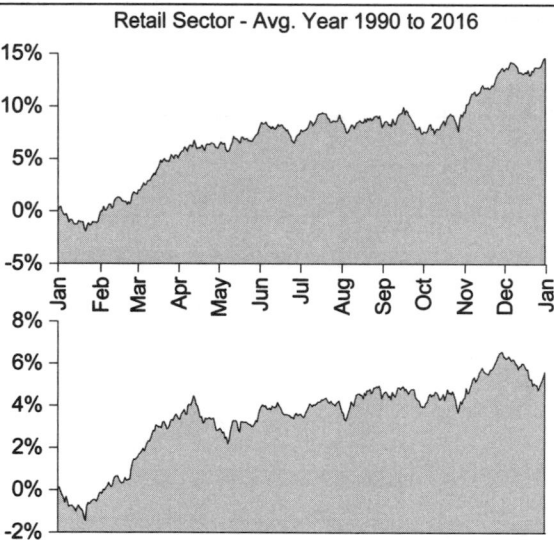

Retail Sector - Avg. Year 1990 to 2016

Retail / S&P 500 Relative Strength - Avg Yr. 1990 - 2016

Retail Sector vs. S&P 500 1990 to 2017			
Jan 21 to Apr 12	S&P 500	Positive Retail	Diff
1990	1.5 %	9.7 %	8.1 %
1991	14.5	29.9	15.4
1992	-2.9	-2.7	0.2
1993	3.5	-0.6	-4.0
1994	-5.8	2.0	7.8
1995	9.1	7.4	-1.8
1996	4.1	19.7	15.7
1997	-5.0	6.0	11.0
1998	13.5	20.1	6.6
1999	8.1	23.4	15.2
2000	1.5	5.8	4.3
2001	-11.8	-0.5	11.3
2002	-1.5	6.7	8.2
2003	-3.7	6.5	10.3
2004	0.6	6.7	6.1
2005	1.1	-1.6	-2.7
2006	2.1	3.4	1.3
2007	1.2	-0.7	-1.9
2008	0.6	3.5	3.0
2009	6.4	25.1	18.7
2010	5.1	15.5	10.4
2011	2.7	4.4	1.7
2012	5.5	12.1	6.6
2013	6.9	10.1	3.2
2014	-1.3	-7.1	-5.8
2015	3.9	15.5	11.5
2016	10.9	9.7	-1.2
2017	3.2	4.6	1.4
Avg.	2.6 %	8.4 %	5.7 %
Fq > 0	75 %	79 %	79 %

Most investors think that the best time to invest in retail stocks is before Black Friday in November. Yes, there is a positive seasonal cycle at this time, but it is not as strong as the cycle from January to April.

The worst month for retail sales is January. Consumers are all shopped out from the holiday season. Investors start becoming attracted to the sector as the prospect of increasing spring sales unfolds. Seasonal investors enter the sector in late January, in order to take advantage of the increasing interest in the sector by other investors that takes place over the next two to three months.

The January retail bounce coincides with the "rosy" stock market analysts' forecasts that tend to occur at the beginning of the year. These forecasts generally rely on healthy consumer spending which makes up approximately 2/3 of the GDP. The retail sector benefits from the optimistic forecasts and tends to outperform the S&P 500.

From a seasonal basis, investors have been best served by exiting the retail sector in April and then returning to it later, at the end of October (see *Retail Shop Early* strategy).

ⓘ *Retail SP GIC Sector # 2550: An index designed to represent a cross section of retail companies*
For more information on the retail sector, see www.standardandpoors.com.

Retail Performance

Retail Monthly Performance (1990-2016)

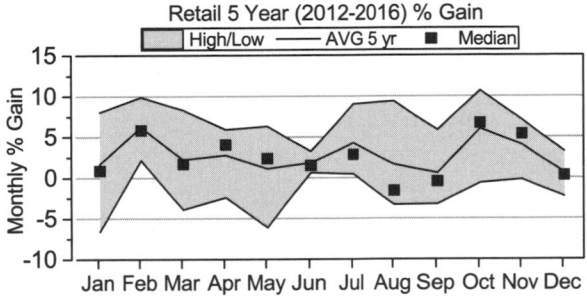

	Jan	Feb	Mar	Apr	May	Jun	Jul	Aug	Sep	Oct	Nov	Dec
Avg. % Gain	-0.1	2.1	3.3	0.8	1.8	-0.5	1.0	-0.5	-0.6	2.1	3.4	0.9
Med. % Gain	0.1	2.0	1.2	0.5	2.3	-0.5	0.8	1.1	-1.1	2.2	3.9	0.0
Fq %>0	50	69	73	58	62	46	58	54	46	69	81	50
Fq %>S&P 500	54	73	73	42	62	58	58	62	46	58	69	35

Retail 5 Year (2012-2016) % Gain

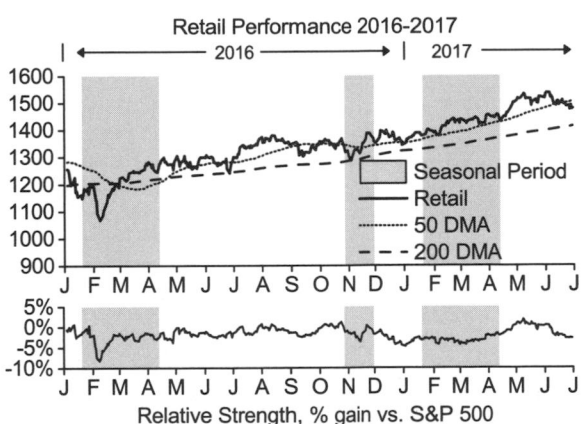

Retail Performance 2016-2017

	WEEK 06	
Market Indices & Rates		
Weekly Values**		
Stock Markets	**2016**	**2017**
Dow	15,918	20,128
S&P500	1,850	2,301
Nasdaq	4,288	5,694
TSX	12,294	15,571
FTSE	5,648	7,207
DAX	8,919	11,582
Nikkei	15,939	19,036
Hang Seng	18,433	23,453
Commodities	**2016**	**2017**
Oil	28.15	52.88
Gold	1211.0	1233.0
Bond Yields	**2016**	**2017**
USA 5 Yr Treasury	1.15	1.86
USA 10 Yr T	1.71	2.39
USA 20 Yr T	2.13	2.73
Moody's Aaa	3.92	3.95
Moody's Baa	5.29	4.64
CAN 5 Yr T	0.52	1.06
CAN 10 Yr T	1.05	1.68
Money Market	**2016**	**2017**
USA Fed Funds	0.50	0.75
USA 3 Mo T-B	0.30	0.54
CAN tgt overnight rate	0.50	0.50
CAN 3 Mo T-B	0.45	0.46
Foreign Exchange	**2016**	**2017**
EUR/USD	1.13	1.07
GBP/USD	1.45	1.25
USD/CAD	1.39	1.31
USD/JPY	114.00	112.51

Relative Strength, % gain vs. S&P 500

FEBRUARY

M	T	W	T	F	S	S
		1	2	3	4
5	6	7	8	9	10	11
12	13	14	15	16	17	18
19	20	21	22	23	24	24
26	27	28				

MARCH

M	T	W	T	F	S	S
			1	2	3	4
5	6	7	8	9	10	11
12	13	14	15	16	17	18
19	20	21	22	23	24	25
26	27	28	29	30	31	

From 1990 to 2016, the two best months of the year on an average basis for the retail sector were March and November. November is the core part of the autumn retail seasonal trade and March is the core part of the spring retail seasonal trade.

On average, over the last five years, from 2012 to 2016, the retail sector has followed its general seasonal pattern with the strongest months being February, April, October and November. These months are part of either the spring seasonal trade or the autumn seasonal trade. In 2017, the retail sector outperformed the S&P 500 in its spring seasonal period.

APRIL

M	T	W	T	F	S	S
						1
2	3	4	5	6	7	8
9	10	11	12	13	14	15
16	17	18	19	20	21	22
23	24	25	26	27	28	29
30						

EASTMAN CHEMICAL COMPANY
①LONG (Jan28-May5)
②SELL SHORT (May30-Oct27)

In 2016, Eastman Chemical performed according to its seasonal trends, outperforming from January 28th to May 5th and underperforming from May 30th to October 27th.

In its positive seasonal period from January 28th to May 5th, Eastman Chemical during the period from 1994 to 2016, has produced an average 13.5% gain and has been positive 87% of the time. In its short sell seasonal period from May 30th to October 27th, in the same yearly period, Eastman Chemical has produced an average loss of 6.4% and has been positive 35% of the time. The short sell seasonal period has not been as successful as the long seasonal period, especially in recent years. Nevertheless, investors should still be aware of the weaker period for Eastman Chemical in the summer months.

20.8% growth & positive 74% of the time

Eastman Chemical, in its 10-K report filed with regulators in 2013, outlines the seasonal trends in its business. "The Company's earnings are typically greater in second and third quarters." This is a bit different than many other cyclical companies, that tend to have weaker earnings over the summer months. The net result is for Eastman Chemical to outperform into May and then underperform at the tail end of Q2, and Q3, as investors anticipate a weaker Q4 earnings report. In Q4, Eastman tends to perform at market.

Eastman Chemical* vs. S&P 500 1994 to 2016

Positive Long ▢　　　　Negative Short ▢

Year	Jan 28 to May 5 S&P 500	Jan 28 to May 5 EMN	May 30 to Oct 27 S&P 500	May 30 to Oct 27 EMN	Compound Growth S&P 500	Compound Growth EMN
1994	-5.4	7.8 %	1.9 %	8.7 %	-3.6 %	-1.6 %
1995	10.6	11.0	10.7	2.6	22.4	8.2
1996	3.2	7.1	4.9	-21.8	8.3	30.5
1997	8.5	-1.1	3.9	2.7	12.8	-3.8
1998	15.1	18.7	-2.3	-15.3	12.4	36.8
1999	8.4	32.1	-0.4	-24.5	8.0	64.4
2000	2.4	21.9	0.1	-19.3	2.6	45.3
2001	-6.5	22.7	-12.9	-33.1	-18.6	63.2
2002	-5.3	13.1	-15.9	-21.2	-20.4	37.0
2003	9.3	-11.4	8.6	-0.6	18.7	-10.9
2004	-2.0	16.4	0.4	-1.9	-1.6	18.6
2005	-0.2	10.5	-1.7	-15.7	-1.8	27.9
2006	3.3	17.3	7.6	5.5	11.1	10.9
2007	5.9	11.8	1.1	-0.1	7.1	11.9
2008	5.8	14.9	-39.3	-55.6	-35.8	78.8
2009	6.9	52.4	15.7	34.3	23.6	0.2
2010	6.2	12.4	8.5	33.0	15.3	-24.7
2011	2.7	9.2	-3.5	-23.1	-0.8	34.5
2012	4.0	0.6	6.0	21.6	10.2	-21.1
2013	7.4	-5.6	6.8	8.4	14.7	-13.5
2014	5.8	15.5	2.2	-15.6	8.1	33.4
2015	3.0	13.1	-2.0	-6.0	0.9	19.9
2016	8.9	21.5	1.6	-8.8	10.7	32.1
Avg.	4.3 %	13.5 %	0.1 %	-6.4 %	4.5 %	20.8 %
Fq>0	78 %	87 %	65 %	35 %	70 %	74 %

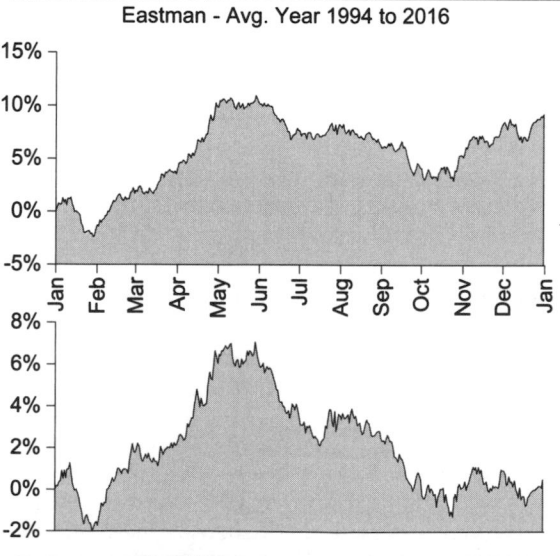

Eastman - Avg. Year 1994 to 2016

Eastman / S&P 500 Rel. Strength- Avg Yr. 1994-2016

Eastman Chemical Performance

EMN Monthly Performance (1994-2016)

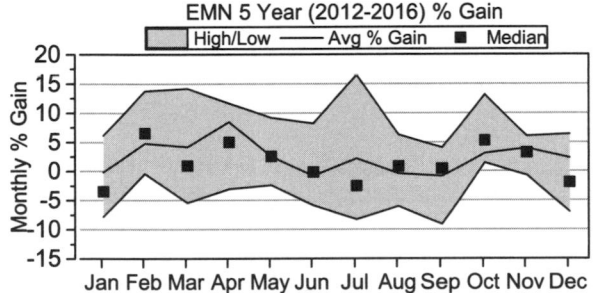

Legend: Avg % Gain, Med % Gain

	Jan	Feb	Mar	Apr	May	Jun	Jul	Aug	Sep	Oct	Nov	Dec
Avg. % Gain	-1.7	3.2	2.6	6.9	0.9	-2.4	0.6	-2.0	-2.4	1.5	2.4	0.7
Med. % Gain	-3.0	5.0	0.8	5.3	1.3	-2.8	-3.4	-1.1	-1.0	-0.2	1.3	-0.1
Fq %>0	30	74	57	74	57	26	39	48	39	43	70	48
Fq %>S&P 500	26	70	57	70	48	26	48	52	30	43	65	43

EMN 5 Year (2012-2016) % Gain

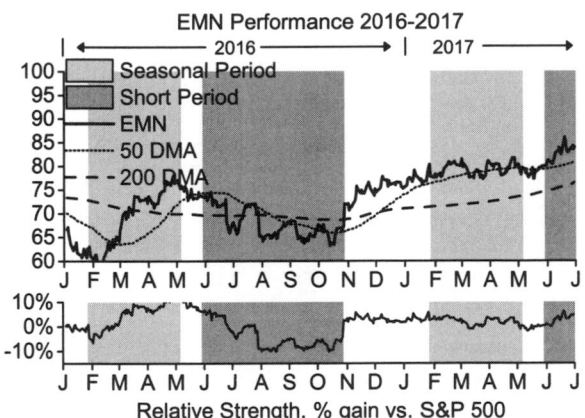

Legend: High/Low, Avg % Gain, Median

EMN Performance 2016-2017

Legend: Seasonal Period, Short Period, EMN, 50 DMA, 200 DMA

Relative Strength, % gain vs. S&P 500

Market Indices & Rates
Weekly Values**

Stock Markets	2016	2017
Dow	16,364	20,554
S&P500	1,915	2,343
Nasdaq	4,490	5,804
TSX	12,792	15,818
FTSE	5,928	7,286
DAX	9,314	11,771
Nikkei	16,015	19,344
Hang Seng	19,123	23,910

Commodities	2016	2017
Oil	30.03	53.20
Gold	1213.8	1232.0

Bond Yields	2016	2017
USA 5 Yr Treasury	1.24	1.96
USA 10 Yr T	1.78	2.46
USA 20 Yr T	2.19	2.80
Moody's Aaa	4.01	3.98
Moody's Baa	5.37	4.66
CAN 5 Yr T	0.61	1.16
CAN 10 Yr T	1.14	1.75

Money Market	2016	2017
USA Fed Funds	0.50	0.75
USA 3 Mo T-B	0.30	0.53
CAN tgt overnight rate	0.50	0.50
CAN 3 Mo T-B	0.46	0.47

Foreign Exchange	2016	2017
EUR/USD	1.11	1.06
GBP/USD	1.44	1.25
USD/CAD	1.38	1.31
USD/JPY	113.73	113.65

FEBRUARY

M	T	W	T	F	S	S
		1	2	3	4	
5	6	7	8	9	10	11
12	13	14	15	16	17	18
19	20	21	22	23	24	24
26	27	28				

MARCH

M	T	W	T	F	S	S
		1	2	3	4	
5	6	7	8	9	10	11
12	13	14	15	16	17	18
19	20	21	22	23	24	25
26	27	28	29	30	31	

APRIL

M	T	W	T	F	S	S
					1	
2	3	4	5	6	7	8
9	10	11	12	13	14	15
16	17	18	19	20	21	22
23	24	25	26	27	28	29
30						

From 1994 to 2016, the best performing months for Eastman Chemical were February and April on an average, median and frequency basis. These months are the cornerstones of the long seasonal trade. On a median basis, the worst performing contiguous months were June through October, as all five months had negative medians. These months make up the bulk of the ideal time to short Eastman Chemical.

Over the last five years, Eastman Chemical has performed well in its seasonally strong period. In 2016 and 2017, the combination of the long and short seasonal periods worked well.

AUTOMOTIVE & COMPONENTS
①LONG (Dec14-Jan7) ②LONG (Feb24-Apr24)
③SELL SHORT (Aug3-Oct3)

The automotive and components sector (auto sector) has its main seasonal period from February 24th to April 24. In this time period, from 1990 to 2016, the sector has produced an average gain of 8.2% and has been positive 74% of the time.

From 1989/90 to 2015/16, the total seasonal strategy of investing in the auto sector on December 14th, exiting on January 7th, reinvesting on February 24th, exiting on April 24th and shorting the sector from August 3rd to October 3rd, has produced an average gain of 20.0%.

20.0% gain & positive 78% of the time

The auto sector tends to rise in the spring, as investors look to benefit from being in this sector ahead of the peak in auto sales in May.

After the peak, auto sales generally decline from May until November (1975-2013, source: BEA). As a result, shorting the sector from August 3rd to October 3rd has proven to be profitable. The trend changes as auto sales increase in December, creating a positive seasonal period from December 14th to January 7th.

Automotive & Components* vs. S&P 500 1989/90 to 2015/16

Negative Short ☐   Positive Long ▨

Year	Dec 14 to Jan 7		Feb 24 to Apr 24		Aug 3 to Oct 3		Compound Growth	
	S&P 500	Auto	S&P 500	Auto	S&P 500	Auto	S&P 500	Auto
1989/90	-0.2 %	-0.8 %	1.9 %	4.4 %	-11.4 %	-19.3 %	-9.8 %	23.6 %
1990/91	-4.2	-4.0	4.7	6.9	-0.7	-6.3	-0.4	9.1
1991/92	8.6	15.7	-0.6	9.1	-3.2	-16.4	4.4	46.8
1992/93	-0.7	3.6	0.5	11.2	2.5	-1.8	2.3	17.3
1993/94	0.9	1.5	-4.9	-11.1	0.3	-9.5	-3.8	-1.2
1994/95	2.3	10.9	5.3	2.7	4.2	-0.5	12.3	14.4
1995/96	-0.8	1.1	-1.4	11.4	4.6	-2.1	2.3	15.0
1996/97	3.4	4.3	-3.8	-4.0	1.9	6.9	1.3	-6.7
1997/98	1.1	0.1	6.7	10.4	-10.5	-23.0	-3.5	35.9
1998/99	8.9	10.0	6.7	5.8	-3.4	-2.8	12.2	19.5
1999/00	1.9	8.5	5.1	22.9	-0.9	1.8	6.1	31.0
2000/01	-4.5	8.7	-2.9	4.0	-12.2	-27.9	-18.6	44.7
2001/02	4.1	4.6	0.3	12.2	-5.2	-12.1	-1.1	31.6
2002/03	3.8	5.2	7.5	10.1	5.1	7.2	17.2	7.5
2003/04	4.9	12.8	0.0	7.0	2.3	-2.8	7.2	24.0
2004/05	-1.0	0.7	-3.3	-22.4	-1.4	-10.5	-5.6	-13.6
2005/06	1.4	0.8	1.6	-0.8	4.4	7.9	7.6	-7.9
2006/07	-0.3	5.1	2.0	-2.5	4.6	2.0	6.4	0.4
2007/08	-4.9	-9.6	2.6	6.1	-12.8	-15.1	-14.8	10.4
2008/09	3.1	1.0	16.5	102.4	3.8	-11.4	24.7	127.8
2009/10	3.2	16.3	11.2	21.3	1.8	-3.1	16.8	45.4
2010/11	2.5	9.8	2.3	2.7	-12.4	-24.0	-8.1	39.8
2011/12	4.3	10.3	0.6	-5.8	6.3	10.8	11.5	-7.3
2012/13	3.0	13.6	4.2	6.9	-1.8	-0.3	5.3	21.8
2013/14	3.5	-1.4	2.3	1.0	2.2	-6.8	8.3	6.3
2014/15	1.2	3.5	0.4	-1.7	-7.3	-4.2	-5.8	5.9
2015/16	-3.4	-9.5	8.9	12.6	0.2	3.9	5.3	-2.0
Avg.	-1.5 %	4.6 %	2.8 %	8.2 %	-1.4 %	-5.9 %	3.0 %	20.0 %
Fq>0	67 %	81 %	74	74 %	52 %	26 %	63 %	78 %

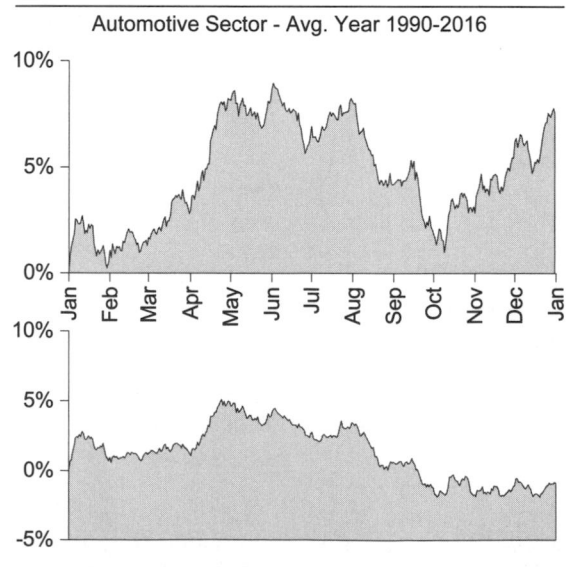

Automotive Sector - Avg. Year 1990-2016

Automotive / S&P 500 Rel. Strength- Avg Yr. 1990-2016

Automotive Performance

Auto Monthly Performance (1990-2016)

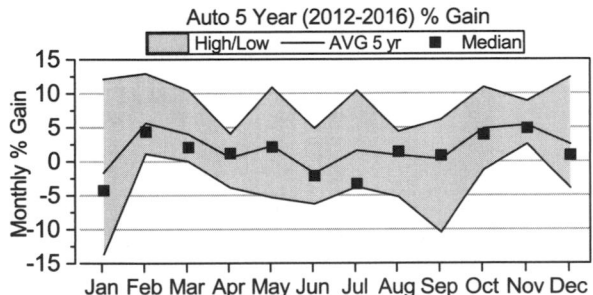

Legend: ☐ Avg % Gain   + Med % Gain

	Jan	Feb	Mar	Apr	May	Jun	Jul	Aug	Sep	Oct	Nov	Dec
Avg. % Gain	0.5	0.7	1.6	5.8	0.3	-1.9	1.4	-3.3	-2.5	0.6	1.7	1.3
Med. % Gain	1.4	-0.3	0.7	1.9	0.0	-1.2	0.5	-1.9	-1.8	1.5	2.7	1.7
Fq %>0	56	41	56	67	52	48	56	37	30	56	63	59
Fq %>S&P 500	48	48	56	52	26	44	52	33	37	41	56	37

Auto 5 Year (2012-2016) % Gain

Legend: ☐ High/Low — AVG 5 yr ■ Median

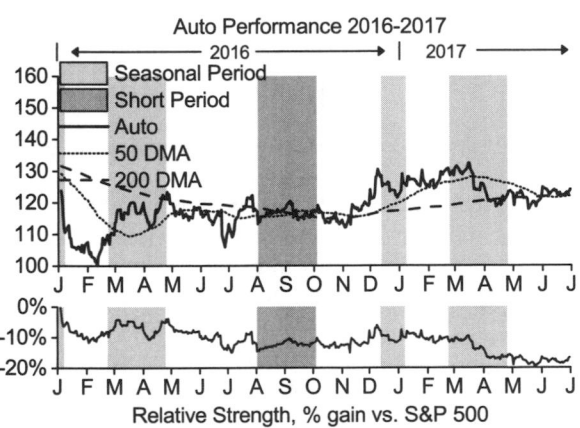

Jan Feb Mar Apr May Jun Jul Aug Sep Oct Nov Dec

Auto Performance 2016-2017

Legend: Seasonal Period, Short Period, Auto, 50 DMA, 200 DMA

Relative Strength, % gain vs. S&P 500

WEEK 08

Market Indices & Rates
Weekly Values**

Stock Markets	2016	2017
Dow	16,575	20,788
S&P500	1,939	2,365
Nasdaq	4,558	5,852
TSX	12,780	15,767
FTSE	5,995	7,278
DAX	9,401	11,909
Nikkei	16,082	19,333
Hang Seng	19,265	24,078

Commodities	2016	2017
Oil	31.38	53.74
Gold	1229.1	1241.7

Bond Yields	2016	2017
USA 5 Yr Treasury	1.22	1.88
USA 10 Yr T	1.75	2.39
USA 20 Yr T	2.17	2.75
Moody's Aaa	3.91	3.91
Moody's Baa	5.31	4.60
CAN 5 Yr T	0.63	1.15
CAN 10 Yr T	1.15	1.69

Money Market	2016	2017
USA Fed Funds	0.50	0.75
USA 3 Mo T-B	0.33	0.52
CAN tgt overnight rate	0.50	0.50
CAN 3 Mo T-B	0.47	0.48

Foreign Exchange	2016	2017
EUR/USD	1.10	1.06
GBP/USD	1.40	1.25
USD/CAD	1.36	1.31
USD/JPY	112.84	112.96

FEBRUARY

M	T	W	T	F	S	S
			1	2	3	4
5	6	7	8	9	10	11
12	13	14	15	16	17	18
19	20	21	22	23	24	24
26	27	28				

MARCH

M	T	W	T	F	S	S
			1	2	3	4
5	6	7	8	9	10	11
12	13	14	15	16	17	18
19	20	21	22	23	24	25
26	27	28	29	30	31	

From 1990 to 2016, April has been the best month of the year for the auto sector on an average and frequency basis. April is the core of the spring seasonal strategy.

Over the last five years, the auto sector has generally followed its seasonal trend of weakness in the summer months and strength in the autumn months. October has been uncharacteristically strong, especially given that the auto sector tends to underperform the S&P 500 at this time of the year. In 2016 and 2017, the combination of long and short trades produced a loss and underperformed the S&P 500.

APRIL

M	T	W	T	F	S	S
						1
2	3	4	5	6	7	8
9	10	11	12	13	14	15
16	17	18	19	20	21	22
23	24	25	26	27	28	29
30						

OIL STOCKS – WINTER/SPRING STRATEGY
February 25th to May 9th

The *Energy- Winter/Spring Strategy* is a strong seasonal performer over the long-term. From 1984 to 2017, for the two and half months starting on February 25th and ending May 9th, the energy sector (XOI) has outperformed the S&P 500 by an average 3.8%.

What is even more impressive are the positive returns, 28 out of 34 times, and the outperformance of the S&P 500, 76% of the time.

3.8% extra and 76% of the time better than the S&P 500, in just over two months

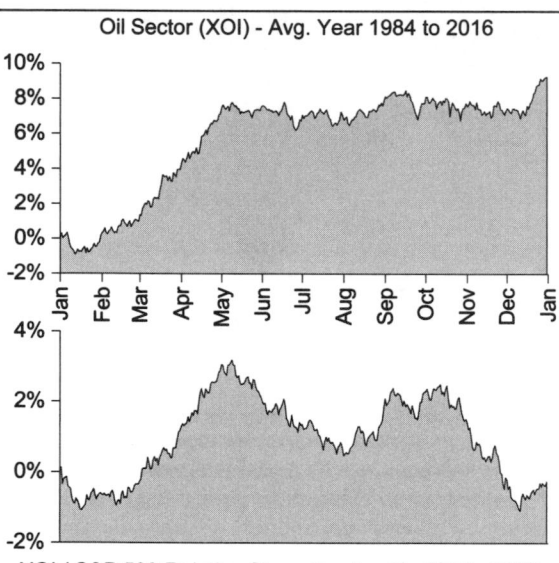

Oil Sector (XOI) - Avg. Year 1984 to 2016

XOI / S&P 500 Relative Strength - Avg Yr. 1984 - 2016

XOI* vs S&P 500 1984 to 2017

Feb 25 to May 9	S&P 500	positive XOI	Diff
1984	1.7 %	5.6 %	3.9 %
1985	1.4	4.9	3.5
1986	6.0	7.7	1.7
1987	3.7	25.5	21.8
1988	-3.0	5.6	8.6
1989	6.3	8.1	1.8
1990	5.8	-0.6	-6.3
1991	4.8	6.8	2.0
1992	0.9	5.8	4.9
1993	0.3	6.3	6.0
1994	-4.7	3.2	7.9
1995	7.3	10.3	3.1
1996	-2.1	2.2	4.3
1997	1.8	4.7	2.9
1998	7.5	9.8	2.3
1999	7.3	35.4	28.1
2000	4.3	22.2	17.9
2001	0.8	10.2	9.4
2002	-1.5	5.3	6.9
2003	12.1	5.7	-6.4
2004	-3.5	4.0	7.5
2005	-1.8	-1.0	0.8
2006	2.8	9.4	6.6
2007	4.2	10.1	5.8
2008	2.6	7.6	5.0
2009	20.2	15.8	-4.4
2010	0.5	-2.3	-2.8
2011	3.1	-0.6	-3.7
2012	-0.8	-13.4	-12.5
2013	7.3	3.8	-3.5
2014	1.7	9.1	7.4
2015	0.3	1.2	1.1
2016	6.7	11.1	4.4
2017	1.3	-4.0	-5.2
Avg	3.1 %	6.9 %	3.8 %
Fq > 0	79 %	82 %	76 %

A lot of investors assume that the time to buy oil stocks is just before the cold winter sets in. The rationale is that oil will climb in price as the temperature drops.

The results in the market have not supported this assumption. The price for a barrel of oil has more to do with oil inventory. Refineries have a choice: they can produce either gasoline or heating oil. As the winter progresses, refineries start to convert their operations from heating oil to gasoline.

In late winter and early spring, as refineries start coming off their conversion and winter maintenance programs, they increase their demand for oil, putting upward pressure on its price. In addition, later in the spring, in April and early May, investors increase their holdings in the oil sector before the driving season kicks off (Memorial Day in May), helping to drive up the price of oil stocks.

(i) *NYSE Arca Oil Index (XOI):* *An index designed to represent a cross section of widely held oil corporations involved in various phases of the oil industry.*

For more information on the XOI index, see www.cboe.com

NYSE Arca Oil Index (XOI) Performance

XOI Monthly Performance (1984-2016)

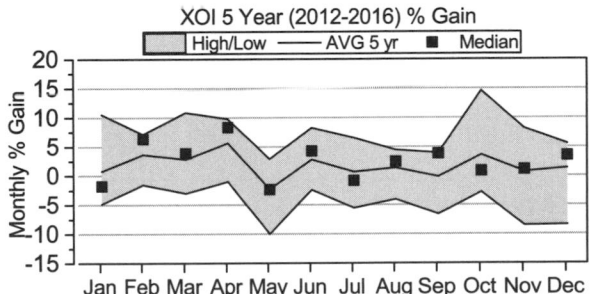

Legend: Avg % Gain, + Med % Gain

	Jan	Feb	Mar	Apr	May	Jun	Jul	Aug	Sep	Oct	Nov	Dec
Avg. % Gain	0.5	0.8	3.1	3.2	0.6	-0.8	0.3	0.8	-0.2	0.3	-0.4	1.8
Med. % Gain	0.1	1.6	2.7	2.5	0.8	-1.8	1.2	0.5	0.0	-0.0	0.8	1.0
Fq %>0	48	55	73	82	61	39	55	58	52	48	55	64
Fq %>S&P 500	33	55	67	64	39	36	48	64	58	52	36	55

XOI 5 Year (2012-2016) % Gain

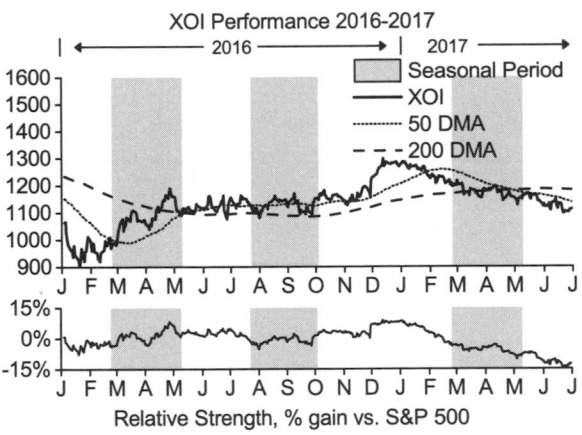

Legend: High/Low, AVG 5 yr, ■ Median

XOI Performance 2016-2017

Relative Strength, % gain vs. S&P 500

Legend: Seasonal Period, XOI, 50 DMA, 200 DMA

Market Indices & Rates
Weekly Values**

Stock Markets	2016	2017
Dow	16,846	20,955
S&P500	1,978	2,379
Nasdaq	4,675	5,865
TSX	13,039	15,522
FTSE	6,145	7,331
DAX	9,713	11,962
Nikkei	16,567	19,331
Hang Seng	19,728	23,745

Commodities	2016	2017
Oil	34.66	53.57
Gold	1247.7	1243.6

Bond Yields	2016	2017
USA 5 Yr Treasury	1.32	1.96
USA 10 Yr T	1.82	2.43
USA 20 Yr T	2.25	2.78
Moody's Aaa	3.80	3.91
Moody's Baa	5.32	4.61
CAN 5 Yr T	0.70	1.14
CAN 10 Yr T	1.23	1.67

Money Market	2016	2017
USA Fed Funds	0.50	0.75
USA 3 Mo T-B	0.32	0.61
CAN tgt overnight rate	0.50	0.50
CAN 3 Mo T-B	0.47	0.48

Foreign Exchange	2016	2017
EUR/USD	1.09	1.06
GBP/USD	1.41	1.23
USD/CAD	1.34	1.33
USD/JPY	113.52	113.53

FEBRUARY

M	T	W	T	F	S	S
			1	2	3	4
5	6	7	8	9	10	11
12	13	14	15	16	17	18
19	20	21	22	23	24	24
26	27	28				

MARCH

M	T	W	T	F	S	S
		1	2	3	4	
5	6	7	8	9	10	11
12	13	14	15	16	17	18
19	20	21	22	23	24	25
26	27	28	29	30	31	

APRIL

M	T	W	T	F	S	S
						1
2	3	4	5	6	7	8
9	10	11	12	13	14	15
16	17	18	19	20	21	22
23	24	25	26	27	28	29
30						

From 1984 to 2016, March and April have been the best performing months for the energy sector on an average, median and frequency basis. Over the last five years, the energy sector has generally followed its seasonal pattern of positive performance in early winter and weaker performance in summer. In 2016, the energy sector underperformed in its February to May seasonal period, but in its secondary seasonal period from July to October, the sector rebounded outperforming the S&P 500. In its 2017 winter/spring seasonal period, the energy sector was negative as it continued a downward trend that started in late 2016.

MARCH

	MONDAY	TUESDAY	WEDNESDAY
WEEK 09	26	27	28
WEEK 10	**5** 26	**6** 25	**7** 24
WEEK 11	**12** 19	**13** 18	**14** 17
WEEK 12	**19** 12	**20** 11	**21** 10
WEEK 13	**26** 5	**27** 4	**28** 3

THURSDAY	FRIDAY
1 30	**2** 29
8 23	**9** 22
15 16	**16** 15
22 9	**23** 8
29 2	**30** 1

USA Market Closed- Good Friday
CAN Market Closed- Good Friday

APRIL

M	T	W	T	F	S	S
						1
2	3	4	5	6	7	8
9	10	11	12	13	14	15
16	17	18	19	20	21	22
23	24	25	26	27	28	29
30						

MAY

M	T	W	T	F	S	S
	1	2	3	4	5	6
7	8	9	10	11	12	13
14	15	16	17	18	19	20
21	22	23	24	25	26	27
28	29	30	31			

JUNE

M	T	W	T	F	S	S
				1	2	3
4	5	6	7	8	9	10
11	12	13	14	15	16	17
18	19	20	21	22	23	24
25	26	27	28	29	30	

JULY

M	T	W	T	F	S	S
						1
2	3	4	5	6	7	8
9	10	11	12	13	14	15
16	17	18	19	20	21	22
23	24	25	26	27	28	29
30	31					

MARCH
S U M M A R Y

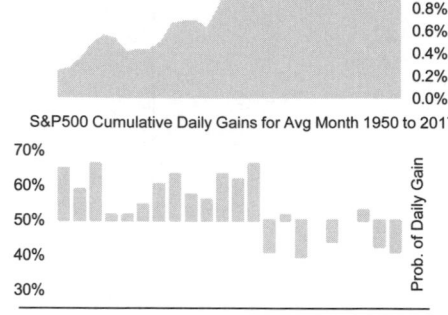

	Dow Jones	S&P 500	Nasdaq	TSX Comp
Month Rank	4	4	7	3
# Up	44	44	28	19
# Down	23	23	17	13
% Pos	66	66	62	59
% Avg. Gain	1.2	1.3	0.8	1.1

Dow & S&P 1950-2016, Nasdaq 1972-2016, TSX 1985-2016

S&P500 Cumulative Daily Gains for Avg Month 1950 to 2017

Prob. of Daily Gain

♦ March tends to be a strong month for stocks, but in 2017 the S&P 500 digested its strong gains from the previous months. ♦ Typically, in March, it is the cyclicals that perform well and the defensive sectors that underperform. ♦ The energy sector is typically the best performing sector in March, but in 2017, the energy sector continued its negative trend from the previous months. ♦ The financial sector typically performs well in March, but in 2017, the sector was negative as it consolidated gains from previous months.

BEST / WORST MARCH BROAD MKTS. 2008-2017

BEST MARCH MARKETS
- ♦ Nasdaq (2009) 10.9%
- ♦ Nikkei 225 (2010) 9.5%
- ♦ Russell 2000 (2009) 8.7%

WORST MARCH MARKETS
- ♦ Nikkei 225 (2011) -8.2%
- ♦ Nikkei 225 (2008) -7.9%
- ♦ FTSE 100 (2014) -3.1%

Index Values End of Month

	2008	2009	2010	2011	2012	2013	2014	2015	2016	2017
Dow	12,263	7,609	10,857	12,320	13,212	14,579	16,458	17,776	17,685	20,663
S&P 500	1,323	798	1,169	1,326	1,408	1,569	1,872	2,068	2,060	2,363
Nasdaq	2,279	1,529	2,398	2,781	3,092	3,268	4,199	4,901	4,870	5,912
TSX	13,350	8,720	12,038	14,116	12,392	12,750	14,335	14,902	13,494	15,548
Russell 1000	720	434	644	737	779	872	1,046	1,157	1,139	1,310
Russell 2000	688	423	679	844	830	952	1,173	1,253	1,114	1,386
FTSE 100	5,702	3,926	5,680	5,909	5,768	6,412	6,598	6,773	6,175	7,323
Nikkei 225	12,526	8,110	11,090	9,755	10,084	12,398	14,828	19,207	16,759	18,909

Percent Gain for March

	2008	2009	2010	2011	2012	2013	2014	2015	2016	2017
Dow	0.0	7.7	5.1	0.8	2.0	3.7	0.8	-2.0	7.1	-0.7
S&P 500	-0.6	8.5	5.9	-0.1	3.1	3.6	0.7	-1.7	6.6	0.0
Nasdaq	0.3	10.9	7.1	0.0	4.2	3.4	-2.5	-1.3	6.8	1.5
TSX	-1.7	7.4	3.5	-0.1	-2.0	-0.6	0.9	-2.2	4.9	1.0
Russell 1000	-0.8	8.5	6.0	0.1	3.0	3.7	0.5	-1.4	6.8	-0.1
Russell 2000	0.3	8.7	8.0	2.4	2.4	4.4	-0.8	1.6	7.8	-0.1
FTSE 100	-3.1	2.5	6.1	-1.4	-1.8	0.8	-3.1	-2.5	1.3	0.8
Nikkei 225	-7.9	7.1	9.5	-8.2	3.7	7.3	-0.1	2.2	4.6	-1.1

March Market Avg. Performance 2008 to 2017[1]

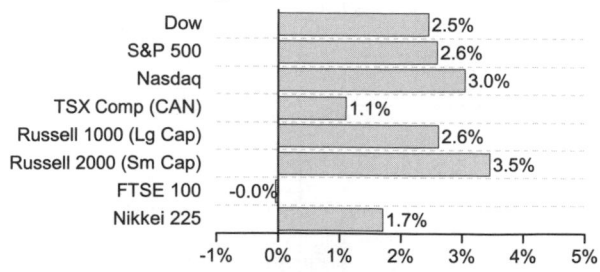

Dow	2.5%
S&P 500	2.6%
Nasdaq	3.0%
TSX Comp (CAN)	1.1%
Russell 1000 (Lg Cap)	2.6%
Russell 2000 (Sm Cap)	3.5%
FTSE 100	-0.0%
Nikkei 225	1.7%

Interest Corner Mar[2]

	Fed Funds % [3]	3 Mo. T-Bill % [4]	10 Yr % [5]	20 Yr % [6]
2017	1.00	0.76	2.40	2.76
2016	0.50	0.21	1.78	2.20
2015	0.25	0.03	1.94	2.31
2014	0.25	0.05	2.73	3.31
2013	0.25	0.07	1.87	2.71

(1) Russell Data provided by Russell (2) Federal Reserve Bank of St. Louis- end of month values (3) Target rate set by FOMC (4)(5)(6) Constant yield maturities.

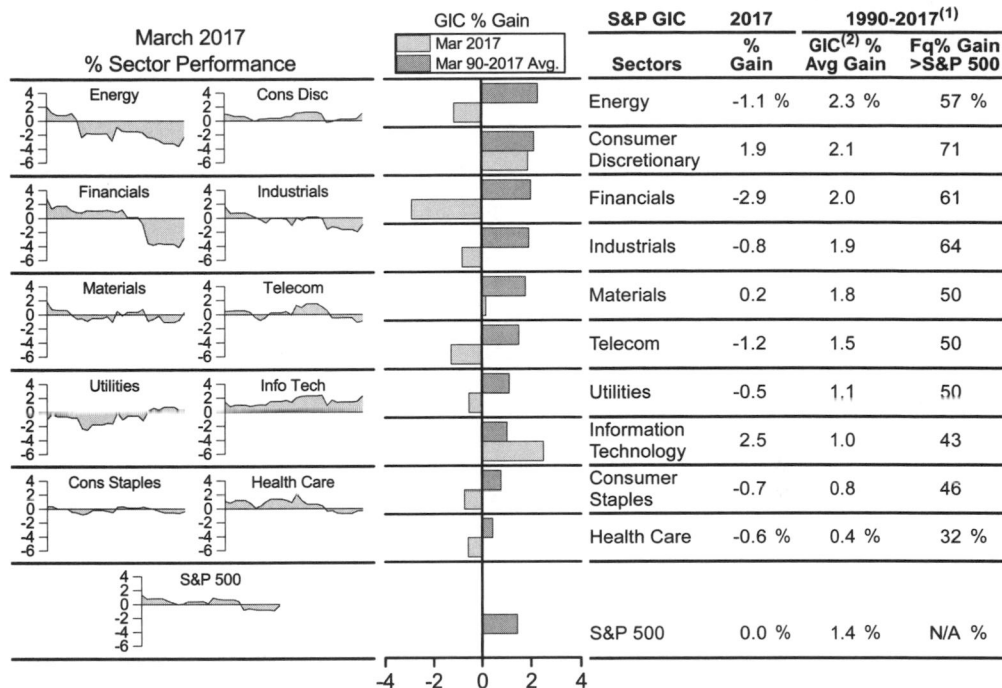

S&P GIC Sectors	2017 % Gain	1990-2017[1] GIC[2] % Avg Gain	Fq% Gain >S&P 500
Energy	-1.1 %	2.3 %	57 %
Consumer Discretionary	1.9	2.1	71
Financials	-2.9	2.0	61
Industrials	-0.8	1.9	64
Materials	0.2	1.8	50
Telecom	-1.2	1.5	50
Utilities	-0.5	1.1	50
Information Technology	2.5	1.0	43
Consumer Staples	-0.7	0.8	46
Health Care	-0.6 %	0.4 %	32 %
S&P 500	0.0 %	1.4 %	N/A %

Sector Commentary

♦ In March 2017, information technology continued its strong rally from the previous months. ♦ Investors became more concerned that Trump's reforms were not going to be implemented or were going to be delayed substantially, and as a result, some of the sectors that were expected to be beneficiaries from the reforms underperformed. ♦ The financial sector underperformed as investors digested the reality that the Federal Reserve was becoming more dovish in their monetary policy stance.

Sub-Sector Commentary

♦ In March 2017, the cyclical sub-sectors were generally underperformers. ♦ Banks were sharply negative for the month, producing a loss of 3.9%. ♦ Homebuilders continued to perform well, producing a gain of 5.0%. ♦ The retail sector bounced back in March, one of the strongest months for retail, producing a gain of 2.2%. ♦ The semi-conductor sub-sector (SOX) produced a strong gain of 4.3% as investors became enamoured with the idea of the sub-sector performing well based upon the increasing use of artificial intelligence (AI) in automobiles.

SELECTED SUB-SECTORS[3]			
Retail	2.2 %	3.4 %	75 %
Steel	-4.6	2.8	61
Chemicals	1.0	2.2	54
Transportation	-3.3	2.0	61
Railroads	-3.6	1.8	54
SOX (1995-2017)	4.3	1.8	48
Silver	-1.2	1.7	46
Banks	-3.9	1.6	50
Automotive & Components	-2.3	1.5	54
Homebuilders	5.0	1.2	50
Metals & Mining	-2.9	1.1	43
Agriculture (1994-2017)	-2.0	0.6	33
Pharma	-0.8	0.5	32
Biotech (1993-2017)	-1.1	-0.2	36
Gold	-0.9	-1.0	32

NIKE – RUNS INTO EARNINGS
①Mar1-Mar20 ②Sep1-Sep25 ③Dec12-Dec24

Nike has had a strong run in the stock market since it went public in 1980. A lot of the gains in the stock price can be accounted for in the two to three week periods leading up to its first, second and third quarters earnings reports.

Nike Inc* Seasonal Gains 1990 to 2016

	Year %	Mar 1 to Mar 20	Sep 1 to Sep 25	Dec 12 to Dec 24	Positive Compound Growth
1990	51.2 %	14.5 %	1.3 %	11.5 %	29.5 %
1991	79.8	-5.7	9.3	12.7	12.4
1992	14.7	-8.4	6.0	-2.9	-6.8
1993	-44.3	5.7	-13.5	0.6	-9.0
1994	61.4	10.4	-7.0	14.5	17.3
1995	86.6	5.3	18.8	10.7	34.4
1996	72.4	22.1	13.7	13.0	56.9
1997	-34.9	-6.1	0.9	-14.1	-18.6
1998	3.8	1.0	18.0	14.8	36.8
1999	22.2	15.6	15.1	18.2	57.3
2000	12.6	16.0	1.5	16.3	37.1
2001	0.8	-2.6	-8.7	3.7	-7.8
2002	-20.9	8.7	2.8	2.1	14.0
2003	53.9	14.0	6.0	4.4	26.1
2004	32.5	4.9	5.8	5.3	17.0
2005	-4.3	-1.8	3.0	1.3	2.5
2006	14.1	-1.5	7.1	2.6	8.3
2007	29.7	4.6	3.8	4.2	13.0
2008	-20.6	11.7	7.3	0.8	20.8
2009	29.5	8.4	5.9	2.2	17.3
2010	29.3	8.8	13.7	-2.0	21.2
2011	12.8	-12.9	2.3	-0.8	-11.6
2012	7.1	3.5	-2.3	6.2	7.4
2013	52.4	0.7	9.7	1.1	11.6
2014	22.3	1.2	1.5	-0.7	2.1
2015	30.0	5.0	11.9	0.1	17.5
2016	-18.7	2.3	-4.3	0.4	-1.8
Avg.	21.3 %	4.7 %	4.8 %	4.7 %	15.4 %

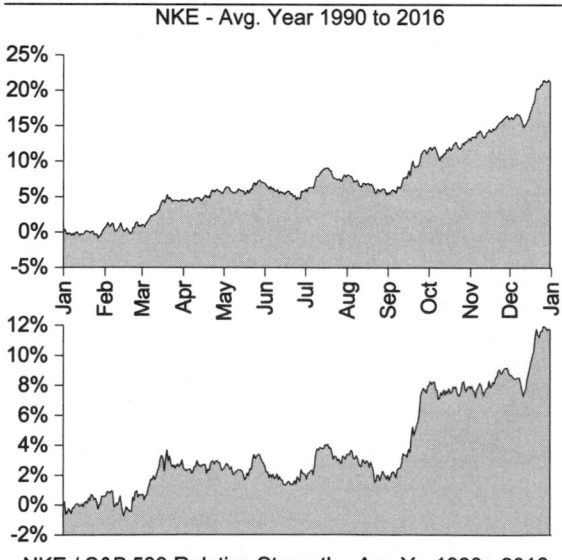

NKE - Avg. Year 1990 to 2016

NKE / S&P 500 Relative Strength - Avg Yr. 1990 - 2016

Nike's year-end is May 31st, and although from year to year the actual report dates for Nike's earnings changes, generally speaking, Nike reports its earnings in the third or fourth week in the months of March, June, September and December.

It is interesting to note that Nike has strong seasonal runs at different times of the year. Stocks typically have similar seasonal patterns as the sector to which they belong. Nike belongs to the consumer discretionary sector and it would be expected that Nike would have a similar seasonal pattern.

There are large differences in Nike's pattern of seasonal strength compared with the seasonal pattern of the consumer discretionary sector. First, Nike has a period of seasonal strength that includes September, a month that is not favorable to consumer discretionary stocks. Second, Nike's outperformance is focused on very short periods in the weeks leading up to three of its earnings reports. In contrast, the consumer discretionary sector has a much longer seasonal period and has a more gradual transition from its favorable seasonal period to its unfavorable seasonal period and vice versa.

From 1990 to 2016, Nike produced an average annual gain of 21.3%. In comparison, its three short seasonal periods within the year have produced an average compound gain of 15.4%. The seasonal periods in total are approximately eight weeks and yet, they have produced most of the average annual gains of Nike. Investors have been well served investing in Nike in its seasonal periods and then running to another investment during its "off-season."

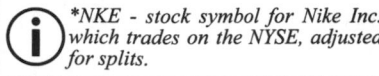

*NKE - stock symbol for Nike Inc. which trades on the NYSE, adjusted for splits.

Nike Performance

NKE Monthly Performance (1990-2016)

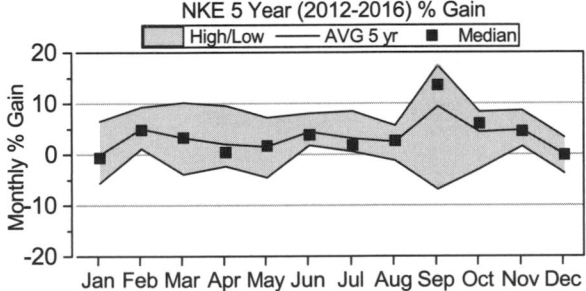

Avg % Gain											

	Jan	Feb	Mar	Apr	May	Jun	Jul	Aug	Sep	Oct	Nov	Dec
Avg. % Gain	0.4	0.2	4.6	0.7	1.4	-1.2	2.6	-2.1	5.2	1.8	2.6	3.9
Med. % Gain	-0.8	3.5	3.3	1.5	2.2	1.3	0.5	-0.2	6.1	2.7	4.1	1.5
Fq %>0	46	69	73	62	58	62	58	46	69	65	69	62
Fq %>S&P 500	50	58	62	46	65	54	58	54	81	58	62	50

NKE 5 Year (2012-2016) % Gain

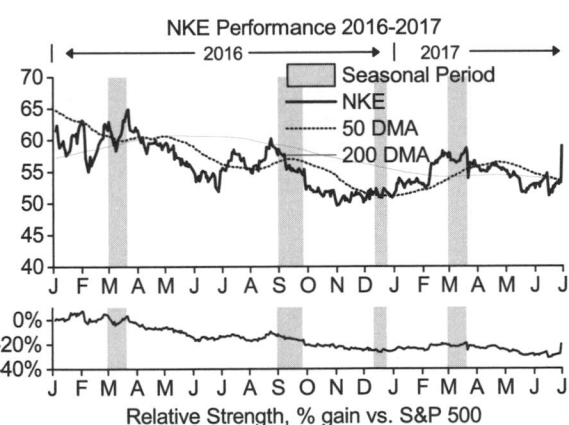

NKE Performance 2016-2017

Relative Strength, % gain vs. S&P 500

From 1990 to 2016, on average, the three best months for Nike were March, September and December, which are all part of the *Nike Runs Into Earnings* strategy. September has been the best month of the three as it has higher average and median values than the other two months. Performing well in September is particularly valuable as the S&P 500 tends not to perform well in this month. On average, over the last five years, Nike has performed extremely well in the month of September. In 2016 and 2017, the Nike combination strategy was negative as the stock has maintained an overall downward trend starting in 2016.

WEEK 10

Market Indices & Rates
Weekly Values**

Stock Markets	2016	2017
Dow	17,049	20,899
S&P500	1,996	2,369
Nasdaq	4,688	5,844
TSX	13,398	15,548
FTSE	6,126	7,336
DAX	9,705	11,967
Nikkei	16,826	19,380
Hang Seng	20,070	23,626

Commodities	2016	2017
Oil	37.81	50.88
Gold	1262.5	1213.2

Bond Yields	2016	2017
USA 5 Yr Treasury	1.42	2.08
USA 10 Yr T	1.91	2.55
USA 20 Yr T	2.28	2.89
Moody's Aaa	3.88	4.05
Moody's Baa	5.25	4.72
CAN 5 Yr T	0.72	1.22
CAN 10 Yr T	1.27	1.77

Money Market	2016	2017
USA Fed Funds	0.50	0.75
USA 3 Mo T-B	0.31	0.74
CAN tgt overnight rate	0.50	0.50
CAN 3 Mo T-B	0.47	0.48

Foreign Exchange	2016	2017
EUR/USD	1.11	1.06
GBP/USD	1.43	1.22
USD/CAD	1.33	1.35
USD/JPY	113.30	114.39

MARCH

M	T	W	T	F	S	S
			1	2	3	4
5	6	7	8	9	10	11
12	13	14	15	16	17	18
19	20	21	22	23	24	25
26	27	28	29	30	31	

APRIL

M	T	W	T	F	S	S
						1
2	3	4	5	6	7	8
9	10	11	12	13	14	15
16	17	18	19	20	21	22
23	24	25	26	27	28	29
30						

MAY

M	T	W	T	F	S	S
	1	2	3	4	5	6
7	8	9	10	11	12	13
14	15	16	17	18	19	20
21	22	23	24	25	26	27
28	29	30	31			

CANADIAN TIRE – MORE THAN TIRES

①SELL SHORT (Jan1-Jan31)
②LONG (Feb11-Apr12) ③LONG (Oct28-Nov30)

Canadian Tire is an iconic Canadian store that has successfully developed a diversified portfolio of retail operations selling a wide range of products including clothing, home products, leisure products, sports equipment and auto repair parts.

16.3% gain & positive 86% of the time

Despite its diversified product approach, Canadian Tire is still a retail operation and generally follows the seasonal trends for the retail sector.

Although Canada does not have an "official" Black Friday, Canadian Tire's stock price tends to peak, relative to the TSX Composite Index at the end of November, after performing well starting in the last few days in October.

Canadian Tire also tends to perform well from February 11th to April 12th, which is similar to the retail sector's seasonal period.

Investors should note that Canadian Tire tends to perform poorly in the month of January, which also happens to be a weak month for the retail sector.

* *Canadian Tire is a diversified retail company that trades on the Toronto exchange under the symbol CTC.A. Data from TSX Exchange, includes stock splits only.*

Canadian Tire* vs. TSX Comp. 1996 to 2016
Negative Short ☐ Positive Long ▨

Year	Jan 1 to Jan 31 TSX Comp	CTC.A	Feb 11 to Apr 12 TSX Comp	CTC.A	Oct 28 to Nov 30 TSX Comp	CTC.A	Compound Growth TSX Comp	CTC.A
1996	5.4 %	-1.7 %	-0.3 %	9.5 %	8.4	16.8 %	13.9 %	30.1 %
1997	3.1	-6.2	-6.5	9.3	-1.3	0.2	-4.9	16.2
1998	0.0	3.4	10.7	9.7	5.8	8.5	17.2	14.9
1999	3.8	3.1	8.4	3.8	7.3	-4.9	20.7	-4.3
2000	0.8	-20.1	-2.9	14.0	-5.4	-2.8	-7.4	33.0
2001	4.4	12.6	-12.5	16.9	6.0	14.2	-3.2	16.6
2002	-0.5	-2.3	2.6	25.2	2.6	3.7	4.7	32.7
2003	-0.7	-9.4	-0.2	4.7	2.6	-0.5	1.7	13.9
2004	3.7	3.9	1.7	3.9	2.7	6.3	8.3	6.0
2005	-0.5	-8.1	1.4	7.7	5.7	12.8	6.6	31.3
2006	6.0	-4.9	4.4	-5.5	3.9	3.1	15.0	2.2
2007	1.0	-3.7	3.2	7.5	-4.3	-15.1	-0.2	-5.3
2008	-4.9	-13.1	5.3	8.1	8.6	7.1	8.8	31.0
2009	-3.3	-5.9	4.2	24.4	3.6	-3.7	4.4	26.8
2010	-5.6	-7.0	7.6	1.3	3.1	8.0	4.8	17.1
2011	0.8	-8.6	-0.3	-4.6	-2.1	7.2	-1.6	11.2
2012	4.2	-2.5	-1.4	5.1	-0.5	-8.2	2.2	-1.2
2013	2.0	0.1	-3.6	3.5	0.0	1.9	-1.7	5.4
2014	0.5	-4.4	3.4	11.6	1.9	3.3	5.9	20.5
2015	0.3	-4.5	1.8	14.1	-1.7	8.0	0.4	28.7
2016	-1.4	-3.4	11.5	17.9	1.7	6.4	11.7	29.6
Avg.	0.9 %	-3.9 %	1.9 %	8.9 %	2.0 %	2.8 %	4.7 %	16.3 %
Fq>0	67 %	24 %	62	90 %	67 %	71 %	71 %	86 %

From 1996 to 2016, short selling in January and then investing from February 11th to April 12th and then once again investing from October 28th to November 30th, has produced an average gain of 16.3% and has been positive 86% of the time.

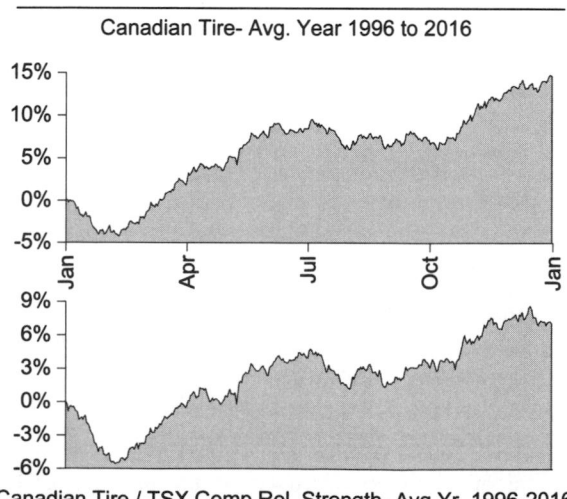

Canadian Tire- Avg. Year 1996 to 2016

Canadian Tire / TSX Comp Rel. Strength- Avg Yr. 1996-2016

33 -

Canadian Tire Performance

Canadian Tire Monthly Performance (1996-2016)

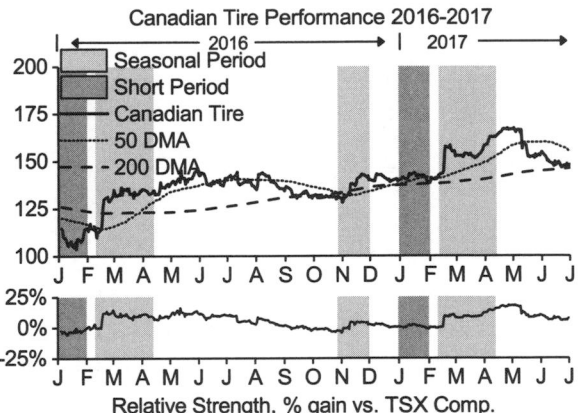

	Jan	Feb	Mar	Apr	May	Jun	Jul	Aug	Sep	Oct	Nov	Dec
Avg. % Gain	-3.9	1.5	4.1	2.6	3.2	0.6	-1.9	0.2	0.6	2.5	2.3	1.7
Med. % Gain	-4.4	0.5	4.2	1.2	3.4	-1.7	-2.5	0.0	2.2	3.1	3.0	2.0
Fq %>0	24	52	76	67	67	43	33	52	62	57	71	62
Fq %>TSX Comp	14	67	76	52	67	52	24	38	57	57	67	52

Canadian Tire 5 Year (2012-2016) % Gain

Canadian Tire Performance 2016-2017

Relative Strength, % gain vs. TSX Comp.

Market Indices & Rates
Weekly Values**

Stock Markets	2016	2017
Dow	17,378	20,904
S&P500	2,031	2,377
Nasdaq	4,763	5,887
TSX	13,495	15,500
FTSE	6,176	7,387
DAX	9,950	12,033
Nikkei	16,997	19,586
Hang Seng	20,431	24,010

Commodities	2016	2017
Oil	38.32	48.50
Gold	1244.4	1213.3

Bond Yields	2016	2017
USA 5 Yr Treasury	1.43	2.07
USA 10 Yr T	1.93	2.55
USA 20 Yr T	2.30	2.91
Moody's Aaa	3.80	4.09
Moody's Baa	5.13	4.75
CAN 5 Yr T	0.74	1.25
CAN 10 Yr T	1.31	1.81

Money Market	2016	2017
USA Fed Funds	0.50	1.00
USA 3 Mo T-B	0.31	0.75
CAN tgt overnight rate	0.50	0.50
CAN 3 Mo T-B	0.46	0.50

Foreign Exchange	2016	2017
EUR/USD	1.12	1.07
GBP/USD	1.43	1.23
USD/CAD	1.31	1.34
USD/JPY	112.50	113.80

MARCH

M	T	W	T	F	S	S
			1	2	3	4
5	6	7	8	9	10	11
12	13	14	15	16	17	18
19	20	21	22	23	24	25
26	27	28	29	30	31	

APRIL

M	T	W	T	F	S	S
						1
2	3	4	5	6	7	8
9	10	11	12	13	14	15
16	17	18	19	20	21	22
23	24	25	26	27	28	29
30						

MAY

M	T	W	T	F	S	S
	1	2	3	4	5	6
7	8	9	10	11	12	13
14	15	16	17	18	19	20
21	22	23	24	25	26	27
28	29	30	31			

From 1990 to 2016, the worst month of the year for Canadian Tire has been January on a median, average and frequency basis. July has also been a poor performer. The best month of the year has been March, which is also a strong month of the year for retail stocks.

Over the last five years, Canadian Tire has generally followed its seasonal trend with January being the worst month of the year and March being one of the stronger months.

In its 2016 autumn seasonal period, Canadian Tire outperformed the TSX Composite. In 2017, both the short sell trade and the long trade were successful.

NATURAL GAS – FIRES UP AND DOWN
①LONG (Mar22-Jun19) ②LONG (Sep5-Dec21)
③SELL SHORT (Dec22-Dec31)

There are two high consumption times for natural gas: winter and summer. The colder it gets in winter, the more natural gas is consumed to keep the furnaces going. The warmer it gets in summer, the more natural gas is used to produce power for air conditioners.

On the supply side, weather plays a large factor in determining price. During the hurricane season in the Gulf of Mexico, the price of natural gas is affected by the number and severity of hurricanes.

Natural Gas (Cash) Henry Hub LA*
Seasonal Gains 1995 to 2016

Year	Pos. Mar 22 to Jun 19	Pos. Sep 5 to Dec 21	Neg. (Short) Dec 22 to Dec 31	Pos. Compound Growth
	%	%		%
1995	99.4	13.0	103.0	1.2	126.7
1996	-27.4	-6.6	170.4	-46.2	269.2
1997	-9.4	16.8	-13.1	-6.3	7.9
1998	-13.0	-2.6	20.9	-6.7	25.7
1999	18.6	28.9	5.3	-11.2	50.9
2000	356.5	57.1	121.9	0.7	246.3
2001	-74.3	-24.1	21.5	1.5	-9.2
2002	70.0	0.6	61.3	-9.1	77.1
2003	26.4	9.5	47.1	-16.3	87.4
2004	3.6	18.2	54.6	-11.6	103.9
2005	58.4	6.3	14.5	-29.6	57.7
2006	-42.2	-1.8	17.4	-9.5	26.3
2007	30.2	9.2	32.7	2.0	42.1
2008	-21.4	52.2	-21.4	-0.9	20.6
2009	3.6	1.5	208.0	0.7	210.4
2010	-27.4	28.6	10.4	2.4	38.6
2011	-29.6	10.0	-26.1	-1.7	-17.3
2012	15.4	18.7	21.7	0.6	43.7
2013	26.3	-1.4	18.2	-0.2	16.8
2014	-31.1	7.7	-11.8	-12.9	7.2
2015	-22.8	-0.5	-36.1	35.6	-59.0
2016	59.2	46.6	21.9	5.8	68.3
Avg.	21.3	13.1	38.7	-4.9	65.8

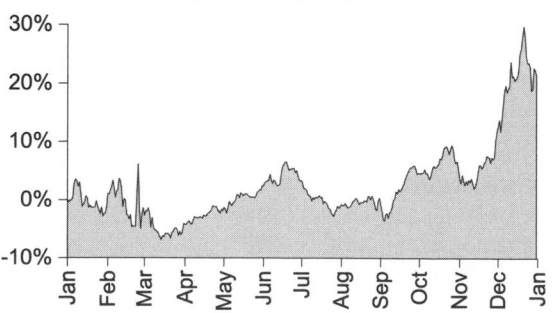

Natural Gas (Henry Hub Spot)- Avg. Year 1995 to 2016

Natural gas prices tend to rise from mid-March to mid-June ahead of the cooling season demands in the summer. From 1995 to 2016, during the period of March 22nd to June 19th, the spot price of natural gas has on average increased 13.1% and has been positive 73% of the time. The price of natural gas also tends to rise between September 5th and December 21st, due to the demands of the heating season. In this period, from 1995 to 2016, natural gas has produced an average gain of 38.7% and has been positive 78% of the time.

Positive 86% of the time

Natural gas tends to fall in price from December 22nd to December 31st. Although this is a short time period, for the years from 1995 to 2016, natural gas has produced an average loss of 4.9% and has only been positive 41% of the time. Also, in this period, when gains did occur, they were relatively small. The poor performance of natural gas at this time is largely driven by southern U.S. refiners dumping inventory on the market to help mitigate year-end taxes on their inventory.

Applying a strategy of investing in natural gas from March 22nd to June 19th, reinvesting the proceeds from September 5th to December 21st, reinvesting the proceeds again to short natural gas from December 22nd to December 31st, has produced a compound average return of 65.8% and has been positive 86% of the time.

Using the natural gas compound strategy has produced returns that are over three times greater than the average annual gain in natural gas. By using the strategy, an investor would have caught most of the large gains and missed most of the large losses.

> ⚠ *Caution: The cash price for natural gas is extremely volatile and extreme caution should be used. Care must be taken to ensure that investments are within risk tolerances.*

> ⓘ *Source: New York Mercantile Exchange. NYMX is an exchange provider of futures and options.*

Natural Gas Performance

NatGas Monthly Performance (1995-2016)

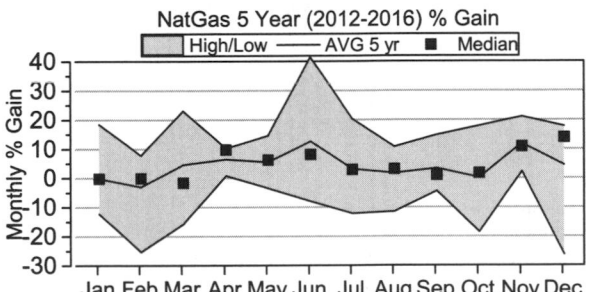

	Jan	Feb	Mar	Apr	May	Jun	Jul	Aug	Sep	Oct	Nov	Dec
Avg. % Gain	-0.9	-1.0	0.8	1.5	3.9	1.1	-1.9	-2.0	3.4	8.3	5.8	5.8
Med. % Gain	-2.9	-4.7	5.9	2.7	3.3	-1.5	-0.4	-4.7	1.5	1.0	5.8	3.7
Fq %>0	41	41	68	64	68	45	41	41	55	50	64	55
Fq %>S&P 500	45	32	64	45	64	41	41	55	45	50	64	50

NatGas 5 Year (2012-2016) % Gain

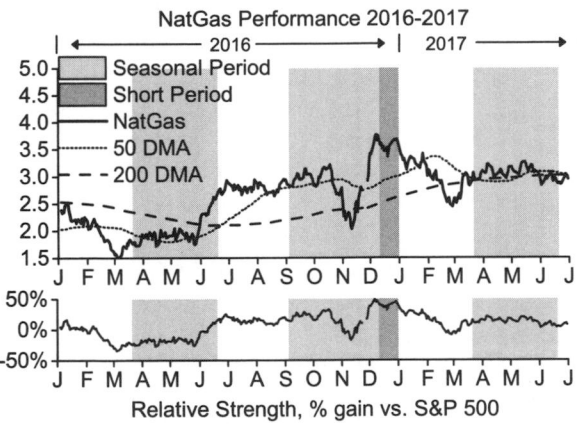

NatGas Performance 2016-2017

Relative Strength, % gain vs. S&P 500

Market Indices & Rates Weekly Values**		
Stock Markets	**2016**	**2017**
Dow	17,556	20,698
S&P500	2,044	2,351
Nasdaq	4,793	5,833
TSX	13,448	15,396
FTSE	6,171	7,362
DAX	9,953	12,005
Nikkei	16,986	19,211
Hang Seng	20,578	24,420
Commodities	**2016**	**2017**
Oil	39.08	47.44
Gold	1234.0	1243.6
Bond Yields	**2016**	**2017**
USA 5 Yr Treasury	1.39	1.96
USA 10 Yr T	1.91	2.42
USA 20 Yr T	2.29	2.78
Moody's Aaa	3.78	3.98
Moody's Baa	5.01	4.65
CAN 5 Yr T	0.73	1.16
CAN 10 Yr T	1.28	1.69
Money Market	**2016**	**2017**
USA Fed Funds	0.50	1.00
USA 3 Mo T-B	0.30	0.77
CAN tgt overnight rate	0.50	0.50
CAN 3 Mo T-B	0.45	0.50
Foreign Exchange	**2016**	**2017**
EUR/USD	1.12	1.08
GBP/USD	1.42	1.25
USD/CAD	1.32	1.34
USD/JPY	112.54	111.54

MARCH

M	T	W	T	F	S	S
			1	2	3	4
5	6	7	8	9	10	11
12	13	14	15	16	17	18
19	20	21	22	23	24	25
26	27	28	29	30	31	

APRIL

M	T	W	T	F	S	S
						1
2	3	4	5	6	7	8
9	10	11	12	13	14	15
16	17	18	19	20	21	22
23	24	25	26	27	28	29
30						

MAY

M	T	W	T	F	S	S
	1	2	3	4	5	6
7	8	9	10	11	12	13
14	15	16	17	18	19	20
21	22	23	24	25	26	27
28	29	30	31			

From 1995 to 2016, on average, September through to December has been the best cluster of positive months for natural gas. Natural gas is a very volatile commodity and as a result there is a large difference between the mean and median performances on a month to month basis.

April and May are also strong months and make up the core of the spring trade. In the last five years, natural gas has generally followed its seasonal trend, with a strong performance in April, a weak performance in summer and a strong performance in autumn. In 2016/2017, the overall return for the combination of natural gas trades was positive.

CANADIANS GIVE 3 CHEERS FOR AMERICAN HOLIDAYS

When I used to work on the retail side of the investment business, I was always amazed at how often the Canadian stock market increased on U.S. holidays, when the U.S. stock market was closed.

The Canadian stock market on U.S. holidays always had light volume, tended not to have large increases or decreases, but usually ended the day with a gain.

1.0% average gain

How the trade works

For the three big holidays in the United States that do not exist in Canada (Memorial, Independence and U.S. Thanksgiving Days), buy at the end of the market day before the holiday (TSX Composite) and sell at the end of the U.S. holiday when the U.S markets are closed.

For U.S. investors to take advantage of this trade, they must have access to the TSX Composite. Unfortunately, SEC regulations do not allow most Americans to purchase foreign ETFs.

Generally, markets perform well around most major U.S. holidays, hence the trading strategies for U.S holidays included in this book. The typical U.S. holiday trade is to get into the stock market the day before the holiday and then exit the day after the holiday.

The main reason for the strong performance around these holidays is a lack of institutional involvement in the markets, allowing bullish retail investors to push up the markets.

On the actual American holidays, economic reports are not released in the U.S. and are very seldom released in Canada. During market hours on U.S. holidays, without any strong influences, the TSX Composite tends to float, as investors wait until the next day before making any significant moves. Despite this laxidasical action during the day, the TSX Composite tends to end the day on a gain. This is true for the three major U.S. holidays: Memorial Day, Independence Day and U.S. Thanksgiving.

From a theoretical perspective, a lot of the gain that is captured on the U.S. holidays in the Canadian stock market is realized the next day when the U.S stock market is open. This does not invalidate the *Canadians Give 3 Cheers* trade – it presents more alternatives for the astute investor.

For example, an investor can allocate a portion of money to a standard U.S. holiday trade and another portion to the *Canadian Give 3 Cheers* version. By spreading out the exit days, the overall risk in the trade is reduced.

S&P/TSX Comp Gain 1977-2016 — Positive

	Memorial	Independence	Thanksgiving	Compound Growth
1977	0.10 %	-0.08 %	0.61 %	0.63 %
1978	-0.05	-0.16	0.57	0.36
1979	1.11	0.23	0.58	1.93
1980	1.64	0.76	0.89	3.32
1981	0.51	-0.15	1.03	1.40
1982	-0.18	-0.01	0.35	0.17
1983	0.29	0.53	0.15	0.97
1984	0.86	-0.11	0.73	1.48
1985	0.61	0.31	0.31	1.24
1986	0.23	-0.02	0.22	0.44
1987	-0.11	1.08	1.57	2.55
1988	0.44	0.08	0.58	1.11
1989	0.10	-0.12	-0.11	-0.13
1990	0.11	0.43	0.02	0.57
1991	0.02	0.18	-0.09	0.11
1992	-0.06	0.35	0.36	0.65
1993	0.42	-0.18	0.14	0.38
1994	-0.19	0.70	0.91	1.43
1995	0.14	0.25	0.29	0.68
1996	0.11	0.25	0.54	0.90
1997	1.08	-0.04	-0.85	0.18
1998	0.56	0.18	0.51	1.25
1999	0.57	1.63	1.14	3.39
2000	0.43	1.04	0.91	2.40
2001	-0.02	-0.23	0.70	0.45
2002	-0.01	0.08	0.38	0.45
2003	0.03	0.03	0.26	0.31
2004	0.84	-0.02	0.55	1.39
2005	0.56	0.39	1.48	2.45
2006	0.70	1.04	0.70	2.46
2007	0.35	-0.03	0.76	1.08
2008	0.24	-0.94	1.28	0.56
2009	0.76	0.36	-1.29	-0.18
2010	0.78	-0.92	0.34	0.19
2011	0.23	0.64	-0.75	0.12
2012	-0.09	0.55	0.44	0.90
2013	0.23	0.17	0.07	0.47
2014	0.05	0.05	-0.77	-0.67
2015	-0.09	0.30	0.16	0.38
2016	-0.13	1.48	-0.04	1.21
Avg	0.33 %	0.25 %	0.39 %	0.97 %
Fq > 0	75 %	65 %	83 %	93 %

Canadians Give 3 Cheers Performance

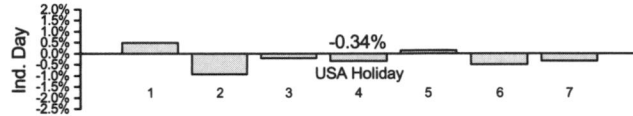

Market Indices & Rates Weekly Values**		
Stock Markets	**2016**	**2017**
Dow	17,673	20,661
S&P500	2,058	2,358
Nasdaq	4,853	5,888
TSX	13,451	15,578
FTSE	6,158	7,341
DAX	9,924	12,184
Nikkei	16,808	19,076
Hang Seng	20,611	24,269
Commodities	**2016**	**2017**
Oil	38.22	49.31
Gold	1228.2	1251.9
Bond Yields	**2016**	**2017**
USA 5 Yr Treasury	1.27	1.94
USA 10 Yr T	1.82	2.40
USA 20 Yr T	2.22	2.76
Moody's Aaa	3.70	3.93
Moody's Baa	4.91	4.63
CAN 5 Yr T	0.68	1.10
CAN 10 Yr T	1.23	1.62
Money Market	**2016**	**2017**
USA Fed Funds	0.50	1.00
USA 3 Mo T-B	0.24	0.78
CAN tgt overnight rate	0.50	0.50
CAN 3 Mo T-B	0.45	0.52
Foreign Exchange	**2016**	**2017**
EUR/USD	1.13	1.08
GBP/USD	1.43	1.25
USD/CAD	1.30	1.33
USD/JPY	112.57	111.23

MARCH

M	T	W	T	F	S	S
			1	2	3	4
5	6	7	8	9	10	11
12	13	14	15	16	17	18
19	20	21	22	23	24	25
26	27	28	29	30	31	

APRIL

M	T	W	T	F	S	S
						1
2	3	4	5	6	7	8
9	10	11	12	13	14	15
16	17	18	19	20	21	22
23	24	25	26	27	28	29
30						

MAY

M	T	W	T	F	S	S
	1	2	3	4	5	6
7	8	9	10	11	12	13
14	15	16	17	18	19	20
21	22	23	24	25	26	27
28	29	30	31			

Canadians Give 3 Cheers Performance

In 2016, the TSX Composite suffered nominal losses on Memorial Day and Thanksgiving Day. The losses were more than offset by the gain on Independence Day. The large gain on Independence Day was partially driven by the Brexit referendum rally that started in late June.

In 2017, the TSX Composite was slightly positive on Memorial Day. On Independence Day, the TSX was nominally negative. Both the Canadian and U.S. stock markets rallied strongly, shortly after the end of the "Canadian Independence Day" trade.

APRIL

	MONDAY	TUESDAY	WEDNESDAY
WEEK 14	**2** 28	**3** 27	**4** 26
WEEK 15	**9** 21	**10** 20	**11** 19
WEEK 16	**16** 14	**17** 13	**18** 12
WEEK 17	**23** 7	**24** 6	**25** 5
WEEK 18	**30**	1	2

THURSDAY		FRIDAY	
5	25	**6**	24
12	18	**13**	17
19	11	**20**	10
26	4	**27**	3
3		4	

MAY

M	T	W	T	F	S	S
	1	2	3	4	5	6
7	8	9	10	11	12	13
14	15	16	17	18	19	20
21	22	23	24	25	26	27
28	29	30	31			

JUNE

M	T	W	T	F	S	S
				1	2	3
4	5	6	7	8	9	10
11	12	13	14	15	16	17
18	19	20	21	22	23	24
25	26	27	28	29	30	

JULY

M	T	W	T	F	S	S
						1
2	3	4	5	6	7	8
9	10	11	12	13	14	15
16	17	18	19	20	21	22
23	24	25	26	27	28	29
30	31					

AUGUST

M	T	W	T	F	S	S
		1	2	3	4	5
6	7	8	9	10	11	12
13	14	15	16	17	18	19
20	21	22	23	24	25	26
27	28	29	30	31		

APRIL SUMMARY

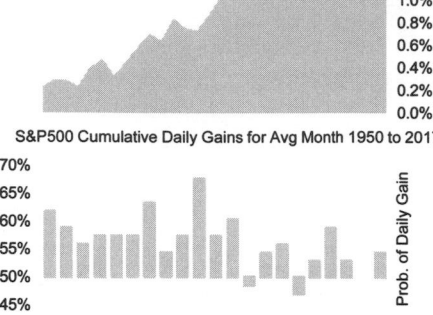

	Dow Jones	S&P 500	Nasdaq	TSX Comp
Month Rank	1	3	4	7
# Up	45	46	28	19
# Down	22	21	17	13
% Pos	67	69	62	59
% Avg. Gain	1.9	1.4	1.2	0.8

Dow & S&P 1950-2016, Nasdaq 1972-2016 TSX 1985-2016

S&P500 Cumulative Daily Gains for Avg Month 1950 to 2017

♦ April, on average, from 1950 to 2017 has been the third strongest month for the S&P 500 with an average gain of 1.5% and a positive frequency of 71%. ♦ The first part of April tends to be the strongest (see *18 Day Earnings Month Effect strategy*). ♦ The last part of April tends to be "flat." ♦ Overall, April tends to be a volatile month with the cyclical sectors outperforming. ♦ When the defensive sectors outperform in April, it often indicates market weakness ahead.

BEST / WORST APRIL BROAD MKTS. 2008-2017

BEST APRIL MARKETS
♦ Russell 2000 (2009) 15.3%
♦ Nasdaq (2009) 12.3%
♦ Nikkei 225 (2013) 11.8%

WORST APRIL MARKETS
♦ Nikkei 225 (2012) -5.6%
♦ Russell 2000 (2014) -3.9%
♦ Nikkei 225 (2014) -3.5%

Index Values End of Month

	2008	2009	2010	2011	2012	2013	2014	2015	2016	2017
Dow	12,820	8,168	11,009	12,811	13,214	14,840	16,581	17,841	17,774	20,941
S&P 500	1,386	873	1,187	1,364	1,398	1,598	1,884	2,086	2,065	2,384
Nasdaq	2,413	1,717	2,461	2,874	3,046	3,329	4,115	4,941	4,775	6,048
TSX	13,937	9,325	12,211	13,945	12,293	12,457	14,652	15,225	13,951	15,586
Russell 1000	756	477	655	758	774	887	1,050	1,164	1,144	1,322
Russell 2000	716	488	717	865	817	947	1,127	1,220	1,131	1,400
FTSE 100	6,087	4,244	5,553	6,070	5,738	6,430	6,780	6,961	6,242	7,204
Nikkei 225	13,850	8,828	11,057	9,850	9,521	13,861	14,304	19,520	16,666	19,197

Percent Gain for April

	2008	2009	2010	2011	2012	2013	2014	2015	2016	2017
Dow	4.5	7.3	1.4	4.0	0.0	1.8	0.7	0.4	0.5	1.3
S&P 500	4.8	9.4	1.5	2.8	-0.7	1.8	0.6	0.9	0.3	0.9
Nasdaq	5.9	12.3	2.6	3.3	-1.5	1.9	-2.0	0.8	-1.9	2.3
TSX	4.4	6.9	1.4	-1.2	-0.8	-2.3	2.2	2.2	3.4	0.2
Russell 1000	5.0	10.0	1.8	2.9	-0.7	1.7	0.4	0.6	0.4	0.9
Russell 2000	4.1	15.3	5.6	2.6	-1.6	-0.4	-3.9	-2.6	1.5	1.0
FTSE 100	6.8	8.1	-2.2	2.7	-0.5	0.3	2.8	2.8	1.1	-1.6
Nikkei 225	10.6	8.9	-0.3	1.0	-5.6	11.8	-3.5	1.6	-0.6	1.5

April Market Avg. Performance 2008 to 2017[1]

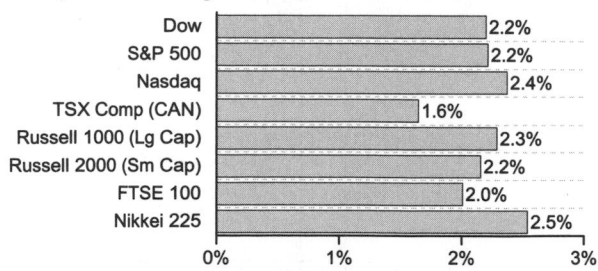

Dow	2.2%
S&P 500	2.2%
Nasdaq	2.4%
TSX Comp (CAN)	1.6%
Russell 1000 (Lg Cap)	2.3%
Russell 2000 (Sm Cap)	2.2%
FTSE 100	2.0%
Nikkei 225	2.5%

Interest Corner Apr[2]

	Fed Funds %[3]	3 Mo. T-Bill %[4]	10 Yr %[5]	20 Yr %[6]
2017	1.00	0.80	2.29	2.67
2016	0.50	0.22	1.83	2.26
2015	0.25	0.01	2.05	2.49
2014	0.25	0.03	2.67	3.22
2013	0.25	0.05	1.70	2.49

(1) Russell Data provided by Russell (2) Federal Reserve Bank of St. Louis- end of month values (3) Target rate set by FOMC (4)(5)(6) Constant yield maturities.

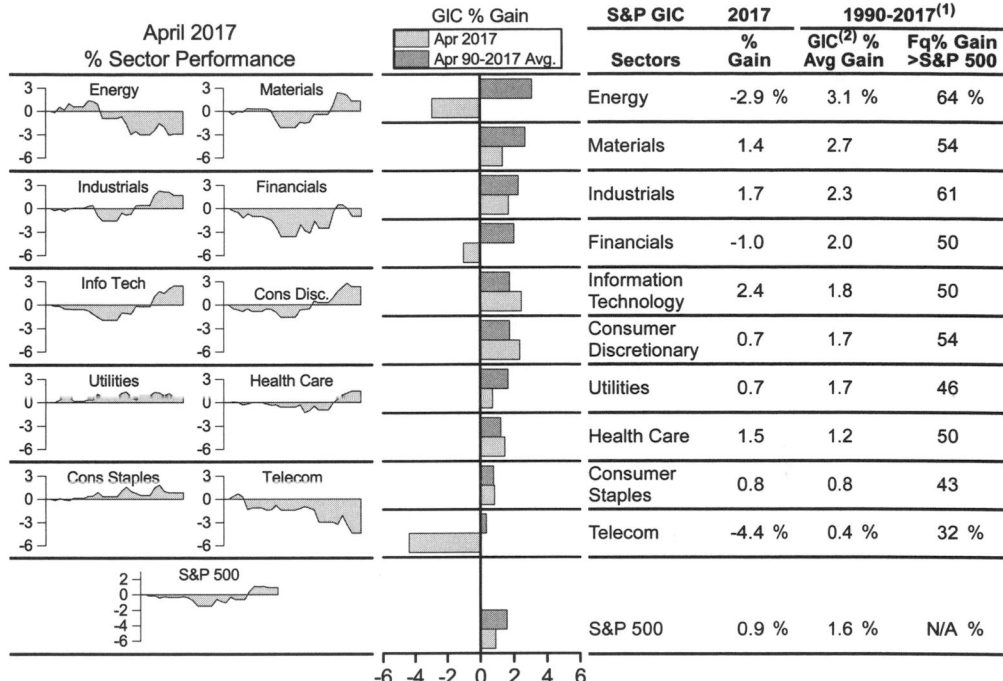

S&P GIC Sectors	2017 % Gain	1990-2017[1] GIC[2] % Avg Gain	1990-2017[1] Fq% Gain >S&P 500
Energy	-2.9 %	3.1 %	64 %
Materials	1.4	2.7	54
Industrials	1.7	2.3	61
Financials	-1.0	2.0	50
Information Technology	2.4	1.8	50
Consumer Discretionary	0.7	1.7	54
Utilities	0.7	1.7	46
Health Care	1.5	1.2	50
Consumer Staples	0.8	0.8	43
Telecom	-4.4 %	0.4 %	32 %
S&P 500	0.9 %	1.6 %	N/A %

April 2017 % Sector Performance — GIC % Gain (Apr 2017, Apr 90-2017 Avg.)

Sector Commentary

♦ On average, April is one of the strongest months of the year for commodities, including oil. ♦ In 2017, the energy sector did not live up to its seasonal trend, and produced a loss of 2.9%. ♦ The information technology sector performed well in April, extending its rally. ♦ For a second month in a row, the financial sector produced a loss and underperformed the S&P 500. ♦ The industrials sector was a strong performer, producing a gain of 1.7%

Sub-Sector Commentary

♦ In April 2017, the railroads sub-sector performed well, producing a gain of 6.4%. ♦ The retail sub-sector performed well, despite investor's concern with Amazon displacing "bricks and mortar" sales. ♦ Homebuilders finally produced a loss, after its recent rally in previous months. ♦ Although gold was positive, silver produced a loss of 3.6%.♦ Pharma produced a loss of 0.4% as investors tried to anticipate the path of Trump's plan for the health care sector.

SELECTED SUB-SECTORS[3]			
Automotive & Components	-1.5 %	5.6 %	50 %
Railroads	6.4	3.5	61
SOX (1995-2017)	-0.6	3.1	48
Chemicals	1.2	3.1	71
Banks	-1.3	2.5	54
Metals & Mining	0.3	2.3	43
Transportation	2.0	2.2	57
Pharma	-0.4	1.7	54
Steel	2.7	1.7	50
Homebuilders	-1.9	1.1	43
Retail	3.1	0.8	46
Gold	1.7	0.4	46
Agriculture (1994-2017)	-0.6	0.4	54
Biotech (1993-2017)	0.5	0.3	40
Silver	-3.6	0.1	39

(1) Sector data provided by Standard and Poors (2) GIC is short form for Global Industry Classification (3) Sub Sector data provided by Standard and Poors, except where marked by symbol.

18 DAY EARNINGS MONTH EFFECT
Markets Outperform 1st 18 Calendar Days of Earnings Months

Earnings season occurs the first month of every quarter. At this time, public companies report their financials for the previous quarter and give guidance on future expectations. As a result, investors tend to bid up stocks, anticipating good earnings. Earnings are a major driver of stock market prices as investors generally get in the stock market early, in anticipation of favorable results, which helps to run stock prices up in the first half of the month.

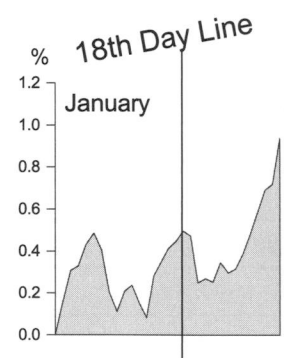

18th Day Line

1st to 18th Day 1950-2016

Avg Gain 0.5%	Fq Pos 61%

The first month of the year generally has a good start. Investors and money managers generally push the market upward as they try to lock in their new positions for the year. The result is that the market tends to increase for the first eighteen days, pause, and then accelerate through the end of the month.

Avg Gain 1.4%	Fq Pos 69%

This month has a reputation of being a strong month. If you look at the graph, you can see that almost all of the gains have come in the first half of the month. It is interesting to note that the month returns tend to peak just after the last day to file tax returns.

Avg Gain 0.9%	Fq Pos 66%

This is the month in which the market can peak in strong bull markets. The returns in the first half of the month can be positive, but investors should be cautious, as the time period following in August and September has a tendency towards negative returns.

Avg Gain 0.8%	Fq Pos 64%

This is the month with a bad reputation. Once again, the first part of the month tends to do well. It is the middle segment, centered around the notorious Black Monday, that brings down the results. Toward the end of the month, investors realize that the world has not ended and start to buy stocks again, providing a strong finish to the month.

1st to 18th Day Gain S&P500			
JAN	APR	JUL	OCT
1950	0.36 %	4.28 %	-3.56 %	2.88 %
1951	4.75	3.41	4.39	1.76
1952	2.02	-3.57	-0.44	-1.39
1953	-2.07	-2.65	0.87	3.38
1954	2.50	3.71	2.91	-1.49
1955	-3.28	4.62	3.24	-4.63
1956	-2.88	-1.53	4.96	2.18
1957	-4.35	2.95	2.45	-4.93
1958	2.78	1.45	1.17	2.80
1959	1.09	4.47	1.23	0.79
1960	-3.34	2.26	-2.14	1.55
1961	2.70	1.75	-0.36	2.22
1962	-4.42	-1.84	2.65	0.12
1963	3.30	3.49	-1.27	2.26
1964	2.05	1.99	2.84	0.77
1965	2.05	2.31	1.87	1.91
1966	1.64	2.63	2.66	2.77
1967	6.80	1.84	3.16	-1.51
1968	-0.94	7.63	1.87	2.09
1969	-1.76	-0.27	-2.82	3.37
1970	-1.24	-4.42	6.83	-0.02
1971	1.37	3.17	0.42	-1.01
1972	1.92	2.40	-1.22	-2.13
1973	0.68	0.02	2.00	1.46
1974	-2.04	0.85	-2.58	13.76
1975	3.50	3.53	-2.09	5.95
1976	7.55	-2.04	0.38	-3.58
1977	-3.85	2.15	0.47	-3.18
1978	-4.77	4.73	1.40	-2.00
1979	3.76	0.11	-1.19	-5.22
1980	2.90	-1.51	6.83	4.83
1981	-0.73	-0.96	-0.34	2.59
1982	-4.35	4.33	1.33	13.54
1983	4.10	4.43	-2.20	1.05
1984	1.59	-0.80	-1.16	1.20
1985	2.44	0.10	1.32	2.72
1986	-1.35	1.46	-5.77	3.25
1987	9.96	-1.64	3.48	-12.16
1988	1.94	0.12	-1.09	2.75
1989	3.17	3.78	4.20	-2.12
1990	-4.30	0.23	1.73	-0.10
1991	0.61	3.53	3.83	1.20
1992	0.42	3.06	1.83	-1.45
1993	0.26	-0.60	-1.06	2.07
1994	1.67	-0.74	2.46	1.07
1995	2.27	0.93	2.52	0.52
1996	-1.25	-0.29	-4.04	3.42
1997	4.78	1.22	3.41	-0.33
1998	-0.92	1.90	4.67	3.88
1999	1.14	2.54	3.36	-2.23
2000	-0.96	-3.80	2.69	-6.57
2001	2.10	6.71	-1.36	2.66
2002	-1.79	-2.00	-10.94	8.48
2003	2.50	5.35	1.93	4.35
2004	2.51	0.75	-3.46	-0.05
2005	-1.32	-2.93	2.50	-4.12
2006	2.55	1.22	0.51	3.15
2007	1.41	4.33	-3.20	1.48
2008	-9.75	5.11	-1.51	-19.36
2009	-5.88	8.99	2.29	2.89
2010	1.88	1.94	3.32	3.81
2011	2.97	-1.56	-1.15	8.30
2012	4.01	-1.66	0.78	1.16
2013	4.2	-1.76	5.17	3.74
2014	-0.52	-0.4	0.92	-4.34
2015	-1.92	0.64	3.08	5.89
2016	-8.0	1.68	3.21	-1.32
Avg	0.51 %	1.37 %	0.90 %	0.83 %

Earnings Month Effect Performance

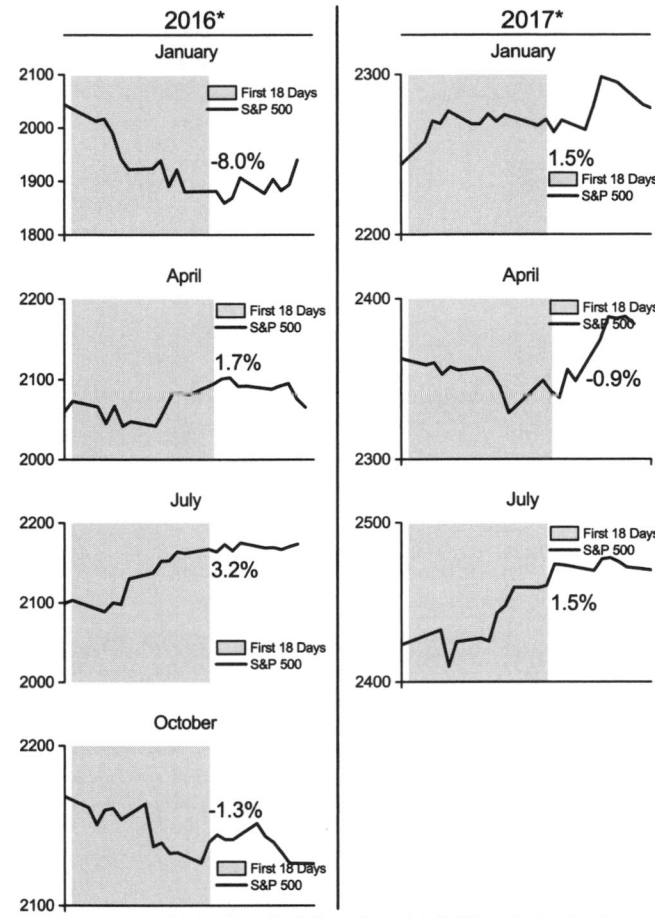

2016*

January
-8.0%
First 18 Days / S&P 500

April
1.7%
First 18 Days / S&P 500

July
3.2%
First 18 Days / S&P 500

October
-1.3%
First 18 Days / S&P 500

2017*

January
1.5%
First 18 Days / S&P 500

April
-0.9%
First 18 Days / S&P 500

July
1.5%
First 18 Days / S&P 500

*Last day of previous month included in graph only, displayed return is for first 18 calendar days of month

Market Indices & Rates
Weekly Values**

Stock Markets	2016	2017
Dow	17,635	20,661
S&P500	2,053	2,357
Nasdaq	4,871	5,883
TSX	13,330	15,652
FTSE	6,152	7,318
DAX	9,633	12,243
Nikkei	15,829	18,783
Hang Seng	20,255	24,301

Commodities	2016	2017
Oil	37.26	51.27
Gold	1230.8	1253.9

Bond Yields	2016	2017
USA 5 Yr Treasury	1.18	1.88
USA 10 Yr T	1.74	2.35
USA 20 Yr T	2.14	2.72
Moody's Aaa	3.63	3.93
Moody's Baa	4.82	4.62
CAN 5 Yr T	0.68	1.08
CAN 10 Yr T	1.20	1.57

Money Market	2016	2017
USA Fed Funds	0.50	1.00
USA 3 Mo T-B	0.23	0.80
CAN tgt overnight rate	0.50	0.50
CAN 3 Mo T-B	0.46	0.54

Foreign Exchange	2016	2017
EUR/USD	1.14	1.06
GBP/USD	1.41	1.25
USD/CAD	1.31	1.34
USD/JPY	109.55	110.85

APRIL

M	T	W	T	F	S	S
						1
2	3	4	5	6	7	8
9	10	11	12	13	14	15
16	17	18	19	20	21	22
23	24	25	26	27	28	29
30						

Earnings Month Effect Performance

In 2016, the first eighteen calendar days of the earnings months were positive two out of four times. The biggest gain occurred in July, as the S&P 500 benefited from the bounce in the stock market after the Brexit referendum.

In 2017, the first eighteen calendar days for the earnings months' phenomenon started off on a positive note as January rallied strongly at the beginning of the month. The first eighteen calendar days in April were negative as investors questioned whether the high stock market valuations could be sustained with less than very strong earnings.

The first eighteen calendar days of July 2017 were strong as investors became enamoured with reports of strengthening worldwide growth and the subsequent impact on earnings.

MAY

M	T	W	T	F	S	S
	1	2	3	4	5	6
7	8	9	10	11	12	13
14	15	16	17	18	19	20
21	22	23	24	25	26	27
28	29	30	31			

JUNE

M	T	W	T	F	S	S
				1	2	3
4	5	6	7	8	9	10
11	12	13	14	15	16	17
18	19	20	21	22	23	24
25	26	27	28	29	30	

The *Consumer Switch* strategy has allowed investors to use a set portion of their account to switch between the two related consumer sectors. To use this strategy, investors take a position in the consumer discretionary sector from October 28th to April 22nd, and then use the proceeds to invest in the consumer staples sector from April 23rd to October 27th, and then repeat the cycle.

The end result has been outperformance compared with buying and holding both consumer sectors, or buying and holding the broad market.

4459% total aggregate gain

The basic premise of the strategy is that the consumer discretionary sector tends to outperform during the favorable six month period for stocks (October 28th to May 5th), when more money flows into the stock market, pushing up stock prices. On the other hand, the consumer staples sector tends to outperform when investors are looking for safety and stability of earnings in the other six months when the market tends to move into a defensive mode.

Consumer Staples & Discretionary Switch Strategy*

Investment Period	Buy @ Beginning of Period	% Gain @ End of Period	% Gain Cumulative
90 Apr23 - 90 Oct29	Staples	7.7%	8%
90 Oct29 - 91 Apr23	Discretionary	41.7	53
91 Apr23 - 91 Oct28	Staples	2.1	56
91 Oct28 - 92 Apr23	Discretionary	15.9	81
92 Apr23 - 92 Oct27	Staples	6.3	92
92 Oct27 - 93 Apr23	Discretionary	6.3	104
93 Apr23 - 93 Oct27	Staples	5.8	116
93 Oct27 - 94 Apr25	Discretionary	-3.7	108
94 Apr25 - 94 Oct27	Staples	10.2	129
94 Oct27 - 95 Apr24	Discretionary	4.4	139
95 Apr24 - 95 Oct27	Staples	15.3	176
95 Oct27 - 96 Apr23	Discretionary	17.3	227
96 Apr23 - 96 Oct27	Staples	12.6	265
96 Oct27 - 97 Apr23	Discretionary	5.1	283
97 Apr23 - 97 Oct27	Staples	2.5	293
97 Oct27 - 98 Apr23	Discretionary	35.9	434
98 Apr23 - 98 Oct27	Staples	-0.7	423
98 Oct27 - 99 Apr23	Discretionary	41.8	651
99 Apr23 - 99 Oct27	Staples	-9.7	578
99 Oct27 - 00 Apr24	Discretionary	11.9	659
00 Apr24 - 00 Oct27	Staples	16.5	785
00 Oct27 - 01 Apr23	Discretionary	9.8	872
01 Apr23 - 01 Oct29	Staples	4.0	910
01 Oct29 - 02 Apr23	Discretionary	16.1	1073
02 Apr23 - 02 Oct28	Staples	-13.9	910
02 Oct28 - 03 Apr23	Discretionary	3.0	941
03 Apr23 - 03 Oct27	Staples	8.4	1028
03 Oct27 - 04 Apr23	Discretionary	9.6	1137
04 Apr23 - 04 Oct27	Staples	-7.4	1045
04 Oct27 - 05 Apr25	Discretionary	-2.0	1021
05 Apr25 - 05 Oct27	Staples	-0.5	1016
05 Oct27 - 06 Apr24	Discretionary	9.2	1119
06 Apr24 - 06 Oct27	Staples	10.6	1249
06 Oct27 - 07 Apr23	Discretionary	6.3	1334
07 Apr23 - 07 Oct29	Staples	4.6	1400
07 Oct29 - 08 Apr23	Discretionary	-13.7	1194
08 Apr23 - 08 Oct27	Staples	-21.5	916
08 Oct27 - 09 Apr23	Discretionary	17.7	1096
09 Apr23 - 09 Oct27	Staples	20.6	1342
09 Oct27 - 10 Apr23	Discretionary	29.7	1770
10 Apr23 - 10 Oct27	Staples	2.4	1815
10 Oct27 - 11 Apr25	Discretionary	13.7	2079
11 Apr25 - 11 Oct27	Staples	2.2	2126
11 Oct27 - 12 Apr23	Discretionary	10.9	2368
12 Apr23 - 12 Oct31	Staples	4.7	2485
12 Oct31 - 13 Apr23	Discretionary	17.5	2938
13 Apr23 - 13 Oct28	Staples	2.3	3006
13 Oct28 - 14 Apr23	Discretionary	1.7	3060
14 Apr23 - 14 Oct27	Staples	5.9	3248
14 Oct27 - 15 Apr23	Discretionary	15.2	3758
15 Apr23 - 15 Oct27	Staples	3.1	3878
15 Oct27 - 16 Apr23	Discretionary	-0.4	3863
16 Apr22 - 16 Oct27	Staples	1.1	3907
16 Oct27 - 17 Apr24	Discretionary	13.8	4459

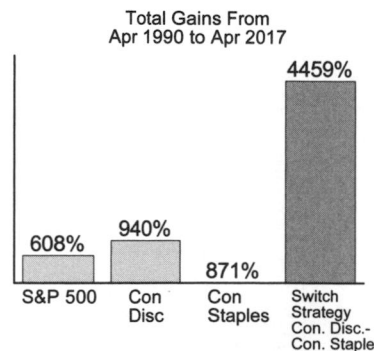

Total Gains From
Apr 1990 to Apr 2017

S&P 500: 608%
Con Disc: 940%
Con Staples: 871%
Switch Strategy Con. Disc.- Con. Staples: 4459%

* If buy date lands on weekend or holiday, then next day is used

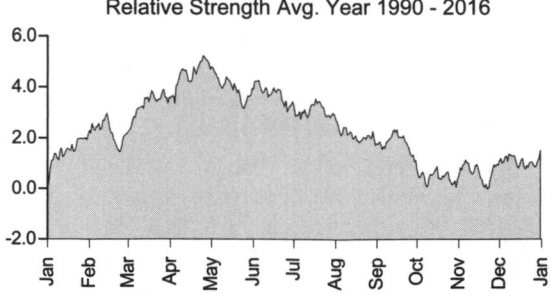

Consumer Discretionary / Consumer Staples
Relative Strength Avg. Year 1990 - 2016

Consumer Switch Performance

2016

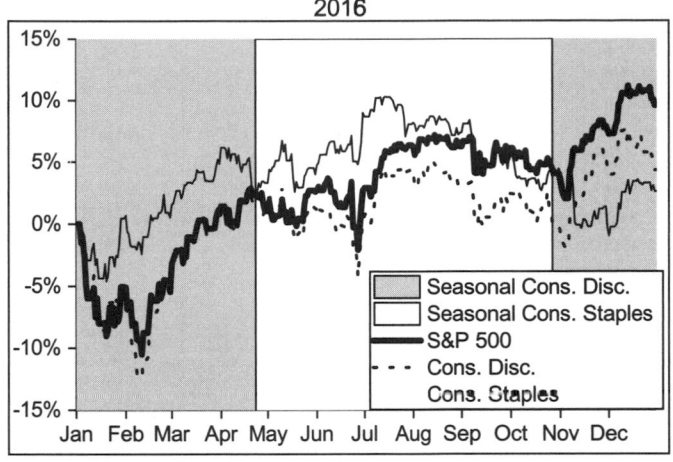

2017

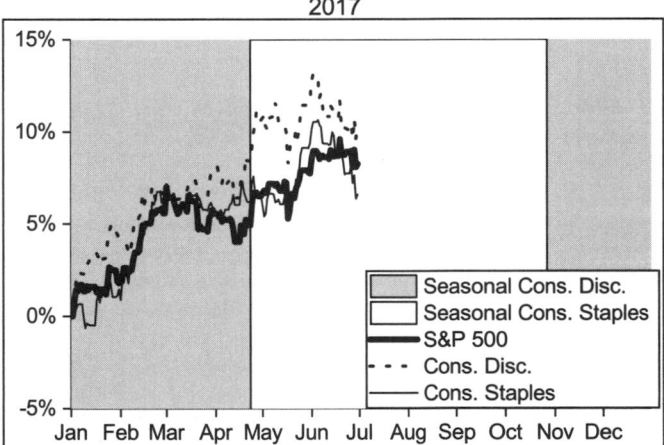

Stock Markets	2016	2017
Dow	17,802	20,589
S&P500	2,070	2,346
Nasdaq	4,907	5,847
TSX	13,596	15,660
FTSE	6,303	7,348
DAX	9,923	12,151
Nikkei	16,364	18,572
Hang Seng	20,952	24,231

Commodities	2016	2017
Oil	41.23	53.19
Gold	1243.2	1265.4

Bond Yields	2016	2017
USA 5 Yr Treasury	1.22	1.83
USA 10 Yr T	1.77	2.30
USA 20 Yr T	2.16	2.67
Moody's Aaa	3.61	3.86
Moody's Baa	4.78	4.56
CAN 5 Yr T	0.75	1.07
CAN 10 Yr T	1.27	1.53

Money Market	2016	2017
USA Fed Funds	0.50	1.00
USA 3 Mo T-B	0.22	0.82
CAN tgt overnight rate	0.50	0.50
CAN 3 Mo T-B	0.48	0.54

Foreign Exchange	2016	2017
EUR/USD	1.13	1.06
GBP/USD	1.42	1.25
USD/CAD	1.28	1.33
USD/JPY	108.80	109.46

In 2016, the consumer discretionary sector performed equal to the S&P 500 in its seasonal period, at the beginning of the year. It underperformed in the seasonal period at the end of the year. In both instances, the S&P 500 was rallying sharply. The consumer staples sector performed equal to the S&P 500 and outperformed the consumer discretionary sector in its seasonal period.

So far in 2017, the consumer discretionary sector has outperformed the S&P 500 in its seasonal period and the consumer staples sector has underperformed the S&P 500 in the first half of its seasonal period.

APRIL

M	T	W	T	F	S	S
						1
2	3	4	5	6	7	8
9	10	11	12	13	14	15
16	17	18	19	20	21	22
23	24	25	26	27	28	29
30						

MAY

M	T	W	T	F	S	S
	1	2	3	4	5	6
7	8	9	10	11	12	13
14	15	16	17	18	19	20
21	22	23	24	25	26	27
28	29	30	31			

JUNE

M	T	W	T	F	S	S
				1	2	3
4	5	6	7	8	9	10
11	12	13	14	15	16	17
18	19	20	21	22	23	24
25	26	27	28	29	30	

U.S. Government Bonds (7-10 Years)
May 6th to Oct 3rd

The following government bond seasonal period analysis has been broken down into two contiguous periods in order to demonstrate the relative strength of the first part of the trade compared with the second part. Although both the May 6th to August 8th and the August 9th to October 3rd periods provide value, the sweet spot to the government bond trade is in the latter period from August 9th to October 3rd.

Bonds outperform from late spring into autumn for three reasons. First, governments and companies tend to raise more money through bond issuance at the beginning of the year to meet their needs for the rest of the year. With more bonds competing in the market for money, bond prices tend to decrease. Less bonds tend to be issued in late spring and early summer during their seasonal period, helping to support bond prices.

6.8% gain & positive 84% of the time

Second, optimistic forecasts at the beginning of the year for stronger GDP growth tend to increase inflation expectations and as a result interest rates respond by increasing. As economic growth expectations tend to decrease in the summer, interest rates respond by retreating.

Third, the stock market often peaks in May and investors rotate their money into bonds. As the demand for bonds increases, interest rates decrease and bonds increase in value. For seasonal investors looking to put their money to work in the unfavorable six months of the year, buying bonds in the summer months fits perfectly.

In periods when the stock market rallies in the early summer months, positive bond performance can be delayed until later in the summer, typically early August, which coincides with the bond seasonal period sweet spot, from August 9th to October 3rd.

Investors should note that government bonds have a track record of appreciating in November and December, but despite their typical positive performance at this time, there are other investments, such as high yield bonds, corporate bonds and equities that have a better return profile.

U.S. Gov. Bonds* vs. S&P 500 1998 to 2016 Positive ▭

Year	May 6 to Aug 8 S&P 500	May 6 to Aug 8 Gov. Bonds	Aug 9 to Oct 3 S&P 500	Aug 9 to Oct 3 Gov. Bonds	Total Growth S&P 500	Total Growth Gov. Bonds
1998	-2.3 %	3.3 %	-8.0 %	8.3 %	-10.1 %	11.9 %
1999	-3.5	-3.0	-1.3	0.9	-4.8	-2.1
2000	3.5	5.8	-3.8	0.9	-0.4	6.7
2001	-6.6	2.6	-9.4	4.4	-15.3	7.1
2002	-15.7	6.5	-9.6	5.0	-23.7	11.9
2003	5.5	-1.3	5.4	1.3	11.2	0.0
2004	-5.1	3.6	6.4	0.8	0.9	4.4
2005	4.3	-0.9	0.3	0.7	4.6	-0.2
2006	-4.1	2.6	4.9	2.7	0.6	5.3
2007	-0.5	-0.3	2.8	3.3	2.3	3.0
2008	-7.9	0.9	-15.2	2.4	-21.9	3.4
2009	11.8	-4.0	1.5	5.4	13.4	1.1
2010	-3.8	7.1	2.2	2.6	-1.7	9.8
2011	-16.2	7.6	-1.8	4.6	-17.7	12.6
2012	2.4	2.3	3.5	0.9	6.0	3.3
2013	5.1	-5.2	-1.1	0.3	4.0	-4.9
2014	2.5	2.3	1.9	0.1	4.4	2.4
2015	-0.6	0.6	-6.1	2.1	-6.6	2.6
2016	6.4	1.6	-0.9	-0.1	5.4	1.6
Avg.	1.3 %	1.7 %	1.5 %	2.5 %	4.2 %	6.8 %
Fq>0	42 %	68 %	47 %	95 %	79 %	84 %

ⓘ *Source: Barclays Capital Inc.*
The U.S. Treasury: 7-10 Year is a total return index, which includes both interest and capital appreciation.
For more information on fixed income indices, see www.barcap.com.

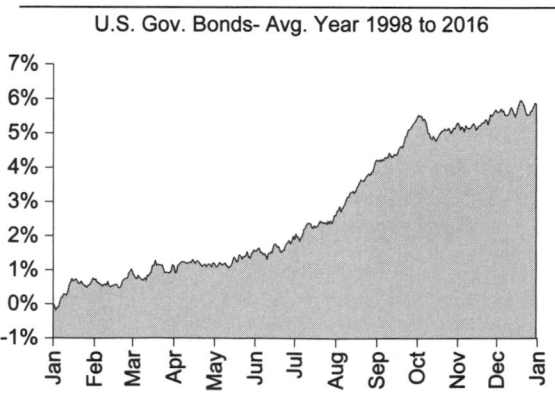

U.S. Gov. Bonds- Avg. Year 1998 to 2016

U.S. Government Bond Performance

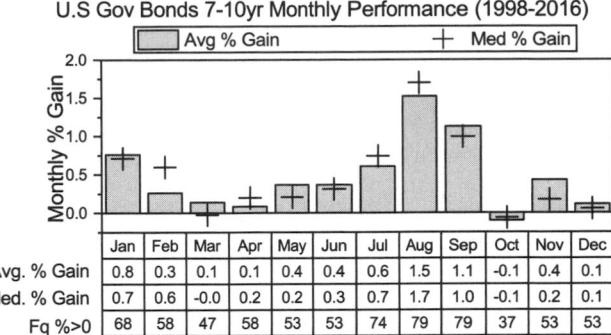

U.S Gov Bonds 7-10yr Monthly Performance (1998-2016)

	Jan	Feb	Mar	Apr	May	Jun	Jul	Aug	Sep	Oct	Nov	Dec
Avg. % Gain	0.8	0.3	0.1	0.1	0.4	0.4	0.6	1.5	1.1	-0.1	0.4	0.1
Med. % Gain	0.7	0.6	-0.0	0.2	0.2	0.3	0.7	1.7	1.0	-0.1	0.2	0.1
Fq %>0	68	58	47	58	53	53	74	79	79	37	53	53

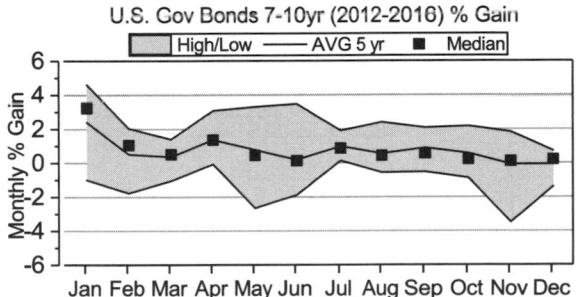

U.S. Gov Bonds 7-10yr (2012-2016) % Gain

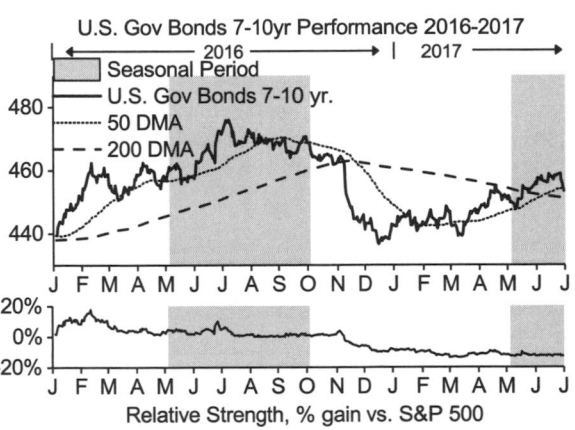

U.S. Gov Bonds 7-10yr Performance 2016-2017

Relative Strength, % gain vs. S&P 500

Market Indices & Rates Weekly Values**

Stock Markets	2016	2017
Dow	18,028	20,538
S&P500	2,096	2,347
Nasdaq	4,940	5,879
TSX	13,851	15,620
FTSE	6,372	7,124
DAX	10,340	12,023
Nikkei	16,999	18,451
Hang Seng	21,385	23,962

Commodities	2016	2017
Oil	41.68	51.01
Gold	1246.8	1280.5

Bond Yields	2016	2017
USA 5 Yr Treasury	1.31	1.76
USA 10 Yr T	1.84	2.23
USA 20 Yr T	2.24	2.60
Moody's Aaa	3.57	3.82
Moody's Baa	4.77	4.51
CAN 5 Yr T	0.82	1.01
CAN 10 Yr T	1.39	1.48

Money Market	2016	2017
USA Fed Funds	0.50	1.00
USA 3 Mo T-B	0.22	0.81
CAN tgt overnight rate	0.50	0.50
CAN 3 Mo T-B	0.55	0.54

Foreign Exchange	2016	2017
EUR/USD	1.13	1.07
GBP/USD	1.43	1.28
USD/CAD	1.27	1.34
USD/JPY	109.82	108.92

APRIL

M	T	W	T	F	S	S
						1
2	3	4	5	6	7	8
9	10	11	12	13	14	15
16	17	18	19	20	21	22
23	24	25	26	27	28	29
30						

MAY

M	T	W	T	F	S	S
	1	2	3	4	5	6
7	8	9	10	11	12	13
14	15	16	17	18	19	20
21	22	23	24	25	26	27
28	29	30	31			

JUNE

M	T	W	T	F	S	S
			1	2	3	
4	5	6	7	8	9	10
11	12	13	14	15	16	17
18	19	20	21	22	23	24
25	26	27	28	29	30	

From 1998 to 2016, U.S. government bonds have performed well from May until October, particularly in August and September which is the sweet spot for the seasonal *U.S. Government Bond Trade*. From 2012 to 2016, the magnitude of the relative gains in the seasonal period compared to the rest of the year have not been as strong as the long-term trend.

In 2016, U.S. government bonds performed well as investors anticipated the Federal Reserve taking a more dovish stance with its monetary policy. In 2017, at the beginning of their seasonal period, U.S. government bonds have been positive.

CANADIAN DOLLAR – STRONG TWICE
①April ②Aug20-Sep25

All other things being equal, if oil increases in price, investors favor the Canadian dollar over the U.S. dollar. They do so with good reason, as Canada is a net exporter of oil and benefits from its rising price.

Oil tends to do well in the month of April, which is the core of the main energy seasonal strategy that lasts from February 25th to May 9th.

April has been a strong month for the Canadian dollar relative to the U.S. dollar. The largest losses have had a tendency to occur in years when the Federal Reserve has been aggressively hiking its target rate.

Since 1971, at some point during the years 1987, 2000, 2004 and 2005, the Federal Reserve increased their target rate by a total of at least 1% in each

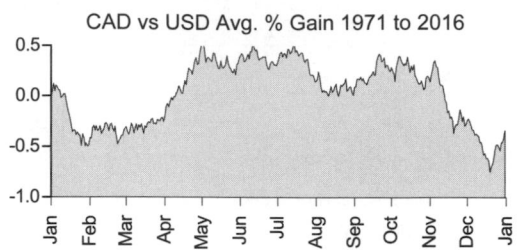

CAD vs USD Avg. % Gain 1971 to 2016

year. Three of these years (1987, 2004 and 2005) were three of the biggest losers for the Canadian dollar in the month of April.

The Canadian dollar also has a second period of seasonality, August 20th to September 25th. It is not a coincidence that oil also has a second period of seasonal strength at this time. Although the August 20th to September 25th seasonal period is not as strong as the April seasonal period, it is still a trade worth considering.

CAD vs USD Apr & Aug 20 to Sep 25 % Gain (1971-2017) Source: Bloomberg   Positive ☐

	Apr1-Apr30	Aug20-Sep25		Apr1-Apr30	Aug20-Sep25		Apr1-Apr30	Aug20-Sep25		Apr1-Apr30	Aug20-Sep25		Apr1-Apr30	Aug20-Sep25
1980	0.29%	-0.15%	1990	0.44%	-0.43%	2000	-1.89%	-0.96%	2010	0.44%	1.32%			
1971	-0.10%	0.46%	1981	-0.74	1.08	1991	0.65	0.86	2001	2.76	-1.76	2011	2.44	-4.20
1972	0.53	0.01	1982	0.89	0.78	1992	-0.48	-3.37	2002	1.77	-0.61	2012	1.05	1.16
1973	-0.41	-0.32	1983	0.64	0.17	1993	-1.02	-0.08	2003	2.50	3.95	2013	1.01	0.39
1974	1.27	-0.40	1984	-0.62	-1.01	1994	0.14	2.22	2004	-4.46	1.57	2014	0.88	-1.58
1975	-1.56	1.33	1985	0.04	-0.32	1995	2.91	0.96	2005	-3.77	3.75	2015	4.67	-1.18
1976	0.55	1.41	1986	1.69	0.35	1996	0.15	0.48	2006	4.17	0.64	2016	3.40	-2.29
1977	0.91	0.31	1987	-2.38	1.41	1997	-0.97	0.79	2007	4.17	6.30	2017	-2.45	
1978	0.09	-3.22	1988	0.41	0.43	1998	-0.85	1.37	2008	1.81	2.59			
1979	1.61	0.15	1989	0.60	0.55	1999	3.53	1.36	2009	5.59	0.46			
Avg.	0.32%	-0.03%		0.06%	0.38%		0.45%	0.51%		1.62%	1.88%		1.60%	-0.97%

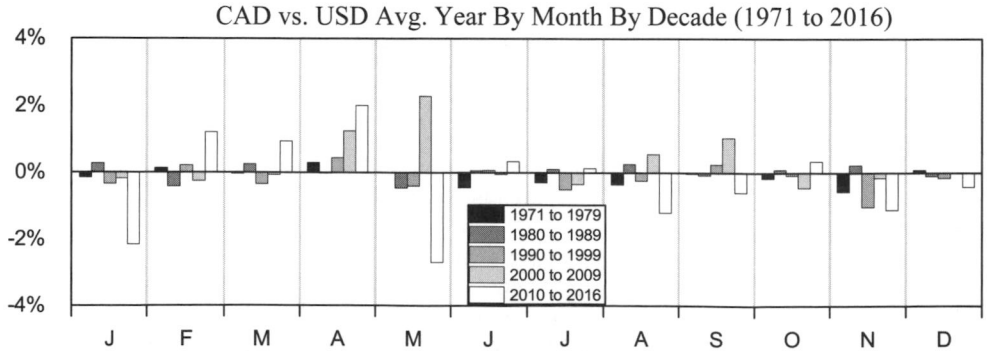

CAD vs. USD Avg. Year By Month By Decade (1971 to 2016)

Legend: 1971 to 1979 · 1980 to 1989 · 1990 to 1999 · 2000 to 2009 · 2010 to 2016

CAD/USD Performance

CAD/USD Monthly Performance (1971-2016)

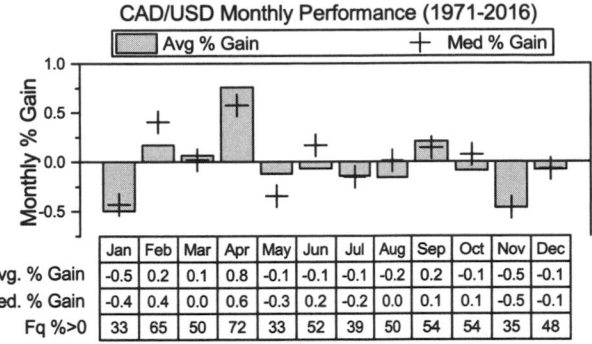

	Jan	Feb	Mar	Apr	May	Jun	Jul	Aug	Sep	Oct	Nov	Dec
Avg. % Gain	-0.5	0.2	0.1	0.8	-0.1	-0.1	-0.1	-0.2	0.2	-0.1	-0.5	-0.1
Med. % Gain	-0.4	0.4	0.0	0.6	-0.3	0.2	-0.2	0.0	0.1	0.1	-0.5	-0.1
Fq %>0	33	65	50	72	33	52	39	50	54	54	35	48

CAD/USD 5 Year (2012-2016) % Gain

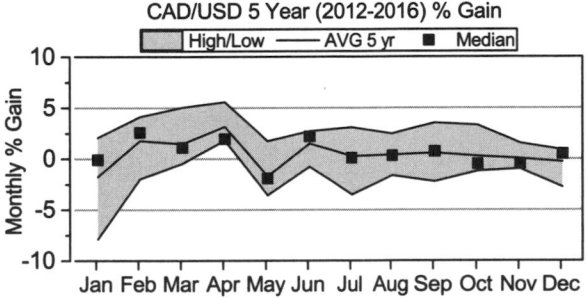

CAD/USD Performance 2016-2017

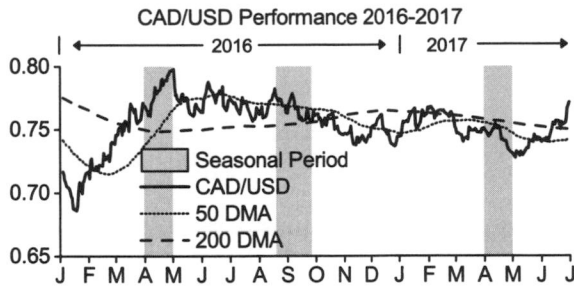

Market Indices & Rates
Weekly Values**

Stock Markets	2016	2017
Dow	17,923	20,931
S&P500	2,083	2,385
Nasdaq	4,846	6,026
TSX	13,866	15,640
FTSE	6,277	7,254
DAX	10,294	12,455
Nikkei	17,187	19,139
Hang Seng	21,306	24,497

Commodities	2016	2017
Oil	44.13	49.20
Gold	1253.4	1265.7

Bond Yields	2016	2017
USA 5 Yr Treasury	1.35	1.83
USA 10 Yr T	1.89	2.31
USA 20 Yr T	2.30	2.68
Moody's Aaa	3.63	3.07
Moody's Baa	4.75	4.58
CAN 5 Yr T	0.89	1.04
CAN 10 Yr T	1.52	1.52

Money Market	2016	2017
USA Fed Funds	0.50	1.00
USA 3 Mo T-B	0.23	0.81
CAN tgt overnight rate	0.50	0.50
CAN 3 Mo T-B	0.56	0.52

Foreign Exchange	2016	2017
EUR/USD	1.13	1.09
GBP/USD	1.46	1.29
USD/CAD	1.26	1.36
USD/JPY	109.72	110.93

APRIL

M	T	W	T	F	S	S
						1
2	3	4	5	6	7	8
9	10	11	12	13	14	15
16	17	18	19	20	21	22
23	24	25	26	27	28	29
30						

MAY

M	T	W	T	F	S	S
1	2	3	4	5	6	
7	8	9	10	11	12	13
14	15	16	17	18	19	20
21	22	23	24	25	26	27
28	29	30	31			

JUNE

M	T	W	T	F	S	S
				1	2	3
4	5	6	7	8	9	10
11	12	13	14	15	16	17
18	19	20	21	22	23	24
25	26	27	28	29	30	

Canadian Dollar Performance (CAD/USD)

From 1971 to 2016, April has been the strongest month of the year for CAD/USD on an average, median and frequency basis. On a median basis, February is the second strongest month. Over the last five years, May has been the worst performing month.

In 2016, the Canadian dollar started the year on a positive note and then turned negative at the beginning of May, just after its seasonal period finished. In 2017, the Canadian dollar started to correct in January and then finished its correction in May. The correction of the Canadian dollar in April was the first in fifteen years.

MAY

	MONDAY	TUESDAY	WEDNESDAY
WEEK 18	30	1 30	2 29
WEEK19	7 24	8 23	9 22
WEEK 20	14 17	15 16	16 15
WEEK 21	21 10 CAN Market Closed- Victoria Day	22 9	23 8
WEEK 22	28 3 USA Market Closed- Memorial Day	29 2	30 1

THURSDAY		FRIDAY	
3	28	**4**	27
10	21	**11**	20
17	14	**18**	13
24	7	**25**	6
31		1	

JUNE

M	T	W	T	F	S	S
				1	2	3
4	5	6	7	8	9	10
11	12	13	14	15	16	17
18	19	20	21	22	23	24
25	26	27	28	29	30	

JULY

M	T	W	T	F	S	S
						1
2	3	4	5	6	7	8
9	10	11	12	13	14	15
16	17	18	19	20	21	22
2	24	25	26	27	28	29
30	31					

AUGUST

M	T	W	T	F	S	S
		1	2	3	4	5
6	7	8	9	10	11	12
13	14	15	16	17	18	19
20	21	22	23	24	25	26
27	28	29	30	31		

SEPTEMBER

M	T	W	T	F	S	S
					1	2
3	4	5	6	7	8	9
10	11	12	13	14	15	16
17	18	19	20	21	22	23
24	25	26	27	28	29	30

MAY
S U M M A R Y

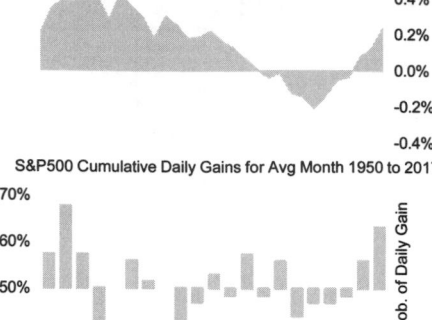

S&P500 Cumulative Daily Gains for Avg Month 1950 to 2017

	Dow Jones	S&P 500	Nasdaq	TSX Comp
Month Rank	9	8	5	2
# Up	35	39	28	20
# Down	32	28	17	12
% Pos	52	58	62	63
% Avg. Gain	0.0	0.2	1.0	1.4

Dow & S&P 1950-2016, Nasdaq 1972-2016, TSX 1985-2016

♦ The S&P 500 often peaks in May, and as a result seasonal investors should start to be more cautious with their investments at this time. ♦ Defensive sectors often perform well in May. ♦ The first few days and the last few days in May tend to be strong and the period in between tends to be negative. ♦ A lot of the cyclical sectors finish their seasonal periods at the beginning of May. ♦ The month of May starts the six month unfavorable period for stocks, which has historically been the weaker six months of the year.

BEST / WORST MAY BROAD MKTS. 2008-2017

BEST MAY MARKETS
- ♦ TSX Comp. (2009) 11.2%
- ♦ Nikkei 225 (2009) 7.9%
- ♦ TSX Comp (2008) 5.6%

WORST MAY MARKETS
- ♦ Nikkei 225 (2010) -11.7%
- ♦ Nikkei 225 (2012) -10.3%
- ♦ Nasdaq (2010) -8.8%

Index Values End of Month

	2008	2009	2010	2011	2012	2013	2014	2015	2016	2017
Dow	12,638	8,500	10,137	12,570	12,393	15,116	16,717	18,011	17,787	21,009
S&P 500	1,400	919	1,089	1,345	1,310	1,631	1,924	2,107	2,097	2,412
Nasdaq	2,523	1,774	2,257	2,835	2,827	3,456	4,243	5,070	4,948	6,199
TSX Comp.	14,715	10,370	11,763	13,803	11,513	12,650	14,604	15,014	14,066	15,350
Russell 1000	768	502	602	749	724	904	1,072	1,177	1,161	1,336
Russell 2000	748	502	662	848	762	984	1,135	1,247	1,155	1,370
FTSE 100	6,054	4,418	5,188	5,990	5,321	6,583	6,845	6,984	6,231	7,520
Nikkei 225	14,339	9,523	9,769	9,694	8,543	13,775	14,632	20,563	17,235	19,651

Percent Gain for May

	2008	2009	2010	2011	2012	2013	2014	2015	2016	2017
Dow	-1.4	4.1	-7.9	-1.9	-6.2	1.9	0.8	1.0	0.1	0.3
S&P 500	1.1	5.3	-8.2	-1.4	-6.3	2.1	2.1	1.0	1.5	1.2
Nasdaq	4.6	3.3	-8.3	-1.3	-7.2	3.8	3.1	2.6	3.6	2.5
TSX Comp.	5.6	11.2	-3.7	-1.0	-6.3	1.6	-0.3	-1.4	0.8	-1.5
Russell 1000	1.6	5.3	-8.1	-1.3	-6.4	2.0	2.1	1.1	1.5	1.0
Russell 2000	4.5	2.9	-7.7	-2.0	-6.7	3.9	0.7	2.2	2.1	-2.2
FTSE 100	-0.6	4.1	-6.6	-1.3	-7.3	2.4	1.0	0.3	-0.2	4.4
Nikkei 225	3.5	7.9	-11.7	-1.6	-10.3	-0.6	2.3	5.3	3.4	2.4

May Market Avg. Performance 2008 to 2017[1]

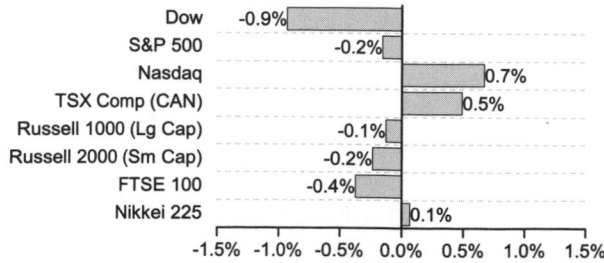

Dow	-0.9%
S&P 500	-0.2%
Nasdaq	0.7%
TSX Comp (CAN)	0.5%
Russell 1000 (Lg Cap)	-0.1%
Russell 2000 (Sm Cap)	-0.2%
FTSE 100	-0.4%
Nikkei 225	0.1%

-1.5% -1.0% -0.5% 0.0% 0.5% 1.0% 1.5%

Interest Corner May[2]

	Fed Funds % [3]	3 Mo. T-Bill % [4]	10 Yr % [5]	20 Yr % [6]
2017	1.00	0.98	2.21	2.60
2016	0.50	0.34	1.84	2.23
2015	0.25	0.01	2.12	2.63
2014	0.25	0.04	2.48	3.05
2013	0.25	0.04	2.16	2.95

(1) Russell Data provided by Russell (2) Federal Reserve Bank of St. Louis- end of month values (3) Target rate set by FOMC (4)(5)(6) Constant yield maturities.

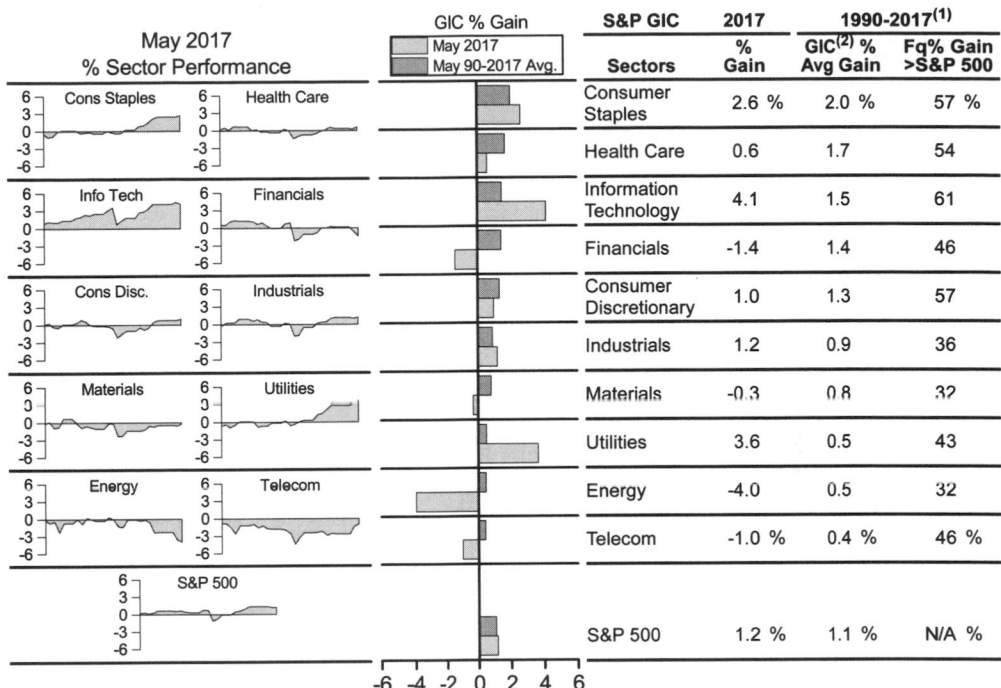

S&P GIC Sectors	2017 % Gain	1990-2017[1]	
		GIC[2] % Avg Gain	Fq% Gain >S&P 500
Consumer Staples	2.6 %	2.0 %	57 %
Health Care	0.6	1.7	54
Information Technology	4.1	1.5	61
Financials	-1.4	1.4	46
Consumer Discretionary	1.0	1.3	57
Industrials	1.2	0.9	36
Materials	-0.3	0.8	32
Utilities	3.6	0.5	43
Energy	-4.0	0.5	32
Telecom	-1.0 %	0.4 %	46 %
S&P 500	1.2 %	1.1 %	N/A %

Sector Commentary

♦ In May 2017, the information technology sector continued with its rally from previous months, producing a 4.1% gain. ♦ The energy sector is typically one of the weaker performing sectors in May, and in 2017 the sector lived up to its reputation, producing a loss of 4.0%. ♦ The consumer staples sector has on average been the best performing sector in May since 1990. In 2017, the sector performed well, with a 2.6% gain. The utilities sector, another defensive sector, also performed well producing a gain of 3.6%.

Sub-Sector Commentary

♦ In May 2017, the semiconductor sub-sector (SOX) produced a strong gain of 8.5%. ♦ Transportation produced a gain of 2.9% as investors speculated that the positive "soft" economic data (business sentiment data) would eventually translate into economic strength. ♦ In addition, the agriculture sub-sector was also sharply negative, producing a loss of 9.1%. The drop was largely the result of falling grain prices.

SELECTED SUB-SECTORS[3]			
Agriculture (1994-2017)	-9.1 %	2.1 %	54 %
Biotech (1993-2017)	-3.9	2.0	68
Banks	-3.3	1.9	50
Retail	1.1	1.7	57
Railroads	2.3	1.3	57
Pharma	0.4	1.3	46
SOX (1995-2017)	8.5	1.1	57
Chemicals	-0.1	0.9	46
Transportation	2.9	0.5	50
Steel	-5.3	0.4	46
Metals & Mining	-4.6	0.3	43
Automotive & Components	-1.4	0.2	25
Gold	0.0	0.1	50
Silver	-0.6	-0.6	43
Home-builders	0.3	-0.8	46

DISNEY–TIME TO STAY AWAY & TIME TO VISIT
①SELL SHORT (Jun5-Sep30) ②LONG(Oct1-Feb15)

Although some children receive Disney stock as a gift to hold onto for life, using a seasonal investment approach to owning the stock has proven to be a better strategy. Disney's stock price has performed like a seasonal roller coaster: on average, up strongly in late autumn, into winter; and down in summer.

Gain of 28.6%

Disney's year-end occurs at the end of September and it typically reports its results in the first week of November. Investors start to increase their positions at the beginning of October in anticipation of positive year-end news.

Investors are particularly attracted to Disney at this time of the year as Q4 tends to be a big revenue reporting quarter.

According to their Form 10-K filed with the Securities and Exchange Commission for the year ended September 29, 2012: "Revenues in our Media Networks segment are subject to seasonal advertising patterns... these commitments are typically satisfied during the second half of the Company's fiscal year." The media segment is the biggest driver of revenue for Disney. In addition, their other business segments are skewed towards revenue generation in the summer.

Do not "visit" the Disney stock from June 5th to September 30th. For the period from 1990 to 2016, Disney produced an average loss of 8.0% and only beat the S&P 500, 11% of the time.

DIS - stock symbol for Walt Disney Company which trades on the NYSE. is a diversified worldwide entertainment company. Price is adjusted for stock splits.

Disney vs. S&P 500 1990/91 to 2016/17

Negative Short ☐   Positive Long ▨

Year	Jun 5 to Sep 30		Oct 1 to Feb 15		Compound Growth	
	S&P 500	Disney	S&P 500	Disney	S&P 500	Disney
1990/91	-16.7 %	-29.4 %	20.6 %	30.1 %	40.7 %	68.4 %
1991/92	0.0	-3.0	6.4	25.4	6.3	29.1
1992/93	1.1	-2.7	6.4	29.7	5.2	33.1
1993/94	2.0	-14.7	3.0	23.9	0.9	42.1
1994/95	0.6	-13.2	4.7	38.5	4.1	56.7
1995/96	9.8	2.7	11.5	11.3	0.6	8.3
1996/97	2.2	5.2	17.6	23.6	15.1	17.1
1997/98	12.8	0.9	7.7	38.2	-6.1	36.9
1998/99	-7.1	-30.4	21.0	39.6	29.6	82.1
1999/00	-3.4	-15.1	9.3	41.9	13.0	63.3
2001/01	-2.8	-5.4	-7.7	-15.3	-5.1	-10.7
2001/02	-17.9	-41.1	6.1	28.4	25.0	81.1
2002/03	-21.7	-31.9	2.4	10.5	24.6	45.8
2003/04	1.0	-2.7	15.0	33.5	13.9	37.1
2004/05	-0.7	-6.3	8.6	31.2	9.3	39.4
2005/06	2.7	-11.7	4.2	11.4	1.3	24.4
2006/07	3.7	1.0	9.1	12.2	5.0	11.1
2007/08	-0.8	-3.7	-11.6	-5.5	-10.9	-2.1
2008/09	-15.3	-10.7	-29.1	-39.7	-18.3	-33.2
2009/10	12.2	9.2	1.7	9.5	-10.6	0.6
2010/11	7.2	-1.8	16.4	30.2	8.0	32.5
2011/12	-13.0	-23.4	18.7	36.8	34.1	68.8
2012/13	12.7	17.7	5.5	6.4	-7.9	-12.5
2013/14	3.1	0.2	9.3	22.9	6.0	22.6
2014/15	2.3	5.7	6.3	17.0	3.9	10.4
2015/16	-8.4	-7.3	-2.9	-10.8	5.3	-4.3
2016/17	3.3	-6.0	8.4	18.7	4.8	25.7
Avg.	-1.2 %	-8.0 %	6.2 %	18.5 %	7.3 %	28.6 %
Fq>0	59 %	30 %	85 %	65 %	78 %	78 %

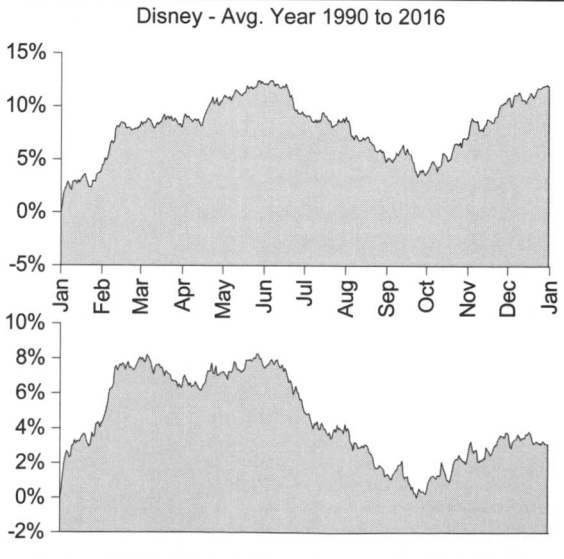

Disney - Avg. Year 1990 to 2016

Disney / S&P 500 Rel. Strength- Avg Yr. 1990-2016

Disney - Performance

DIS Monthly Performance (1990-2016)

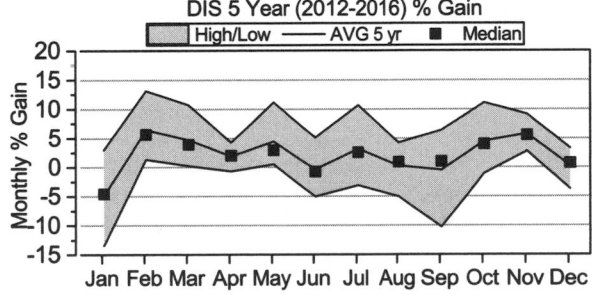

Legend: ☐ Avg % Gain   + Med % Gain

Monthly % Gain

	Jan	Feb	Mar	Apr	May	Jun	Jul	Aug	Sep	Oct	Nov	Dec
Avg. % Gain	0.5	0.7	1.6	5.8	0.3	-1.9	1.4	-3.3	-2.5	0.6	1.7	1.3
Med. % Gain	1.4	-0.3	0.7	1.9	0.0	-1.2	0.5	-1.9	-1.8	1.5	2.7	1.7
Fq %>0	56	41	56	67	52	48	56	37	30	56	63	59
Fq %>S&P 500	48	48	56	52	26	44	52	33	37	41	56	37

DIS 5 Year (2012-2016) % Gain

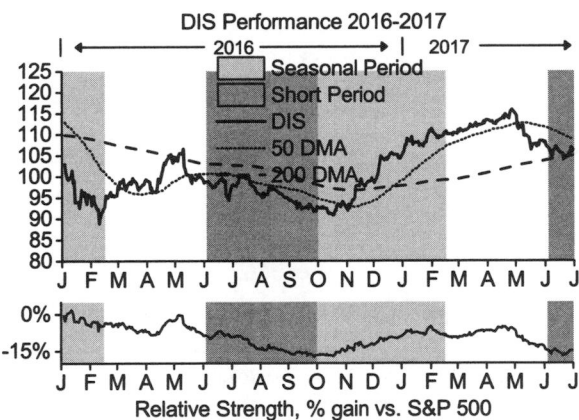

Legend: ☐ High/Low — AVG 5 yr ■ Median

Monthly % Gain — Jan Feb Mar Apr May Jun Jul Aug Sep Oct Nov Dec

DIS Performance 2016-2017

2016 — 2017

Legend: ☐ Seasonal Period, ☐ Short Period, — DIS, ⋯ 50 DMA, — 200 DMA

J F M A M J J A S O N D J F M A M J J

Relative Strength, % gain vs. S&P 500

From 1990 to 2016, Disney has on average been negative from June to September and positive from October into February. The transition from the short sell period to the long period is best navigated with technical analysis. Over the last five years, Disney has generally followed its seasonal trend. October, November and February have been the strongest months (included in the long seasonal period) and June has been one of the weakest months (included in the short sell seasonal period). In 2016, Disney was negative in its short sell seasonal period. In 2017, Disney was positive in its long seasonal period.

WEEK 18

Market Indices & Rates
Weekly Values**

Stock Markets	2016	2017
Dow	17,739	20,956
S&P500	2,061	2,391
Nasdaq	4,752	6,087
TSX	13,708	15,543
FTSE	6,135	7,258
DAX	9,920	12,600
Nikkei	16,127	19,378
Hang Seng	20,441	24,619

Commodities	2016	2017
Oil	44.24	47.21
Gold	1286.6	1240.6

Bond Yields	2016	2017
USA 5 Yr Treasury	1.25	1.86
USA 10 Yr T	1.81	2.33
USA 20 Yr T	2.23	2.71
Moody's Aaa	3.66	3.89
Moody's Baa	4.66	4.60
CAN 5 Yr T	0.78	0.99
CAN 10 Yr T	1.42	1.54

Money Market	2016	2017
USA Fed Funds	0.50	1.00
USA 3 Mo T-B	0.20	0.85
CAN tgt overnight rate	0.50	0.50
CAN 3 Mo T-B	0.53	0.51

Foreign Exchange	2016	2017
EUR/USD	1.15	1.09
GBP/USD	1.45	1.29
USD/CAD	1.28	1.37
USD/JPY	106.88	112.35

MAY

M	T	W	T	F	S	S
	1	2	3	4	5	6
7	8	9	10	11	12	13
14	15	16	17	18	19	20
21	22	23	24	25	26	27
28	29	30	31			

JUNE

M	T	W	T	F	S	S
					1	2	3
4	5	6	7	8	9	10
11	12	13	14	15	16	17
18	19	20	21	22	23	24
25	26	27	28	29	30	

JULY

M	T	W	T	F	S	S
						1
2	3	4	5	6	7	8
9	10	11	12	13	14	15
16	17	18	19	20	21	22
23	24	25	26	27	28	29
30	31					

Several times in the last few years, the stock market has corrected sharply in spring, which has prompted many pundits to release reports in the media on "Sell in May and Go Away." But most pundits do not grasp the full value of the favorable six month period for stocks from October 28th to May 5th, compared with the other six months: the unfavorable six month period.

Not only does the favorable period on average have bigger gains more frequently and smaller losses, but also on a yearly basis, outperforms the unfavorable period 72% of the time (last column in the table with YES values). There is no question which six month period seasonal investors should favor.

$1,639,048 gain on $10,000

The accompanying table uses the S&P 500 to compare the returns made from Oct 28th to May 5th, to the returns made during the remainder of the year.

Starting with $10,000 and investing from October 28th to May 5th every year (October 28th, 1950, to May 5th, 2016) has produced a gain of $1,639,048. On the flip side, being invested from May 6th to October 27th, has actually lost money. An initial investment of $10,000 has lost $2,015 over the same time period.

S&P 500 Unfavorable 6 Month Avg. Gain vs Favorable 6 Month Avg. Gain (1950-2016)

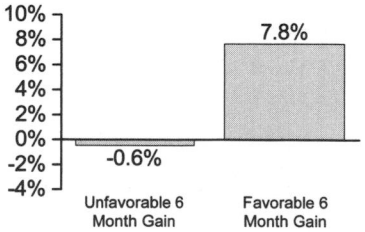

The above growth rates are geometric averages in order to represent the cumulative growth of a dollar investment over time. These figures differ from the arithmetic mean calculations used in the Six 'N' Six Take a Break Strategy, which are used to represent an average year.

	S&P 500 % May 6 to Oct 27	$10,000 Start	S&P 500 % Oct 28 to May 5	$10,000 Start	Oct28-May5 > May6-Oct27
1950/51	8.5%	10,851	15.2%	11,517	YES
1951/52	0.2	10,870	3.7	11,947	YES
1952/53	1.8	11,067	3.9	12,413	YES
1953/54	-3.1	10,727	16.6	14,475	YES
1954/55	13.2	12,141	18.1	17,097	YES
1955/56	11.4	13,528	15.1	19,681	YES
1956/57	-4.6	12,903	0.2	19,711	YES
1957/58	-12.4	11,302	7.9	21,265	YES
1958/59	15.1	13,013	14.5	24,356	
1959/60	-0.6	12,939	-4.5	23,270	
1960/61	-2.3	12,647	24.1	28,869	YES
1961/62	2.7	12,993	-3.1	27,982	
1962/63	-17.7	10,698	28.4	35,929	YES
1963/64	5.7	11,306	9.3	39,264	YES
1964/65	5.1	11,882	5.5	41,440	YES
1965/66	3.1	12,253	-5.0	39,388	
1966/67	-8.8	11,180	17.7	46,364	YES
1967/68	0.6	11,241	3.9	48,171	YES
1968/69	5.6	11,872	0.2	48,249	
1969/70	-6.2	11,141	-19.7	38,722	
1970/71	5.8	11,782	24.9	48,346	YES
1971/72	-9.6	10,647	13.7	54,965	YES
1972/73	3.7	11,046	0.3	55,154	
1973/74	0.3	11,084	-18.0	45,205	
1974/75	-23.2	8,513	28.5	58,073	YES
1975/76	-0.4	8,480	12.4	65,290	YES
1976/77	0.9	8,554	-1.6	64,231	
1977/78	-7.8	7,890	4.5	67,146	YES
1978/79	-2.0	7,732	6.4	71,476	YES
1979/80	-0.1	7,723	5.8	75,605	YES
1980/81	20.2	9,283	1.9	77,047	
1981/82	-8.5	8,498	-1.4	76,001	YES
1982/83	15.0	9,769	21.4	92,293	YES
1983/84	0.3	9,803	-3.5	89,085	
1984/85	3.9	10,183	8.9	97,057	YES
1985/86	4.1	10,604	26.8	123,044	YES
1986/87	0.4	10,651	23.7	152,196	YES
1987/88	-21.0	8,409	11.0	168,904	YES
1988/89	7.1	9,010	10.9	187,380	YES
1989/90	8.9	9,814	1.0	189,242	
1990/91	-10.0	8,837	25.0	236,498	YES
1991/92	0.9	8,916	8.5	256,590	YES
1992/93	0.4	8,952	6.2	272,550	YES
1993/94	4.5	9,356	-2.8	264,789	
1994/95	3.2	9,656	11.6	295,636	YES
1995/96	11.5	10,762	10.7	327,219	
1996/97	9.2	11,757	18.5	387,591	YES
1997/98	5.6	12,419	27.2	493,003	YES
1998/99	-4.5	11,860	26.5	623,489	YES
1999/00	-3.8	11,415	10.5	688,842	YES
2000/01	-3.7	10,992	-8.2	632,435	
2001/02	-12.8	9,586	-2.8	614,583	YES
2002/03	-16.4	8,016	3.2	634,369	YES
2003/04	11.3	8,921	8.8	689,985	
2004/05	0.3	8,952	4.2	718,942	YES
2005/06	0.5	9,000	12.5	808,503	YES
2006/07	3.9	9,350	9.3	883,804	YES
2007/08	2.0	9,534	-8.3	810,240	
2008/09	-39.7	5,750	6.5	862,619	YES
2009/10	17.7	6,766	9.6	934,470	
2010/11	1.4	6,862	12.9	1,067,851	YES
2011/12	-3.8	6,602	6.6	1,138,103	YES
2012/13	3.1	6,809	14.3	1,301,313	YES
2013/14	9.0	7,422	7.1	1,393,667	
2014/15	4.1	7,725	6.5	1,484,478	YES
2015/16	-1.1	7,638	-0.7	1,473,513	YES
2016/17	4.0	7,985	12.5	1,649,048	YES
Total Gain (Loss)		**($2,015)**		**$1,639,048**	

6 'n' 6 Strategy Performance

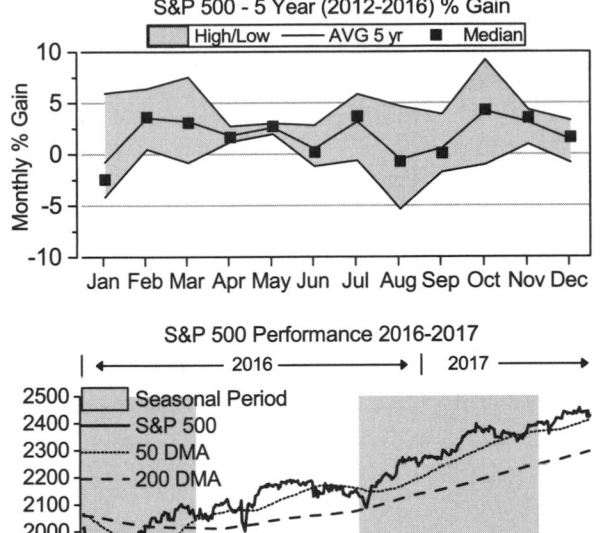

S&P 500 - 5 Year (2012-2016) % Gain

High/Low —— AVG 5 yr ■ Median

S&P 500 Performance 2016-2017

Seasonal Period
S&P 500
50 DMA
200 DMA

Favorable vs. Unfavorable Seasons 2015-2017 (S&P 500)

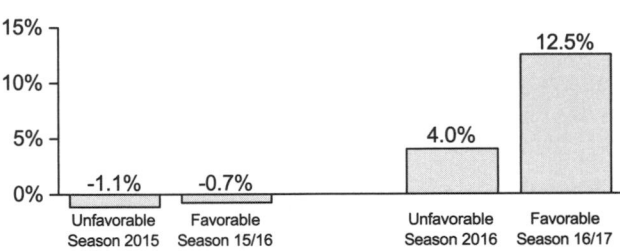

-1.1% Unfavorable Season 2015
-0.7% Favorable Season 15/16
4.0% Unfavorable Season 2016
12.5% Favorable Season 16/17

WEEK 19

Market Indices & Rates
Weekly Values**

Stock Markets	2016	2017
Dow	17,720	20,949
S&P500	2,064	2,396
Nasdaq	4,755	6,118
TSX	13,733	15,589
FTSE	6,135	7,370
DAX	9,963	12,737
Nikkei	16,484	19,897
Hang Seng	20,018	24,953

Commodities	2016	2017
Oil	45.45	47.06
Gold	1270.0	1225.5

Bond Yields	2016	2017
USA 5 Yr Treasury	1.21	1.91
USA 10 Yr T	1.75	2.39
USA 20 Yr T	2.17	2.77
Moody's Aaa	3.63	3.92
Moody's Baa	4.64	4.62
CAN 5 Yr T	0.69	1.04
CAN 10 Yr T	1.31	1.60

Money Market	2016	2017
USA Fed Funds	0.50	1.00
USA 3 Mo T-B	0.26	0.90
CAN tgt overnight rate	0.50	0.50
CAN 3 Mo T-B	0.51	0.50

Foreign Exchange	2016	2017
EUR/USD	1.14	1.09
GBP/USD	1.44	1.29
USD/CAD	1.29	1.37
USD/JPY	108.73	113.75

MAY

M	T	W	T	F	S	S
	1	2	3	4	5	6
7	8	9	10	11	12	13
14	15	16	17	18	19	20
21	22	23	24	25	26	27
28	29	30	31			

JUNE

M	T	W	T	F	S	S
					1	2	3
4	5	6	7	8	9	10
11	12	13	14	15	16	17
18	19	20	21	22	23	24
25	26	27	28	29	30	

JULY

M	T	W	T	F	S	S
						1
2	3	4	5	6	7	8
9	10	11	12	13	14	15
16	17	18	19	20	21	22
23	24	25	26	27	28	29
30	31					

Over the last five years, the six month seasonal strategy for the stock market has generally followed its seasonal pattern. The months in the six month favorable seasonal period have generally been better than the other six months of the year. The big exception to this has been the performance of January, which has been the worst month of the year on a median basis. July, although one of the better months of the year over the last five years, is part of "eye of the storm" trade, when the stock market tends to perform well from the last few days in June until July 18th.

In 2015/16, although the favorable six month period produced a nominal loss, it outperformed the unfavorable six month period, which produced a larger loss. In 2016/17, the favorable six month period strongly outperformed the unfavorable six month period.

CANADIAN SIX 'N' SIX
Take a Break for Six Months - May 6th to October 27th

In analyzing long-term trends for the broad markets such as the S&P 500 or the TSX Composite, a large data set is preferable because it incorporates various economic cycles. The daily data set for the TSX Composite starts in 1977.

Over this time period, investors have been rewarded for following the six month cycle of investing from October 28th to May 5th, versus the other unfavorable six month period, May 6th to October 27th.

Starting with an investment of $10,000 in 1977, investing in the unfavorable six months has produced a loss of $3,324, versus investing in the favorable six month period which has produced a gain of $222,470.

$222,470 gain on $10,000 since 1977

The TSX Composite Average Year 1977 to 2016 graph (below), indicates that the market tended to peak in mid-July or the end of August. In our book *Time In Time Out, Outsmart the Stock Market Using Calendar Investment Strategies*, Bruce Lindsay and I analyzed a number of market trends and peaks over different decades.

What we found was that the markets tend to peak at the beginning of May or mid-July. The mid-July peak was usually the result of a strong bull market in place that had a lot of momentum.

The main reason that the TSX Composite data shows a peak occurring in July-August is that the data is primarily from the biggest bull market in history, starting in 1982.

TSX Composite % Gain Avg. Year 1977 to 2016

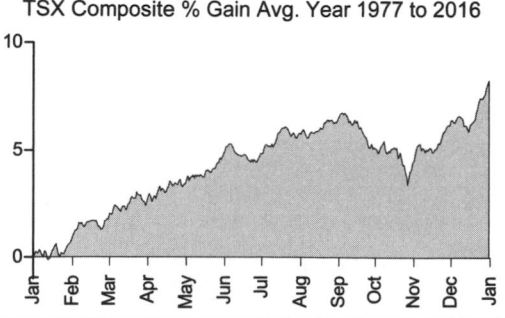

Does a later average peak in the stock market mean that the best six month cycle does not work? No. Dividing the year up into six month

intervals, the period from October to May is far superior compared with the other half of the year.

The table below illustrates the superiority of the best six months over the worst six months. Going down the table year by year, the period from October 28 to May 5th outperforms the period from May 6th to October 27 on a regular basis.

In a strong bull market, investors always have the choice of using a stop loss or technical indicators to help extend the exit point past the May date.

	TSX Comp May 6 to Oct 27	$10,000 Start	TSX Comp Oct 28 to May 5	$10,000 Start
1977/78	-3.9%	9,608	13.1%	11,313
1978/79	12.1	10,775	21.3	13,728
1979/80	2.9	11,084	23.0	16,883
1980/81	22.5	13,579	-2.4	16,479
1981/82	-17.0	11,272	-18.2	13,488
1982/83	16.6	13,138	34.6	18,150
1983/84	-0.9	13,015	-1.9	17,811
1984/85	1.6	13,226	10.7	19,718
1985/86	0.5	13,299	16.5	22,978
1986/87	-1.9	13,045	24.8	28,666
1987/88	-23.4	9,992	15.3	33,050
1988/89	2.7	10,260	5.7	34,939
1989/90	7.9	11,072	-13.3	30,294
1990/91	-8.4	10,148	13.1	34,266
1991/92	-1.6	9,982	-2.0	33,571
1992/93	-2.3	9,750	15.3	38,704
1993/94	10.8	10,801	1.7	39,365
1994/95	-0.1	10,792	0.3	39,483
1995/96	1.3	10,936	18.2	46,671
1996/97	8.3	11,843	10.8	51,725
1997/98	7.3	12,707	17.0	60,510
1998/99	-22.3	9,870	17.1	70,871
1999/00	-0.2	9,853	36.9	97,009
2000/01	-2.9	9,570	-14.4	83,062
2001/02	-12.2	8,399	9.4	90,875
2002/03	-16.4	7,020	4.0	94,476
2003/04	15.1	8,079	10.3	104,252
2004/05	3.9	8,398	7.8	112,379
2005/06	8.1	9,080	19.8	134,587
2006/07	0.0	9,079	12.2	151,053
2007/08	3.8	9,426	-0.2	150,820
2008/09	-40.2	5,638	15.7	174,551
2009/10	11.9	6,307	7.4	187,526
2010/11	5.8	6,674	7.1	200,778
2011/12	-7.4	6,183	-4.8	191,207
2012/13	3.6	6,407	1.1	193,348
2013/14	7.7	6,902	9.7	212,072
2014/15	-1.6	6,795	4.9	222,404
2015/16	-9.7	6,135	-4.9	221,307
2016/17	8.8	6,676	5.0	232,470
Total Gain (Loss)	**($3,324)**			**$222,470**

6n6 Canada Strategy Performance

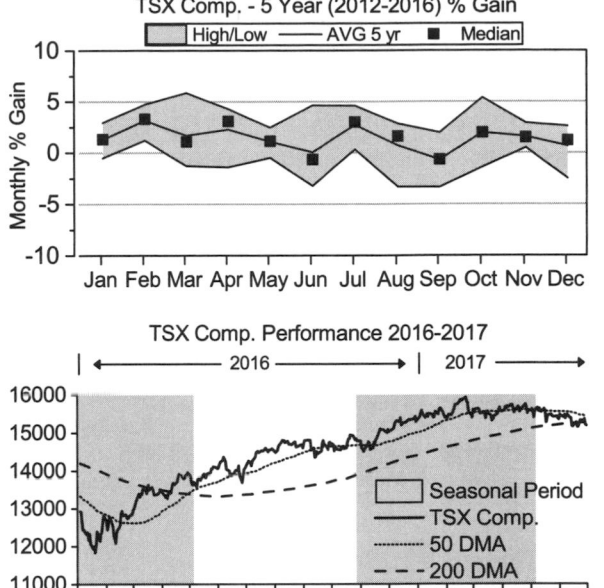

TSX Comp. - 5 Year (2012-2016) % Gain

High/Low —— AVG 5 yr ■ Median

TSX Comp. Performance 2016-2017

| ← 2016 → | 2017 → |

Seasonal Period
—— TSX Comp.
········· 50 DMA
- - - 200 DMA

Market Indices & Rates
Weekly Values**

Stock Markets	2016	2017
Dow	17,541	20,807
S&P500	2,051	2,381
Nasdaq	4,742	6,094
TSX	13,875	15,436
FTSE	6,139	7,477
DAX	9,886	12,694
Nikkei	16,629	19,750
Hang Seng	19,875	25,263

Commodities	2016	2017
Oil	48.03	49.25
Gold	1267.2	1246.6

Bond Yields	2016	2017
USA 5 Yr Treasury	1.34	1.81
USA 10 Yr T	1.82	2.27
USA 20 Yr T	2.22	2.68
Moody's Aaa	3.65	3.81
Moody's Baa	4.69	4.52
CAN 5 Yr T	0.74	0.97
CAN 10 Yr T	1.34	1.51

Money Market	2016	2017
USA Fed Funds	0.50	1.00
USA 3 Mo T-B	0.30	0.91
CAN tgt overnight rate	0.50	0.50
CAN 3 Mo T-B	0.51	0.51

Foreign Exchange	2016	2017
EUR/USD	1.13	1.11
GBP/USD	1.45	1.30
USD/CAD	1.30	1.36
USD/JPY	109.69	112.10

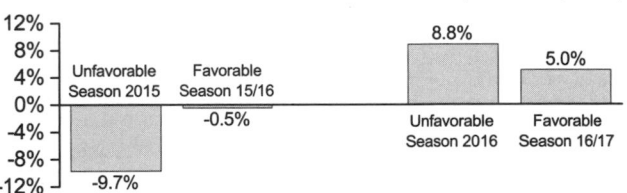

Favorable vs. Unfavorable Seasons 2015-2017 (TSX Composite)

Unfavorable Season 2015: -9.7%
Favorable Season 15/16: -0.5%
Unfavorable Season 2016: 8.8%
Favorable Season 16/17: 5.0%

MAY

M	T	W	T	F	S	S
	1	2	3	4	5	6
7	8	9	10	11	12	13
14	15	16	17	18	19	20
21	22	23	24	25	26	27
28	29	30	31			

JUNE

M	T	W	T	F	S	S
			1	2	3	
4	5	6	7	8	9	10
11	12	13	14	15	16	17
18	19	20	21	22	23	24
25	26	27	28	29	30	

JULY

M	T	W	T	F	S	S
						1
2	3	4	5	6	7	8
9	10	11	12	13	14	15
16	17	18	19	20	21	22
23	24	25	26	27	28	29
30	31					

Over the last five years, the TSX Composite has generally followed its six month favorable/unfavorable cycle. The worst two months of the year on an average and median basis have been June and September, which are in the unfavorable six month period. The best months of the year have been February, April and July. February and April are in the favorable six month period. Although July is in the unfavorable six month period, it is part of the "eye of the storm" trade, which lasts from the last few days in June until eighteen calendar days into July.

In 2015, the unfavorable six month period produced a loss of 9.7% for the TSX Composite. The following six month favorable period produced a nominal loss of 0.5%. In 2016, the unfavorable period produced a large gain of 8.8% for the TSX Composite, which was greater than the gain in the 2016/17 favorable period.

COSTCO – BUY AT A DISCOUNT
COST ①May26-Jun30 ②Oct4-Dec1

Shoppers are attracted to Costco because of its consistently low prices. They take comfort in the fact that although the prices may not always be the lowest, they are consistently in the lower range.

Costco performs well in late spring into early summer, and in autumn into early winter. These two periods are considered to be transition periods where the stock market is moving to and from its unfavorable and favorable seasons. Companies such as Costco that have stable earnings are desirable at these times.

There are two times when Costco is a seasonal bargain: May 26th to June 30th and October 4th to December 1st. From 1990 to 2016, during the period of May 26th to June 30th, Costco has averaged a gain of 5.3% and has been positive 67% of the time. From October 4th to December 1st, Costco has averaged a gain of 9.4% and has been positive 81% of the time.

15.3% gain & positive 93% of the time

Putting both seasonal periods together has produced a 93% positive success rate and an average gain of 15.3%. Although the earlier strong years in the 1990's skews the data to the high-side, Costco has still maintained its strong seasonal performances in both the May to June and the October to December time periods. When investors go shopping for stocks, Costco is one consumer staples company that should be on their list, at least in its favorable seasonal periods.

(i) *COST - stock symbol for Costco which trades on the Nasdaq exchange. Stock data adjusted for stock splits.*

Costco* vs. S&P 500 1990 to 2016 Positive ☐

Year	May 26 to Jun 30 S&P 500	May 26 to Jun 30 COST	Oct 4 to Dec 1 S&P 500	Oct 4 to Dec 1 COST	Compound Growth S&P 500	Compound Growth COST
1990	1.0	16.5%	3.5	26.5%	4.5	47.3%
1991	-1.7	-2.0	-2.4	-3.7	-4.0	-5.6
1992	-1.4	-2.2	5.0	22.7	3.5	20.0
1993	0.4	17.2	0.1	13.4	0.5	24.6
1994	-2.6	10.7	-2.8	-6.3	-5.3	3.7
1995	3.1	19.3	4.2	-2.2	7.4	16.7
1996	-1.2	9.5	9.3	15.5	8.0	26.5
1997	4.5	3.1	1.0	16.5	5.6	20.2
1998	2.1	17.6	17.2	41.1	19.7	66.0
1999	6.9	8.1	9.0	30.7	16.5	41.3
2000	5.3	10.0	-7.8	-3.6	-2.9	6.1
2001	-4.2	9.3	6.3	12.3	1.8	22.6
2002	-8.7	-0.8	14.3	4.6	4.4	3.8
2003	4.4	5.3	3.9	13.5	8.5	19.4
2004	2.5	10.3	5.3	17.4	7.9	29.4
2005	0.1	-1.5	3.1	13.9	3.2	12.2
2006	-0.2	5.0	4.7	6.0	4.5	11.3
2007	-0.8	3.8	-3.8	8.9	-4.6	12.9
2008	-7.0	-1.7	-25.8	-23.5	-30.9	-24.7
2009	3.6	-5.2	8.2	7.5	12.1	1.9
2010	-4.0	-3.0	5.2	5.0	1.0	1.9
2011	0.0	1.2	13.2	6.7	13.2	7.9
2012	3.4	12.5	-2.4	4.3	0.9	17.3
2013	-2.6	-3.3	7.6	9.6	4.7	6.0
2014	3.1	0.2	4.4	11.7	7.6	11.9
2015	-3.0	-6.0	7.8	10.6	4.6	3.9
2016	0.4	8.7	1.4	0.5	1.8	9.2
Avg.	0.1%	5.3%	3.3%	9.4%	3.5%	15.3%
Fq>0	55%	67%	78%	81%	81%	93%

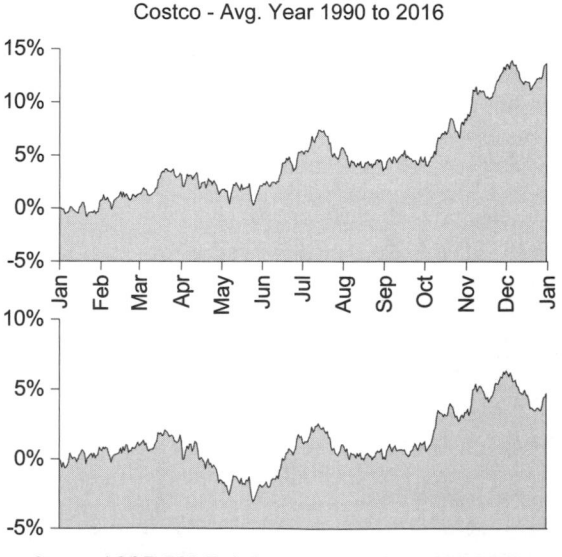

Costco - Avg. Year 1990 to 2016

Costco / S&P 500 Rel. Strength- Avg Yr. 1990-2016

MAY

Costco Performance

COST Monthly Performance (1990-2016)

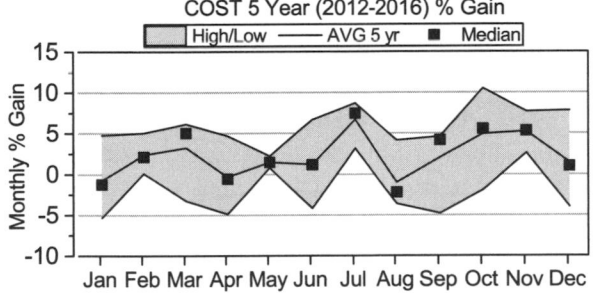

	Jan	Feb	Mar	Apr	May	Jun	Jul	Aug	Sep	Oct	Nov	Dec
Avg. % Gain	0.6	0.9	1.9	-2.0	0.9	3.4	0.4	-1.9	0.8	4.2	4.1	0.4
Med. % Gain	0.8	-0.5	3.1	-0.3	0.9	3.3	1.1	-3.0	1.5	4.8	3.3	0.0
Fq %>0	52	48	56	48	63	56	59	41	59	67	74	52
Fq %>S&P 500	48	52	48	37	52	70	41	41	48	63	63	41

COST 5 Year (2012-2016) % Gain

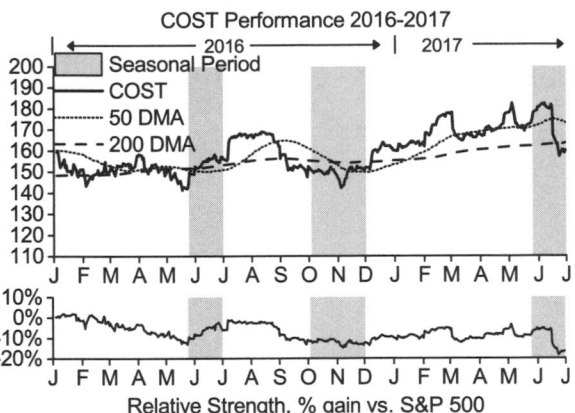

COST Performance 2016-2017

Relative Strength, % gain vs. S&P 500

From 1990 to 2016, October and November have been the best two contiguous months for Costco on an average, median and frequency basis. This has been mainly driven by Costco releasing its year-end earnings at the end of September. The other strong month is June, which occurs right after Costco typically announces its Q3 results. Over the last five years, on average, July has been Costco's best month (not in seasonal period) followed by August, which has been its worst month.

In 2016, Costco underperformed the S&P 500 in its Oct. 4th to Dec. 1st seasonal period, and also more recently in its first seasonal period in 2017.

WEEK 21

Market Indices & Rates Weekly Values**

Stock Markets	2016	2017
Dow	17,750	21,002
S&P500	2,081	2,406
Nasdaq	4,871	6,170
TSX	14,040	15,431
FTSE	6,221	7,512
DAX	10,133	12,629
Nikkei	16,704	19,707
Hang Seng	20,196	25,499

Commodities	2016	2017
Oil	48.54	50.29
Gold	1231.8	1258.7

Bond Yields	2016	2017
USA 5 Yr Treasury	1.40	1.80
USA 10 Yr T	1.86	2.26
USA 20 Yr T	2.25	2.65
Moody's Aaa	3.66	3.82
Moody's Baa	4.71	4.50
CAN 5 Yr T	0.77	0.97
CAN 10 Yr T	1.36	1.47

Money Market	2016	2017
USA Fed Funds	0.50	1.00
USA 3 Mo T-B	0.33	0.93
CAN tgt overnight rate	0.50	0.50
CAN 3 Mo T-B	0.52	0.51

Foreign Exchange	2016	2017
EUR/USD	1.12	1.12
GBP/USD	1.46	1.29
USD/CAD	1.31	1.35
USD/JPY	109.90	111.55

MAY
M	T	W	T	F	S	S
	1	2	3	4	5	6
7	8	9	10	11	12	13
14	15	16	17	18	19	20
21	22	23	24	25	26	27
28	29	30	31			

JUNE
M	T	W	T	F	S	S
			1	2	3	
4	5	6	7	8	9	10
11	12	13	14	15	16	17
18	19	20	21	22	23	24
25	26	27	28	29	30	

JULY
M	T	W	T	F	S	S
						1
2	3	4	5	6	7	8
9	10	11	12	13	14	15
16	17	18	19	20	21	22
23	24	25	26	27	28	29
30	31					

SUPER SEVEN DAYS
7 Best Days of the Month

The end of the month tends to be an excellent time to invest: portfolio managers "window dress" (adjust their portfolios to look good for month end reports), investors stop procrastinating and invest their extra cash, and brokers try to increase their commissions by investing their clients' extra cash.

From 1950 to 2016
All 7 days better
than market average

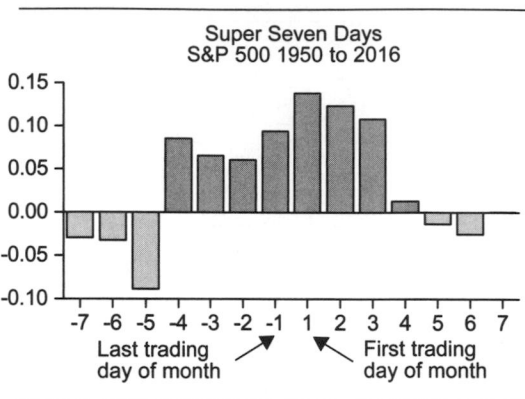

All of these factors tend to produce above average returns in the market during the days on either side of month end.

The above graph illustrates the strength of the *Super Seven* days. The *Super Seven* days are the last four trading days of the month and the first three trading days of the next month, represented by the dark columns from day -4 to day 3. All of the *Super Seven* days have daily average gains above the daily market average gain of 0.03% since 1950.

% Gain Super Seven Day Period From 2007 to 2016

	2007	2008	2009	2010	2011	2012	2013	2014	2015	2016	Avg.
Jan	1.6 %	-4.5 %	-0.5 %	0.0 %	1.2 %	1.4 %	0.6 %	-1.7 %	-0.8	1.9	-0.1 %
Feb	-5.6	-2.8	4.1	1.0	1.2	0.1	1.6	1.4	-0.5	3.8	-0.4
Mar	0.1	1.2	3.5	2.0	1.4	-1.2	-0.2	1.2	0.9	0.5	1.0
Apr	1.5	1.3	4.3	-3.8	0.9	1.4	2.3	0.3	-1.3	-1.8	0.5
May	1.6	0.1	5.0	2.7	-1.2	-2.7	-2.5	1.4	-0.6	1.1	0.5
Jun	1.8	-3.9	-0.2	-4.2	5.6	4.1	2.7	1.8	-1.9	3.1	0.9
Jul	-5.6	2.2	2.1	1.1	-5.8	4.0	1.0	-2.9	1.6	-0.2	-0.3
Aug	0.8	-2.4	-2.4	4.7	0.5	1.5	-0.1	0.0	4.5	0.6	0.8
Sep	1.4	-7.3	-1.0	1.1	-1.6	-0.4	-1.1	-1.5	2.8	0.6	-0.7
Oct	-0.8	12.2	-1.9	1.0	2.6	0.3	0.2	3.2	1.5	-2.5	1.6
Nov	5.5	8.8	-0.6	3.7	8.2	0.2	-0.7	0.5	-1.8	0.0	2.4
Dec	-5.7	7.7	0.9	1.5	1.2	2.8	-0.4	-3.8	-3.4	0.2	0.1
Avg.	-0.3 %	1.1 %	0.4 %	0.9 %	1.2 %	1.0 %	0.3 %	0.0 %	0.1	0.6	0.5 %

From 2006 to 2016, the *Super Seven* strategy has worked very well and has produced an average gain of 0.5% per month. On an annualized basis, this return is greater than 6% per year.

Given that the *Super Seven* strategy has seven trading days and the average month has twenty-two trading days, the *Super Seven* strategy has investors in the market for less than one third of the time. Adjusting returns for the amount of time in the market, the strategy has produced much greater gains per day than a buy and hold discipline.

If there is one time of the month that investors should be concentrating on investing, it is the last four trading days of the current month and the first three of the next month.

Super Seven Strategy Performance

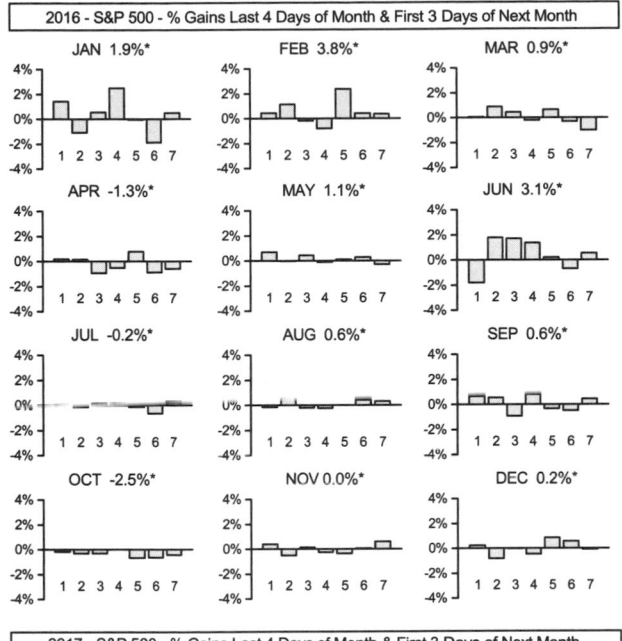

2016 - S&P 500 - % Gains Last 4 Days of Month & First 3 Days of Next Month

JAN 1.9%* FEB 3.8%* MAR 0.9%*
APR -1.3%* MAY 1.1%* JUN 3.1%*
JUL -0.2%* AUG 0.6%* SEP 0.6%*
OCT -2.5%* NOV 0.0%* DEC 0.2%*

2017 - S&P 500 - % Gains Last 4 Days of Month & First 3 Days of Next Month

JAN 0.0%* FEB 0.9%* MAR 0.5%*
APR 0.6%* MAY 1.3%* JUN -1.2%*

*% Cumulative Gain Return over full 7 days, **Scale changed due to magnitude of gains

Market Indices & Rates Weekly Values**

Stock Markets	2016	2017
Dow	17,806	21,097
S&P500	2,100	2,423
Nasdaq	4,954	6,239
TSX	14,116	15,411
FTSE	6,204	7,534
DAX	10,195	12,666
Nikkei	16,893	19,810
Hang Seng	20,802	25,774

Commodities	2016	2017
Oil	48.98	48.50
Gold	1219.9	1267.2

Bond Yields	2016	2017
USA 5 Yr Treasury	1.34	1.75
USA 10 Yr T	1.80	2.20
USA 20 Yr T	2.18	2.59
Moody's Aaa	3.59	3.75
Moody's Baa	4.64	4.44
CAN 5 Yr T	0.71	0.94
CAN 10 Yr T	1.28	1.41

Money Market	2016	2017
USA Fed Funds	0.50	1.00
USA 3 Mo T-B	0.31	0.97
CAN tgt overnight rate	0.50	0.50
CAN 3 Mo T-B	0.53	0.52

Foreign Exchange	2016	2017
EUR/USD	1.12	1.12
GBP/USD	1.45	1.29
USD/CAD	1.31	1.35
USD/JPY	109.36	110.93

MAY

M	T	W	T	F	S	S
	1	2	3	4	5	6
7	8	9	10	11	12	13
14	15	16	17	18	19	20
21	22	23	24	25	26	27
28	29	30	31			

JUNE

M	T	W	T	F	S	S
				1	2	3
4	5	6	7	8	9	10
11	12	13	14	15	16	17
18	19	20	21	22	23	24
25	26	27	28	29	30	

JULY

M	T	W	T	F	S	S
						1
2	3	4	5	6	7	8
9	10	11	12	13	14	15
16	17	18	19	20	21	22
23	24	25	26	27	28	29
30	31					

Super Seven Performance

The *Super Seven* strategy produced gains in 2016 and started 2017 with every month being positive except June.

In 2016, the S&P 500 was successful nine out of twelve *Super Seven* trades. On average, the positive results were larger than the negative results, leading to an overall gain for the *Super Seven* strategy.

In 2017, so far the *Super Seven* strategy has been positive five out of the six times. June has been the only negative month as the stock market turned down at the end of the month as it entered into the first part of the *18 Calendar Earnings Month Trade*.

JUNE

	MONDAY	TUESDAY	WEDNESDAY
WEEK 22	28	29	30
WEEK 23	4 26	5 25	6 24
WEEK 24	11 19	12 18	13 17
WEEK 25	18 12	19 11	20 10
WEEK 26	25 5	26 4	27 3

THURSDAY	FRIDAY
31	1 29
7 23	8 22
14 16	15 15
21 9	22 8
28 2	29 1

JULY

M	T	W	T	F	S	S
						1
2	3	4	5	6	7	8
9	10	11	12	13	14	15
16	17	18	19	20	21	22
23	24	25	26	27	28	29
30	31					

AUGUST

M	T	W	T	F	S	S
	1	2	3	4	5	
6	7	8	9	10	11	12
13	14	15	16	17	18	19
20	21	22	23	24	25	26
27	28	29	30	31		

SEPTEMBER

M	T	W	T	F	S	S
					1	2
3	4	5	6	7	8	9
10	11	12	13	14	15	16
17	18	19	20	21	22	23
24	25	26	27	28	29	30

OCTOBER

M	T	W	T	F	S	S
1	2	3	4	5	6	7
8	9	10	11	12	13	14
15	16	17	18	19	20	21
22	23	24	25	26	27	28
29	30	31				

JUNE SUMMARY

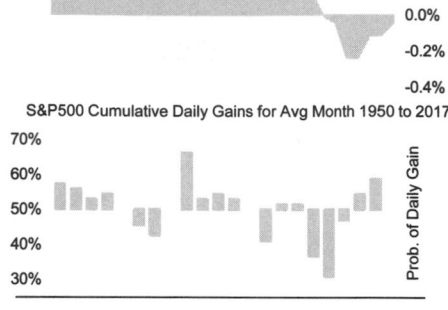

	Dow Jones	S&P 500	Nasdaq	TSX Comp
Month Rank	11	10	8	11
# Up	31	35	25	14
# Down	36	32	20	18
% Pos	46	52	56	44
% Avg. Gain	-0.3	0.0	0.7	-0.4

Dow & S&P 1950-2016, Nasdaq 1972-2016, TSX 1985-2016

S&P500 Cumulative Daily Gains for Avg Month 1950 to 2017

♦ On average, June is not a strong month for the S&P 500. From 1950 to 2017, it was the third worst month of the year, producing a flat return of 0.0%. ♦ From year to year, different sectors of the market tend to lead in June as there is not a strong consistent outperforming major sector. ♦ On average, the bio-tech sector starts its seasonal run in late June. ♦ The last few days of June, the start of the successful *Independence Day Trade,* tend to be positive.

BEST / WORST JUNE BROAD MKTS. 2008-2017

BEST JUNE MARKETS
♦ Nikkei 225 (2012) 5.4%
♦ Russell 2000 (2014) 5.2%
♦ Russell 2000 (2012) 4.8%

WORST JUNE MARKETS
♦ Dow (2008) -10.2%
♦ Nikkei 225 (2016) - 9.6%
♦ Nasdaq (2008) -9.1%

Index Values End of Month

	2008	2009	2010	2011	2012	2013	2014	2015	2016	2017
Dow	11,350	8,447	9,774	12,414	12,880	14,910	16,827	17,620	17,930	21,350
S&P 500	1,280	919	1,031	1,321	1,362	1,606	1,960	2,063	2,099	2,423
Nasdaq	2,293	1,835	2,109	2,774	2,935	3,403	4,408	4,987	4,843	6,140
TSX Comp.	14,467	10,375	11,294	13,301	11,597	12,129	15,146	14,553	14,065	15,182
Russell 1000	703	502	567	734	751	891	1,095	1,153	1,162	1,344
Russell 2000	690	508	609	827	798	977	1,193	1,254	1,152	1,415
FTSE 100	5,626	4,249	4,917	5,946	5,571	6,215	6,744	6,521	6,504	7,313
Nikkei 225	13,481	9,958	9,383	9,816	9,007	13,677	15,162	20,236	15,576	20,033

Percent Gain for June

	2008	2009	2010	2011	2012	2013	2014	2015	2016	2017
Dow	-10.2	-0.6	-3.6	-1.2	3.9	-1.4	0.7	-2.2	0.8	1.6
S&P 500	-8.6	0.0	-5.4	-1.8	4.0	-1.5	1.9	-2.1	0.1	0.5
Nasdaq	-9.1	3.4	-6.5	-2.2	3.8	-1.5	3.9	-1.6	-2.1	-0.9
TSX Comp.	-1.7	0.0	-4.0	-3.6	0.7	-4.1	3.7	-3.1	0.0	-1.1
Russell 1000	-8.5	0.1	-5.7	-1.9	3.7	-1.5	2.1	-2.0	0.1	0.5
Russell 2000	-7.8	1.3	-7.9	-2.5	4.8	-0.7	5.2	0.6	-0.2	3.3
FTSE 100	-7.1	-3.8	-5.2	-0.7	4.7	-5.6	-1.5	-6.6	4.4	-2.8
Nikkei 225	-6.0	4.6	-4.0	1.3	5.4	-0.7	3.6	-1.6	-9.6	1.9

June Market Avg. Performance 2008 to 2017[1]

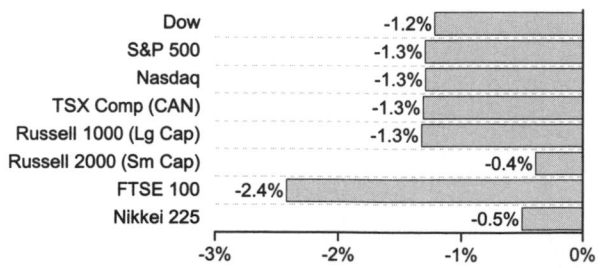

	Dow	-1.2%
	S&P 500	-1.3%
	Nasdaq	-1.3%
	TSX Comp (CAN)	-1.3%
	Russell 1000 (Lg Cap)	-1.3%
	Russell 2000 (Sm Cap)	-0.4%
	FTSE 100	-2.4%
	Nikkei 225	-0.5%

Interest Corner Jun[2]

	Fed Funds % [3]	3 Mo. T-Bill % [4]	10 Yr % [5]	20 Yr % [6]
2017	1.25	1.03	2.31	2.61
2016	0.50	0.26	1.49	1.86
2015	0.25	0.01	2.35	2.83
2014	0.25	0.04	2.53	3.08
2013	0.25	0.04	2.52	3.22

(1) Russell Data provided by Russell (2) Federal Reserve Bank of St. Louis- end of month values (3) Target rate set by FOMC (4)(5)(6) Constant yield maturities.

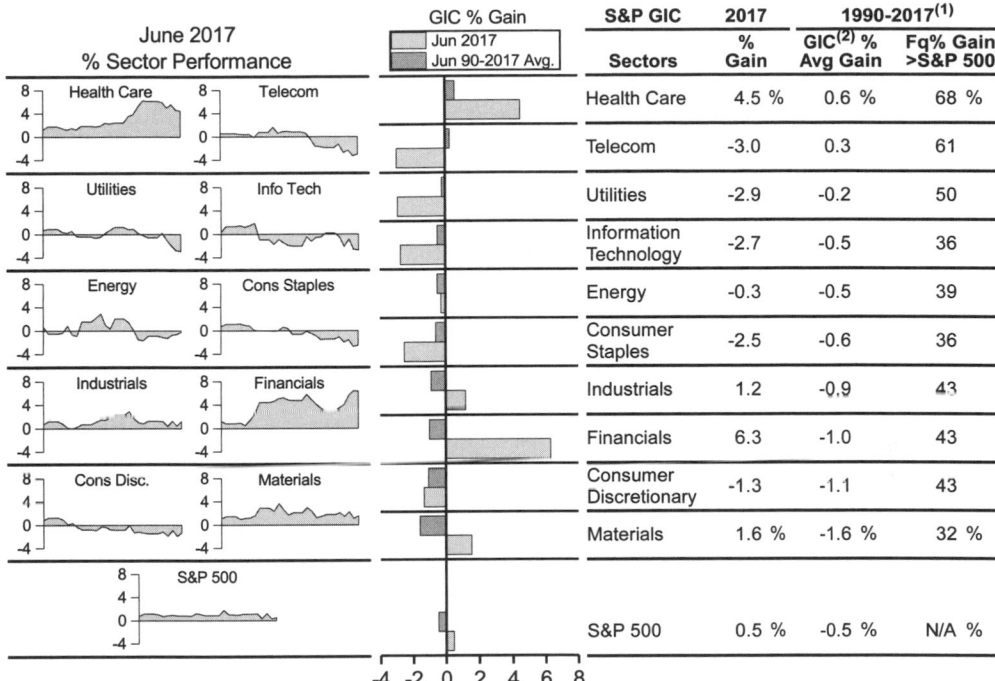

S&P GIC	2017	1990-2017[1]	
Sectors	**% Gain**	**GIC[2] % Avg Gain**	**Fq% Gain >S&P 500**
Health Care	4.5 %	0.6 %	68 %
Telecom	-3.0	0.3	61
Utilities	-2.9	-0.2	50
Information Technology	-2.7	-0.5	36
Energy	-0.3	-0.5	39
Consumer Staples	-2.5	-0.6	36
Industrials	1.2	-0.9	43
Financials	6.3	-1.0	43
Consumer Discretionary	-1.3	-1.1	43
Materials	1.6 %	-1.6 %	32 %
S&P 500	0.5 %	-0.5 %	N/A %

SELECTED SUB-SECTORS[3]			
Pharma	2.6 %	0.7 %	68 %
Gold	-1.9	-0.2	50
Retail	-2.5	-0.6	54
Biotech (1993-2017)	10.1	-0.6	48
Metals & Mining	-0.6	-0.8	54
Home-builders	5.6	-1.0	46
Railroads	-0.2	-1.0	39
SOX (1995-2017)	-5.2	-1.2	35
Steel	-0.4	-1.2	43
Transportation	3.1	-1.2	32
Agriculture (1994-2017)	-0.5	-1.6	33
Chemicals	1.4	-1.7	32
Automotive & Components	1.7	-1.7	46
Silver	-4.9	-1.9	39
Banks	8.5	-1.9	32

Sector Commentary

♦ In June 2017, the financials sector produced a strong gain of 6.3%. Investor interest in the sector strengthened as the Federal Reserve was perceived as becoming more hawkish. ♦ The health care sector produced a gain of 4.5%, as investors were attracted to the sector largely based on the increased perception of possible favorable health care reform. ♦ Two other defensive sectors of the stock market, consumer staples and utilities, both produced losses as investors looked for returns in higher beta sectors.

Sub-Sector Commentary

♦ In June 2017, silver and gold were negative for the month. June tends to be one of the weaker months of the year for silver. ♦ The semiconductor sector (SOX) pulled back after having a strong run in previous months. ♦ The biotech sector performed well in June, the start of its seasonal period. ♦ Banks do not typically perform well in June, but in 2017, they managed to buck the trend, producing a gain of 8.5%.

(1) Sector data provided by Standard and Poors (2) GIC is short form for Global Industry Classification (3) Sub Sector data provided by Standard and Poors, except where marked by symbol.

BIOTECH SUMMER SOLSTICE
June 23rd to September 13th

The *Biotech Summer Solstice* trade starts on June 23rd and lasts until September 13th. The trade is aptly named as its outperformance starts approximately when summer solstice starts– the longest day of the year.

There are two main drivers of the trade: biotech is a good substitute for technology stocks in the summer, and investors want to take a position in the biotech sector before the autumn conferences.

> ***10.9% extra & 88% of the time better than the S&P 500***

Biotech* vs. S&P 500 1992 to 2016

Jun 23 to Sep 13	S&P 500	Biotech	Positive	Diff
1992	4.0 %	17.9 %		13.8 %
1993	3.6	3.6		0.0
1994	3.2	24.2		21.0
1995	5.0	31.5		26.5
1996	2.1	7.0		4.9
1997	2.8	-18.9		-21.7
1998	-8.5	20.6		29.1
1999	0.6	64.3		63.7
2000	2.3	7.6		5.4
2001	-10.8	-3.6		7.2
2002	-10.0	8.1		18.2
2003	2.3	6.4		4.1
2004	-0.8	8.9		9.6
2005	1.4	26.0		24.5
2006	5.8	7.4		1.6
2007	-1.2	6.0		7.2
2008	-5.0	11.4		16.5
2009	16.8	7.7		-9.1
2010	2.4	2.8		0.4
2011	-8.9	-3.7		5.2
2012	9.4	15.6		6.2
2013	6.0	24.9		18.9
2014	1.2	14.8		13.6
2015	-7.6	-7.2		0.5
2016	2.0	7.3		5.3
Avg	0.7 %	11.6 %		10.9 %
Fq>0	68 %	84 %		88 %

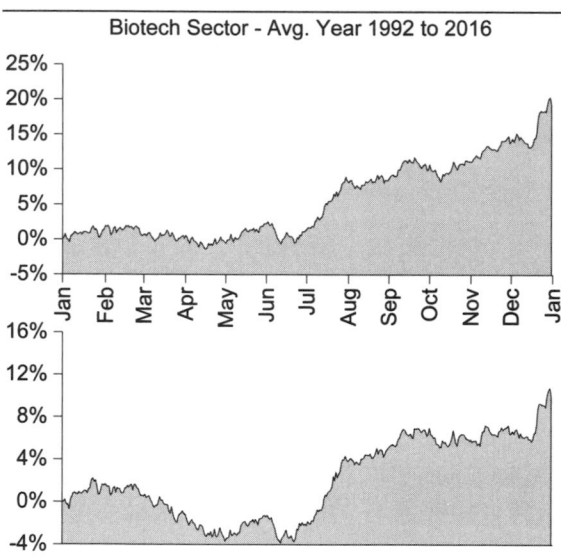

Biotech Sector - Avg. Year 1992 to 2016

Biotech / S&P 500 Relative Strength - Avg Yr. 1992 - 2016

As a result, in the summer months when investors tend to be more cautious, they are more willing to commit speculative money into the biotech sector, compared with the technology sector.

The biotech sector is one of the few sectors that starts its outperformance in June. This is in part because of the biotech conferences that occur in autumn and with the possibility of positive announcements, the price of biotech companies can increase dramatically. As a result, investors try to lock in positions early.

The biotechnology sector is often considered the cousin of the technology sector, a good place for speculative investments. The sectors are similar as both include concept companies (companies without a product but with good potential).

Despite their similarity, investors view the sectors differently. The technology sector is viewed as being much more dependent on the economy compared with the biotech sector. The end product of biotechnology companies is mainly medicine, which is not economically sensitive.

> **Biotech SP GIC Sector # 352010: Companies primarily engaged in the research, development, manufacturing and/or marketing of products based on genetic analysis and genetic engineering. This includes companies specializing in protein-based therapeutics to treat human diseases.*

Biotech Performance

Biotech Monthly Performance (1992-2016)

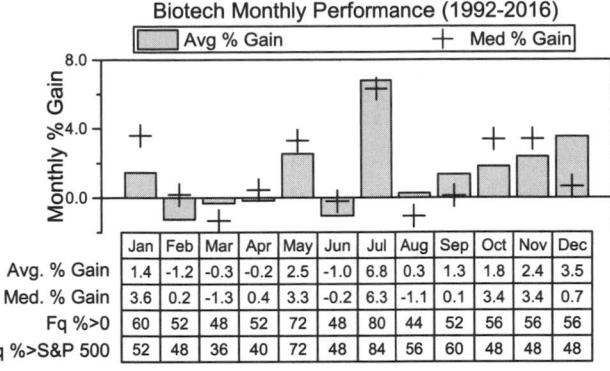

	Jan	Feb	Mar	Apr	May	Jun	Jul	Aug	Sep	Oct	Nov	Dec
Avg. % Gain	1.4	-1.2	-0.3	-0.2	2.5	-1.0	6.8	0.3	1.3	1.8	2.4	3.5
Med. % Gain	3.6	0.2	-1.3	0.4	3.3	-0.2	6.3	-1.1	0.1	3.4	3.4	0.7
Fq %>0	60	52	48	52	72	48	80	44	52	56	56	56
Fq %>S&P 500	52	48	36	40	72	48	84	56	60	48	48	48

Biotech 5 Year (2012-2016) % Gain

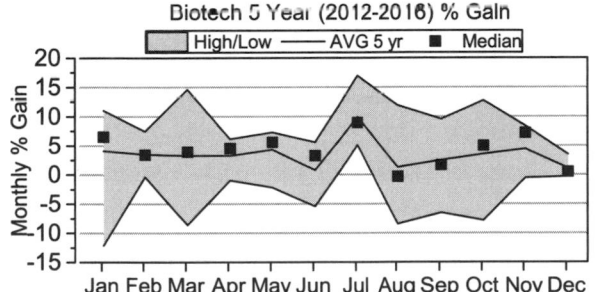

Biotech Performance 2016-2017

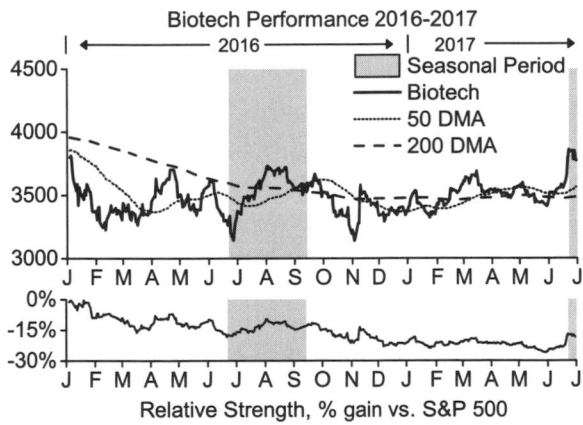

Relative Strength, % gain vs. S&P 500

From 1992 to 2016, the best month for the biotech sector has been July on an average, median and frequency basis. The start of the seasonal period for the sector is late June and runs into the middle of September. On the whole, June is actually a negative month, but the tail end of the month often provides a good buying opportunity. Although August has been positive on an average absolute basis, it can be a weaker month and investors should be prepared to exit the sector before the seasonal period finishes. Over the last five years, the sector has demonstrated superior performance in July. In 2016, the sector outperformed the S&P 500 during its seasonal period.

WEEK 23

Market Indices & Rates
Weekly Values**

Stock Markets	2016	2017
Dow	17,943	21,190
S&P500	2,110	2,433
Nasdaq	4,952	6,280
TSX	14,246	15,429
FTSE	6,241	7,501
DAX	10,110	12,723
Nikkei	16,671	20,012
Hang Seng	21,175	25,986

Commodities	2016	2017
Oil	50.18	46.56
Gold	1257.5	1280.8

Bond Yields	2016	2017
USA 5 Yr Treasury	1.22	1.74
USA 10 Yr T	1.70	2.18
USA 20 Yr T	2.07	2.56
Moody's Aaa	3.61	3.72
Moody's Baa	4.55	4.41
CAN 5 Yr T	0.62	0.94
CAN 10 Yr T	1.20	1.41

Money Market	2016	2017
USA Fed Funds	0.50	1.00
USA 3 Mo T-B	0.27	0.99
CAN tgt overnight rate	0.50	0.50
CAN 3 Mo T-B	0.50	0.51

Foreign Exchange	2016	2017
EUR/USD	1.13	1.12
GBP/USD	1.44	1.29
USD/CAD	1.28	1.35
USD/JPY	107.20	110.00

JUNE

M	T	W	T	F	S	S
				1	2	3
4	5	6	7	8	9	10
11	12	13	14	15	16	17
18	19	20	21	22	23	24
25	26	27	28	29	30	

JULY

M	T	W	T	F	S	S
						1
2	3	4	5	6	7	8
9	10	11	12	13	14	15
16	17	18	19	20	21	22
23	24	25	26	27	28	29
30	31					

AUGUST

M	T	W	T	F	S	S
	1	2	3	4	5	
6	7	8	9	10	11	12
13	14	15	16	17	18	19
20	21	22	23	24	25	26
27	28	29	30	31		

CAMECO— CHARGES DOWN AND UP

CCO ①SELL SHORT (June 5-Aug7)
②LONG (Oct4-Jan24)

Cameco is the world's largest publically traded uranium company. It trades on both the NYSE stock exchange (ticker: CCJ) and the Toronto Stock Exchange (ticker: CCO).

Cameco has a very narrow market for its product: countries that need uranium to power their nuclear reactors. Mining operations do not vary much throughout the year, so supply is fairly constant. In addition actual usage of uranium does not change much throughout the year as nuclear reactors are run most efficiently at one constant level over time. Yet, there is a seasonal tendency for Cameco to perform well from October 4th to January 24th. In this time period, from 1995 to 2017, Cameco has produced an average gain of 15.9%. Also, in the same yearly period, from June 5th to August 7th, Cameco has performed poorly, producing an average loss of 7.8%.

24.5% growth & positive 82% of the time

Some of the seasonal trend for Cameco can be explained by the overall tendency of the stock market to perform well during Cameco's strong seasonal period, and poorly during Cameco's weak seasonal period.

The seasonal trend for Cameco can also be explained somewhat with buyer behavior. The World Nuclear Association (WNA) has an annual conference that takes place in the middle of September of each year. As a result of the conference, buyers tend to be reassured of the future demand of uranium, helping to give

> *Cameco Corporation is in the materials sector. Its stock symbol is CCO, which trades on the Toronto Stock Exchange, adjusted for splits.*

Cameco vs. TSX Composite Index - 1995/96 to 2016/17

Negative Short [ ]   Positive Long [ ]

Year	Jun 5 to Aug 7		Oct 4 to Jan 24		Compound Growth	
	TSX	CCO	TSX	CCO	TSX	CCO
1995/96	5.2 %	0.6 %	6.5	42.7 %	12.0 %	41.9 %
1996/97	-1.3	-6.1	11.2	-16.5	9.8	-11.5
1997/98	13.2	1.1	-0.8	-22.6	12.3	-23.4
1998/99	-0.5	-22.2	22.2	44.4	21.6	76.5
1999/00	-2.1	-16.9	9.3	-24.8	7.0	-12.1
2000/01	0.1	-13.7	-4.4	25.0	-4.2	42.1
2001/02	-5.0	-20.3	5.6	14.6	0.4	37.9
2002/03	-15.8	-28.6	5.2	27.9	-11.4	64.5
2003/04	-1.2	4.9	10.9	35.7	9.5	29.1
2004/05	-5.2	8.9	2.9	30.6	-2.5	19.0
2005/06	2.5	5.7	3.3	38.3	5.9	30.4
2006/07	-1.0	-9.1	8.0	18.6	6.9	29.4
2007/08	-4.1	-30.2	-12.2	-15.7	-15.7	9.8
2008/09	-8.1	-15.0	-24.3	-6.5	-30.4	7.5
2009/10	7.2	0.5	6.5	6.2	14.2	5.6
2010/11	5.3	11.2	12.6	35.6	18.6	20.4
2011/12	-7.8	-13.7	19.6	29.0	10.3	46.6
2012/13	9.6	9.0	3.0	12.6	13.0	2.4
2013/14	3.7	-10.3	6.7	29.6	10.5	42.9
2014/15	-1.0	-3.1	4.3	-8.9	3.3	-6.1
2015/16	-0.9	-6.2	-2.3	-2.9	-3.1	5.3
2016/17	4.0	-17.3	5.5	54.0	9.7	80.7
Avg.	-0.1 %	-7.8 %	4.5	15.9 %	4.4 %	24.5 %
Fq>0	41 %	36 %	77 %	68 %	73 %	82 %

Cameco a boost starting in October. Likewise, investors often have a low interest level in Cameco in the summer months ahead of the WNA conference in mid-September.

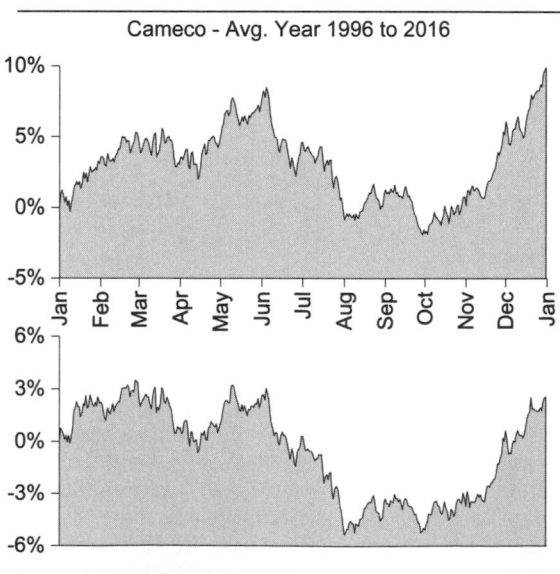

Cameco - Avg. Year 1996 to 2016

Cameco / TSX Comp. Rel. Strength- Avg Yr. 1996-2016

Cameco Performance

Cameco Monthly Performance (1996-2016)

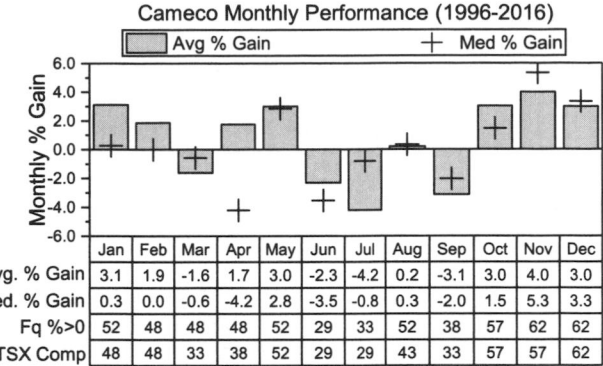

	Jan	Feb	Mar	Apr	May	Jun	Jul	Aug	Sep	Oct	Nov	Dec
Avg. % Gain	3.1	1.9	-1.6	1.7	3.0	-2.3	-4.2	0.2	-3.1	3.0	4.0	3.0
Med. % Gain	0.3	0.0	-0.6	-4.2	2.8	-3.5	-0.8	0.3	-2.0	1.5	5.3	3.3
Fq %>0	52	48	48	48	52	29	33	52	38	57	62	62
Fq %>TSX Comp	48	48	33	38	52	29	29	43	33	57	57	62

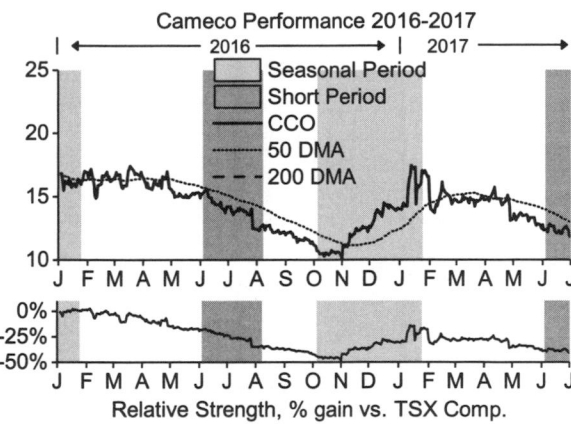

Cameco 5 Year (2012-2016) % Gain

Cameco Performance 2016-2017

Relative Strength, % gain vs. TSX Comp.

Market Indices & Rates
Weekly Values**

Stock Markets	2016	2017
Dow	17,691	21,337
S&P500	2,075	2,435
Nasdaq	4,834	6,182
TSX	13,917	15,257
FTSE	5,981	7,474
DAX	9,593	12,741
Nikkei	15,766	19,893
Hang Seng	20,315	25,726

Commodities	2016	2017
Oil	47.91	45.29
Gold	1290.5	1262.8

Bond Yields	2016	2017
USA 5 Yr Treasury	1.12	1.76
USA 10 Yr T	1.61	2.18
USA 20 Yr T	1.99	2.55
Moody's Aaa	3.45	3.70
Moody's Baa	4.49	4.38
CAN 5 Yr T	0.57	1.12
CAN 10 Yr T	1.11	1.52

Money Market	2016	2017
USA Fed Funds	0.50	1.25
USA 3 Mo T-B	0.27	1.01
CAN tgt overnight rate	0.50	0.50
CAN 3 Mo T-B	0.51	0.54

Foreign Exchange	2016	2017
EUR/USD	1.13	1.12
GBP/USD	1.42	1.27
USD/CAD	1.29	1.33
USD/JPY	105.36	110.28

JUNE

M	T	W	T	F	S	S
				1	2	3
4	5	6	7	8	9	10
11	12	13	14	15	16	17
18	19	20	21	22	23	24
25	26	27	28	29	30	

JULY

M	T	W	T	F	S	S
						1
2	3	4	5	6	7	8
9	10	11	12	13	14	15
16	17	18	19	20	21	22
23	24	25	26	27	28	29
30	31					

AUGUST

M	T	W	T	F	S	S
	1	2	3	4	5
6	7	8	9	10	11	12
13	14	15	16	17	18	19
20	21	22	23	24	25	26
27	28	29	30	31		

From 1996 to 2016, October to January has been the strongest four month contiguous period for Cameco on an average basis. It is important to note that Cameco, on an average basis has performed well in January, but on a median basis, it has only been slightly positive. In other words, a few large returns skewed performance. Generally, over the last five years, Cameco has followed its seasonal pattern with October through February being strong months and June through July being weak months. In 2016 and 2017, Cameco was positive and outperformed the S&P 500 in its seasonal strong period.

INDEPENDENCE DAY – THE FULL TRADE PROFIT BEFORE & AFTER FIREWORKS
Two Market Days Before June Month End To 5 Market Days After Independence Day

The beginning of July is a time for celebration and the markets tend to agree.

Based on previous market data, the best way to take advantage of this trend is to be invested for the two market days prior to June month end and hold until five market days after Independence Day. This time period has produced above average returns on a fairly consistent basis.

Since 1950, 0.9% avg. gain & 72% of the time positive

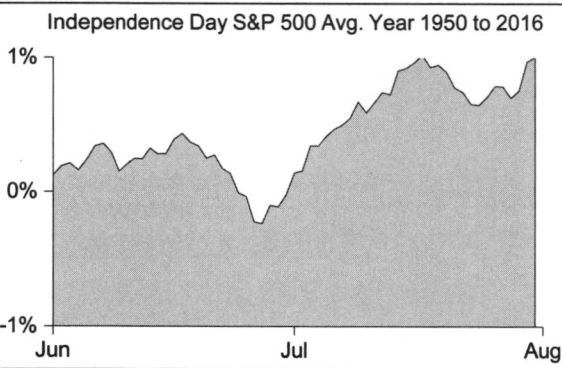

Independence Day S&P 500 Avg. Year 1950 to 2016

The typical strategy to take advantage of the tendency of positive performance around Independence Day has been to invest one or two days before the holiday and take profits one or two days after the holiday.

Although this strategy has produced profits, it has left a lot of money on the table. This strategy misses out on the positive days at the end of June and on the full slate of positive days after Independence Day.

The beginning part of the *Independence Day Trade* positive trend is driven by portfolio managers who "window dress" their portfolios, buying stocks at month end that have a favorable perception in the market in order to make their portfolios look good on month and quarter end statements. This is particularly true at quarter ends. The result is typically increased buying pressure that lifts the stock market.

Depending on market conditions at the time, investors should consider extending the exit date of the *Independence Day Trade* until eighteen calendar days in July. With July being an earnings month, the market can continue to rally until mid-month (see *18 Day Earnings Month Strategy*).

> *History of Independence Day: Independence Day is celebrated on July 4th because that is the day when the Continental Congress adopted the final draft of the Declaration of Independence in 1776. Independence Day was made an official holiday at the end of the War of Independence in 1783. In 1941 Congress declared the 4th of July a federal holiday.*

S&P 500, 2 Market Days Before June Month End To 5 Market Days after Independence Day % Gain 1950 to 2016   Positive ☐

1950	-4.4 %	1960	-0.1 %	1970	1.5 %	1980	1.4 %	1990	1.7 %	2000	1.8 %	2010	0.4 %
1951	1.5	1961	1.7	1971	3.2	1981	-2.4	1991	1.4	2001	-2.6	2011	1.8
1952	0.9	1962	9.8	1972	0.3	1982	-0.6	1992	2.8	2002	-4.7	2012	0.7
1953	0.8	1963	0.5	1973	2.1	1983	1.5	1993	-0.6	2003	1.2	2013	4.5
1954	2.9	1964	2.3	1974	-8.8	1984	-0.7	1994	0.4	2004	-1.7	2014	0.5
1955	4.9	1965	5.0	1975	-0.2	1985	1.5	1995	1.8	2005	1.5	2015	-1.2
1956	3.4	1966	2.1	1976	2.4	1986	-2.6	1996	-2.8	2006	2.1	2016	5.0
1957	3.8	1967	1.3	1977	-0.6	1987	0.4	1997	3.7	2007	0.8	2017	0.2
1958	2.0	1968	2.3	1978	0.6	1988	-0.6	1998	2.7	2008	-3.4		
1959	3.3	1969	-1.5	1979	1.3	1989	0.9	1999	5.1	2009	-4.3		
Avg.	1.9 %		2.3 %		0.2 %		-0.1 %		1.8 %		-0.9 %		1.5 %

Independence Day Strategy Performance

 Independence Day Trade

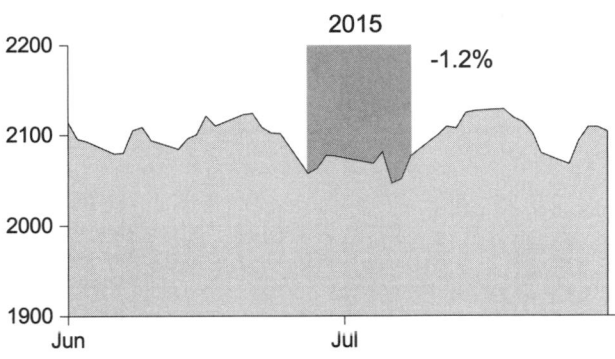

2015 -1.2%

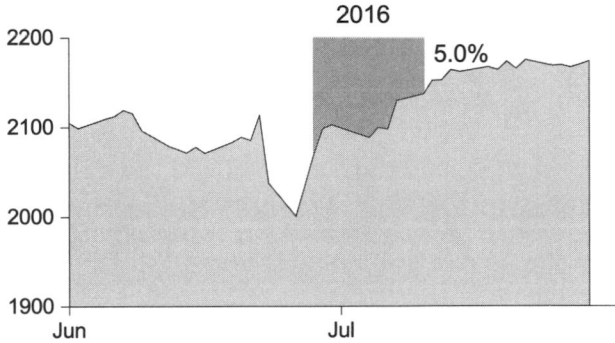

2016 5.0%

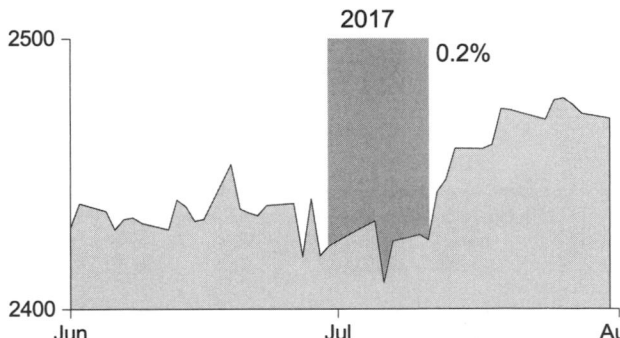

2017 0.2%

Market Indices & Rates
Weekly Values**

Stock Markets	2016	2017
Dow	17,765	21,440
S&P500	2,082	2,440
Nasdaq	4,826	6,233
TSX	14,011	15,221
FTSE	6,234	7,462
DAX	9,973	12,801
Nikkei	15,878	20,136
Hang Seng	20,620	25,761

Commodities	2016	2017
Oil	48.56	43.02
Gold	1279.4	1247.9

Bond Yields	2016	2017
USA 5 Yr Treasury	1.18	1.78
USA 10 Yr T	1.68	2.16
USA 20 Yr T	2.05	2.49
Moody's Aaa	3.66	3.62
Moody's Baa	4.56	4.32
CAN 5 Yr T	0.69	1.14
CAN 10 Yr T	1.23	1.50

Money Market	2016	2017
USA Fed Funds	0.50	1.25
USA 3 Mo T-B	0.28	0.99
CAN tgt overnight rate	0.50	0.50
CAN 3 Mo T-B	0.50	0.59

Foreign Exchange	2016	2017
EUR/USD	1.13	1.12
GBP/USD	1.45	1.27
USD/CAD	1.28	1.33
USD/JPY	104.30	111.39

JUNE

M	T	W	T	F	S	S
				1	2	3
4	5	6	7	8	9	10
11	12	13	14	15	16	17
18	19	20	21	22	23	24
25	26	27	28	29	30	

JULY

M	T	W	T	F	S	S
						1
2	3	4	5	6	7	8
9	10	11	12	13	14	15
16	17	18	19	20	21	22
23	24	25	26	27	28	29
30	31					

AUGUST

M	T	W	T	F	S	S
	1	2	3	4	5
6	7	8	9	10	11	12
13	14	15	16	17	18	19
20	21	22	23	24	25	26
27	28	29	30	31		

In 2015, the S&P 500 declined in June and continued its decline into the *Independence Day Trade* to produce a loss of 1.2%.

In 2016, the S&P 500 benefited from the post Brexit rally. The rally started a few days before the end of June, but tapered off after the *Independence Day Trade*.

In 2017, the S&P 500 produced a nominal return of 0.2% during the *Independence Day Trade* period. After the *Independence Day Trade* finished, the S&P 500 rallied sharply.

Ryder— Rolls Down & Up

R ①LONG (Jan1-Jun2)
②SELL SHORT (June3-Oct27)

Ryder System Inc. is a supplier of transportation and supply chain management products. It is mainly known for its fleet of rental trucks.

A large part of its revenue is derived from its services and products that are provided when its customers need to be able to meet their busy seasonal demands.

> ### 19.2% growth & positive 78% of the time

The first few months of the year tend to be positive for Ryder as the economy tends to expand at this time and many companies outsource their logistical needs.

From 1990 to 2016, in the period from January 1st to June 2nd, Ryder has produced an average gain of 11.2% and been positive 74% of the time.

For most of the second half of the year, Ryder tends to perform poorly. At this time, expectations for economic growth tend to moderate. The fourth quarter of the year tends to be the weakest revenue producer for Ryder.

The end result is that Ryder tends to underperform from June 3rd to October 27th. In this period, from 1990 to 2016, Ryder has produced an average loss of 5.9% and has only been positive 30% of the time.

Short selling Ryder in its weak seasonal period and buying it in its strong seasonal period, from 1990 to 2016 has produced an average gain of 19.2% and has been positive 78% of the time.

(i) *Ryder is in the transportation sector. Its stock symbol is R. which trades on the NYSE, adjusted for splits.*

Ryder vs. S&P 500 1990 to 2016

Positive Long ▢   Negative Short ▢

Year	Jan1 to Jun 2 S&P 500	Jan1 to Jun 2 R	Jun 3 to Oct 27 S&P 500	Jun 3 to Oct 27 R	Compound Growth S&P 500	Compound Growth R
1990	2.8	11.6 %	-16.1 %	-44.8 %	-13.8 %	61.6 %
1991	18.1	37.5	-1.4	-7.3	16.4	47.5
1992	-0.9	27.6	1.2	-8.2	0.3	38.0
1993	4.2	3.2	2.4	-1.8	6.6	5.0
1994	-1.9	-8.5	1.8	-1.0	-0.1	-7.5
1995	16.0	13.6	8.9	-3.0	26.2	17.0
1996	8.6	18.2	4.8	-0.9	13.8	19.2
1997	14.3	19.1	3.6	2.2	18.4	16.4
1998	12.7	5.2	-2.6	-28.7	9.8	35.3
1999	5.3	-2.2	0.2	-18.9	5.5	16.4
2000	0.6	-18.4	-6.6	-16.3	-6.1	-5.1
2001	-4.5	32.0	-12.4	-10.2	-16.3	45.4
2002	-7.1	35.0	-15.9	-20.9	-21.8	63.2
2003	9.9	18.7	6.6	10.7	17.2	6.0
2004	1.2	9.1	0.0	31.1	1.2	-24.9
2005	-0.6	-22.7	-2.1	0.1	-2.7	-22.8
2006	3.2	34.2	6.9	-3.1	10.3	38.2
2007	8.3	5.9	-0.1	-12.4	8.2	19.0
2008	-5.6	55.4	-38.7	-49.5	-42.2	132.4
2009	4.6	-23.7	12.6	44.8	17.7	-57.9
2010	-1.5	8.1	7.7	-2.0	6.0	10.2
2011	4.4	1.2	-2.2	-3.6	2.1	4.9
2012	1.6	-21.6	10.5	7.5	12.3	-27.4
2013	14.3	26.3	7.9	3.7	23.4	21.7
2014	4.1	18.0	1.9	-2.4	6.1	20.8
2015	2.5	-0.8	-2.1	-25.9	0.3	24.9
2016	3.0	21.4	1.3	0.3	4.4	21.1
Avg.	4.4 %	11.2 %	-0.8 %	-5.9 %	3.8 %	19.2 %
Fq>0	74 %	74 %	59 %	30 %	74 %	78 %

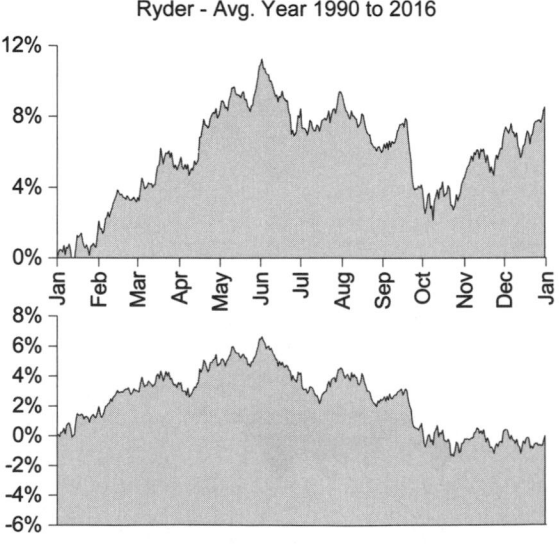

Ryder - Avg. Year 1990 to 2016

Ryder / S&P 500 Rel. Strength- Avg Yr. 1990-2016

Ryder Strategy Performance

Ryder Monthly Performance (1990-2016)

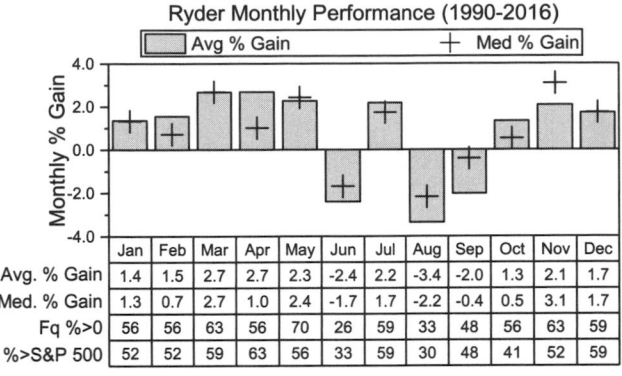

	Jan	Feb	Mar	Apr	May	Jun	Jul	Aug	Sep	Oct	Nov	Dec
Avg. % Gain	1.4	1.5	2.7	2.7	2.3	-2.4	2.2	-3.4	-2.0	1.3	2.1	1.7
Med. % Gain	1.3	0.7	2.7	1.0	2.4	-1.7	1.7	-2.2	-0.4	0.5	3.1	1.7
Fq %>0	56	56	63	56	70	26	59	33	48	56	63	59
Fq %>S&P 500	52	52	59	63	56	33	59	30	48	41	52	59

Ryder 5 Year (2012-2016) % Gain

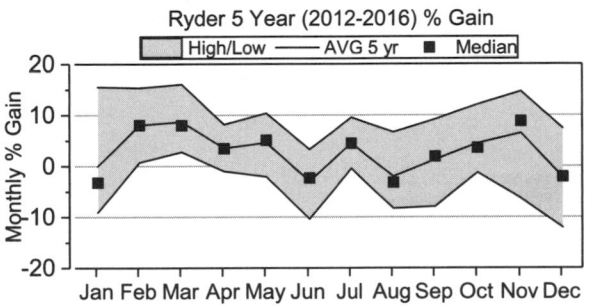

Ryder Performance 2016-2017

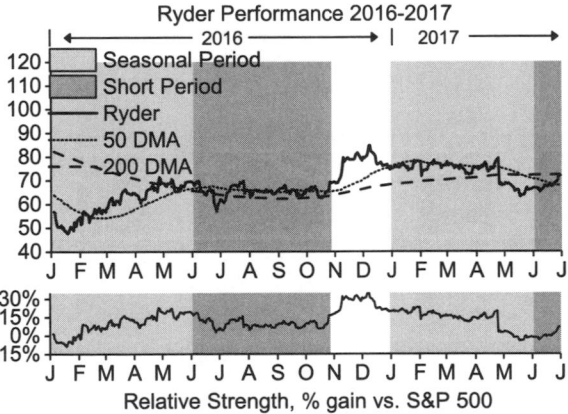

Relative Strength, % gain vs. S&P 500

Market Indices & Rates
Weekly Values**

Stock Markets	2016	2017
Dow	17,625	21,362
S&P500	2,062	2,428
Nasdaq	4,754	6,183
TSX	13,908	15,270
FTSE	6,313	7,386
DAX	9,557	12,566
Nikkei	15,492	20,153
Hang Seng	20,408	25,825

Commodities	2016	2017
Oil	48.28	44.67
Gold	1323.3	1245.7

Bond Yields	2016	2017
USA 5 Yr Treasury	1.01	1.83
USA 10 Yr T	1.47	2.23
USA 20 Yr T	1.84	2.55
Moody's Aaa	3.39	3.65
Moody's Baa	4.39	4.35
CAN 5 Yr T	0.58	1.27
CAN 10 Yr T	1.08	1.62

Money Market	2016	2017
USA Fed Funds	0.50	1.25
USA 3 Mo T-B	0.27	1.02
CAN tgt overnight rate	0.50	0.50
CAN 3 Mo T-B	0.49	0.68

Foreign Exchange	2016	2017
EUR/USD	1.11	1.14
GBP/USD	1.33	1.29
USD/CAD	1.30	1.31
USD/JPY	102.66	112.22

JUNE

M	T	W	T	F	S	S
				1	2	3
4	5	6	7	8	9	10
11	12	13	14	15	16	17
18	19	20	21	22	23	24
25	26	27	28	29	30	

JULY

M	T	W	T	F	S	S
						1
2	3	4	5	6	7	8
9	10	11	12	13	14	15
16	17	18	19	20	21	22
23	24	25	26	27	28	29
30	31					

AUGUST

M	T	W	T	F	S	S
	1	2	3	4	5	
6	7	8	9	10	11	12
13	14	15	16	17	18	19
20	21	22	23	24	25	26
27	28	29	30	31		

From 1990 to 2016, Ryder has been positive from January to May, negative from June to September (other than July) and positive from October to December. Although October to December has been positive, Ryder has not strongly outperformed the S&P 500 at this time.

From 2012 to 2016, the summer months have generally been weak. The strongest month has been October. In its 2016 long seasonal period, Ryder strongly outperformed the S&P 500. In its short sell seasonal period, the trade was not successful as Ryder was slightly positive.

JULY

	MONDAY	TUESDAY	WEDNESDAY
WEEK 27	**2** 29 CAN Market Closed- Canada Day	**3** 28	**4** 27 USA Market Closed - Independence Day
WEEK 28	**9** 22	**10** 21	**11** 20
WEEK 29	**16** 15	**17** 14	**18** 13
WEEK 30	**23** 8	**24** 7	**25** 6
WEEK 31	**30** 1	**31**	1

THURSDAY		FRIDAY	
5	26	**6**	25
12	19	**13**	18
19	12	**20**	11
26	5	**27**	4
2		3	

AUGUST

M	T	W	T	F	S	S
		1	2	3	4	5
6	7	8	9	10	11	12
13	14	15	16	17	18	19
20	21	22	23	24	25	26
27	28	29	30	31		

SEPTEMBER

M	T	W	T	F	S	S
					1	2
3	4	5	6	7	8	9
10	11	12	13	14	15	16
17	18	19	20	21	22	23
24	25	26	27	28	29	30

OCTOBER

M	T	W	T	F	S	S
1	2	3	4	5	6	7
8	9	10	11	12	13	14
15	16	17	18	19	20	21
22	23	24	25	26	27	28
29	30	31				

NOVEMBER

M	T	W	T	F	S	S
			1	2	3	4
5	6	7	8	9	10	11
12	13	14	15	16	17	18
19	20	21	22	23	24	25
26	27	28	29	30		

JULY SUMMARY

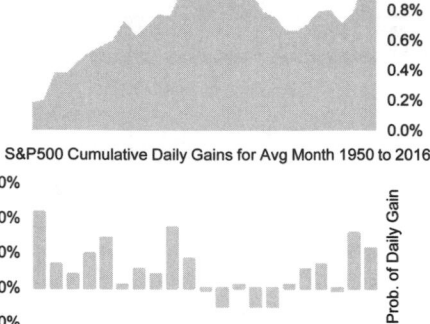

S&P500 Cumulative Daily Gains for Avg Month 1950 to 2016

	Dow Jones	S&P 500	Nasdaq	TSX Comp
Month Rank	5	5	10	6
# Up	42	37	24	21
# Down	25	30	21	11
% Pos	63	55	53	66
% Avg. Gain	1.1	1.0	0.4	0.9

Dow & S&P 1950-2016, Nasdaq 1972-2016, TSX 1985-2016

♦ When a summer rally occurs in the stock market, the gains are usually made in July. ♦ Typically, it is the first part of July that produces the gains as the market tends to rally before Independence Day and into the first eighteen calendar days (see the *18 Days Earnings Month Effect*). In 2016, July produced a strong gain of 3.2% during its first eighteen calendar days. ♦ On average, volatility starts to increase in July and continues this trend into October. ♦ August and September, the two months following July tend to be seasonally weak.

BEST / WORST JULY BROAD MKTS. 2007-2016

BEST JULY MARKETS
- ♦ Russell 2000 (2009) 9.5%
- ♦ Dow (2009) 8.6%
- ♦ FTSE 100 (2009) 8.5%

WORST JULY MARKETS
- ♦ Russell 2000 (2007) -6.9%
- ♦ Russell 2000 (2014) -6.1%
- ♦ TSX Comp (2008) -6.0%

Index Values End of Month

	2007	2008	2009	2010	2011	2012	2013	2014	2015	2016
Dow	13,212	11,378	9,172	10,466	12,143	13,009	15,500	16,563	17,690	18,432
S&P 500	1,455	1,267	987	1,102	1,292	1,379	1,686	1,931	2,104	2,174
Nasdaq	2,546	2,326	1,979	2,255	2,756	2,940	3,626	4,370	5,128	5,162
TSX Comp.	13,869	13,593	10,787	11,713	12,946	11,665	12,487	15,331	14,468	14,583
Russell 1000	792	694	540	606	718	759	937	1,076	1,174	1,204
Russell 2000	776	715	557	651	797	787	1,045	1,120	1,239	1,220
FTSE 100	6,360	5,412	4,608	5,258	5,815	5,635	6,621	6,730	6,696	6,724
Nikkei 225	17,249	13,377	10,357	9,537	9,833	8,695	13,668	15,621	20,585	16,569

Percent Gain for July

	2007	2008	2009	2010	2011	2012	2013	2014	2015	2016
Dow	-1.5	0.2	8.6	7.1	-2.2	1.0	4.0	-1.6	0.4	2.8
S&P 500	-3.2	-1.0	7.4	6.9	-2.1	1.3	4.9	-1.5	2.0	3.6
Nasdaq	-2.2	1.4	7.8	6.9	-0.6	0.2	6.6	-0.9	2.8	6.6
TSX Comp.	-0.3	-6.0	4.0	3.7	-2.7	0.6	2.9	1.2	-0.6	3.7
Russell 1000	-3.2	-1.3	7.5	6.8	-2.3	1.1	5.2	-1.7	1.8	3.7
Russell 2000	-6.9	3.6	9.5	6.8	-3.7	-1.4	6.9	-6.1	-1.2	5.9
FTSE 100	-3.8	-3.8	8.5	6.9	-2.2	1.2	6.5	-0.2	2.7	3.4
Nikkei 225	-4.9	-0.8	4.0	1.6	0.2	-3.5	-0.1	3.0	1.7	6.4

July Market Avg. Performance 2007 to 2016[1]

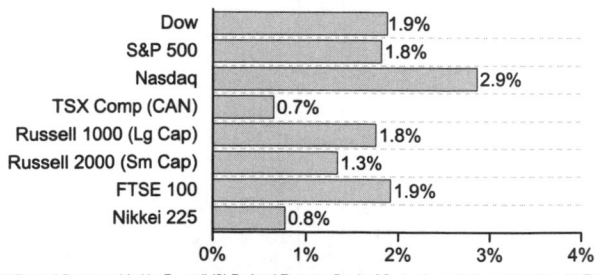

- Dow 1.9%
- S&P 500 1.8%
- Nasdaq 2.9%
- TSX Comp (CAN) 0.7%
- Russell 1000 (Lg Cap) 1.8%
- Russell 2000 (Sm Cap) 1.3%
- FTSE 100 1.9%
- Nikkei 225 0.8%

Interest Corner Jul[2]

	Fed Funds % [3]	3 Mo. T-Bill % [4]	10 Yr % [5]	20 Yr % [6]
2016	0.50	0.28	1.46	1.78
2015	0.25	0.08	2.20	2.61
2014	0.25	0.03	2.58	3.07
2013	0.25	0.04	2.60	3.34
2012	0.25	0.11	1.51	2.21

(1) Russell Data provided by Russell (2) Federal Reserve Bank of St. Louis- end of month values (3) Target rate set by FOMC (4)(5)(6) Constant yield maturities.

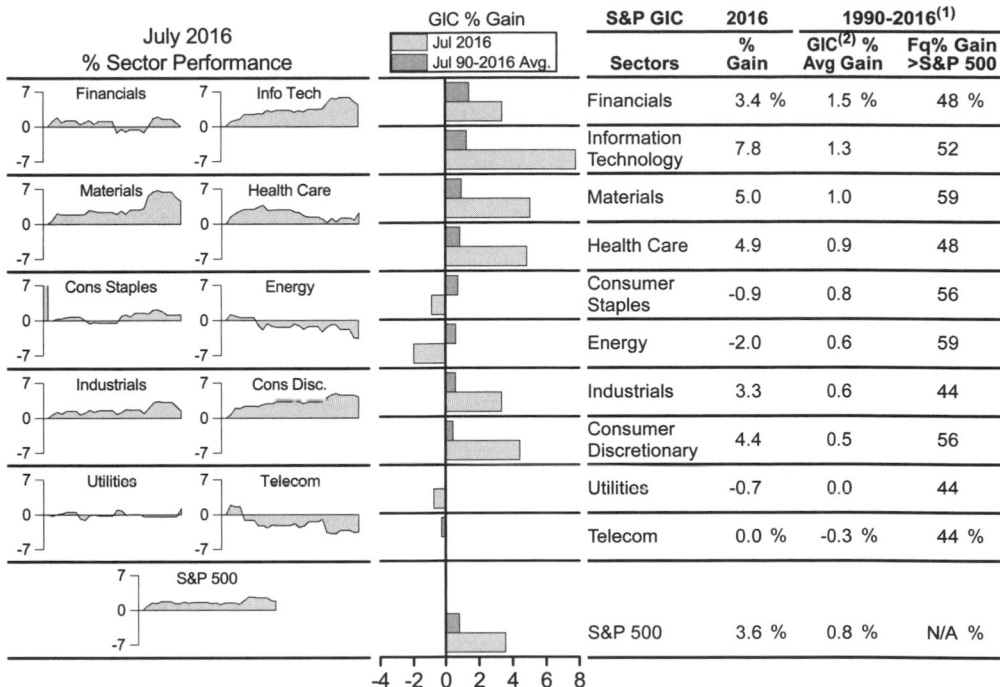

S&P GIC	2016	1990-2016[1]	
Sectors	% Gain	GIC[2] % Avg Gain	Fq% Gain >S&P 500
Financials	3.4 %	1.5 %	48 %
Information Technology	7.8	1.3	52
Materials	5.0	1.0	59
Health Care	4.9	0.9	48
Consumer Staples	-0.9	0.8	56
Energy	-2.0	0.6	59
Industrials	3.3	0.6	44
Consumer Discretionary	4.4	0.5	56
Utilities	-0.7	0.0	44
Telecom	0.0 %	-0.3 %	44 %
S&P 500	3.6 %	0.8 %	N/A %

Sector Commentary

♦ July is an earnings month and the S&P 500 performed positively into the start of the earnings season in July 2016. ♦ The information technology sector performed well in January as the "FANG" stocks helped to propel the sector higher. ♦ Health care performed well with a gain of 4.9%. ♦ The consumer discretionary sector performed well as consumers continued to spend money despite a weaker than expected economy.

Sub-Sector Commentary

♦ In July 2016, the biotech sub-sector continued its run from June with a gain of 9.3%. ♦ The semiconductor sub-sector (SOX) continued its rally with a gain of 10.9%. The semiconductor sub-sector does not typically perform well in the summer months. ♦ The metals and mining sub-sector was also a strong performer, producing a gain of 12.8%. ♦ Overall, investors were in a risk-on mode, attracted to investments with higher betas.

SELECTED SUB-SECTORS[3]			
Biotech (1993-2016)	9.3 %	6.8 %	83 %
Railroads	6.8	2.5	63
Silver	9.2	1.6	63
Banks	3.9	1.5	67
Automotive & Components	6.6	1.4	52
Transportation	5.3	1.3	48
Chemicals	3.9	1.3	56
Retail	6.4	1.2	59
Homebuilders	4.5	0.8	48
SOX (1995-2016)	10.9	0.4	41
Pharma	4.0	0.4	52
Gold	1.6	0.3	48
Metals & Mining	12.8	0.1	48
Steel	8.6	-0.2	48
Agriculture (1994-2016)	5.1	-0.8	48

(1) Sector data provided by Standard and Poors (2) GIC is short form for Global Industry Classification (3) Sub Sector data provided by Standard and Poors, except where marked by symbol.

GOLD SHINES
(Metal) Gold (Metal) Outperforms – July 12th to October 9th

In the 1990's, gold was thought to be a dead investment. It was only the "gold bugs" that espoused the virtues of investing in the precious metal. Investors were mesmerized with technology stocks, and central bankers confident of their currencies, were selling gold, "left, right and center."

3.3% gain & positive 64% of the time

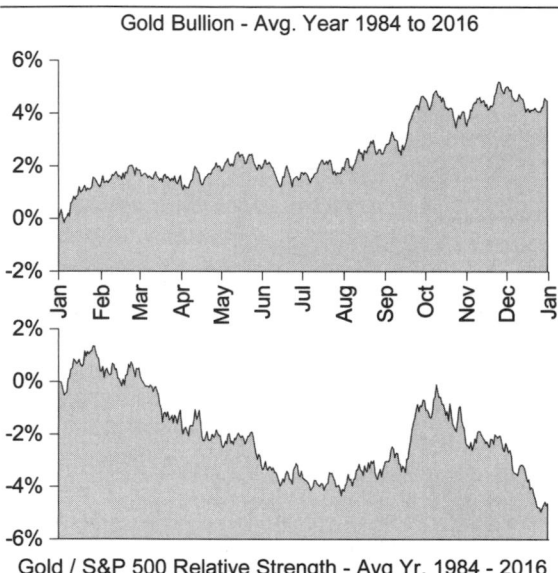

Gold Bullion - Avg. Year 1984 to 2016

Gold / S&P 500 Relative Strength - Avg Yr. 1984 - 2016

**Gold (Metal) London PM* vs S&P 500
1984 to 2016**

Jul 12 to Oct 9th	S&P 500	Positive Gold	Diff
1984	7.4 %	0.5 %	-6.9 %
1985	-5.4	4.1	9.5
1986	-2.6	25.2	27.8
1987	0.9	3.9	3.0
1988	2.8	-7.5	-10.3
1989	9.4	-4.2	-13.6
1990	-15.5	12.1	27.6
1991	0.0	-2.9	-2.8
1992	-2.9	0.4	3.3
1993	2.7	-8.8	-11.5
1994	1.6	1.6	0.0
1995	4.3	-0.1	-4.3
1996	7.9	-0.4	-8.3
1997	5.9	4.4	-1.5
1998	-15.5	2.8	18.2
1999	-4.8	25.6	30.4
2000	-5.3	-4.5	0.8
2001	-10.5	8.4	18.8
2002	-16.2	1.7	17.9
2003	4.1	7.8	3.8
2004	0.8	3.8	2.9
2005	-1.9	11.4	13.4
2006	6.1	-8.8	-14.9
2007	3.1	11.0	8.0
2008	-26.6	-8.2	18.4
2009	21.9	15.2	- 6.7
2010	8.1	11.0	2.9
2011	-12.4	6.2	18.6
2012	7.5	12.5	5.0
2013	-1.1	1.5	2.6
2014	-2.0	-8.1	-6.1
2015	-3.0	-0.7	2.3
2016	0.8	-7.3	-8.0
Avg.	**-0.9 %**	**3.3 %**	**4.3 %**
Fq > 0	**52 %**	**64 %**	**64 %**

In the early 2000's, investors started to take a shine to gold, boosting its returns. On a seasonal basis, on average from 1984 to 2016, gold has performed well relative to the stock market from July 12th to October 9th. The reasons for gold's seasonal changes in price are largely related to jewelery production and European Central banks selling cycles (see *Golden Times* strategy page).

The movement of gold stock prices, represented by the index (XAU) on the Philadelphia Exchange, coincides closely with the price of gold. Although there is a strong correlation between gold and gold stocks, there are other factors, such as company operations and hedging policies, which determine each company's price in the market. Gold has typically started its seasonal strong period a few weeks earlier than gold miners and finished just after gold miners have turned down.

October has typically been a weak month for gold (see *Golden Times* strategy).

Although November tends to be a positive month for gold, producing an average gain of 1.2% and being positive 64% of the time (1984 to 2016), the trouble is in the following month.

December has a history of being negative for gold, producing an average loss of 0.5% and only being positive 39% of the time. This compares with the S&P 500, which over the same time period has produced a 1.8% average gain and has been positive 79% of the time in December.

 Source: Bank of England- London PM represents the close value of gold in afternoon trading in London.

Gold Performance

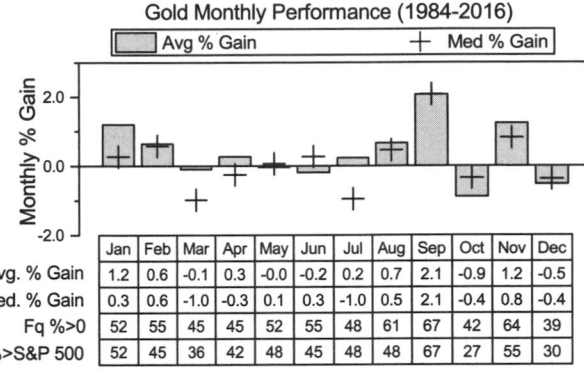

Gold Monthly Performance (1984-2016)

Legend: Avg % Gain | + Med % Gain

	Jan	Feb	Mar	Apr	May	Jun	Jul	Aug	Sep	Oct	Nov	Dec
Avg. % Gain	1.2	0.6	-0.1	0.3	-0.0	-0.2	0.2	0.7	2.1	-0.9	1.2	-0.5
Med. % Gain	0.3	0.6	-1.0	-0.3	0.1	0.3	-1.0	0.5	2.1	-0.4	0.8	-0.4
Fq %>0	52	55	45	45	52	55	48	61	67	42	64	39
Fq %>S&P 500	52	45	36	42	48	45	48	48	67	27	55	30

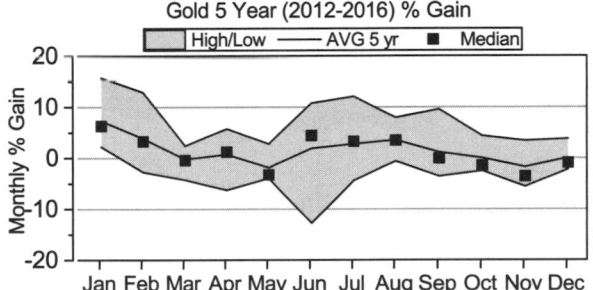

Gold 5 Year (2012-2016) % Gain

Legend: High/Low — AVG 5 yr ■ Median

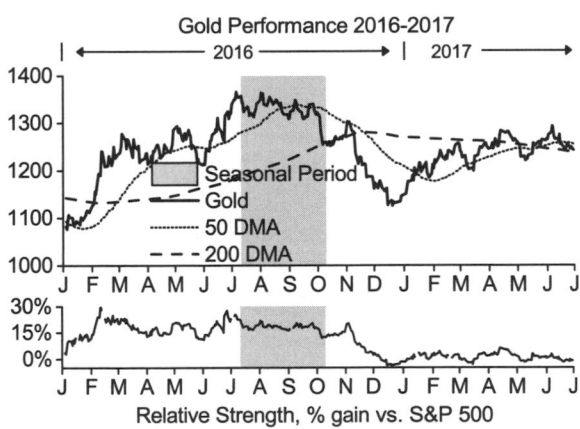

Gold Performance 2016-2017

Legend: Seasonal Period / Gold / 50 DMA / 200 DMA

Relative Strength, % gain vs. S&P 500

From 1984 to 2016, the best month for gold bullion on average, median and frequency basis has been September. On average the worst month of the year has been October. With the juxtaposition of the best and worst months, investors have to be cautious.

Over the last five years, gold has performed above average in July and August, but has performed poorly in September.

In 2016, gold was negative in its seasonal period, and underperformed the S&P 500.

WEEK 27

Market Indices & Rates
Weekly Values**

Stock Markets	2015	2016
Dow	17,676	17,950
S&P500	2,069	2,104
Nasdaq	4,992	4,879
TSX	14,591	14,221
FTSE	6,593	6,531
DAX	11,073	9,533
Nikkei	20,347	15,441
Hang Seng	26,141	20,715

Commodities	2015	2016
Oil	57.92	46.15
Gold	1169.6	1355.7

Bond Yields	2015	2016
USA 5 Yr Treasury	1.65	0.95
USA 10 Yr T	2.38	1.38
USA 20 Yr T	2.87	1.71
Moody's Aaa	4.23	3.21
Moody's Baa	5.22	4.19
CAN 5 Yr T	0.84	0.54
CAN 10 Yr T	1.71	0.99

Money Market	2015	2016
USA Fed Funds	0.25	0.50
USA 3 Mo T-B	0.01	0.28
CAN tgt overnight rate	0.75	0.50
CAN 3 Mo T-B	0.57	0.48

Foreign Exchange	2015	2016
EUR/USD	1.11	1.11
GBP/USD	1.56	1.30
USD/CAD	1.25	1.30
USD/JPY	122.81	101.39

JULY

M	T	W	T	F	S	S
						1
2	3	4	5	6	7	8
9	10	11	12	13	14	15
16	17	18	19	20	21	22
23	24	25	26	27	28	29
30	31					

AUGUST

M	T	W	T	F	S	S
	1	2	3	4	5	
6	7	8	9	10	11	12
13	14	15	16	17	18	19
20	21	22	23	24	25	26
27	28	29	30	31		

SEPTEMBER

M	T	W	T	F	S	S
					1	2
3	4	5	6	7	8	9
10	11	12	13	14	15	16
17	18	19	20	21	22	23
24	25	26	27	28	29	30

GOLDEN TIMES

(Stocks) ## Gold Miners Outperform – July 27th to September 25th

On average from 1984 (start of the XAU index) to 2016, gold miners as represented by the XAU index, have outperformed the S&P 500 from July 27th to September 25th.

One factor that has led to a rise in the price of gold miners in August and September is the Indian festival and wedding season that starts in October and finishes in November during Diwali. The Indian culture places a great emphasis on gold as a store of value and a lot of it is "consumed" as jewelery during the festival and wedding season. The price of gold tends to increase in the months preceding this season, as the jewelery fabricators purchase gold to make their final product.

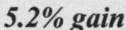

5.2% gain

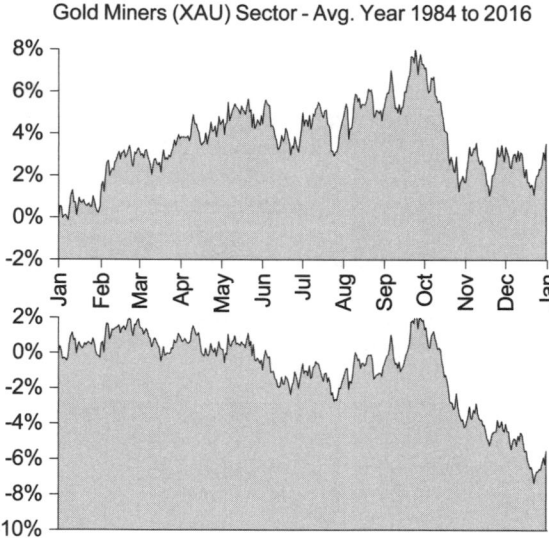

Gold Miners (XAU) Sector - Avg. Year 1984 to 2016

XAU / S&P 500 Relative Strength - Avg Yr. 1984-2016

Jul 27 to Sep 25	S&P 500	Gold	XAU
XAU>S&P 500			
XAU>Gold			
1984	10.4 %	0.3 %	20.8 %
1985	-6.1	3.6	-5.5
1986	-3.5	23.0	36.9
1987	3.5	1.9	23.0
1988	1.7	-7.2	-11.9
1989	1.8	-1.3	10.5
1990	-13.4	9.5	3.8
1991	1.6	-3.1	-11.9
1992	0.7	-2.2	-3.8
1993	1.9	-8.7	-7.3
1994	1.4	2.5	18.2
1995	3.6	-0.8	-1.0
1996	7.9	-0.7	-1.0
1997	-0.1	0.2	8.7
1998	-8.4	1.2	12.0
1999	-5.2	6.5	16.9
2000	-0.9	-2.3	-2.8
2001	-15.8	7.7	3.2
2002	-1.5	6.6	29.8
2003	0.5	7.6	11.0
2004	2.4	4.4	16.5
2005	-1.3	9.3	20.5
2006	4.6	-4.8	-11.9
2007	2.3	8.7	14.0
2008	-3.9	-3.5	-18.5
2009	6.7	4.2	6.0
2010	3.0	9.6	14.7
2011	-14.7	4.7	-13.7
2012	6.0	9.5	23.4
2013	0.1	-0.6	-5.5
2014	-0.6	-6.3	-16.4
2015	-7.1	6.1	-2.6
2016	-0.2	1.2	-7.0
Avg.	-0.7 %	2.6 %	5.2 %
Fq > 0	55 %	64 %	55 %

XAU (Gold Miners)* vs S&P 500 and Gold (1984 to 2016)

The August-September increase in gold miners coincides with the time that a lot of investors are pulling their money out of the broad market and are looking for a place to invest. This makes gold a very attractive investment at this time of the year.

Be careful. Just as the gold miners tend to go up in August and September, they also tend to go down in October. Historically, this negative trend has been caused by European Central banks selling some of their gold holdings in autumn when their annual allotment of possible sales is renewed yearly. In recent years, European Central banks have reduced gold sales and have even become net buyers. This has muted gold's negative trend in October. Nevertheless, gold miners have still underperformed. From October 1st to October 27th, for the period 1984 to 2016, XAU has produced an average loss of 4.7% and has only been positive 36% of the time.

(i) *XAU- PHLX Gold Silver Index consists of 12 precious metal mining companies.*

Gold Miners Performance

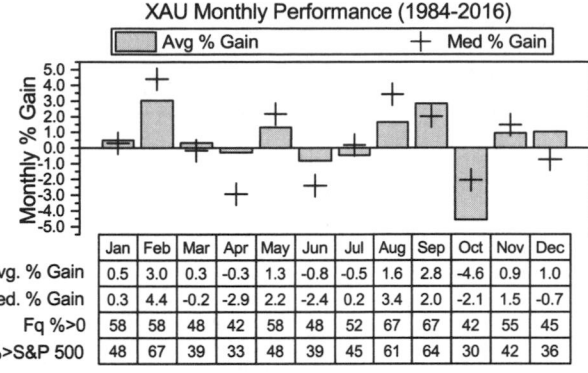

XAU Monthly Performance (1984-2016)

	Jan	Feb	Mar	Apr	May	Jun	Jul	Aug	Sep	Oct	Nov	Dec
Avg. % Gain	0.5	3.0	0.3	-0.3	1.3	-0.8	-0.5	1.6	2.8	-4.6	0.9	1.0
Med. % Gain	0.3	4.4	-0.2	-2.9	2.2	-2.4	0.2	3.4	2.0	-2.1	1.5	-0.7
Fq %>0	58	58	48	42	58	48	52	67	67	42	55	45
Fq %>S&P 500	48	67	39	33	48	39	45	61	64	30	42	36

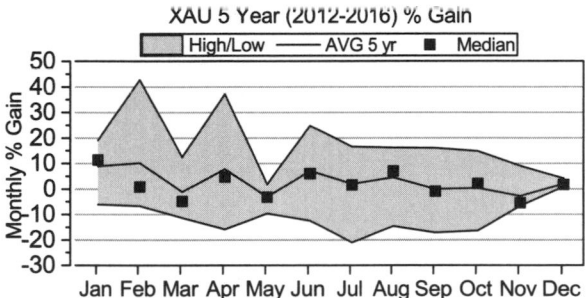

XAU 5 Year (2012-2016) % Gain

Market Indices & Rates
Weekly Values**

Stock Markets	2015	2016
Dow	17,657	18,394
S&P500	2,065	2,153
Nasdaq	4,964	5,016
TSX	14,464	14,466
FTSE	6,543	6,672
DAX	10,925	9,973
Nikkei	19,972	16,184
Hang Seng	24,604	21,330

Commodities	2015	2016
Oil	52.41	45.59
Gold	1160.9	1338.6

Bond Yields	2015	2016
USA 5 Yr Treasury	1.57	1.09
USA 10 Yr T	2.31	1.51
USA 20 Yr T	2.78	1.81
Moody's Aaa	4.15	3.27
Moody's Baa	5.17	4.21
CAN 5 Yr T	0.73	0.59
CAN 10 Yr T	1.60	1.04

Money Market	2015	2016
USA Fed Funds	0.25	0.50
USA 3 Mo T-B	0.02	0.31
CAN tgt overnight rate	0.75	0.50
CAN 3 Mo T-B	0.54	0.47

Foreign Exchange	2015	2016
EUR/USD	1.11	1.11
GBP/USD	1.55	1.32
USD/CAD	1.27	1.30
USD/JPY	121.99	104.44

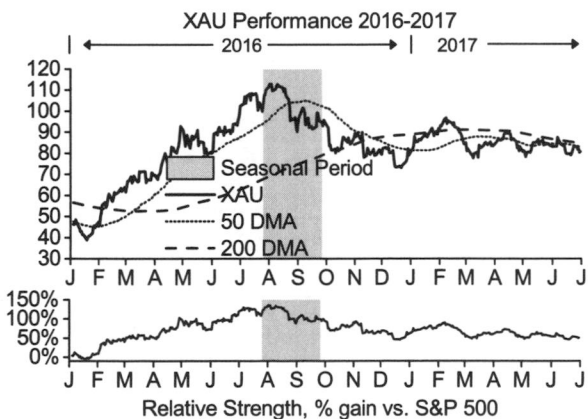

XAU Performance 2016-2017

Relative Strength, % gain vs. S&P 500

JULY

M	T	W	T	F	S	S
						1
2	3	4	5	6	7	8
9	10	11	12	13	14	15
16	17	18	19	20	21	22
23	24	25	26	27	28	29
30	31					

AUGUST

M	T	W	T	F	S	S
	1	2	3	4	5	
6	7	8	9	10	11	12
13	14	15	16	17	18	19
20	21	22	23	24	25	26
27	28	29	30	31		

SEPTEMBER

M	T	W	T	F	S	S
					1	2
3	4	5	6	7	8	9
10	11	12	13	14	15	16
17	18	19	20	21	22	23
24	25	26	27	28	29	30

From 1984 to 2016, gold miners have performed well in September on an average, median and frequency basis. The following month, October, has been the worst performing month for gold miners.

Over the last five years, January has been one of the strongest months for gold miners. In recent years, Chinese gold buying has increased at the beginning of the year, pushing up gold prices and gold miners.

In 2016, gold miners corrected in its seasonal period after a rally starting at the beginning of the year.

VIX Volatility Index
July 3rd to October 9th

The Chicago Board Options Exchange Market Volatility Index (VIX) is often referred to as a fear index as it measures investors' expectations of market volatility over the next thirty day period. The higher the VIX value, the greater the expectation of volatility and vice versa.

From 1990 to June 2017, the long-term average of the VIX is 19.5. In this time period, the VIX has bottomed at approximately 10 in the mid-90's, and the mid-2000's. In both cases, the VIX dropped below 10 for a few days.

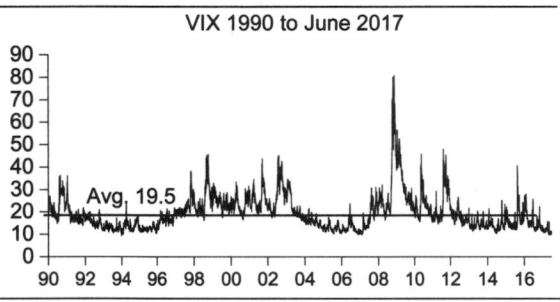
VIX 1990 to June 2017

VIX - Avg. Year 1990 to 2016

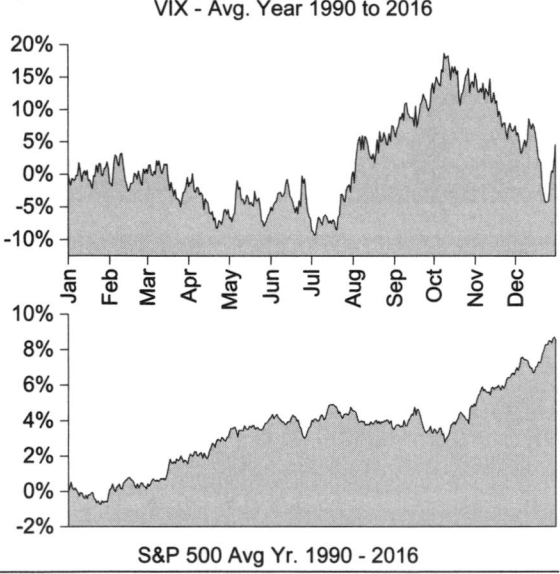
S&P 500 Avg Yr. 1990 - 2016

VIX* vs. S&P 500 1990 to 2016

July 3 to Oct 9	S&P 500	VIX %Gain (Positive)
1990	-15.1%	88.9%
1991	-0.2	5.2
1992	-2.2	47.8
1993	3.3	6.3
1994	2.0	3.9
1995	6.2	30.5
1996	3.4	13.4
1997	7.4	13.3
1998	-14.1	138.8
1999	-4.0	9.8
2000	-3.6	22.9
2001	-14.6	85.7
2002	-18.1	45.5
2003	4.5	-1.1
2004	-0.3	-0.2
2005	0.1	28.0
2006	6.3	-10.7
2007	3.0	4.7
2008	-27.9	146.6
2009	19.5	-17.3
2010	13.9	-31.2
2011	-13.8	128.1
2012	5.6	-2.6
2013	2.6	19.2
2014	-2.4	73.4
2015	-2.9	1.7
2016	2.4	-8.7
Avg	-1.4%	31.2%
Fq > 0	52%	74%

From 1990 to 2016, during the period of July 3rd to October 9th, the VIX has increased 74% of the time. On average, the VIX tends to start increasing in July, particularly after the earnings season gets underway. After mid-July, without the expectation of strong earnings ahead, investors tend to focus on economic forecasts that often become more dire in the second half of the year.

In addition, stock market analysts tend to reduce their earnings forecasts at this time. Both of these effects tend to add volatility in the markets, increasing the VIX. The VIX tends to peak in October as the stock market often starts to establishing a rising trend at this time.

Levels below 15 are often associated with investor complacency, as investors are expecting very little volatility. Very often when a stock market correction occurs in this state, it can be sharp and severe. Knowing the trends of the VIX can be useful in adjusting the amount of risk in a portfolio.

(i) *VIX - ticker symbol for the Chicago Board Options Exchange Market Volatility Index, measure implied volatility of S&P 500 index options*

VIX Performance

2016

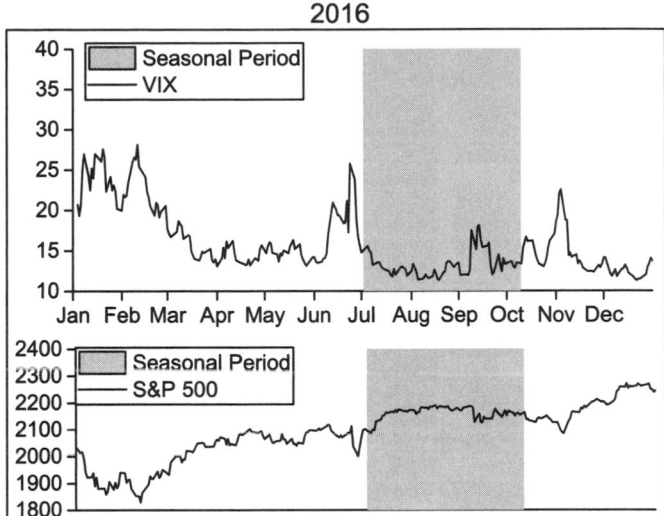

2017

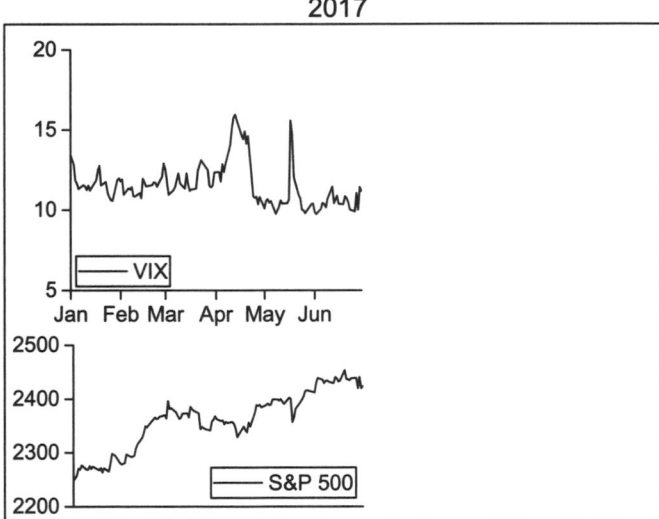

Market Indices & Rates Weekly Values**		
Stock Markets	**2015**	**2016**
Dow	18,058	18,555
S&P500	2,113	2,169
Nasdaq	5,130	5,071
TSX	14,634	14,551
FTSE	6,763	6,710
DAX	11,586	10,098
Nikkei	20,438	16,711
Hang Seng	25,196	21,865
Commodities	**2015**	**2016**
Oil	51.69	44.45
Gold	1147.2	1324.7
Bond Yields	**2015**	**2016**
USA 5 Yr Treasury	1.67	1.13
USA 10 Yr T	2.38	1.58
USA 20 Yr T	2.85	1.90
Moody's Aaa	4.22	3.34
Moody's Baa	5.27	4.24
CAN 5 Yr T	0.73	0.65
CAN 10 Yr T	1.62	1.10
Money Market	**2015**	**2016**
USA Fed Funds	0.25	0.50
USA 3 Mo T-B	0.02	0.32
CAN tgt overnight rate	0.50	0.50
CAN 3 Mo T-B	0.49	0.50
Foreign Exchange	**2015**	**2016**
EUR/USD	1.09	1.10
GBP/USD	1.56	1.32
USD/CAD	1.29	1.30
USD/JPY	123.77	106.22

An increase in volatility typically occurs at the beginning of July, just ahead of earnings season. Despite the pickup in volatility ahead of earnings, the S&P 500 tends to perform well for the first half of July.

In 2016, the VIX started at a high level and then dissipated to levels below 15 in March. In June the VIX once again rose as the stock market pulled back from its April highs. The VIX fell from July into the beginning of October.

In 2017, volatility maintained an overall downward trend for the first half of the year, and occasionally dropped below 10.

JULY

M	T	W	T	F	S	S
						1
2	3	4	5	6	7	8
9	10	11	12	13	14	15
16	17	18	19	20	21	22
23	24	25	26	27	28	29
30	31					

AUGUST

M	T	W	T	F	S	S
	1	2	3	4	5	
6	7	8	9	10	11	12
13	14	15	16	17	18	19
20	21	22	23	24	25	26
27	28	29	30	31		

SEPTEMBER

M	T	W	T	F	S	S
					1	2
3	4	5	6	7	8	9
10	11	12	13	14	15	16
17	18	19	20	21	22	23
24	25	26	27	28	29	30

Oil stocks tend to outperform the market from July 24th to October 3rd. Earlier in the year, there is another seasonal period of outperformance from late February to early May. Although the first seasonal period has had an incredible record of outperformance, the second seasonal period in July is still noteworthy.

While the seasonal period for oil stocks has more to do with oil inventories during the switch from producing heating oil to gasoline, the second seasonal period is more related to the conversion of production from gasoline to heating oil and the effects of the hurricane season.

1.5% extra

Oil (XOI) Sector - Avg. Year 1984 to 2016

Oil (XOI) / S&P 500 Relative Strength - Avg Yr. 1984 - 2016

XOI* vs. S&P 500 1984 to 2016			
Jul 24 to Oct 3	S&P 500	Positive XOI	Diff
1984	9.1 %	9.0 %	-0.1 %
1985	-4.3	6.7	11.0
1986	-2.1	15.7	17.7
1987	6.6	-1.2	-7.8
1988	3.0	-3.6	-6.6
1989	5.6	5.7	0.1
1990	-12.4	-0.5	11.8
1991	1.3	0.7	-0.7
1992	-0.4	2.9	3.3
1993	3.2	7.8	4.6
1994	1.9	-3.6	-5.5
1995	5.2	-2.2	-7.4
1996	10.5	7.7	-2.8
1997	3.0	8.9	5.9
1998	-12.0	1.4	13.5
1999	-5.5	-2.1	3.3
2000	-3.6	12.2	15.8
2001	-10.0	-5.1	4.8
2002	2.7	7.3	4.6
2003	4.2	5.5	1.4
2004	4.2	10.9	6.7
2005	-0.6	14.3	14.9
2006	7.6	-8.5	-16.9
2007	-0.1	-4.2	-4.1
2008	-14.3	-18.1	-3.8
2009	5.0	3.0	-2.0
2010	4.0	8.5	4.5
2011	-18.3	-26.0	-7.7
2012	7.4	6.1	-1.3
2013	-0.8	-0.8	0.0
2014	-1.0	-10.8	-9.8
2015	-7.2	-9.6	-2.4
2016	-0.6	2.2	2.8
Avg	-0.6 %	1.2 %	1.5 %
Fq > 0	52 %	58 %	55 %

First, there is a large difference between how heating oil and gasoline are stored and consumed. For individuals and businesses, gasoline is consumed in an immediate fashion. It is stored by the local distributor and the supplies are drawn upon as needed. Heating oil, on the other hand, is largely inventoried by individuals, farms and business operations in rural areas.

The inventory process starts before the cold weather arrives. The production facilities have to start switching from gasoline to heating oil, dropping their inventory levels and boosting prices. Second, the hurricane season can play havoc with the production of oil and

drive up prices substantially. The official duration of the hurricane season in the Gulf of Mexico is from June 1st to November 30th, but most major hurricanes occur in September and early October.

The threat of a strong hurricane can shut down the oil platforms temporarily, interrupting production. If a strong hurricane strikes the platforms, it can do significant damage and put the them out of commission for an extended period of time.

*NYSE Arca Oil Index (XOI): An index designed to represent a cross section of widely held oil corporations involved in various phases of the oil industry. For more information on the XOI index, see www.cboe.com

NYSE Arca Oil Index (XOI) Performance

XOI Monthly Performance (1984-2016)

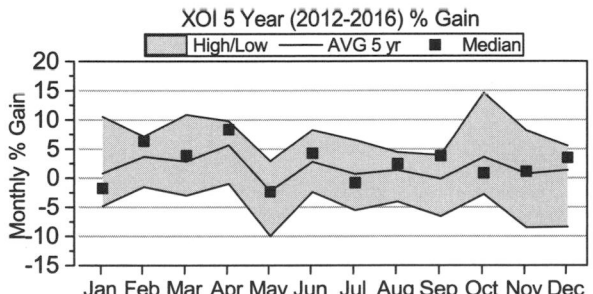

	Jan	Feb	Mar	Apr	May	Jun	Jul	Aug	Sep	Oct	Nov	Dec
Avg. % Gain	0.5	0.8	3.1	3.2	0.6	-0.8	0.3	0.8	-0.2	0.3	-0.4	1.8
Med. % Gain	0.1	1.6	2.7	2.5	0.8	-1.8	1.2	0.5	0.0	-0.0	0.8	1.0
Fq %>0	48	55	73	82	61	39	55	58	52	48	55	64
Fq %>S&P 500	33	55	67	64	39	36	48	64	58	52	36	55

XOI 5 Year (2012-2016) % Gain

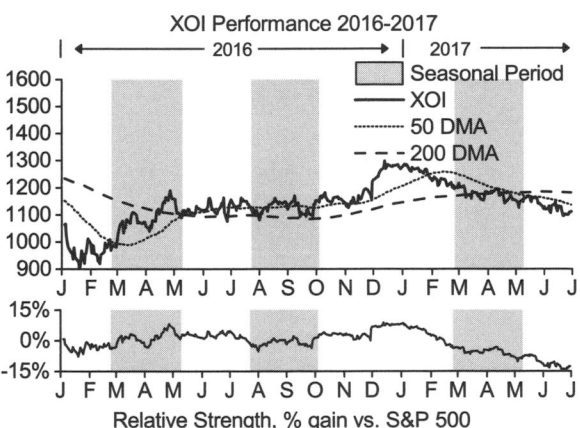

XOI Performance 2016-2017

Relative Strength, % gain vs. S&P 500

Market Indices & Rates Weekly Values**

Stock Markets	2015	2016
Dow	17,834	18,466
S&P500	2,109	2,170
Nasdaq	5,167	5,133
TSX	14,312	14,546
FTSE	6,692	6,726
DAX	11,544	10,276
Nikkei	20,666	16,543
Hang Seng	25,350	22,082

Commodities	2015	2016
Oil	49.12	41.99
Gold	1095.4	1329.8

Bond Yields	2015	2016
USA 5 Yr Treasury	1.68	1.10
USA 10 Yr T	2.32	1.53
USA 20 Yr T	2.73	1.85
Moody's Aaa	4.13	3.29
Moody's Baa	5.18	4.20
CAN 5 Yr T	0.73	0.65
CAN 10 Yr T	1.54	1.08

Money Market	2015	2016
USA Fed Funds	0.25	0.50
USA 3 Mo T-B	0.04	0.29
CAN tgt overnight rate	0.50	0.50
CAN 3 Mo T-B	0.42	0.52

Foreign Exchange	2015	2016
EUR/USD	1.09	1.11
GBP/USD	1.56	1.32
USD/CAD	1.30	1.32
USD/JPY	123.97	104.64

From 1984 to 2016, oil stocks have had a secondary seasonal period from late July to early October. The returns in this secondary seasonal period have largely been focused in August.

Over the last five years, the returns in the secondary seasonal period have on average been negative.

In 2016, oil stocks advanced during their secondary seasonal period. After a rally from October to December, oil stocks corrected into 2017.

JULY

M	T	W	T	F	S	S
						1
2	3	4	5	6	7	8
9	10	11	12	13	14	15
16	17	18	19	20	21	22
23	24	25	26	27	28	29
30	31					

AUGUST

M	T	W	T	F	S	S
	1	2	3	4	5	
6	7	8	9	10	11	12
13	14	15	16	17	18	19
20	21	22	23	24	25	26
27	28	29	30	31		

SEPTEMBER

M	T	W	T	F	S	S
					1	2
3	4	5	6	7	8	9
10	11	12	13	14	15	16
17	18	19	20	21	22	23
24	25	26	27	28	29	30

Seasonal Investment Timeline[1]

Investment	Season		
Core Positions			
S&P 500	Oct 28 - May 5		
TSX Composite	Oct 28 - May 5		
Cash	May 6 - Oct 27		
Primary Sectors			
[4]Consumer Staples	Jan 1 - Jan 22 (S)	Apr 23 - Oct 27	
Financials	Dec 15 - Apr 13		
Energy	Feb 25 - May 9	Jul 24 - Oct 3	
[2]Utilities	Jul 17 - Oct 3	Jan 1 - Mar 13 (S)	
Health Care	Aug 15 - Oct 18		
Information Tech	Oct 9 - Jan 17	Apr 16 - Apr 30	
Consumer Disc.	Oct 28 - Apr 22		
Industrials	Oct 28 - Dec 31	Jan 23- May 5	
Materials	Oct 28 - Jan 6	Jan 23 - May 5	
Small Cap	Dec 19 - Mar 7		
Secondary Sectors			
Silver Bullion	Jan - Mar & Sep & Nov		
[2]Platinum	Jan 1 - May 31		
Software Jan1 - Jan19	Jun 1 - Jun 30	Oct 10 - Dec 5	
[3]Semiconductors	Jan 1 - Mar 7	Oct 28 - Nov 6	
Canadian Dollar	Apr 1 - Apr 30	Aug 20 - Sep 25	
Biotech	Jun 23 - Sep 13		
Gold Bullion	Jul 12 - Oct 9		
Gold Stocks (XAU)	Jul 27 - Sep 25		
Agriculture	Sep 26 - Nov 11		
Transportation Jan23-Apr16	Aug 3 - Oct 9 (S)	Oct 10 - Nov 13	
Natural Gas Mar22 - Jun19	Sep 6 - Dec 21	Dec 22 - Dec 31(S)	
Airlines	Oct 3 - Nov 6	Aug 1- Aug 31 (S)	
Canadian Banks	Oct 10 - Dec 31	Jan 23 - Apr 13	
Retail	Oct 28 - Nov 29	Jan 21 - Apr 12	
Homebuilders	Oct 28 - Feb 3	Apr 27- Jun 13(S)	
Metals & Mining	Nov 19 - Jan 5	Jan 23 - May 5	
Emerging Markets	Nov 24 - April 18		
Aerospace & Defense	Dec 12 - May 5		
Automotive Dec14 - Jan7	Feb 24 - Apr 24	Aug 3- Oct 3 (S)	
Other Market / Sector Trades			
Nikkei 225	May 6 - Nov 19 (S)		
VIX (CBOE)	Jul 3 - Oct 9		
Canadian Snowbird Trade	Oct 28 - Dec 18		
Currency			
CAD / USD	Apr 1 - Apr 30	Aug 20 - Sep 25	
EUR / USD	Nov 17 - Dec 31		
USD / EUR	Jan 1 - Feb 7		
Fixed Income			
[3]U.S. Gov. Bonds	May 9 - Oct 3		
[3]U.S. High Yield	Nov 24 - Jan 8		

2017   2018

O N D J F M A M J J A S O N D

Long Investment ▨▨▨   Short Investment (S) ▭   [1] Holiday, End of Month, Witches' Hangover, - et al not included.
[2]Thackray's 2012 Investor's Guide [3]Thackray's 2013 Investor's Guide [4]Thackray's 2014 Investor's Guide [5]Thackray's 2015 Investor's Guide
[6]Thackray's 2016 Investor's Guide [7]Thackray's 2017 Investor's Guide

Seasonal Investment Timeline[1]

Investment	Season		
Stocks			

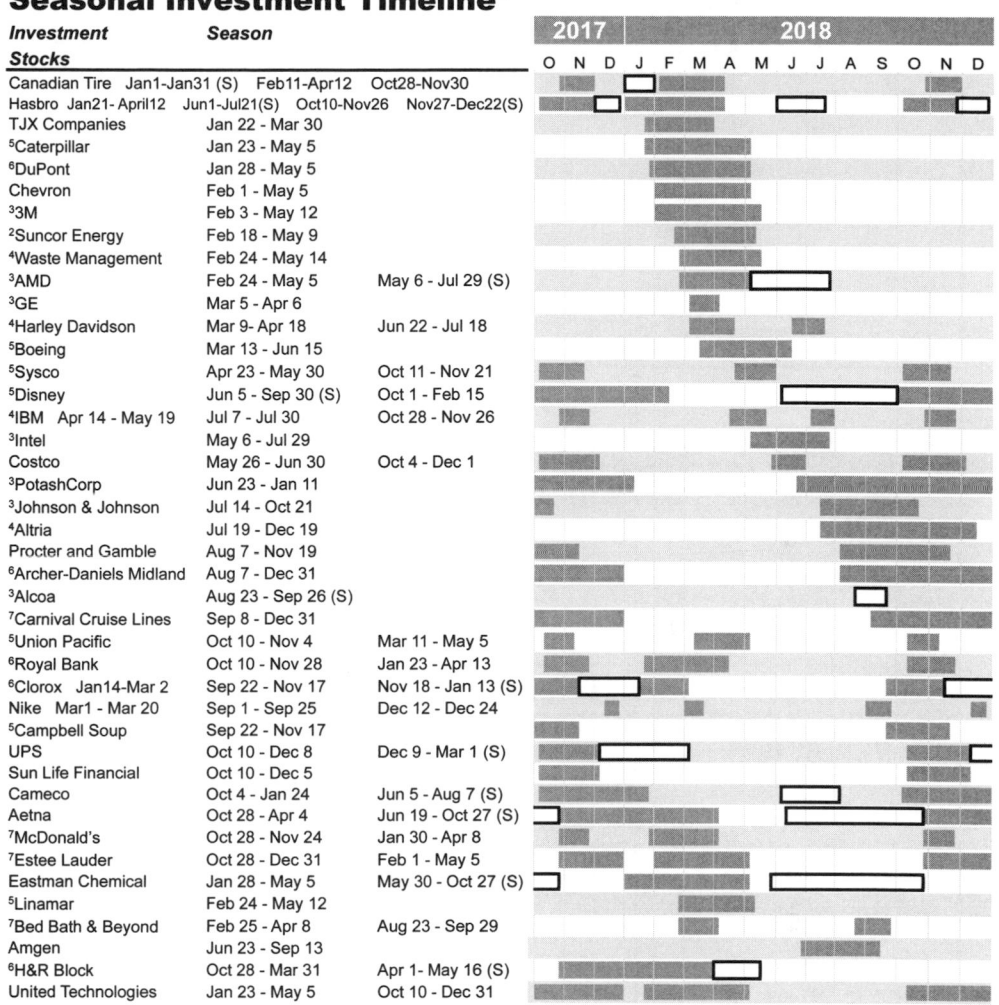

Investment	Season		
Canadian Tire Jan1-Jan31 (S)	Feb11-Apr12	Oct28-Nov30	
Hasbro Jan21- April12	Jun1-Jul21(S)	Oct10-Nov26	Nov27-Dec22(S)
TJX Companies	Jan 22 - Mar 30		
[5]Caterpillar	Jan 23 - May 5		
[6]DuPont	Jan 28 - May 5		
Chevron	Feb 1 - May 5		
[3]3M	Feb 3 - May 12		
[2]Suncor Energy	Feb 18 - May 9		
[4]Waste Management	Feb 24 - May 14		
[3]AMD	Feb 24 - May 5	May 6 - Jul 29 (S)	
[3]GE	Mar 5 - Apr 6		
[4]Harley Davidson	Mar 9- Apr 18	Jun 22 - Jul 18	
[5]Boeing	Mar 13 - Jun 15		
[5]Sysco	Apr 23 - May 30	Oct 11 - Nov 21	
[5]Disney	Jun 5 - Sep 30 (S)	Oct 1 - Feb 15	
[4]IBM Apr 14 - May 19	Jul 7 - Jul 30	Oct 28 - Nov 26	
[3]Intel	May 6 - Jul 29		
Costco	May 26 - Jun 30	Oct 4 - Dec 1	
[3]PotashCorp	Jun 23 - Jan 11		
[3]Johnson & Johnson	Jul 14 - Oct 21		
[4]Altria	Jul 19 - Dec 19		
Procter and Gamble	Aug 7 - Nov 19		
[6]Archer-Daniels Midland	Aug 7 - Dec 31		
[3]Alcoa	Aug 23 - Sep 26 (S)		
[7]Carnival Cruise Lines	Sep 8 - Dec 31		
[5]Union Pacific	Oct 10 - Nov 4	Mar 11 - May 5	
[6]Royal Bank	Oct 10 - Nov 28	Jan 23 - Apr 13	
[6]Clorox Jan14-Mar 2	Sep 22 - Nov 17	Nov 18 - Jan 13 (S)	
Nike Mar1 - Mar 20	Sep 1 - Sep 25	Dec 12 - Dec 24	
[5]Campbell Soup	Sep 22 - Nov 17		
UPS	Oct 10 - Dec 8	Dec 9 - Mar 1 (S)	
Sun Life Financial	Oct 10 - Dec 5		
Cameco	Oct 4 - Jan 24	Jun 5 - Aug 7 (S)	
Aetna	Oct 28 - Apr 4	Jun 19 - Oct 27 (S)	
[7]McDonald's	Oct 28 - Nov 24	Jan 30 - Apr 8	
[7]Estee Lauder	Oct 28 - Dec 31	Feb 1 - May 5	
Eastman Chemical	Jan 28 - May 5	May 30 - Oct 27 (S)	
[5]Linamar	Feb 24 - May 12		
[7]Bed Bath & Beyond	Feb 25 - Apr 8	Aug 23 - Sep 29	
Amgen	Jun 23 - Sep 13		
[6]H&R Block	Oct 28 - Mar 31	Apr 1- May 16 (S)	
United Technologies	Jan 23 - May 5	Oct 10 - Dec 31	

Long Investment ▓▓▓ Short Investment (S) ▭ [1] Holiday, End of Month, Witches' Hangover, - et al not included.

[2]Thackray's 2012 Investor's Guide [3]Thackray's 2013 Investor's Guide [4]Thackray's 2014 Investor's Guide [5]Thackray's 2015 Investor's Guide
[6]Thackray's 2016 Investor's Guide [7]Thackray's 2017 Investor's Guide

AUGUST

	MONDAY	TUESDAY	WEDNESDAY
WEEK 31	30	31	1 30
WEEK 32	6 25 CAN Market Closed- Civic Day	7 24	8 23
WEEK 33	13 18	14 17	15 16
WEEK 34	20 11	21 10	22 9
WEEK 35	27 4	28 3	29 2

THURSDAY   FRIDAY

2	29	**3**	28

9	22	**10**	21

16	15	**17**	14

23	8	**24**	7

30	1	**31**	

SEPTEMBER

M	T	W	T	F	S	S
					1	2
3	4	5	6	7	8	9
7	11	12	13	14	15	16
17	18	19	20	21	22	23
24	25	26	27	28	29	30

OCTOBER

M	T	W	T	F	S	S
1	2	3	4	5	6	7
8	9	10	11	12	13	14
15	16	17	18	19	20	21
22	23	24	25	26	27	28
29	30	31				

NOVEMBER

M	T	W	T	F	S	S
			1	2	3	4
5	6	7	8	9	10	11
12	13	14	15	16	17	18
19	20	21	22	23	24	25
26	27	28	29	30		

DECEMBER

M	T	W	T	F	S	S
					1	2
3	4	5	6	7	8	9
10	11	12	13	14	15	16
17	18	19	20	21	22	23
24	25	26	27	28	29	30
31						

AUGUST
SUMMARY

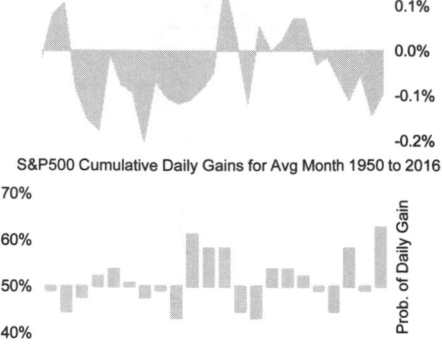

	Dow Jones	S&P 500	Nasdaq	TSX Comp
Month Rank	10	11	11	10
# Up	37	36	24	18
# Down	30	31	21	14
% Pos	55	54	53	56
% Avg. Gain	-0.2	-0.1	0.1	-0.2

Dow & S&P 1950-2016, Nasdaq 1972-2016, TSX 1985-2016

S&P500 Cumulative Daily Gains for Avg Month 1950 to 2016

♦ August is typically a marginal month and has been the fourth worst month for the S&P 500 from 1950 to 2016. ♦ If there is a summer rally in July, it is often in jeopardy in August. ♦ In 2016, the S&P 500 rallied in July and then faded in August, producing a nominal loss of 0.1% in August. ♦ The TSX Composite is usually one of the better performing markets in August, but its strength is largely dependent on oil and gold stocks.

BEST / WORST AUGUST BROAD MKTS. 2007-2016

BEST AUGUST MARKETS
- ♦ FTSE 100 (2009) 6.5%
- ♦ Russell 2000 (2014) 4.8%
- ♦ Nasdaq (2014) 4.8%

WORST AUGUST MARKETS
- ♦ Nikkei 225 (2011) -8.9%
- ♦ Russell 2000 (2011) -8.8%
- ♦ Nikkei 225 (2015) - 8.2%

Index Values End of Month

	2007	2008	2009	2010	2011	2012	2013	2014	2015	2016
Dow	13,358	11,544	9,496	10,015	11,614	13,091	14,810	17,098	16,528	18,401
S&P 500	1,474	1,283	1,021	1,049	1,219	1,407	1,633	2,003	1,972	2,171
Nasdaq	2,596	2,368	2,009	2,114	2,579	3,067	3,590	4,580	4,777	5,213
TSX Comp.	13,660	13,771	10,868	11,914	12,769	11,949	12,654	15,626	13,859	14,598
Russell 1000	803	702	558	578	675	775	909	1,118	1,101	1,203
Russell 2000	793	740	572	602	727	812	1,011	1,174	1,159	1,240
FTSE 100	6,303	5,637	4,909	5,225	5,395	5,711	6,413	6,820	6,248	6,782
Nikkei 225	16,569	13,073	10,493	8,824	8,955	8,840	13,389	15,425	18,890	16,887

Percent Gain for August

	2007	2008	2009	2010	2011	2012	2013	2014	2015	2016
Dow	1.1	1.5	3.5	-4.3	-4.4	0.6	-4.4	3.2	-6.6	-0.2
S&P 500	1.3	1.2	3.4	-4.7	-5.7	2.0	-3.1	3.8	-6.3	-0.1
Nasdaq	2.0	1.8	1.5	-6.2	-6.4	4.3	-1.0	4.8	-6.9	1.0
TSX Comp.	-1.5	1.3	0.8	1.7	-1.4	2.4	1.3	1.9	-4.2	0.1
Russell 1000	1.4	1.2	3.4	-4.7	-6.0	2.2	-3.0	3.9	-6.2	-0.1
Russell 2000	2.2	3.5	2.8	-7.5	-8.8	3.2	-3.3	4.8	-6.4	1.6
FTSE 100	-0.9	4.2	6.5	-0.6	-7.2	1.4	-3.1	1.3	-6.7	0.8
Nikkei 225	-3.9	-2.3	1.3	-7.5	-8.9	1.7	-2.0	-1.3	-8.2	1.9

August Market Avg. Performance 2007 to 2016[1]

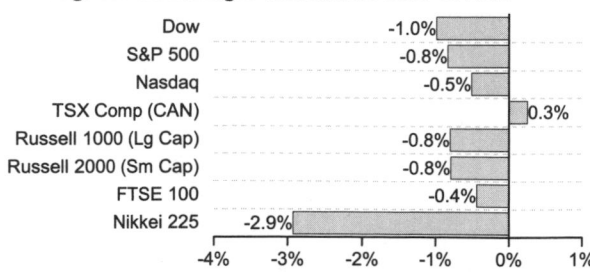

Dow	-1.0%
S&P 500	-0.8%
Nasdaq	-0.5%
TSX Comp (CAN)	0.3%
Russell 1000 (Lg Cap)	-0.8%
Russell 2000 (Sm Cap)	-0.8%
FTSE 100	-0.4%
Nikkei 225	-2.9%

Interest Corner Aug[2]

	Fed Funds % [3]	3 Mo. T-Bill % [4]	10 Yr % [5]	20 Yr % [6]
2016	0.50	0.33	1.58	1.90
2015	0.25	0.08	2.21	2.64
2014	0.25	0.03	2.35	2.83
2013	0.25	0.03	2.78	3.46
2012	0.25	0.09	1.57	2.29

(1) Russell Data provided by Russell (2) Federal Reserve Bank of St. Louis- end of month values (3) Target rate set by FOMC (4)(5)(6) Constant yield maturities.

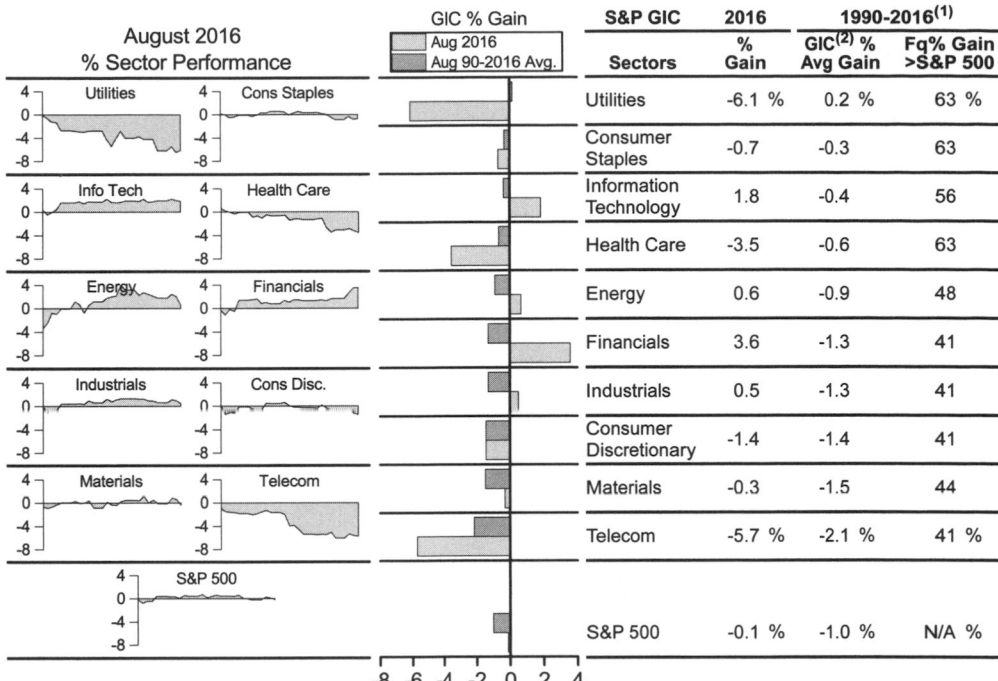

S&P GIC Sectors	2016 % Gain	1990-2016[1] GIC[2] % Avg Gain	Fq% Gain >S&P 500
Utilities	-6.1 %	0.2 %	63 %
Consumer Staples	-0.7	-0.3	63
Information Technology	1.8	-0.4	56
Health Care	-3.5	-0.6	63
Energy	0.6	-0.9	48
Financials	3.6	-1.3	41
Industrials	0.5	-1.3	41
Consumer Discretionary	-1.4	-1.4	41
Materials	-0.3	-1.5	44
Telecom	-5.7 %	-2.1 %	41 %
S&P 500	-0.1 %	-1.0 %	N/A %

Sector Commentary

♦ In August 2016, the S&P 500 lost a nominal 0.1%. ♦ The financial sector put in a strong performance for the month, with a gain of 3.6%. ♦ Information technology continued its rally with a gain of 1.8%. ♦ The health care sector produced a large loss of 3.5% as investors questioned the possible actions of an upcoming new president and the resulting impact on the health care sector. ♦ The other defensive sectors of the market (consumer staples, utilities and telecom) also produced losses as investors remained committed to higher beta sectors in the stock market, such as technology.

Sub-Sector Commentary

♦ In August 2016, the metals and mining sub-sector produced a large loss of 12.4%. ♦ The steel sub-sector followed suit with a loss of 9.6% which is often weak in the summer months. ♦ Pharma also produced a fairly large loss as the overall health care sector was weak during August. ♦ The semiconductor sub-sector (SOX) once again had a strong month, with a gain of 4.5% to continue its 2016 rally.

SELECTED SUB-SECTORS[3]			
Gold	-2.4 %	0.6 %	48 %
Biotech (1993-2016)	-1.9	0.4	58
Agriculture (1994-2016)	-2.9	0.2	52
Home-builders	-0.5	0.1	56
SOX (1995-2016)	4.5	-0.3	55
Retail	-1.7	-0.5	59
Silver	-6.5	-0.6	48
Pharma	-5.4	-0.8	56
Banks	7.1	-1.1	37
Chemicals	1.6	-1.5	44
Metals & Mining	-12.4	-1.6	48
Railroads	2.3	-2.4	44
Transportation	1.2	-2.7	33
Automotive & Components	0.1	-3.3	33
Steel	-9.6	-3.6	48

(1) Sector data provided by Standard and Poors (2) GIC is short form for Global Industry Classification (3) Sub Sector data provided by Standard and Poors, except where marked by symbol.

AIRLINES – DESCEND IN AUGUST SOAR IN OCTOBER
①SELL SHORT (August) ②LONG (Oct3-Nov6)

Airline flights are seasonal based upon the time of year that flights are taken. Airline flights are often used in statistics classes to demonstrate time series seasonality. There are differences between the seasonality of different airlines depending on their business model. International charter airlines have somewhat different seasonality trends compared to domestic airlines.

Overall, airlines book most of their seats in the summer, particularly July and around the holidays.

12.0% growth & positive 81% of the time

It is typically best to avoid the airline sector in August; although it is still considered part of the airlines "high season," it is at the back end of the season and any benefits have probably already been incorporated into the price of stocks in the sector. From 1990 to 2016, the airline sector in August has produced an average loss of 4.6% and has only been positive 30% of the time.

Historically, the best time for the sector has been from October 3rd to November 6th. Although this is a relatively short period, this is the sweet spot for airline sector performance. One factor driving performance at this time is that this period, on average, is one of the worst seasonal periods for oil prices. Oil is a large part of the cost of running airlines. Also, expectations for stronger economic growth in the next year, tend to surface at this time, helping to boost economically sensitive sectors.

*The SP GICS Airlines Sector encompasses a wide range airline based companies.
For more information, see www.standardandpoors.com

Airlines vs. S&P 500 1990 to 2016

Positive Long ▨   Negative Short ☐

Year	Aug 1 to Aug 31 S&P 500	Aug 1 to Aug 31 Air-lines	Oct 3 to Nov 6 S&P 500	Oct 3 to Nov 6 Air-lines	Compound Growth S&P 500	Compound Growth Air-lines
1990	-9.4 %	-21.1 %	-1.1 %	0.0 %	-10.5 %	21.1 %
1991	2.0	-6.9	0.4	4.8	2.4	12.0
1992	-2.4	-11.6	1.7	14.4	-0.7	27.7
1993	3.4	3.0	-0.4	8.3	3.1	5.0
1994	3.8	2.1	-0.1	5.0	3.7	2.8
1995	0.0	-7.5	1.2	0.7	1.1	8.3
1996	1.9	0.4	4.4	5.6	6.4	5.2
1997	-5.7	-5.5	-2.3	9.3	-7.9	15.3
1998	-14.6	-20.7	13.8	16.4	-2.8	40.5
1999	-0.6	-11.4	6.8	12.6	6.1	25.4
2000	6.1	-5.4	-0.3	14.6	5.8	20.8
2001	-6.4	-11.4	6.4	3.9	-0.4	15.7
2002	0.5	2.8	11.6	31.4	12.1	27.7
2003	1.8	4.6	3.7	3.0	5.6	-1.7
2004	0.2	1.1	3.1	19.1	3.3	17.8
2005	-1.1	-7.8	-0.7	9.8	-1.8	18.3
2006	2.1	-3.7	3.6	-11.4	5.8	-8.1
2007	1.3	-3.5	-1.7	-8.8	-0.4	-5.6
2008	1.2	-2.3	-18.8	-17.2	-17.8	-15.3
2009	3.4	4.2	4.3	-6.0	7.8	-9.9
2010	-4.7	-8.3	7.0	9.7	1.9	18.8
2011	-5.7	-13.5	10.8	6.1	4.5	20.4
2012	2.0	-2.7	-1.2	1.9	0.8	4.7
2013	-3.1	-7.4	4.5	14.3	1.2	22.8
2014	3.8	8.5	4.4	19.6	8.3	9.4
2015	-6.3	-1.0	7.6	17.7	0.8	18.9
2016	-0.1	0.0	-3.8	7.4	-3.9	7.4
Avg.	-1.0 %	-4.6 %	2.4 %	7.1 %	1.3 %	12.0 %
Fq>0	52 %	30 %	63 %	81 %	67 %	81 %

From 1990 to 2016, short selling the airline sector for the month of August and then investing in the sector from October 3rd to November 6th has produced an average gain of 12.0%

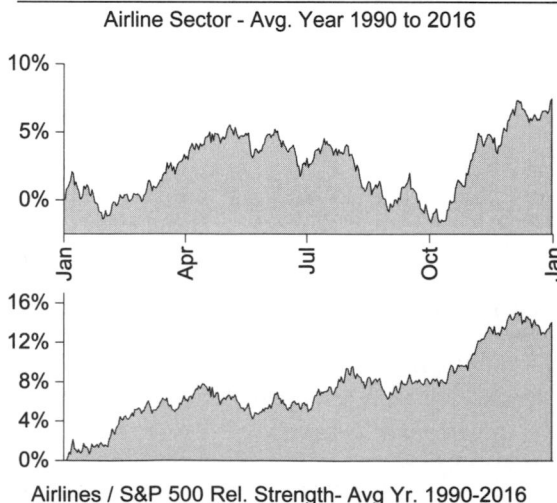

Airline Sector - Avg. Year 1990 to 2016

Airlines / S&P 500 Rel. Strength- Avg Yr. 1990-2016

Airlines Performance

Airlines Monthly Performance (1990-2016)

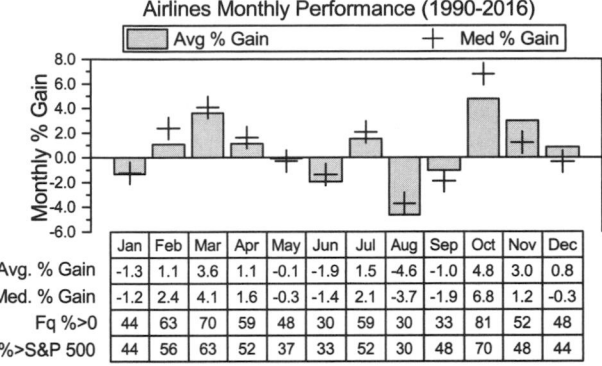

	Jan	Feb	Mar	Apr	May	Jun	Jul	Aug	Sep	Oct	Nov	Dec
Avg. % Gain	-1.3	1.1	3.6	1.1	-0.1	-1.9	1.5	-4.6	-1.0	4.8	3.0	0.8
Med. % Gain	-1.2	2.4	4.1	1.6	-0.3	-1.4	2.1	-3.7	-1.9	6.8	1.2	-0.3
Fq %>0	44	63	70	59	48	30	59	30	33	81	52	48
Fq %>S&P 500	44	56	63	52	37	33	52	30	48	70	48	44

Airlines 5 Year (2012-2016) % Gain

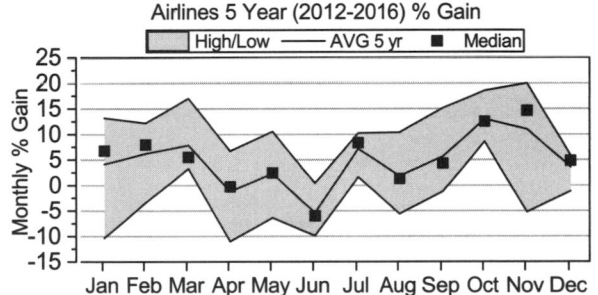

Airlines Performance 2016-2017

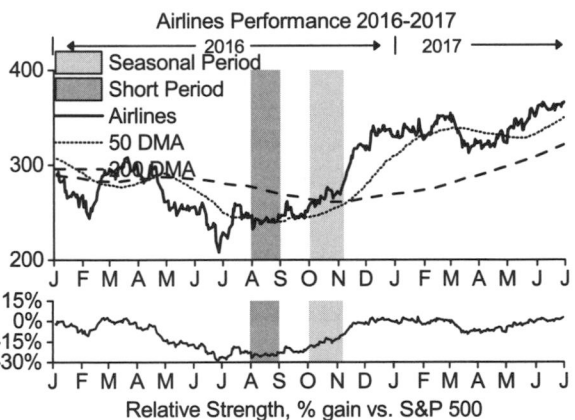

Relative Strength, % gain vs. S&P 500

Market Indices & Rates Weekly Values**

Stock Markets	2015	2016
Dow	17,652	18,394
S&P500	2,096	2,168
Nasdaq	5,100	5,174
TSX	14,246	14,542
FTSE	6,611	6,701
DAX	11,202	10,248
Nikkei	20,418	16,324
Hang Seng	24,522	21,962
Commodities	2015	2016
Oil	47.96	40.83
Gold	1094.5	1355.1
Bond Yields	2015	2016
USA 5 Yr Treasury	1.59	1.07
USA 10 Yr T	2.25	1.54
USA 20 Yr T	2.65	1.87
Moody's Aaa	4.06	3.40
Moody's Baa	5.16	4.29
CAN 5 Yr T	0.80	0.62
CAN 10 Yr T	1.48	1.06
Money Market	2015	2016
USA Fed Funds	0.25	0.50
USA 3 Mo T-B	0.06	0.28
CAN tgt overnight rate	0.50	0.50
CAN 3 Mo T-B	0.41	0.52
Foreign Exchange	2015	2016
EUR/USD	1.10	1.12
GBP/USD	1.56	1.32
USD/CAD	1.30	1.31
USD/JPY	123.76	101.51

AUGUST

M	T	W	T	F	S	S
	1	2	3	4	5	
6	7	8	9	10	11	12
13	14	15	16	17	18	19
20	21	22	23	24	25	26
27	28	29	30	31		

SEPTEMBER

M	T	W	T	F	S	S
					1	2
3	4	5	6	7	8	9
10	11	12	13	14	15	16
17	18	19	20	21	22	23
24	25	26	27	28	29	30

OCTOBER

M	T	W	T	F	S	S
1	2	3	4	5	6	7
8	9	10	11	12	13	14
15	16	17	18	19	20	21
22	23	24	25	26	27	28
29	30	31				

From 1990 to 2016, August has been the worst month of the year for the airline sector based upon average, median and frequency measurements. On the other hand, October has been the strongest month.

Over the last five years, the airline sector has generally followed its seasonal trend: October and November have been the two best months, August has been one of the weaker months of the year.

In 2016, the airline sector was nominally negative in its weak seasonal period and positive in its strong seasonal period.

TRANSPORTATION – ON A ROLL

①LONG (Jan23-Apr16) ②SELL SHORT (Aug1-Oct9)
③LONG (Oct10-Nov13)

The transportation sector can provide a "hilly" ride as the seasonal trends rise and fall throughout the year.

Activity in the transportation sub-sectors; railroads, airlines and freight, tends to bottom in February.

15.9% gain & positive 89% of the time

Increased transportation activity in the spring, coupled with a typically positive economic outlook in the first part of the year, creates a positive seasonal trend, starting January 23rd and lasting until April 16th.

The next seasonal period is a weak period, giving investors an opportunity to sell short the sector and profit from its decline. This negative seasonal period lasts from August 1st to October 9th and is largely the result of investors questioning economic growth at this time of the year.

The third seasonal period is positive and occurs from October 10th to November 13th. This trend is the result of a generally improved economic outlook at this time of the year and investors wanting to get into the sector ahead of earnings announcements.

The SP GICS Transportation Sector encompasses a wide range transportation based companies. For more information, see www.standardandpoors.com

Transportation Sector* vs. S&P 500 1990 to 2016

Negative Short ☐   Positive Long ▨

Year	Jan 23 to Apr 16		Aug 1 to Oct 9		Oct 10 to Nov 13		Compound Growth	
	S&P 500	Trans port	S&P 500	Trans port	S&P 500	Trans port	S&P 500	Trans port
1990	4.4 %	4.1 %	-14.3 %	-19.2 %	4.1 %	3.3 %	-6.9 %	28.1 %
1991	18.1	11.4	-2.8	0.5	5.5	9.6	21.0	21.5
1992	-0.5	3.7	-5.1	-9.1	4.9	14.1	-0.9	29.1
1993	2.9	9.1	2.7	-0.3	1.1	6.4	6.9	16.5
1994	-6.0	-10.7	-0.7	-9.3	1.6	0.8	-5.2	-1.6
1995	9.6	10.5	2.9	-1.3	2.4	5.0	15.5	17.6
1996	5.2	9.4	8.9	4.9	4.9	6.1	20.1	10.4
1997	-2.9	-2.0	1.7	0.9	-5.6	-5.4	-6.7	-8.2
1998	15.1	12.2	-12.2	-16.5	14.4	12.5	15.6	47.0
1999	7.7	17.7	0.6	-11.0	4.5	4.0	13.1	35.8
2000	-5.9	-2.7	-2.0	-6.0	-3.6	13.0	-11.1	16.6
2001	12.2	0.1	-12.8	-20.0	7.8	14.1	-17.4	37.0
2002	0.8	6.9	-14.8	-11.2	13.6	8.2	-2.4	28.6
2003	0.2	0.6	4.9	4.9	1.9	8.0	7.1	3.3
2004	-0.8	-2.9	1.9	6.6	5.5	11.1	6.6	0.7
2005	-2.2	-5.1	-3.1	-0.5	3.3	9.0	-2.1	3.9
2006	2.2	13.2	5.8	6.4	2.5	3.8	10.8	9.9
2007	3.2	4.8	7.6	-0.2	-5.4	-2.9	5.0	1.9
2008	4.1	19.1	-28.2	-23.5	0.2	4.0	-25.1	52.9
2009	4.6	7.2	8.5	6.7	2.1	5.9	15.8	5.9
2010	9.2	17.4	5.8	7.9	2.9	2.5	18.9	10.9
2011	2.8	2.2	-10.6	-11.8	9.4	11.4	0.6	26.9
2012	4.1	-2.0	4.5	-3.5	-4.6	-1.1	3.8	0.3
2013	5.5	3.5	-1.7	1.8	7.6	10.9	11.5	12.7
2014	1.0	1.7	-0.1	2.6	5.8	14.9	6.6	13.8
2015	2.0	-10.0	-4.2	-0.7	0.4	-2.0	-1.9	-11.2
2016	9.1	16.4	-0.9	4.3	0.5	6.4	8.7	18.6
Avg.	3.0 %	5.0 %	-2.1 %	-3.6 %	3.2 %	6.4 %	4.0 %	15.9 %
Fq>0	74 %	74 %	44 %	41 %	85 %	85 %	63 %	89 %

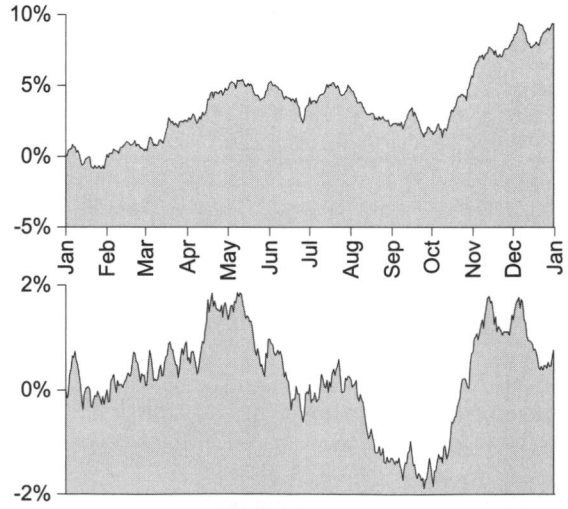

Transportation Sector - Avg. Year 1990 to 2016

Transportation / S&P 500 Rel. Strength- Avg Yr. 1990-2016

Transportation Performance

Transportation Monthly Performance (1990-2016)

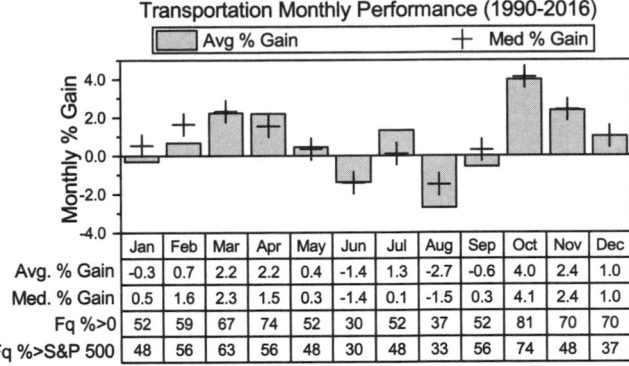

	Jan	Feb	Mar	Apr	May	Jun	Jul	Aug	Sep	Oct	Nov	Dec
Avg. % Gain	-0.3	0.7	2.2	2.2	0.4	-1.4	1.3	-2.7	-0.6	4.0	2.4	1.0
Med. % Gain	0.5	1.6	2.3	1.5	0.3	-1.4	0.1	-1.5	0.3	4.1	2.4	1.0
Fq %>0	52	59	67	74	52	30	52	37	52	81	70	70
Fq %>S&P 500	48	56	63	56	48	30	48	33	56	74	48	37

Transportation 5 Year (2012-2016) % Gain

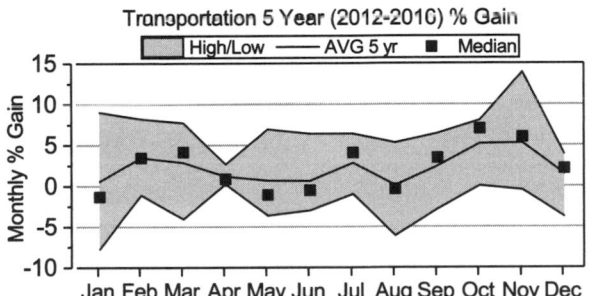

Transportation Performance 2016-2017

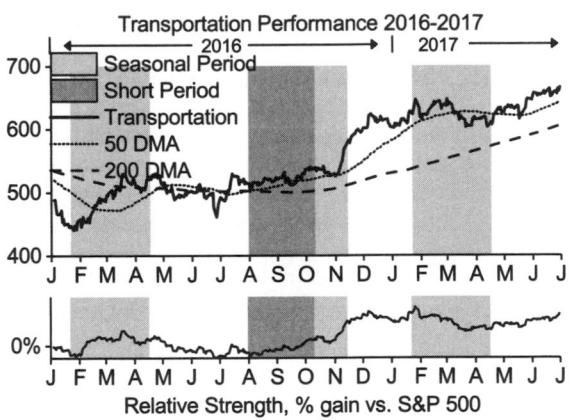

Relative Strength, % gain vs. S&P 500

Market Indices & Rates
Weekly Values**

Stock Markets	2015	2016
Dow	17,496	18,550
S&P500	2,090	2,182
Nasdaq	5,092	5,221
TSX	14,426	14,775
FTSE	6,719	6,872
DAX	11,522	10,646
Nikkei	20,614	16,768
Hang Seng	24,452	22,560

Commodities	2015	2016
Oil	44.92	43.10
Gold	1090.2	1346.5

Bond Yields	2015	2016
USA 5 Yr Treasury	1.60	1.12
USA 10 Yr T	2.22	1.54
USA 20 Yr T	2.58	1.87
Moody's Aaa	4.02	3.34
Moody's Baa	5.12	4.25
CAN 5 Yr T	0.78	0.60
CAN 10 Yr T	1.44	1.02

Money Market	2015	2016
USA Fed Funds	0.25	0.50
USA 3 Mo T-B	0.07	0.29
CAN tgt overnight rate	0.50	0.50
CAN 3 Mo T-B	0.39	0.51

Foreign Exchange	2015	2016
EUR/USD	1.09	1.11
GBP/USD	1.56	1.30
USD/CAD	1.32	1.31
USD/JPY	124.45	101.78

AUGUST

M	T	W	T	F	S	S
	1	2	3	4	5	
6	7	8	9	10	11	12
13	14	15	16	17	18	19
20	21	22	23	24	25	26
27	28	29	30	31		

SEPTEMBER

M	T	W	T	F	S	S
					1	2
3	4	5	6	7	8	9
10	11	12	13	14	15	16
17	18	19	20	21	22	23
24	25	26	27	28	29	30

OCTOBER

M	T	W	T	F	S	S
1	2	3	4	5	6	7
8	9	10	11	12	13	14
15	16	17	18	19	20	21
22	23	24	25	26	27	28
29	30	31				

The transportation sector has a roller coaster seasonal trend. In the early part of the year it typically outperforms, and then underperforms in the summer, and then outperforms at the end of the year. From 1990 to 2016, October has been the best month for the transportation sector on an average, median and frequency basis. Over the last five years, on average, generally the transportation sector has followed its seasonal pattern throughout the year. In 2016, the transportation sector outperformed the S&P 500 during two of its three seasonal periods. In 2017, the transportation sector was negative and underperformed the S&P 500 in its first seasonal period.

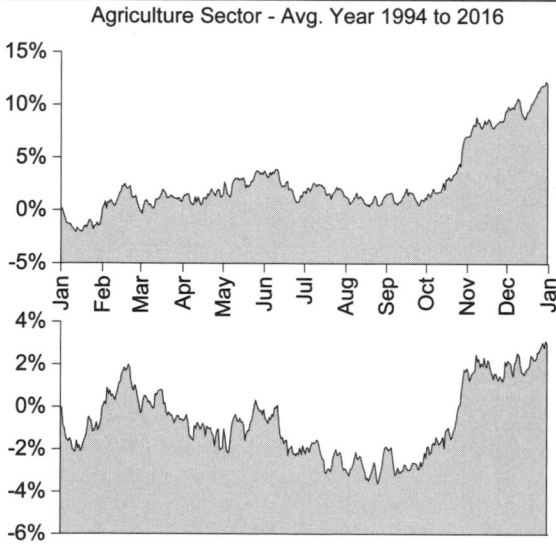

AGRICULTURE MOOOVES
September 26th to November 11th

Note: The seasonal period for the agriculture sector has been adjusted from previous books to reflect the sweet spot of the seasonal trade (September 26th to November 11th).

Agriculture* vs. S&P 500 1994 to 2016			
Sep 26 to Nov 11	S&P 500	Positive Agri	Diff
1994	1.0 %	6.5 %	5.5 %
1995	1.9	12.0	10.2
1996	6.6	23.7	17.1
1997	-1.8	-5.5	-3.7
1998	8.0	-2.2	-10.2
1999	7.5	0.3	-7.2
2000	-5.1	35.3	40.4
2001	10.7	18.1	7.5
2002	6.6	16.0	9.4
2003	4.4	9.2	4.8
2004	4.8	25.1	20.3
2005	1.3	7.1	5.8
2006	4.1	-5.7	-9.9
2007	-4.2	12.6	16.8
2008	-24.0	-0.2	23.8
2009	4.7	19.4	14.8
2010	6.1	-4.6	-10.7
2011	9.1	14.7	5.6
2012	-4.3	-8.2	-3.9
2013	4.6	13.0	8.4
2014	3.7	0.6	-3.1
2015	7.8	-4.4	-12.2
2016	0.1	6.4	6.3
Avg.	2.3 %	8.2 %	5.9 %
Fq > 0	78 %	70 %	65 %

The agriculture seasonal trade is the result of the major summer growing season in the northern hemisphere producing cash for growers and subsequently, increasing sales for farming suppliers typically in the fourth quarter of the year. The seasonal period for the agriculture sector occurs towards the beginning of the fourth quarter.

65% of the time better than the S&P 500

Although this sector can represent a good opportunity, investors should be wary of the wide performance swings. Out of the twenty-three cycles from 1994 to 2016, during its seasonal period, the agriculture sector has had ten years of returns greater than +10%. In other words, this sector is very volatile.

Agriculture Sector - Avg. Year 1994 to 2016

Agriculture / S&P 500 Relative Strength - Avg Yr. 1994-2016

In the 2000's, after realizing that technology stocks were not going to grow to the sky, investors started to have an epiphany– that the world might be running out of food, and as a result interest in the agriculture sector started to pick up.

The world population is still increasing and imbalances in food supply and demand will continue to exist in the future, helping to support the agriculture seasonal trade.

On a year by year basis, the agriculture sector has on average produced its biggest gains during its seasonally strong period. In 2000, the agriculture sector produced a gain of 35.3%. It is interesting to note that this is the same year that the technology sector's bubble burst.

*The SP GICS Agriculture Sector # 30202010
For more information on the agriculture sector, see www.standardandpoors.com

- 99 -

Agriculture Performance

Agriculture Monthly Performance (1994-2016)

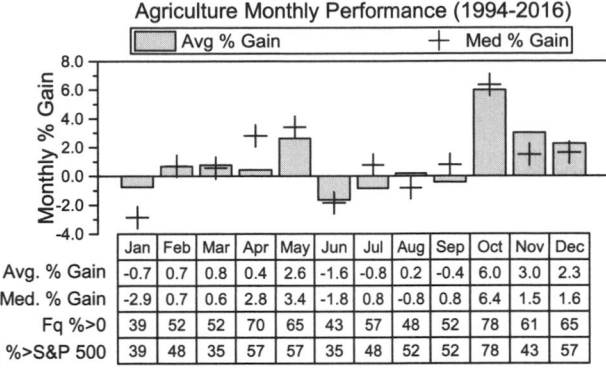

	Jan	Feb	Mar	Apr	May	Jun	Jul	Aug	Sep	Oct	Nov	Dec
Avg. % Gain	-0.7	0.7	0.8	0.4	2.6	-1.6	-0.8	0.2	-0.4	6.0	3.0	2.3
Med. % Gain	-2.9	0.7	0.6	2.8	3.4	-1.8	0.8	-0.8	0.8	6.4	1.5	1.6
Fq %>0	39	52	52	70	65	43	57	48	52	78	61	65
Fq %>S&P 500	39	48	35	57	57	35	48	52	52	78	43	57

Agriculture 5 Year (2012-2016) % Gain

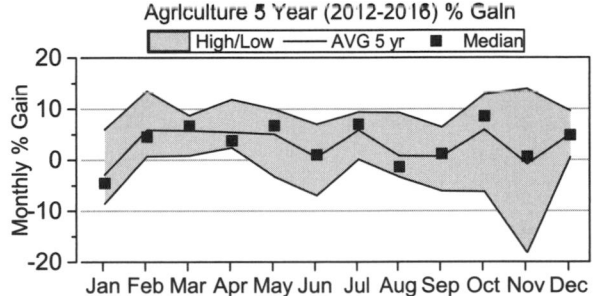

Agriculture Performance 2016-2017

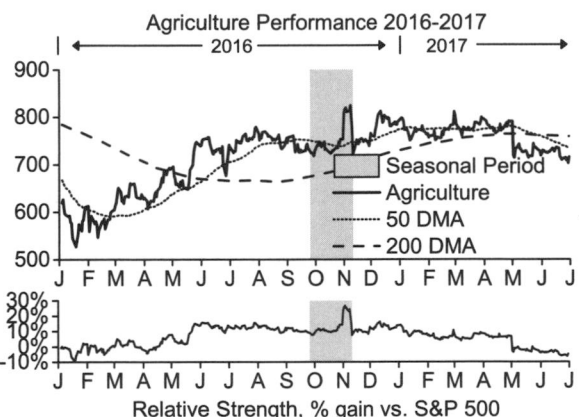

Relative Strength, % gain vs. S&P 500

Market Indices & Rates
Weekly Values**

Stock Markets	2015	2016
Dow	17,461	18,582
S&P500	2,090	2,184
Nasdaq	5,053	5,239
TSX	14,347	14,712
FTSE	6,618	6,884
DAX	11,165	10,620
Nikkei	20,607	16,649
Hang Seng	24,189	22,921

Commodities	2015	2016
Oil	43.21	47.17
Gold	1111.9	1344.6

Bond Yields	2015	2016
USA 5 Yr Treasury	1.57	1.15
USA 10 Yr T	2.18	1.56
USA 20 Yr T	2.54	1.91
Moody's Aaa	4.02	3.31
Moody's Baa	5.14	4.25
CAN 5 Yr T	0.75	0.66
CAN 10 Yr T	1.41	1.06

Money Market	2015	2016
USA Fed Funds	0.25	0.50
USA 3 Mo T-B	0.10	0.30
CAN tgt overnight rate	0.50	0.50
CAN 3 Mo T-B	0.39	0.49

Foreign Exchange	2015	2016
EUR/USD	1.11	1.13
GBP/USD	1.56	1.30
USD/CAD	1.30	1.29
USD/JPY	124.54	100.39

AUGUST

M	T	W	T	F	S	S
	1	2	3	4	5	
6	7	8	9	10	11	12
13	14	15	16	17	18	19
20	21	22	23	24	25	26
27	28	29	30	31		

SEPTEMBER

M	T	W	T	F	S	S
					1	2
3	4	5	6	7	8	9
10	11	12	13	14	15	16
17	18	19	20	21	22	23
24	25	26	27	28	29	30

OCTOBER

M	T	W	T	F	S	S
1	2	3	4	5	6	7
8	9	10	11	12	13	14
15	16	17	18	19	20	21
22	23	24	25	26	27	28
29	30	31				

From 1994 to 2016, October has been the best month of the year on an average, median and frequency basis.

Over the last five years, on average, the general seasonal trend provided nominal benefits.

In 2016, the agriculture sector was positive in its seasonal period and outperformed the S&P 500.

AMGEN
June 23rd to September 13th

Biotech has a period of seasonal strength from June 23rd to September 13th (see *Biotech Summer Solstice* strategy). Amgen is considered one of the major biotech companies and has a similar seasonal trend. Amgen has an additional benefit during the biotech seasonal period, as it typically releases its second quarter earnings towards the end of July. This gives Amgen a seasonal boost as investors buy Amgen ahead of their earnings in anticipation of any possible good news.

Strong earnings are particularly welcome in the second quarter, as the first quarter tends to be the weakest quarter of the year for Amgen. The first quarter of the year tends to be weak due to slower sales and the effects of wholesale inventory over-stocking at the end of the previous year.

14.8% gain & positive 81% of the time

From 1990 to 2016, in its seasonal period, Amgen has produced an average gain of 14.8% and has been positive 81% of the time. During this same time period, it has beaten the S&P 500 by an average 14.4% and has outperformed it 85% of the time. This is a strong track record of outperformance, especially the percentage of times that Amgen has beaten the S&P 500.

AMGN* vs. S&P 500 - 1990 to 2016

Jun 23 to Sep 13	S&P 500	AGMN	Diff
1990	-10.4%	29.8%	40.2%
1991	1.6	42.0	40.5
1992	4.0	17.9	13.9
1993	3.6	3.6	-0.1
1994	3.2	24.2	21.0
1995	5.0	31.5	26.5
1996	2.1	7.0	4.9
1997	2.8	-18.9	-21.7
1998	-8.5	20.6	29.1
1999	0.6	64.3	63.7
2000	2.3	7.9	5.6
2001	-10.8	-1.6	9.3
2002	-10.0	12.9	23.0
2003	2.3	5.4	3.1
2004	-0.8	9.1	9.8
2005	1.4	36.0	34.5
2006	5.8	6.4	0.6
2007	-1.2	2.1	3.3
2008	-5.0	39.2	44.2
2009	16.8	14.8	-1.9
2010	2.4	-3.1	-5.5
2011	-8.9	-5.6	3.3
2012	9.4	15.1	5.7
2013	6.0	17.0	11.0
2014	1.2	14.0	12.8
2015	-7.6	-5.6	2.1
2016	2.0	13.0	11.0
Avg	0.3%	14.8%	14.4%
Fq > 0	67%	81%	85%

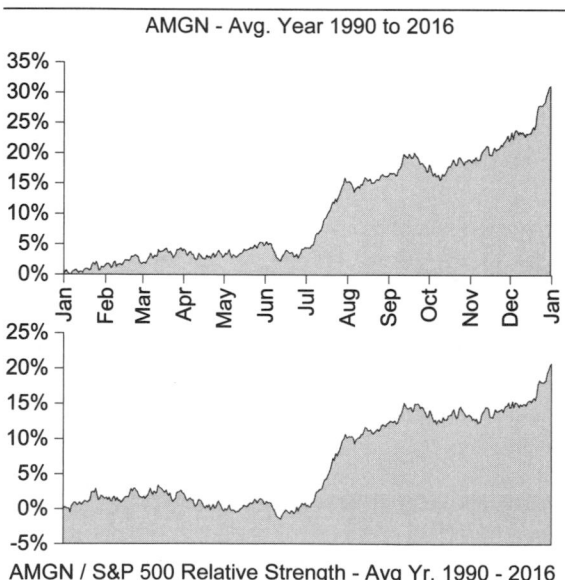

AMGN - Avg. Year 1990 to 2016

AMGN / S&P 500 Relative Strength - Avg Yr. 1990 - 2016

place in the summer months when the stock market typically does not have strong results and the selection of seasonal long trades are limited.

The seasonal trade for Amgen focuses on the sweet spot of its best performance, producing an average large gain over a very short period of time. Like the biotech sector, on average the second half of the year for Amgen is much stronger than the first half of the year. From July 1st to December 31st, for the yearly period 1990 to 2016, Amgen has produced an average gain of 21.6% and has been positive 78% of the time. This compares to the weaker first half of the year, where the average gain over the same yearly period is 4.5% and the frequency of positive performance is 48%.

The Amgen seasonal trade is a valued trade not just because of its strong results, but also because of the time of year when the trade occurs. The trade takes

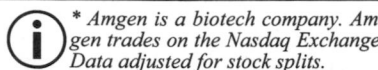

Amgen is a biotech company. Amgen trades on the Nasdaq Exchange. Data adjusted for stock splits.

Amgen Performance

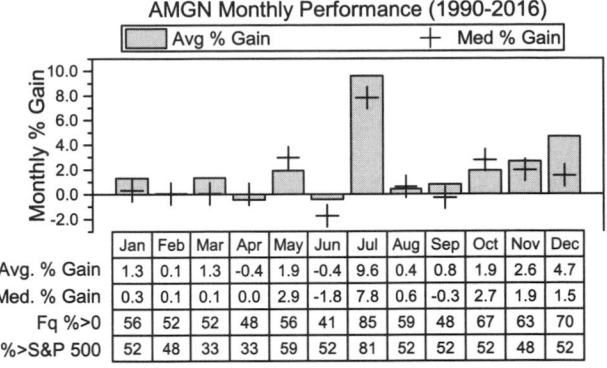

AMGN Monthly Performance (1990-2016)

Legend: Avg % Gain · Med % Gain

	Jan	Feb	Mar	Apr	May	Jun	Jul	Aug	Sep	Oct	Nov	Dec
Avg. % Gain	1.3	0.1	1.3	-0.4	1.9	-0.4	9.6	0.4	0.8	1.9	2.6	4.7
Med. % Gain	0.3	0.1	0.1	0.0	2.9	-1.8	7.8	0.6	-0.3	2.7	1.9	1.5
Fq %>0	56	52	52	48	56	41	85	59	48	67	63	70
Fq %>S&P 500	52	48	33	33	59	52	81	52	52	52	48	52

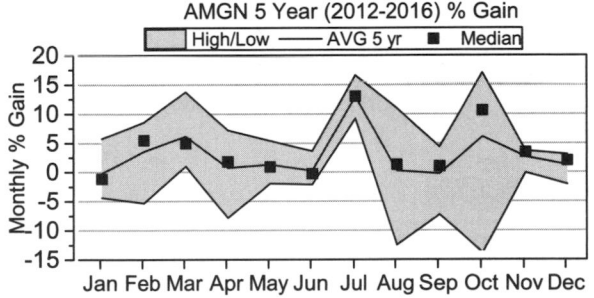

AMGN 5 Year (2012-2016) % Gain

Legend: High/Low — AVG 5 yr ■ Median

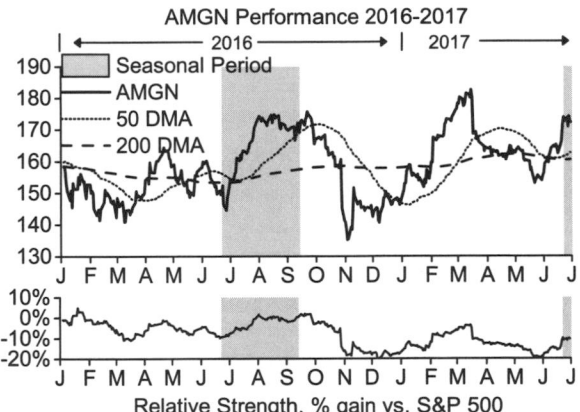

AMGN Performance 2016-2017

Legend: Seasonal Period · AMGN · 50 DMA · 200 DMA

Relative Strength, % gain vs. S&P 500

Market Indices & Rates
Weekly Values**

Stock Markets	2015	2016
Dow	17,171	18,480
S&P500	2,057	2,177
Nasdaq	4,951	5,231
TSX	13,939	14,682
FTSE	6,407	6,838
DAX	10,619	10,566
Nikkei	20,173	16,522
Hang Seng	23,125	22,908

Commodities	2015	2016
Oil	41.33	47.15
Gold	1126.0	1329.0

Bond Yields	2015	2016
USA 5 Yr Treasury	1.53	1.16
USA 10 Yr T	2.13	1.57
USA 20 Yr T	2.49	1.90
Moody's Aaa	3.99	3.26
Moody's Baa	5.16	4.21
CAN 5 Yr T	0.67	0.68
CAN 10 Yr T	1.33	1.05

Money Market	2015	2016
USA Fed Funds	0.25	0.50
USA 3 Mo T-B	0.05	0.31
CAN tgt overnight rate	0.50	0.50
CAN 3 Mo T-B	0.38	0.51

Foreign Exchange	2015	2016
EUR/USD	1.12	1.13
GBP/USD	1.57	1.32
USD/CAD	1.31	1.29
USD/JPY	123.61	100.68

AUGUST

M	T	W	T	F	S	S
	1	2	3	4	5	
6	7	8	9	10	11	12
13	14	15	16	17	18	19
20	21	22	23	24	25	26
27	28	29	30	31		

SEPTEMBER

M	T	W	T	F	S	S
					1	2
3	4	5	6	7	8	9
10	11	12	13	14	15	16
17	18	19	20	21	22	23
24	25	26	27	28	29	30

OCTOBER

M	T	W	T	F	S	S
1	2	3	4	5	6	7
8	9	10	11	12	13	14
15	16	17	18	19	20	21
22	23	24	25	26	27	28
29	30	31				

From 1990 to 2016, the best month of the year for Amgen was July on an average, median and frequency basis. The gains in July were substantially above the other months of the year.

Over the last five years, the seasonal trade has worked well, mainly with the strong support from July's results.

In 2016, Amgen was underperforming the stock market coming into its seasonal period. Shortly after its seasonal period started, Amgen started to perform well, outperforming the S&P 500 in its seasonal period.

HEALTH CARE
AUGUST PRESCRIPTION RENEWAL
August 15th to October 18th

Health care stocks have traditionally been classified as defensive stocks because of their stable earnings. Pharmaceutical and other health care companies typically still perform relatively well in an economic downturn.

Even in tough times, people still need to take their medication. As a result, investors have typically found comfort in this sector starting in the late summer when the stock market is often volatile.

2.1% extra & 17 out of 27 times better than the S&P 500

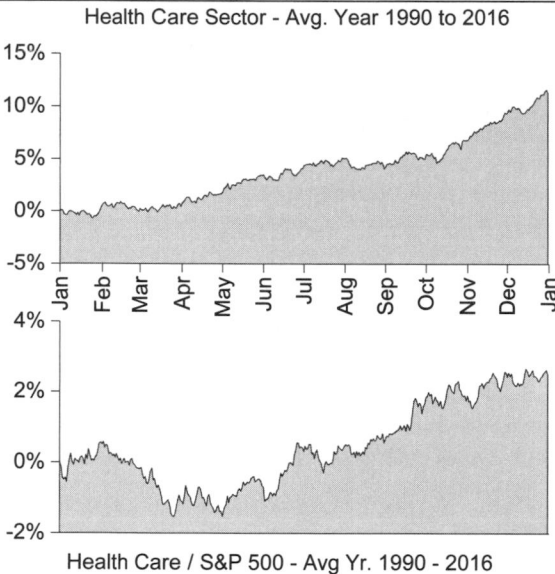

Health Care Sector - Avg. Year 1990 to 2016

Health Care / S&P 500 - Avg Yr. 1990 - 2016

Aug 15 to Oct 18	S&P 500	Positive Health Care	Diff
1990	-9.9 %	-1.3 %	8.6 %
1991	0.7	1.3	0.6
1992	-1.9	-9.0	-7.1
1993	4.1	13.5	9.5
1994	1.2	7.2	6.0
1995	4.9	11.7	6.7
1996	7.4	9.4	2.1
1997	2.1	5.8	3.7
1998	-0.6	3.0	3.6
1999	-5.5	-0.5	5.0
2000	-10.0	6.9	16.9
2001	-10.0	-0.4	9.6
2002	-3.8	2.4	6.2
2003	4.9	-0.5	-5.4
2004	4.6	-0.8	-5.4
2005	-4.2	-3.1	1.2
2006	7.7	6.4	-1.3
2007	8.0	6.0	-2.0
2008	-27.3	-20.4	6.8
2009	8.3	5.1	-3.3
2010	9.8	8.2	-1.6
2011	4.0	3.2	-0.8
2012	3.8	6.9	3.1
2013	3.5	4.3	0.8
2014	-3.5	-1.1	2.5
2015	-2.8	-7.4	-4.6
2016	-2.0	-6.1	-4.1
Avg	-0.3 %	1.9 %	2.1 %
Fq > 0	56 %	59 %	63 %

Health Care* vs. S&P 500
Performance 1990 to 2016

From 1990 to 2016, the health care sector has typically outperformed the S&P 500 during the period from August 15th to October 18th.

During this time period, the broad market (S&P 500) produced an average loss of 0.3%, compared with the health care sector's gain of 1.9%.

Despite legal problems which required some drugs to be withdrawn from the market in the early 2000's, the sector has beaten the S&P 500 seventeen out of twenty-seven times from 1990 to 2016 in its seasonal period.

The real benefit of investing in the health care sector has been the positive returns that have been generated when the market has typically been negative.

Since 1950, August and September have been the worst two-month combination for gains in the broad stock market.

Having an alternative sector to invest in during the summer and early autumn is a valuable asset.

> *Alternate Strategy—As the health care sector has had a tendency to perform at par with the broad market from late October to early December, an alternative strategy is to continue holding the health care sector during this time period if the fundamentals or technicals are favorable.*

> **Health Care SP GIC Sector# 35: An index designed to represent a cross section of health care companies. For more information on the health care sector, see www.standardandpoors.com.*

S&P500 Cumulative Daily Gains for Avg Month 1950 to 2016

Dow Jones	S&P 500	Nasdaq	TSX Comp
12	12	12	12
26	29	24	13
41	38	21	19
39	43	53	41
-0.8	-0.5	-0.6	-1.6

-2016, Nasdaq 1972-2016, TSX 1985-2016

...er has the reputation of being the worst month of the ...e S&P 500. From 1950 to 2016, September has pro- ...verage loss of 0.5% and has only been positive 43% ... ♦ In particular, the last part of September has been ... The defensive sectors of the stock market are typi- ... performing sectors in September as investors seek ... earnings in a month that is often volatile ♦ The ma- ...or on average performs poorly in September and has ...ed the S&P 500 only 22% of the time since 1990.

BEST / WORST SEPTEMBER BROAD MKTS. 2007-2016

BEST SEPTEMBER MARKETS
- ♦ Russell 2000 (2010) 12.3%
- ♦ Nasdaq (2010) 12.0%
- ♦ Russell 1000 (2010) 9.0%

WORST SEPTEMBER MARKETS
- ♦ TSX Comp. (2008) -14.7%
- ♦ Nikkei 225 (2008) -13.9%
- ♦ FTSE 100 (2008) -13.0%

Index Values End of Month

2007	2008	2009	2010	2011	2012	2013	2014	2015	2016
13,896	10,851	9,712	10,788	10,913	13,437	15,130	17,043	16,285	18,308
1,527	1,166	1,057	1,141	1,131	1,441	1,682	1,972	1,920	2,168
2,702	2,092	2,122	2,369	2,415	3,116	3,771	4,493	4,620	5,312
14,099	11,753	11,395	12,369	11,624	12,317	12,787	14,961	13,307	14,726
831	633	580	630	623	794	940	1,096	1,068	1,202
805	680	604	676	644	837	1,074	1,102	1,101	1,252
6,467	4,902	5,134	5,549	5,128	5,742	6,462	6,623	6,062	6,899
16,786	11,260	10,133	9,369	8,700	8,870	14,456	16,174	17,388	16,450

Percent Gain for September

2007	2008	2009	2010	2011	2012	2013	2014	2015	2016
4.0	-6.0	2.3	7.7	-6.0	2.6	2.2	-0.3	-1.5	-0.5
3.6	-9.1	3.6	8.8	-7.2	2.4	3.0	-1.6	-2.6	-0.1
4.0	-11.6	5.6	12.0	-6.4	1.6	5.1	-1.9	-3.3	1.9
3.2	-14.7	4.8	3.8	-9.0	3.1	1.1	-4.3	-4.0	0.9
3.5	-9.8	3.9	9.0	-7.6	2.4	3.3	-1.9	-2.9	-0.1
1.6	-8.1	5.6	12.3	-11.4	3.1	6.2	-6.2	-5.1	0.9
2.6	-13.0	4.6	6.2	-4.9	0.5	0.8	-2.9	-3.0	1.7
1.3	-13.9	-3.4	6.2	-2.8	0.3	8.0	4.9	-8.0	-2.6

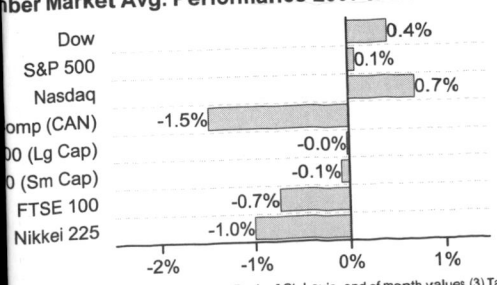

...ber Market Avg. Performance 2007 to 2016(1)

Dow	0.4%
S&P 500	0.1%
Nasdaq	0.7%
...omp (CAN)	-1.5%
...00 (Lg Cap)	-0.0%
...0 (Sm Cap)	-0.1%
FTSE 100	-0.7%
Nikkei 225	-1.0%

Interest Corner Sep(2)

	Fed Funds %(3)	3 Mo. T-Bill %(4)	10 Yr %(5)	20 Yr %(6)
2016	0.50	0.29	1.60	1.99
2015	0.25	0.00	2.06	2.51
2014	0.25	0.02	2.52	2.98
2013	0.25	0.02	2.64	3.41
2012	0.25	0.10	1.65	2.42

...vided by Russell (2) Federal Reserve Bank of St. Louis- end of month values (3) Target rate set by FOMC (4)(5)(6) Constant yield maturities.

Health Care Performance

Health Care Monthly Performance (1990-2016)

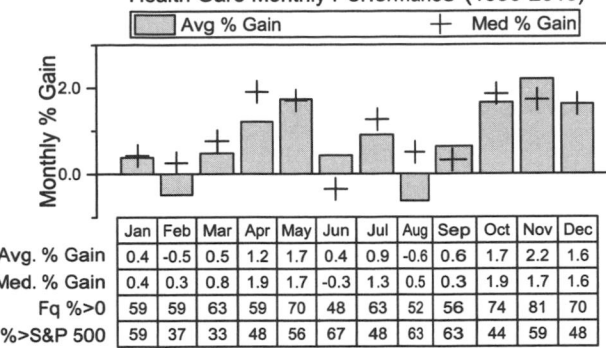

	Jan	Feb	Mar	Apr	May	Jun	Jul	Aug	Sep	Oct	Nov	Dec
Avg. % Gain	0.4	-0.5	0.5	1.2	1.7	0.4	0.9	-0.6	0.6	1.7	2.2	1.6
Med. % Gain	0.4	0.3	0.8	1.9	1.7	-0.3	1.3	0.5	0.3	1.9	1.7	1.6
Fq %>0	59	59	63	59	70	48	63	52	56	74	81	70
Fq %>S&P 500	59	37	33	48	56	67	48	63	63	44	59	48

Health Care 5 Year (2012-2016) % Gain

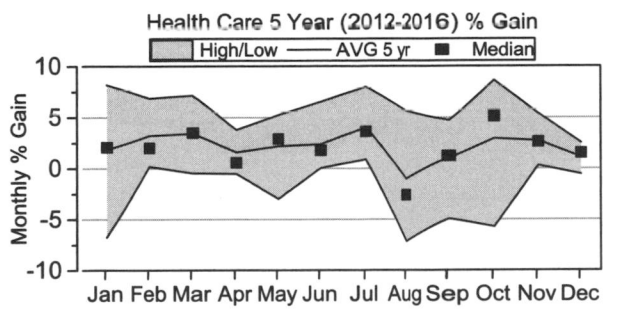

Health Care Performance 2016-2017

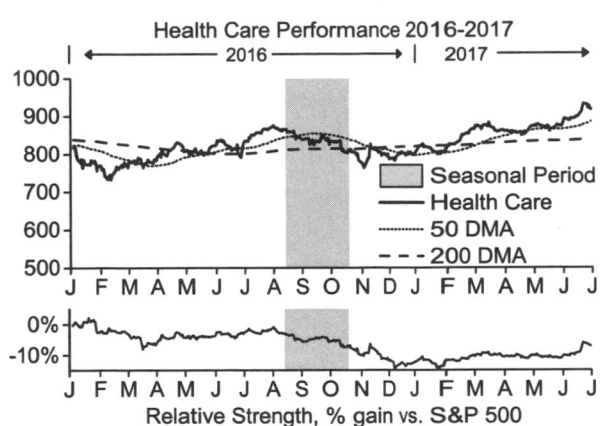

Relative Strength, % gain vs. S&P 500

WEEK 35

Market Indices & Rates Weekly Values**

Stock Markets	2015	2016
Dow	16,224	18,454
S&P500	1,936	2,176
Nasdaq	4,674	5,229
TSX	13,443	14,689
FTSE	6,080	6,811
DAX	10,098	10,603
Nikkei	18,487	16,841
Hang Seng	21,438	23,049

Commodities	2015	2016
Oil	41.38	45.13
Gold	1135.8	1315.4

Bond Yields	2015	2016
USA 5 Yr Treasury	1.47	1.19
USA 10 Yr T	2.14	1.58
USA 20 Yr T	2.56	1.91
Moody's Aaa	4.09	3.24
Moody's Baa	5.29	4.19
CAN 5 Yr T	0.68	0.67
CAN 10 Yr T	1.39	1.03

Money Market	2015	2016
USA Fed Funds	0.25	0.50
USA 3 Mo T-B	0.06	0.33
CAN tgt overnight rate	0.50	0.50
CAN 3 Mo T-B	0.37	0.51

Foreign Exchange	2015	2016
EUR/USD	1.14	1.12
GBP/USD	1.55	1.32
USD/CAD	1.33	1.31
USD/JPY	119.98	103.09

AUGUST

M	T	W	T	F	S	S
				1	2	3	4	5
6	7	8	9	10	11	12
13	14	15	16	17	18	19
20	21	22	23	24	25	26
27	28	29	30	31		

SEPTEMBER

M	T	W	T	F	S	S
					1	2
3	4	5	6	7	8	9
10	11	12	13	14	15	16
17	18	19	20	21	22	23
24	25	26	27	28	29	30

OCTOBER

M	T	W	T	F	S	S
1	2	3	4	5	6	7
8	9	10	11	12	13	14
15	16	17	18	19	20	21
22	23	24	25	26	27	28
29	30	31				

Over the long-term, on average, August is one of the worst performing months for the health care sector, and yet the middle of the month starts off the sector's seasonal period. In this case, averages can be deceiving. Since 1990, not only is the median positive in August, but also the frequency of outperformance relative to the S&P 500 is high, at 63%. Nevertheless, the second half of August is the better performing half. Over the last five years, the health care sector's average performance throughout the year has placed August as the weakest month of the year, and the best performing month as October. In 2016, the health care sector produced a loss in its seasonal period, and underperformed the S&P 500.

	MONDAY		TUESDAY		WEDNESDAY	
WEEK 36	**3** 27		**4** 26		**5** 25	
	USA Market Closed- Labor Day CAN Market Closed- Labor Day					
WEEK 37	**10** 20		**11** 19		**12** 18	
WEEK 38	**17** 13		**18** 12		**19** 11	
WEEK 39	**24** 6		**25** 5		**26** 4	
WEEK 40	1		2		3	

	THURSDAY		FRIDAY	
	6 24	**7** 23	
	13 17	**14** 16	
	20 10	**21** 9	
	27 3	**28** 2	
	4	5	

S
S

Month Rank

Up

Down

% Pos

% Avg. Gain

Dow & S&P 1950

◆ Septemb
year for the
duced an a
of the time
negative. ◆
cally better
more stable
terials secto
outperform

Dow
S&P 500
Nasdaq
TSX Comp.
Russell 1000
Russell 2000
FTSE 100
Nikkei 225

Dow
S&P 500
Nasdaq
TSX Comp.
Russell 1000
Russell 2000
FTSE 100
Nikkei 225

Septem

TSX C
Russell 10
Russell 200

(1) Russell Data pr

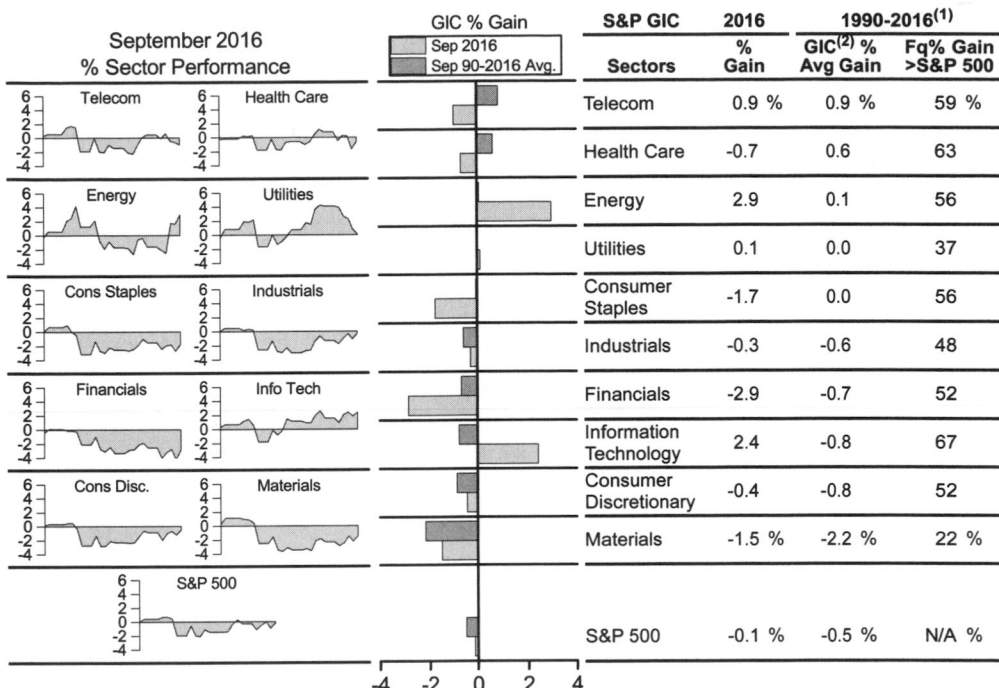

September 2016 % Sector Performance

GIC % Gain
Sep 2016
Sep 90-2016 Avg.

S&P GIC Sectors	2016 % Gain	1990-2016[1] GIC[2] % Avg Gain	Fq% Gain >S&P 500
Telecom	0.9 %	0.9 %	59 %
Health Care	-0.7	0.6	63
Energy	2.9	0.1	56
Utilities	0.1	0.0	37
Consumer Staples	-1.7	0.0	56
Industrials	-0.3	-0.6	48
Financials	-2.9	-0.7	52
Information Technology	2.4	-0.8	67
Consumer Discretionary	-0.4	-0.8	52
Materials	-1.5 %	-2.2 %	22 %
S&P 500	-0.1 %	-0.5 %	N/A %

Sector Commentary

♦ In September 2016, the energy sector produced a gain of 2.9%. The sector is typically one of the better performing sectors in September. ♦ The information technology sector produced a gain of 2.4%. Although the sector has outperformed the S&P 500, 67% of the time from 1990 to 2016 in September, the sector has previously had some large losses in the month, making an investment in this sector typically volatile. ♦ The financial sector produced a loss of 2.9% as investors viewed that the Federal Reserve was becoming more dovish in its monetary policy.

Sub-Sector Commentary

♦ September is typically the month when precious metals tend to perform well. In September 2016, gold produced a gain of 0.1% and silver a gain of 3.3%. ♦ The transportation sub-sector typically starts its period of seasonal strength in October, but in 2016 it was positive in September, producing a gain of 2.9%. ♦ September tends to be a weak month for the chemicals sub-sector and in 2016, the sector produced a loss of 2.5%.

SELECTED SUB-SECTORS[3]

Gold	0.1 %	2.4 %	67 %
Silver	3.3	1.7	70
Biotech (1993-2016)	-0.9	1.4	63
Pharma	-1.6	0.7	59
Agriculture (1994-2016)	-3.6	-0.4	52
Retail	1.0	-0.6	48
Transportation	2.9	-0.6	56
Railroads	3.0	-0.6	41
Banks	-4.1	-1.1	52
Homebuilders	-7.5	-1.1	56
Metals & Mining	2.6	-1.9	44
Chemicals	-2.5	-2.0	30
Automotive & Components	-0.6	-2.5	37
SOX (1995-2016)	4.3	-2.6	45
Steel	1.9	-3.6	44

(1) Sector data provided by Standard and Poors (2) GIC is short form for Global Industry Classification (3) Sub Sector data provided by Standard and Poors, except where marked by symbol.

PROCTER AND GAMBLE
SOMETHING FOR EVERYONE – Aug 7 to Nov 19

In the investors' eyes, Procter and Gamble is a relatively defensive investment, as the company is in the consumer packaged goods business and its revenues are generated in over 180 countries. Defensive stocks have a reputation of producing sub-par performance compared with the broad market. This is not the case with PG, as on average, it has outperformed the S&P 500 over the last twenty-seven years during its seasonally strong period.

7.6% gain & positive 78% of the time

Interestingly, on average, the gains that have been produced are largely in the second half of the year. In the first half of the year, PG has been relatively flat and has underperformed the S&P 500.

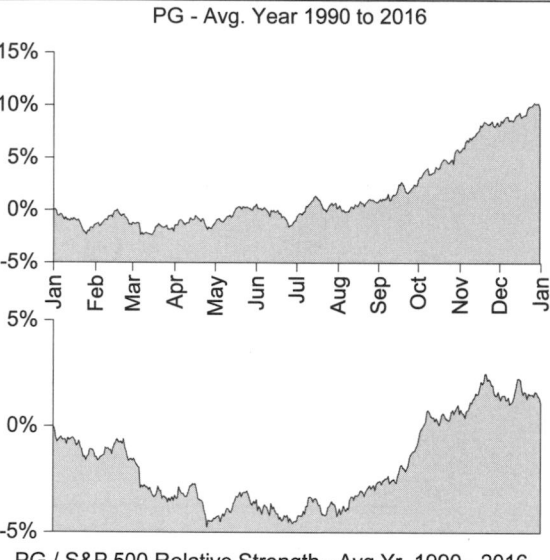

PG - Avg. Year 1990 to 2016

PG / S&P 500 Relative Strength - Avg Yr. 1990 - 2016

PG* vs. S&P 500 - 1990 to 2016

Aug 7 to Nov 19	S&P 500	PG	Positive Diff
1990	-4.5%	8.4%	12.8%
1991	-2.9	-2.1	0.7
1992	0.7	10.1	9.4
1993	3.1	17.7	14.6
1994	1.0	19.5	18.3
1995	7.4	27.8	20.4
1996	12.0	18.4	6.5
1997	-1.6	0.3	1.9
1998	5.8	14.0	8.2
1999	9.4	18.9	9.3
2000	-6.5	32.0	38.3
2001	-4.1	11.2	15.3
2002	4.3	-0.7	-5.0
2003	7.8	8.2	0.4
2004	10.0	2.5	-7.5
2005	1.8	6.2	4.4
2006	9.5	7.4	-2.1
2007	-2.3	12.0	14.4
2008	-37.4	-8.1	29.3
2009	9.8	20.8	11.0
2010	7.0	6.7	-0.3
2011	1.4	4.4	3.0
2012	-0.5	3.2	3.7
2013	5.3	3.2	-2.2
2014	6.7	9.4	2.7
2015	-0.1	0.6	0.8
2016	0.0	-4.4	-4.4
Avg	1.6%	9.2%	7.6%
Fq > 0	63%	85%	78%

This trend benefits PG as more investors switch over to defensive companies. PG's outperformance, on average, starts to occur just after it releases its fourth quarter earnings at the beginning of August.

PG continues to outperform the S&P 500 through September and October. For the S&P 500, September on average is the worst month of the year and October is the most volatile month. The outperformance of PG continues into mid-November.

From a seasonal perspective, the best time to invest in PG has been from August 7th to November 19th. During this period, from 1990 to 2016, PG on average produced a gain of 9.2% and was positive 85% of the time. In addition, it substantially outperformed the S&P 500, generating an extra profit of 7.6% and beating its performance 78% of the time.

Investors will often seek sanctuary in defensive stocks in late summer and early autumn. Although August is not typically the worst month of the year, it does have a weak risk-reward profile. With the dreaded month of September falling right after August, investors become "gun shy" and start to become more conservative in August.

PG's seasonally strong period extends past the seasonal period for the consumer staples sector. It is possible that investors wait until after PG's first quarter results are released in the beginning of November before adjusting their portfolios.

 The Procter and Gamble Company is a consumer packaged goods company. Data adjusted for stock splits.

Procter & Gamble Performance

PG Monthly Performance (1990-2016)

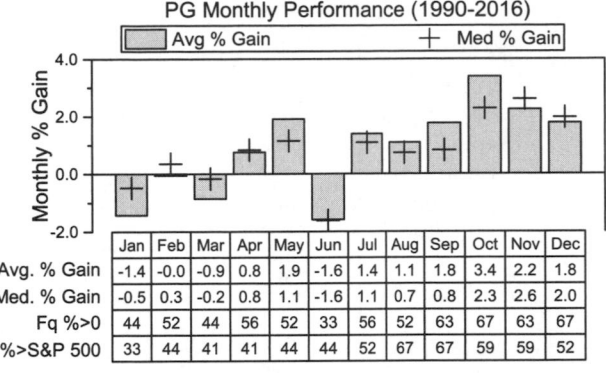

	Jan	Feb	Mar	Apr	May	Jun	Jul	Aug	Sep	Oct	Nov	Dec
Avg. % Gain	-1.4	-0.0	-0.9	0.8	1.9	-1.6	1.4	1.1	1.8	3.4	2.2	1.8
Med. % Gain	-0.5	0.3	-0.2	0.8	1.1	-1.6	1.1	0.7	0.8	2.3	2.6	2.0
Fq %>0	44	52	44	56	52	33	56	52	63	67	63	67
Fq %>S&P 500	33	44	41	41	44	44	52	67	67	59	59	52

PG 5 Year (2012-2016) % Gain

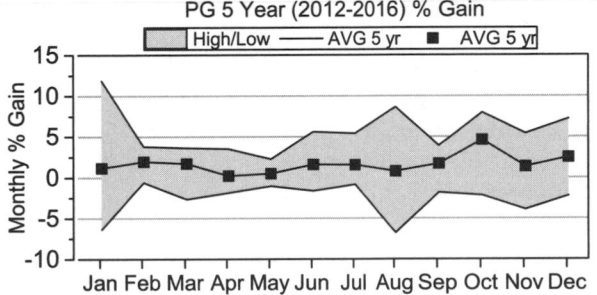

PG Performance 2016-2017

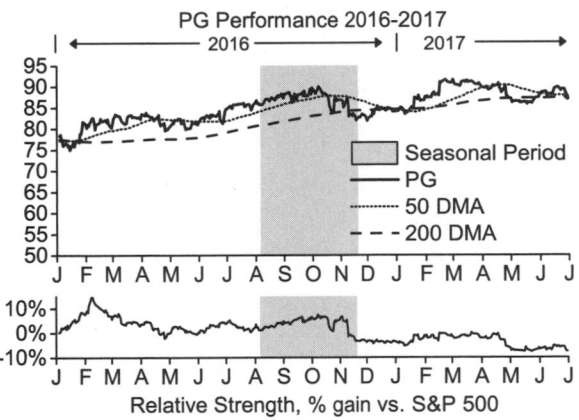

Relative Strength, % gain vs. S&P 500

From 1990 to 2016, October was the strongest month for Procter & Gamble on an average and frequency basis. Over the same time period, June was the weakest month.

Over the last five years, Procter & Gamble has generally followed its average seasonal trend.

In 2016, Proctor and Gamble was positive in the first portion of the year leading up to its seasonal period, but underperformed the S&P 500. In its seasonal period, Procter & Gamble declined and underperformed the S&P 500.

Market Indices & Rates
Weekly Values**

Stock Markets	2015	2016
Dow	16,283	18,407
S&P500	1,941	2,170
Nasdaq	4,716	5,236
TSX	13,592	14,738
FTSE	6,095	6,838
DAX	10,136	10,672
Nikkei	18,225	17,011
Hang Seng	21,158	23,840

Commodities	2015	2016
Oil	46.73	45.96
Gold	1131.6	1337.2

Bond Yields	2015	2016
USA 5 Yr Treasury	1.50	1.17
USA 10 Yr T	2.18	1.59
USA 20 Yr T	2.63	1.96
Moody's Aaa	4.12	3.33
Moody's Baa	5.34	4.25
CAN 5 Yr T	0.75	0.67
CAN 10 Yr T	1.46	1.07

Money Market	2015	2016
USA Fed Funds	0.25	0.50
USA 3 Mo T-B	0.04	0.34
CAN tgt overnight rate	0.50	0.50
CAN 3 Mo T-B	0.37	0.50

Foreign Exchange	2015	2016
EUR/USD	1.12	1.12
GBP/USD	1.53	1.33
USD/CAD	1.32	1.29
USD/JPY	120.00	102.47

SEPTEMBER

M	T	W	T	F	S	S
					1	2
3	4	5	6	7	8	9
10	11	12	13	14	15	16
17	18	19	20	21	22	23
24	25	26	27	28	29	30

OCTOBER

M	T	W	T	F	S	S
1	2	3	4	5	6	7
8	9	10	11	12	13	14
15	16	17	18	19	20	21
22	23	24	25	26	27	28
29	30	31				

NOVEMBER

M	T	W	T	F	S	S
			1	2	3	4
5	6	7	8	9	10	11
12	13	14	15	16	17	18
19	20	21	22	23	24	25
26	27	28	29	30		

CARNIVAL CRUISE LINES
CRUISING FOR RETURNS– Sep 8 to Dec 31

The cruise industry is a seasonal business. The first quarter has the highest number of bookings and the third quarter has the highest number of voyages.

Investors look to be invested in Carnival Cruise Lines (Carnival) ahead of its booking season, increasing the relative performance of the stock price from September 8th until December 31st. In this time period, from 1990 to 2016, Carnival has produced an average return of 13.6% and has been positive 78% of the time.

13.6% gain & positive 78% of the time

The cruise industry has a large number of variables affecting its performance which can be fairly volatile. In the last decade, demand for cruise trips have been adversely affected by news stories of outbreaks of sickness, on-board fires immobilizing ships and general ship breakdowns at sea. Although these problems have adversely affected the stock prices of cruise companies in the short-term, the cruise companies have worked hard at preventing future problems and the stock prices have responded positively.

CCL* vs. S&P 500 - 1990 to 2016

Sep 8 to Dec 31	S&P 500	CCL	Diff
		Positive	
1990	2.1%	-20.5%	-22.6%
1991	7.2	26.4	19.2
1992	4.5	23.0	18.5
1993	1.7	15.5	13.8
1994	-2.5	-2.9	-0.4
1995	8.0	12.8	4.8
1996	13.0	20.0	7.0
1997	4.5	20.6	16.1
1998	26.2	83.8	57.6
1999	8.8	8.7	-0.1
2000	-12.1	56.5	68.6
2001	5.7	-3.3	-9.1
2002	-1.6	3.1	4.7
2003	8.9	15.2	6.3
2004	8.1	22.7	14.6
2005	1.0	7.2	6.3
2006	9.6	16.5	6.9
2007	1.0	-0.5	-1.5
2008	-27.3	-37.6	-10.3
2009	9.7	8.0	-1.7
2010	15.2	36.1	21.0
2011	4.9	2.5	-2.4
2012	-0.8	-0.8	0.1
2013	11.7	12.0	0.4
2014	2.6	15.3	12.7
2015	6.4	11.3	5.0
2016	2.4	14.9	12.5
Avg	4.4%	13.6%	9.1%
Fq > 0	81%	78%	70%

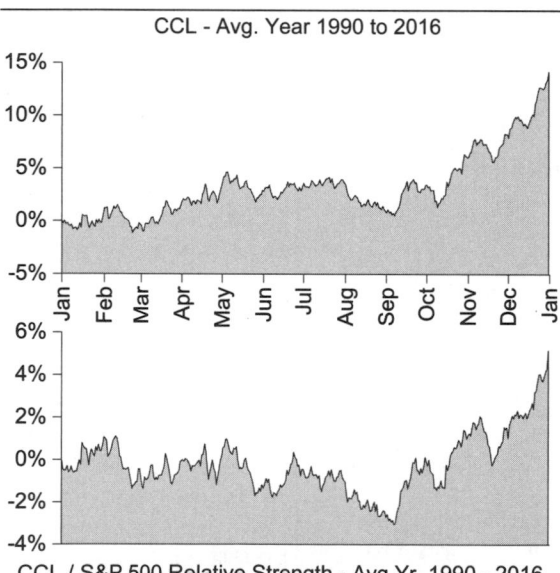

CCL - Avg. Year 1990 to 2016

CCL / S&P 500 Relative Strength - Avg Yr. 1990 - 2016

losses of 10% or greater, which have only occurred twice in the same time period.

August tends to be a weaker month of the year for Carnival and given that its seasonal period starts the following month, investors should be cautious on timing the entry into the seasonal trade. This is particularly true as September tends to be a negative month for the S&P 500 and any large corrections would have a high likelihood of having a negative influence on Carnival.

In its seasonal period, Carnival has on average outperformed the S&P 500 by 9.1% from 1990 to 2016. Although Carnival's 83.8% return in its 1998 seasonal period helps to skew the average higher for the seasonal period, Carnival has had returns of 10% or greater, sixteen times since 1990. This compares to

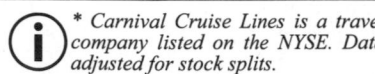

Carnival Cruise Lines is a travel company listed on the NYSE. Data adjusted for stock splits.

CCL Performance

CCL Monthly Performance (1990-2016)

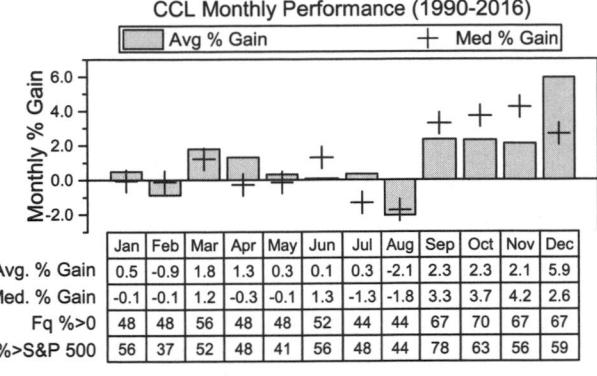

	Jan	Feb	Mar	Apr	May	Jun	Jul	Aug	Sep	Oct	Nov	Dec
Avg. % Gain	0.5	-0.9	1.8	1.3	0.3	0.1	0.3	-2.1	2.3	2.3	2.1	5.9
Med. % Gain	-0.1	-0.1	1.2	-0.3	-0.1	1.3	-1.3	-1.8	3.3	3.7	4.2	2.6
Fq %>0	48	48	56	48	48	52	44	44	67	70	67	67
Fq %>S&P 500	56	37	52	48	41	56	48	44	78	63	56	59

CCL 5 Year (2012-2016) % Gain

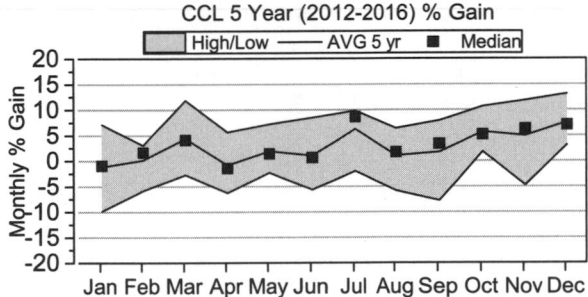

CCL Performance 2016-2017

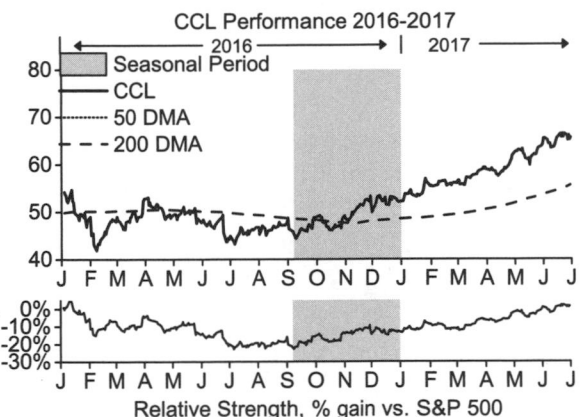

Relative Strength, % gain vs. S&P 500

Market Indices & Rates Weekly Values**

Stock Markets	2015	2016
Dow	16,377	18,153
S&P500	1,956	2,140
Nasdaq	4,797	5,207
TSX	13,548	14,453
FTSE	6,145	6,696
DAX	10,203	10,381
Nikkei	18,124	16,588
Hang Seng	21,408	23,258

Commodities	2015	2016
Oil	45.16	44.34
Gold	1112.1	1317.8

Bond Yields	2015	2016
USA 5 Yr Treasury	1.53	1.22
USA 10 Yr T	2.21	1.70
USA 20 Yr T	2.65	2.10
Moody's Aaa	4.09	3.49
Moody's Baa	5.33	4.41
CAN 5 Yr T	0.77	0.73
CAN 10 Yr T	1.47	1.19

Money Market	2015	2016
USA Fed Funds	0.25	0.50
USA 3 Mo T-B	0.04	0.33
CAN tgt overnight rate	0.50	0.50
CAN 3 Mo T-B	0.38	0.50

Foreign Exchange	2015	2016
EUR/USD	1.12	1.12
GBP/USD	1.54	1.32
USD/CAD	1.33	1.32
USD/JPY	120.16	102.25

SEPTEMBER

M	T	W	T	F	S	S
					1	2
3	4	5	6	7	8	9
10	11	12	13	14	15	16
17	18	19	20	21	22	23
24	25	26	27	28	29	30

OCTOBER

M	T	W	T	F	S	S
1	2	3	4	5	6	7
8	9	10	11	12	13	14
15	16	17	18	19	20	21
22	23	24	25	26	27	28
29	30	31				

NOVEMBER

M	T	W	T	F	S	S
			1	2	3	4
5	6	7	8	9	10	11
12	13	14	15	16	17	18
19	20	21	22	23	24	25
26	27	28	29	30		

From 1990 to 2016, the best four contiguous months of the year for Carnival on an average, median and frequency basis were September through December.

From 2012 to 2016, Carnival has followed its general seasonal pattern with the last four months of the year being strong.

In 2016, Carnival started to outperform the S&P 500 at the beginning of its seasonal period and continued its outperformance into the first half of 2017.

INFORMATION TECHNOLOGY
①Oct9-Dec5 ②Dec15-Jan17

Info Tech Interim Seasonal Period

The interim seasonal period (Dec 6th, to Dec 14th) is not part of the technology sector as it has produced an average loss of 1.9% and has only been positive 25% of the time from 1989 to 2016.

From 1989 to 2016, during its seasonal period of October 9th to December 5th, the information technology sector has produced an average gain of 7.4% and has been positive 71% of the time. From 1989/90 to 2016/17, during the second seasonal period of December 15th to January 17th, the information technology sector has produced an average gain of 3.2% and has been positive 71% of the time. The combined seasonal gains have been 11.2% and has been positive 71% of the time.

11.2% gain

Information technology stocks tend to get bid up at the end of the year for three reasons.

First, a lot of companies operate with year end budgets and if they do not spend the money in their budget, they lose it. In the last few months of the year, whatever money they have, they tend to spend. The number one purchase item for this budget flush is technology equipment. Second, consumers indirectly help push up technology stocks by purchasing electronic items during the holiday season.

Third, the "Conference Effect" helps maintain the momentum of the information technology sector in January. This phenomenon is the result of investors increasing positions in a sector ahead of major conferences in order to benefit from positive announcements. In the case of the information technology sector, investors increase their holdings ahead of the Las Vegas Consumer Electronics Conference that typically occurs in the second week of January.

Info Tech* vs. S&P 500 1989/90 to 2016/17 Positive▢

Year	Oct 9 to Dec 5 S&P 500	IT	Dec 15 to Jan 17 S&P 500	IT	Compound Growth S&P 500	IT
1989/90	-2.6 %	-5.7 %	-3.9 %	3.8 %	-6.3 %	-2.1 %
1990/91	5.2	11.2	0.4	5.5	5.6	17.3
1991/92	-0.9	-1.4	8.9	17.6	8.0	16.0
1992/93	6.0	6.8	1.0	7.4	7.0	14.7
1993/94	1.0	6.9	2.2	8.8	3.2	16.3
1994/95	-0.4	8.5	3.3	9.6	2.9	18.9
1995/96	6.0	3.2	-1.7	-8.0	4.2	-5.1
1996/97	6.2	14.4	6.5	7.3	13.2	22.8
1997/98	1.0	-8.1	0.9	4.0	1.9	-4.4
1998/99	22.7	46.8	8.9	18.7	33.6	74.2
1999/00	7.3	18.7	4.4	9.7	12.0	30.3
2000/01	-2.3	-12.8	-0.9	-3.3	-3.1	-15.7
2001/02	10.2	31.9	1.4	2.3	11.7	34.8
2002/03	13.5	37.2	1.4	-0.6	15.1	36.4
2003/04	2.7	2.3	6.1	11.1	9.0	13.6
2004/05	6.2	11.7	-1.6	-4.1	4.5	7.1
2005/06	5.5	8.4	0.8	1.5	6.4	10.0
2006/07	4.8	6.5	0.4	0.8	5.2	7.4
2007/08	-4.4	-2.6	-9.2	-12.7	-13.1	-14.9
2008/09	-11.1	-14.2	-3.4	-1.9	-14.0	-15.8
2009/10	3.8	6.3	2.0	2.7	5.8	9.2
2010/11	5.1	7.0	4.2	4.9	9.5	12.3
2011/12	8.8	7.6	6.8	4.9	16.1	12.8
2012/13	-3.2	-6.4	4.8	4.0	1.4	-2.6
2013/14	7.8	10.2	3.6	5.5	11.7	16.3
2014/15	5.4	6.8	0.9	-0.7	6.3	6.1
2015/16	3.9	8.2	-7.0	-9.4	-3.4	-1.9
2016/17	2.4	-1.5	0.7	1.5	3.0	0.0
Avg.	4.0 %	7.4 %	1.5 %	3.2 %	5.6 %	11.2 %
Fq > 0	75 %	71 %	75 %	71 %	82 %	71 %

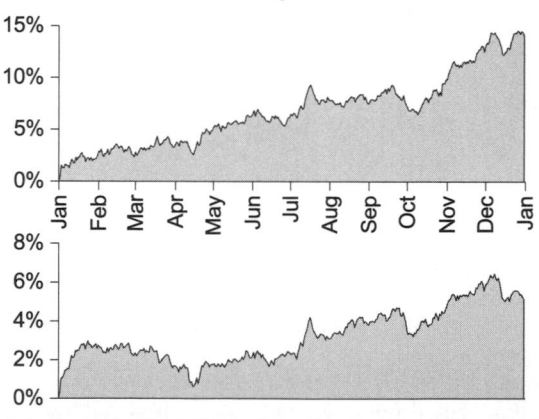

Info Tech Sector - Avg. Year 1990 to 2016

Info Tech / S&P 500 Rel. Strength - Avg Yr. 1990 - 2016

> *Alternate Strategy*— Investors can bridge the gap between the two positive seasonal trends for the information technology sector by holding from October 9th to January 17th. Longer term investors may prefer this strategy, shorter term investors can use technical tools to determine the appropriate strategy.

> *The SP GICS Information Technology Sector. For more information on the information technology sector, see www.standardandpoors.com

Information Technology Performance

Info Tech Monthly Performance (1990-2016)

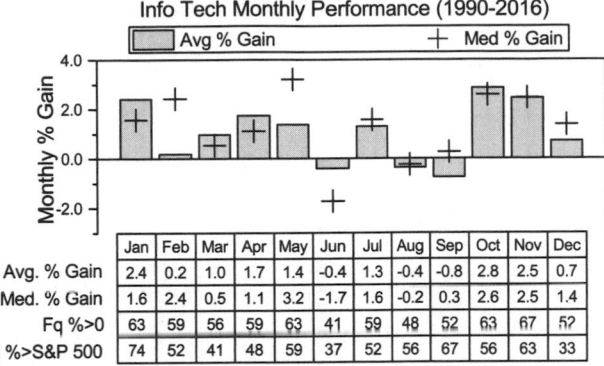

	Jan	Feb	Mar	Apr	May	Jun	Jul	Aug	Sep	Oct	Nov	Dec
Avg. % Gain	2.4	0.2	1.0	1.7	1.4	-0.4	1.3	-0.4	-0.8	2.8	2.5	0.7
Med. % Gain	1.6	2.4	0.5	1.1	3.2	-1.7	1.6	-0.2	0.3	2.6	2.5	1.4
Fq %>0	63	59	56	59	63	41	59	48	52	63	67	52
Fq %>S&P 500	74	52	41	48	59	37	52	56	67	56	63	33

Info Tech 5 Year (2012-2016) % Gain

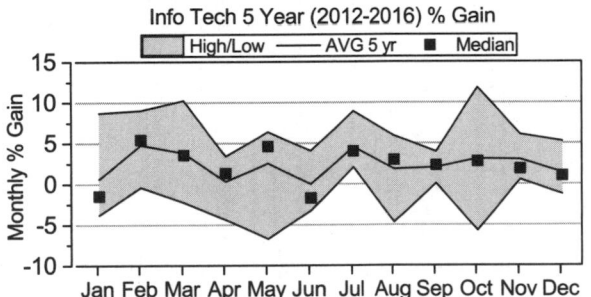

Info Tech Performance 2016-2017

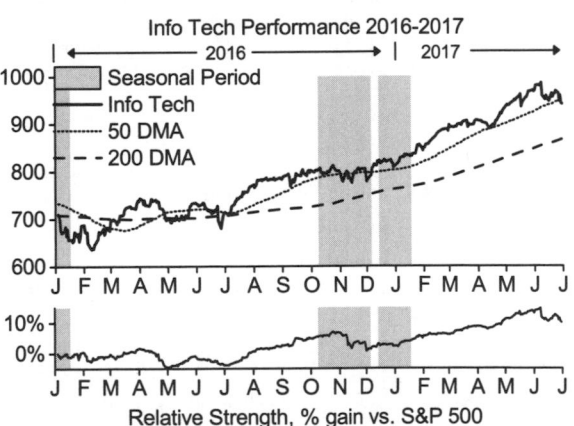

Relative Strength, % gain vs. S&P 500

Market Indices & Rates
Weekly Values**

Stock Markets	2015	2016
Dow	16,554	18,240
S&P500	1,975	2,157
Nasdaq	4,855	5,283
TSX	13,603	14,645
FTSE	6,149	6,860
DAX	10,139	10,501
Nikkei	18,133	16,685
Hang Seng	21,752	23,639

Commodities	2015	2016
Oil	45.46	44.48
Gold	1117.5	1326.5

Bond Yields	2015	2016
USA 5 Yr Treasury	1.54	1.19
USA 10 Yr T	2.22	1.66
USA 20 Yr T	2.67	2.06
Moody's Aaa	4.10	3.47
Moody's Baa	5.37	4.35
CAN 5 Yr T	0.82	0.70
CAN 10 Yr T	1.53	1.13

Money Market	2015	2016
USA Fed Funds	0.25	0.50
USA 3 Mo T-B	0.04	0.24
CAN tgt overnight rate	0.50	0.50
CAN 3 Mo T-B	0.39	0.53

Foreign Exchange	2015	2016
EUR/USD	1.13	1.12
GBP/USD	1.55	1.30
USD/CAD	1.32	1.31
USD/JPY	120.24	101.15

From 1990 to 2016, on average, the technology sector performed well from October to January.

Over the last five years, the technology sector has on average followed its seasonal trend. The largest anomaly has been the weak performance in January. February has been the strongest month and also has had a wide dispersion in returns.

In its 2016/17 seasonal periods, the technology sector was positive, but underperformed the S&P 500.

SEPTEMBER

M	T	W	T	F	S	S
					1	2
3	4	5	6	7	8	9
10	11	12	13	14	15	16
17	18	19	20	21	22	23
24	25	26	27	28	29	30

OCTOBER

M	T	W	T	F	S	S
1	2	3	4	5	6	7
8	9	10	11	12	13	14
15	16	17	18	19	20	21
22	23	24	25	26	27	28
29	30	31				

NOVEMBER

M	T	W	T	F	S	S
		1	2	3	4
5	6	7	8	9	10	11
12	13	14	15	16	17	18
19	20	21	22	23	24	25
26	27	28	29	30		

Canadian banks have their year-end on October 31st. Why does this matter? In the past Canadian banks have announced most of their dividend increases and stock splits when they announce their typically optimistic full year fiscal reports at the end of November and beginning of December. This helps to push up the sector at this time.

11.1% gain & positive 82% of the time

The Canadian bank sector, from October 10th to December 31st for the years 1989/1990 to 2016/2017, has been positive 79% of the time and has produced an average gain of 5.4%. From January 23rd to April 13th, the sector has been positive 71% of the time and has produced an average gain of 5.5%. On a compound basis, the strategy has been positive 82% of the time and produced an average gain of 11.1%.

In the table above, Canadian bank returns in December have been separated out to show the impact of bank earnings on returns. In December, Canadian banks on average have provided gains 75% of the time, but they have underperformed the TSX Composite. If Canadian banks have performed well leading into their earnings, they often pause in December.

ⓘ *Banks SP GIC Canadian Sector Level 2 Represents a cross section of Canadian banking companies.*

Canadian Banks* vs. S&P 500 1989/90 to 2016/17
Positive ▢

	Oct 10 to Dec 31		Jan 23 to Apr 13		Compound Growth		Dec 1 Dec 31 (1989 to 2016)	
Year	TSX-Comp	Cdn. Banks	TSX-Comp	Cdn. Banks	TSX-Comp	Cdn. Banks	TSX-Comp	Cdn. Banks
89/90	-1.7 %	-1.8 %	-6.3 %	-9.1 %	-7.9 %	-10.8 %	0.7 %	-1.4 %
90/91	3.7	8.9	9.8	14.6	13.9	24.8	3.4	5.5
91/92	5.2	10.2	-6.8	-11.6	-2.0	-2.6	1.9	4.6
92/93	4.1	2.5	10.7	14.4	15.2	17.3	2.1	1.8
93/94	6.3	6.8	-5.6	-13.3	0.3	-7.4	3.4	5.1
94/95	-1.8	3.4	5.0	10.0	3.1	13.8	2.9	0.9
95/96	4.9	3.5	3.6	-3.2	8.6	0.1	1.1	1.5
96/97	9.0	15.1	-6.2	0.7	2.3	15.9	-1.5	-1.9
97/98	-6.1	7.6	19.9	38.8	12.6	49.4	2.9	4.2
98/99	18.3	28.0	4.8	13.0	24.0	44.6	2.2	3.0
99/00	18.2	5.1	3.8	22.1	22.8	28.3	11.8	0.7
00/01	-14.4	1.7	-14.1	-6.7	-26.4	-5.1	1.3	9.6
01/02	11.9	6.5	2.3	8.2	14.5	15.1	3.5	3.4
02/03	16.1	21.3	-4.3	2.6	11.1	24.4	0.7	2.6
03/04	8.1	5.1	2.0	2.1	10.3	7.4	4.6	2.0
04/05	4.9	6.2	4.5	6.9	9.6	13.5	2.4	4.7
05/06	6.2	8.4	5.5	2.7	12.1	11.3	4.1	2.1
06/07	10.4	8.4	6.9	3.2	18.0	11.8	1.2	3.7
07/08	-3.0	-10.4	8.2	-3.5	5.0	-13.5	1.1	-7.7
08/09	-6.4	-14.8	9.4	24.4	2.4	6.1	-3.1	-11.2
09/10	2.7	2.4	6.7	15.2	9.6	18.0	2.6	0.1
10/11	7.2	-0.2	4.3	9.1	11.9	8.9	3.8	-0.5
11/12	3.2	3.1	-2.9	1.1	0.2	4.2	-2.0	2.7
12/13	1.3	4.4	-3.8	-2.0	-2.5	2.3	1.6	1.5
13/14	7.0	9.0	1.9	1.6	9.1	10.7	1.7	0.9
14/15	1.2	-0.9	4.2	4.4	5.4	3.5	-0.8	-4.3
15/16	-6.8	-1.5	10.4	11.0	2.8	9.4	-3.4	-3.6
16/17	5.0	11.8	-0.1	-1.5	4.9	10.2	1.4	4.3
Avg.	4.1 %	5.4 %	2.6 %	5.5 %	6.8 %	11.1 %	1.8 %	1.2 %
Fq>0	75 %	79 %	68 %	71 %	86 %	82 %	82 %	75 %

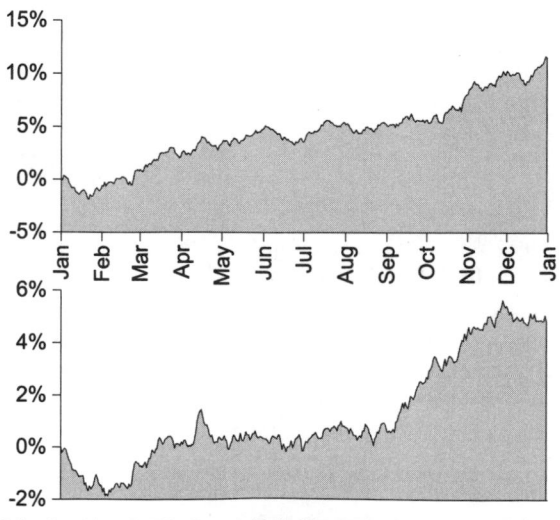

Canadian Banking Sector - Avg. Year 1990 to 2016

Cdn. Banking / TSX Comp Rel. Strength- Avg Yr. 1990-2016

Health Care Performance

Health Care Monthly Performance (1990-2016)

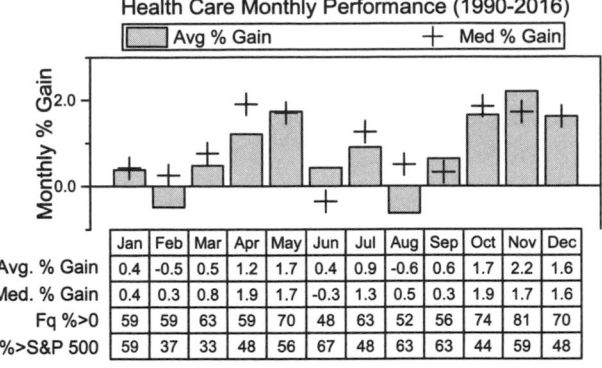

	Jan	Feb	Mar	Apr	May	Jun	Jul	Aug	Sep	Oct	Nov	Dec
Avg. % Gain	0.4	-0.5	0.5	1.2	1.7	0.4	0.9	-0.6	0.6	1.7	2.2	1.6
Med. % Gain	0.4	0.3	0.8	1.9	1.7	-0.3	1.3	0.5	0.3	1.9	1.7	1.6
Fq %>0	59	59	63	59	70	48	63	52	56	74	81	70
Fq %>S&P 500	59	37	33	48	56	67	48	63	63	44	59	48

Health Care 5 Year (2012-2016) % Gain

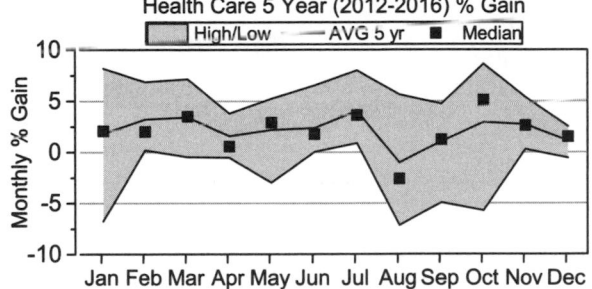

Health Care Performance 2016-2017

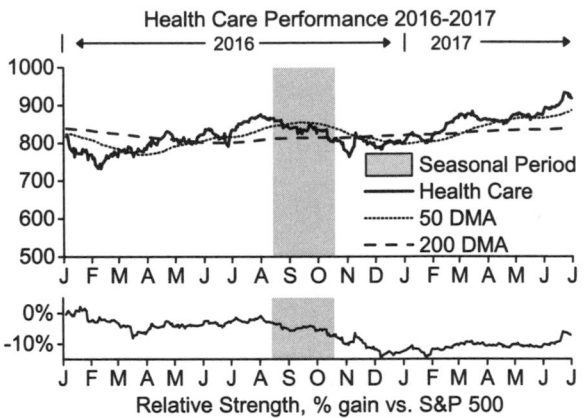

Relative Strength, % gain vs. S&P 500

Market Indices & Rates
Weekly Values**

Stock Markets	2015	2016
Dow	16,224	18,454
S&P500	1,936	2,176
Nasdaq	4,674	5,229
TSX	13,443	14,689
FTSE	6,080	6,811
DAX	10,098	10,603
Nikkei	18,487	16,841
Hang Seng	21,438	23,049

Commodities	2015	2016
Oil	41.38	45.13
Gold	1135.8	1315.4

Bond Yields	2015	2016
USA 5 Yr Treasury	1.47	1.19
USA 10 Yr T	2.14	1.58
USA 20 Yr T	2.56	1.91
Moody's Aaa	4.00	3.24
Moody's Baa	5.29	4.19
CAN 5 Yr T	0.68	0.67
CAN 10 Yr T	1.39	1.03

Money Market	2015	2016
USA Fed Funds	0.25	0.50
USA 3 Mo T-B	0.06	0.33
CAN tgt overnight rate	0.50	0.50
CAN 3 Mo T-B	0.37	0.51

Foreign Exchange	2015	2016
EUR/USD	1.14	1.12
GBP/USD	1.55	1.32
USD/CAD	1.33	1.31
USD/JPY	119.98	103.09

AUGUST

M	T	W	T	F	S	S
		1	2	3	4	5
6	7	8	9	10	11	12
13	14	15	16	17	18	19
20	21	22	23	24	25	26
27	28	29	30	31		

SEPTEMBER

M	T	W	T	F	S	S
					1	2
3	4	5	6	7	8	9
10	11	12	13	14	15	16
17	18	19	20	21	22	23
24	25	26	27	28	29	30

OCTOBER

M	T	W	T	F	S	S
1	2	3	4	5	6	7
8	9	10	11	12	13	14
15	16	17	18	19	20	21
22	23	24	25	26	27	28
29	30	31				

Over the long-term, on average, August is one of the worst performing months for the health care sector, and yet the middle of the month starts off the sector's seasonal period. In this case, averages can be deceiving. Since 1990, not only is the median positive in August, but also the frequency of outperformance relative to the S&P 500 is high, at 63%. Nevertheless, the second half of August is the better performing half. Over the last five years, the health care sector's average performance throughout the year has placed August as the weakest month of the year, and the best performing month as October. In 2016, the health care sector produced a loss in its seasonal period, and underperformed the S&P 500.

SEPTEMBER

	MONDAY	TUESDAY	WEDNESDAY
WEEK 36	**3** 27 USA Market Closed- Labor Day CAN Market Closed- Labor Day	**4** 26	**5** 25
WEEK 37	**10** 20	**11** 19	**12** 18
WEEK 38	**17** 13	**18** 12	**19** 11
WEEK 39	**24** 6	**25** 5	**26** 4
WEEK 40	1	2	3

THURSDAY	FRIDAY
6 24	**7** 23
13 17	**14** 16
20 10	**21** 9
27 3	**28** 2
4	5

OCTOBER

M	T	W	T	F	S	S
1	2	3	4	5	6	7
8	9	10	11	12	13	14
15	16	17	18	19	20	21
22	23	24	25	26	27	28
29	30	31				

NOVEMBER

M	T	W	T	F	S	S
			1	2	3	4
5	6	7	8	9	10	11
12	13	14	15	16	17	18
19	20	21	22	23	24	25
26	27	28	29	30		

DECEMBER

M	T	W	T	F	S	S
					1	2
3	4	5	6	7	8	9
10	11	12	13	14	15	16
17	18	19	20	21	22	23
24	25	26	27	28	29	30
31						

JANUARY

M	T	W	T	F	S	S
	1	2	3	4	5	6
7	8	9	10	11	12	13
14	15	16	17	18	19	20
21	22	23	24	25	26	27
28	29	30	31			

SEPTEMBER
S U M M A R Y

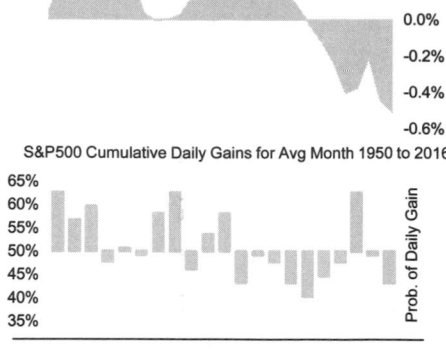

S&P500 Cumulative Daily Gains for Avg Month 1950 to 2016

	Dow Jones	S&P 500	Nasdaq	TSX Comp
Month Rank	12	12	12	12
# Up	26	29	24	13
# Down	41	38	21	19
% Pos	39	43	53	41
% Avg. Gain	-0.8	-0.5	-0.6	-1.6

Dow & S&P 1950-2016, Nasdaq 1972-2016, TSX 1985-2016

♦ September has the reputation of being the worst month of the year for the S&P 500. From 1950 to 2016, September has produced an average loss of 0.5% and has only been positive 43% of the time. ♦ In particular, the last part of September has been negative. ♦ The defensive sectors of the stock market are typically better performing sectors in September as investors seek more stable earnings in a month that is often volatile ♦ The materials sector on average performs poorly in September and has outperformed the S&P 500 only 22% of the time since 1990.

BEST / WORST SEPTEMBER BROAD MKTS. 2007-2016

BEST SEPTEMBER MARKETS
♦ Russell 2000 (2010) 12.3%
♦ Nasdaq (2010) 12.0%
♦ Russell 1000 (2010) 9.0%

WORST SEPTEMBER MARKETS
♦ TSX Comp. (2008) -14.7%
♦ Nikkei 225 (2008) -13.9%
♦ FTSE 100 (2008) -13.0%

Index Values End of Month

	2007	2008	2009	2010	2011	2012	2013	2014	2015	2016
Dow	13,896	10,851	9,712	10,788	10,913	13,437	15,130	17,043	16,285	18,308
S&P 500	1,527	1,166	1,057	1,141	1,131	1,441	1,682	1,972	1,920	2,168
Nasdaq	2,702	2,092	2,122	2,369	2,415	3,116	3,771	4,493	4,620	5,312
TSX Comp.	14,099	11,753	11,395	12,369	11,624	12,317	12,787	14,961	13,307	14,726
Russell 1000	831	633	580	630	623	794	940	1,096	1,068	1,202
Russell 2000	805	680	604	676	644	837	1,074	1,102	1,101	1,252
FTSE 100	6,467	4,902	5,134	5,549	5,128	5,742	6,462	6,623	6,062	6,899
Nikkei 225	16,786	11,260	10,133	9,369	8,700	8,870	14,456	16,174	17,388	16,450

Percent Gain for September

	2007	2008	2009	2010	2011	2012	2013	2014	2015	2016
Dow	4.0	-6.0	2.3	7.7	-6.0	2.6	2.2	-0.3	-1.5	-0.5
S&P 500	3.6	-9.1	3.6	8.8	-7.2	2.4	3.0	-1.6	-2.6	-0.1
Nasdaq	4.0	-11.6	5.6	12.0	-6.4	1.6	5.1	-1.9	-3.3	1.9
TSX Comp.	3.2	-14.7	4.8	3.8	-9.0	3.1	1.1	-4.3	-4.0	0.9
Russell 1000	3.5	-9.8	3.9	9.0	-7.6	2.4	3.3	-1.9	-2.9	-0.1
Russell 2000	1.6	-8.1	5.6	12.3	-11.4	3.1	6.2	-6.2	-5.1	0.9
FTSE 100	2.6	-13.0	4.6	6.2	-4.9	0.5	0.8	-2.9	-3.0	1.7
Nikkei 225	1.3	-13.9	-3.4	6.2	-2.8	0.3	8.0	4.9	-8.0	-2.6

September Market Avg. Performance 2007 to 2016[1]

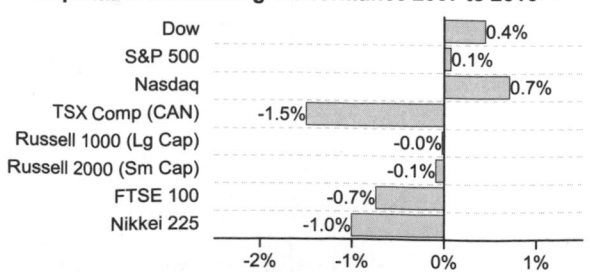

Dow	0.4%
S&P 500	0.1%
Nasdaq	0.7%
TSX Comp (CAN)	-1.5%
Russell 1000 (Lg Cap)	-0.0%
Russell 2000 (Sm Cap)	-0.1%
FTSE 100	-0.7%
Nikkei 225	-1.0%

Interest Corner Sep[2]

	Fed Funds % [3]	3 Mo. T-Bill % [4]	10 Yr % [5]	20 Yr % [6]
2016	0.50	0.29	1.60	1.99
2015	0.25	0.00	2.06	2.51
2014	0.25	0.02	2.52	2.98
2013	0.25	0.02	2.64	3.41
2012	0.25	0.10	1.65	2.42

(1) Russell Data provided by Russell (2) Federal Reserve Bank of St. Louis- end of month values (3) Target rate set by FOMC (4)(5)(6) Constant yield maturities.

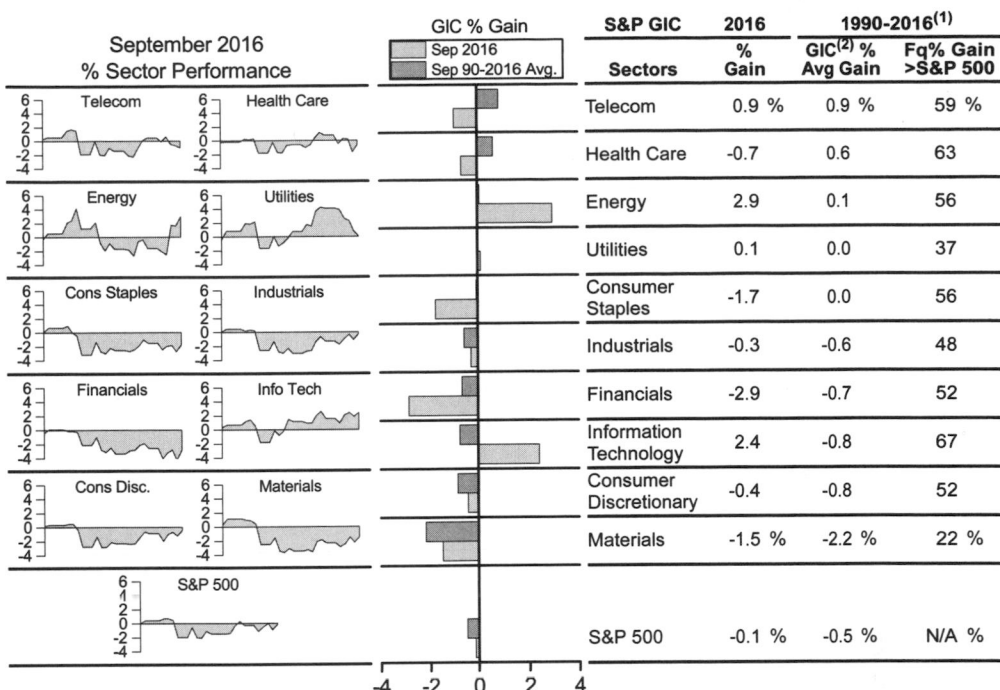

S&P GIC Sectors	2016 % Gain	1990-2016[1] GIC[2] % Avg Gain	1990-2016[1] Fq% Gain >S&P 500
Telecom	0.9 %	0.9 %	59 %
Health Care	-0.7	0.6	63
Energy	2.9	0.1	56
Utilities	0.1	0.0	37
Consumer Staples	-1.7	0.0	56
Industrials	-0.3	-0.6	48
Financials	-2.9	-0.7	52
Information Technology	2.4	-0.8	67
Consumer Discretionary	-0.4	-0.8	52
Materials	-1.5 %	-2.2 %	22 %
S&P 500	-0.1 %	-0.5 %	N/A %

September 2016 % Sector Performance — Telecom, Health Care, Energy, Utilities, Cons Staples, Industrials, Financials, Info Tech, Cons Disc., Materials, S&P 500

GIC % Gain — Sep 2016, Sep 90-2016 Avg.

Sector Commentary

♦ In September 2016, the energy sector produced a gain of 2.9%. The sector is typically one of the better performing sectors in September. ♦ The information technology sector produced a gain of 2.4%. Although the sector has outperformed the S&P 500, 67% of the time from 1990 to 2016 in September, the sector has previously had some large losses in the month, making an investment in this sector typically volatile. ♦ The financial sector produced a loss of 2.9% as investors viewed that the Federal Reserve was becoming more dovish in its monetary policy.

Sub-Sector Commentary

♦ September is typically the month when precious metals tend to perform well. In September 2016, gold produced a gain of 0.1% and silver a gain of 3.3%. ♦ The transportation sub-sector typically starts its period of seasonal strength in October, but in 2016 it was positive in September, producing a gain of 2.9%. ♦ September tends to be a weak month for the chemicals sub-sector and in 2016, the sector produced a loss of 2.5%.

SELECTED SUB-SECTORS[3]

	2016 % Gain	GIC % Avg Gain	Fq% Gain >S&P 500
Gold	0.1 %	2.4 %	67 %
Silver	3.3	1.7	70
Biotech (1993-2016)	-0.9	1.4	63
Pharma	-1.6	0.7	59
Agriculture (1994-2016)	-3.6	-0.4	52
Retail	1.0	-0.6	48
Transportation	2.9	-0.6	56
Railroads	3.0	-0.6	41
Banks	-4.1	-1.1	52
Homebuilders	-7.5	-1.1	56
Metals & Mining	2.6	-1.9	44
Chemicals	-2.5	-2.0	30
Automotive & Components	-0.6	-2.5	37
SOX (1995-2016)	4.3	-2.6	45
Steel	1.9	-3.6	44

(1) Sector data provided by Standard and Poors (2) GIC is short form for Global Industry Classification (3) Sub Sector data provided by Standard and Poors, except where marked by symbol.

PROCTER AND GAMBLE
SOMETHING FOR EVERYONE – Aug 7 to Nov 19

In the investors' eyes, Procter and Gamble is a relatively defensive investment, as the company is in the consumer packaged goods business and its revenues are generated in over 180 countries. Defensive stocks have a reputation of producing sub-par performance compared with the broad market. This is not the case with PG, as on average, it has outperformed the S&P 500 over the last twenty-seven years during its seasonally strong period.

7.6% gain & positive 78% of the time

Interestingly, on average, the gains that have been produced are largely in the second half of the year. In the first half of the year, PG has been relatively flat and has underperformed the S&P 500.

PG* vs. S&P 500 - 1990 to 2016

Aug 7 to Nov 19	S&P 500	PG	Diff
		Positive	
1990	-4.5%	8.4%	12.8%
1991	-2.9	-2.1	0.7
1992	0.7	10.1	9.4
1993	3.1	17.7	14.6
1994	1.0	19.5	18.3
1995	7.4	27.8	20.4
1996	12.0	18.4	6.5
1997	-1.6	0.3	1.9
1998	5.8	14.0	8.2
1999	9.4	18.9	9.3
2000	-6.5	32.0	38.3
2001	-4.1	11.2	15.3
2002	4.3	-0.7	-5.0
2003	7.8	8.2	0.4
2004	10.0	2.5	-7.5
2005	1.8	6.2	4.4
2006	9.5	7.4	-2.1
2007	-2.3	12.0	14.4
2008	-37.4	-8.1	29.3
2009	9.8	20.8	11.0
2010	7.0	6.7	-0.3
2011	1.4	4.4	3.0
2012	-0.5	3.2	3.7
2013	5.3	3.2	-2.2
2014	6.7	9.4	2.7
2015	-0.1	0.6	0.8
2016	0.0	-4.4	-4.4
Avg	1.6%	9.2%	7.6%
Fq > 0	63%	85%	78%

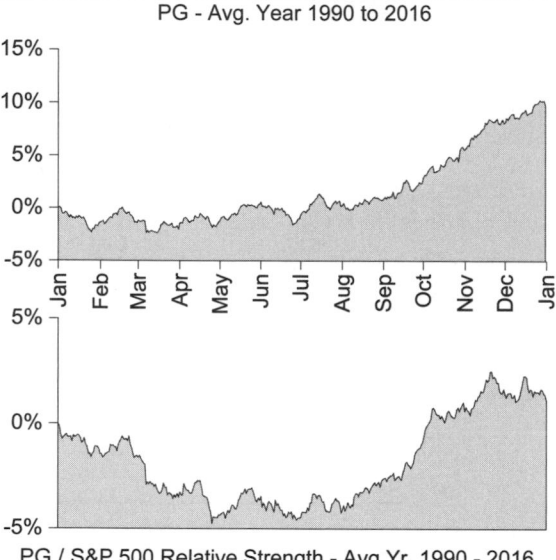

PG - Avg. Year 1990 to 2016

PG / S&P 500 Relative Strength - Avg Yr. 1990 - 2016

From a seasonal perspective, the best time to invest in PG has been from August 7th to November 19th. During this period, from 1990 to 2016, PG on average produced a gain of 9.2% and was positive 85% of the time. In addition, it substantially outperformed the S&P 500, generating an extra profit of 7.6% and beating its performance 78% of the time.

Investors will often seek sanctuary in defensive stocks in late summer and early autumn. Although August is not typically the worst month of the year, it does have a weak risk-reward profile. With the dreaded month of September falling right after August, investors become "gun shy" and start to become more conservative in August.

This trend benefits PG as more investors switch over to defensive companies. PG's outperformance, on average, starts to occur just after it releases its fourth quarter earnings at the beginning of August.

PG continues to outperform the S&P 500 through September and October. For the S&P 500, September on average is the worst month of the year and October is the most volatile month. The outperformance of PG continues into mid-November.

PG's seasonally strong period extends past the seasonal period for the consumer staples sector. It is possible that investors wait until after PG's first quarter results are released in the beginning of November before adjusting their portfolios.

 The Procter and Gamble Company is a consumer packaged goods company. Data adjusted for stock splits.

Procter & Gamble Performance

PG Monthly Performance (1990-2016)

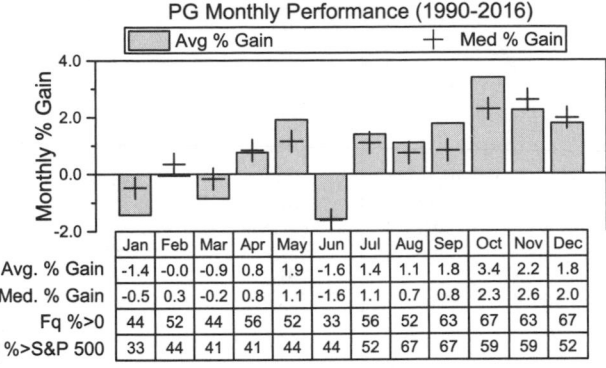

	Jan	Feb	Mar	Apr	May	Jun	Jul	Aug	Sep	Oct	Nov	Dec
Avg. % Gain	-1.4	-0.0	-0.9	0.8	1.9	-1.6	1.4	1.1	1.8	3.4	2.2	1.8
Med. % Gain	-0.5	0.3	-0.2	0.8	1.1	-1.6	1.1	0.7	0.8	2.3	2.6	2.0
Fq %>0	44	52	44	56	52	33	56	52	63	67	63	67
Fq %>S&P 500	33	44	41	41	44	44	52	67	67	59	59	52

PG 5 Year (2012-2016) % Gain

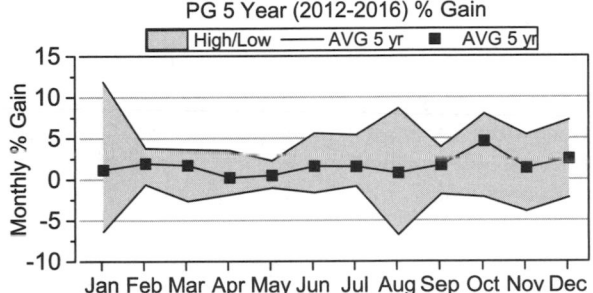

PG Performance 2016-2017

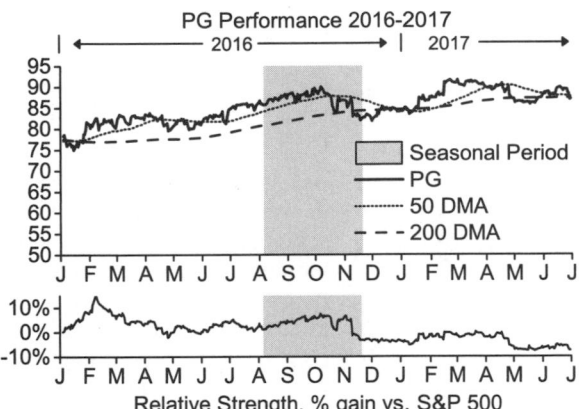

Relative Strength, % gain vs. S&P 500

From 1990 to 2016, October was the strongest month for Procter & Gamble on an average and frequency basis. Over the same time period, June was the weakest month.

Over the last five years, Procter & Gamble has generally followed its average seasonal trend.

In 2016, Proctor and Gamble was positive in the first portion of the year leading up to its seasonal period, but underperformed the S&P 500. In its seasonal period, Procter & Gamble declined and underperformed the S&P 500.

WEEK 36

Market Indices & Rates
Weekly Values**

Stock Markets	2015	2016
Dow	16,283	18,407
S&P500	1,941	2,170
Nasdaq	4,716	5,236
TSX	13,592	14,738
FTSE	6,095	6,838
DAX	10,136	10,672
Nikkei	18,225	17,011
Hang Seng	21,158	23,840

Commodities	2015	2016
Oil	46.73	45.96
Gold	1131.6	1337.2

Bond Yields	2015	2016
USA 5 Yr Treasury	1.50	1.17
USA 10 Yr T	2.18	1.59
USA 20 Yr T	2.63	1.96
Moody's Aaa	4.12	3.33
Moody's Baa	5.34	4.25
CAN 5 Yr T	0.75	0.67
CAN 10 Yr T	1.46	1.07

Money Market	2015	2016
USA Fed Funds	0.25	0.50
USA 3 Mo T-B	0.04	0.34
CAN tgt overnight rate	0.50	0.50
CAN 3 Mo T-D	0.37	0.50

Foreign Exchange	2015	2016
EUR/USD	1.12	1.12
GBP/USD	1.53	1.33
USD/CAD	1.32	1.29
USD/JPY	120.00	102.47

SEPTEMBER

M	T	W	T	F	S	S
					1	2
3	4	5	6	7	8	9
10	11	12	13	14	15	16
17	18	19	20	21	22	23
24	25	26	27	28	29	30

OCTOBER

M	T	W	T	F	S	S
1	2	3	4	5	6	7
8	9	10	11	12	13	14
15	16	17	18	19	20	21
22	23	24	25	26	27	28
29	30	31				

NOVEMBER

M	T	W	T	F	S	S
				1	2	3	4
5	6	7	8	9	10	11
12	13	14	15	16	17	18
19	20	21	22	23	24	25
26	27	28	29	30		

CARNIVAL CRUISE LINES
CRUISING FOR RETURNS– Sep 8 to Dec 31

The cruise industry is a seasonal business. The first quarter has the highest number of bookings and the third quarter has the highest number of voyages.

Investors look to be invested in Carnival Cruise Lines (Carnival) ahead of its booking season, increasing the relative performance of the stock price from September 8th until December 31st. In this time period, from 1990 to 2016, Carnival has produced an average return of 13.6% and has been positive 78% of the time.

13.6% gain & positive 78% of the time

The cruise industry has a large number of variables affecting its performance which can be fairly volatile. In the last decade, demand for cruise trips have been adversely affected by news stories of outbreaks of sickness, on-board fires immobilizing ships and general ship breakdowns at sea. Although these problems have adversely affected the stock prices of cruise companies in the short-term, the cruise companies have worked hard at preventing future problems and the stock prices have responded positively.

CCL* vs. S&P 500 - 1990 to 2016

Sep 8 to Dec 31	S&P 500	CCL	Diff
		Positive	
1990	2.1%	-20.5%	-22.6%
1991	7.2	26.4	19.2
1992	4.5	23.0	18.5
1993	1.7	15.5	13.8
1994	-2.5	-2.9	-0.4
1995	8.0	12.8	4.8
1996	13.0	20.0	7.0
1997	4.5	20.6	16.1
1998	26.2	83.8	57.6
1999	8.8	8.7	-0.1
2000	-12.1	56.5	68.6
2001	5.7	-3.3	-9.1
2002	-1.6	3.1	4.7
2003	8.9	15.2	6.3
2004	8.1	22.7	14.6
2005	1.0	7.2	6.3
2006	9.6	16.5	6.9
2007	1.0	-0.5	-1.5
2008	-27.3	-37.6	-10.3
2009	9.7	8.0	-1.7
2010	15.2	36.1	21.0
2011	4.9	2.5	-2.4
2012	-0.8	-0.8	0.1
2013	11.7	12.0	0.4
2014	2.6	15.3	12.7
2015	6.4	11.3	5.0
2016	2.4	14.9	12.5
Avg	4.4%	13.6%	9.1%
Fq > 0	81%	78%	70%

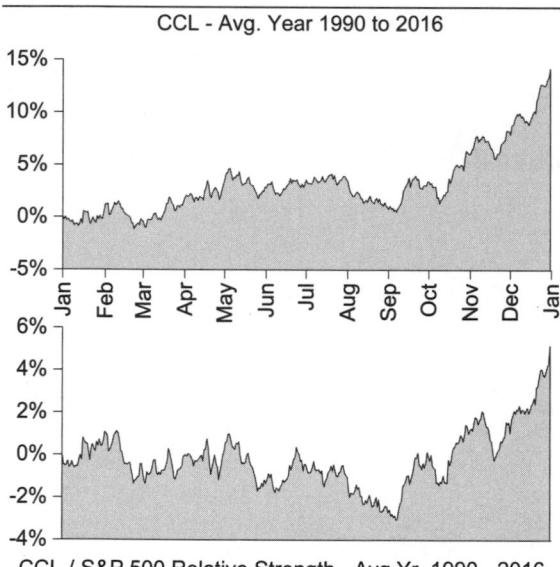

CCL - Avg. Year 1990 to 2016

CCL / S&P 500 Relative Strength - Avg Yr. 1990 - 2016

losses of 10% or greater, which have only occurred twice in the same time period.

August tends to be a weaker month of the year for Carnival and given that its seasonal period starts the following month, investors should be cautious on timing the entry into the seasonal trade. This is particularly true as September tends to be a negative month for the S&P 500 and any large corrections would have a high likelihood of having a negative influence on Carnival.

In its seasonal period, Carnival has on average outperformed the S&P 500 by 9.1% from 1990 to 2016. Although Carnival's 83.8% return in its 1998 seasonal period helps to skew the average higher for the seasonal period, Carnival has had returns of 10% or greater, sixteen times since 1990. This compares to

i * Carnival Cruise Lines is a travel company listed on the NYSE. Data adjusted for stock splits.

CCL Performance

CCL Monthly Performance (1990-2016)

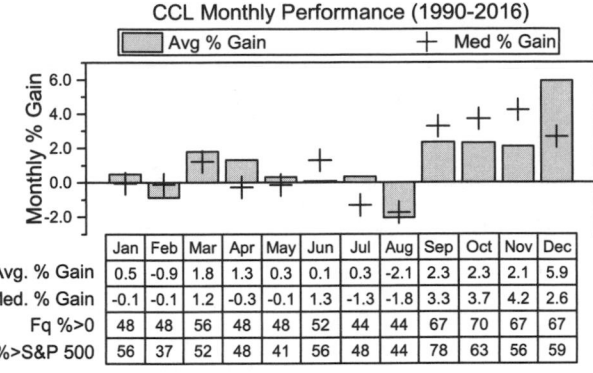

	Jan	Feb	Mar	Apr	May	Jun	Jul	Aug	Sep	Oct	Nov	Dec
Avg. % Gain	0.5	-0.9	1.8	1.3	0.3	0.1	0.3	-2.1	2.3	2.3	2.1	5.9
Med. % Gain	-0.1	-0.1	1.2	-0.3	-0.1	1.3	-1.3	-1.8	3.3	3.7	4.2	2.6
Fq %>0	48	48	56	48	48	52	44	44	67	70	67	67
Fq %>S&P 500	56	37	52	48	41	56	48	44	78	63	56	59

CCL 5 Year (2012-2016) % Gain

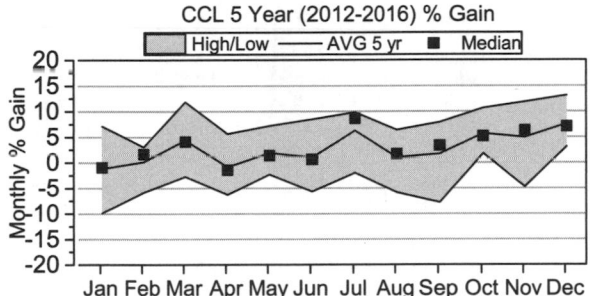

Market Indices & Rates
Weekly Values**

Stock Markets	2015	2016
Dow	16,377	18,153
S&P500	1,956	2,140
Nasdaq	4,797	5,207
TSX	13,548	14,453
FTSE	6,145	6,696
DAX	10,203	10,381
Nikkei	18,124	16,588
Hang Seng	21,408	23,258

Commodities	2015	2016
Oil	45.16	44.34
Gold	1112.1	1317.8

Bond Yields	2015	2016
USA 5 Yr Treasury	1.53	1.22
USA 10 Yr T	2.21	1.70
USA 20 Yr T	2.65	2.10
Moody's Aaa	4.09	3.49
Moody's Baa	5.33	4.41
CAN 5 Yr T	0.77	0.73
CAN 10 Yr T	1.47	1.19

Money Market	2015	2016
USA Fed Funds	0.25	0.50
USA 3 Mo T-B	0.04	0.33
CAN tgt overnight rate	0.50	0.50
CAN 3 Mo T-B	0.38	0.50

Foreign Exchange	2015	2016
EUR/USD	1.12	1.12
GBP/USD	1.54	1.32
USD/CAD	1.33	1.32
USD/JPY	120.16	102.25

CCL Performance 2016-2017

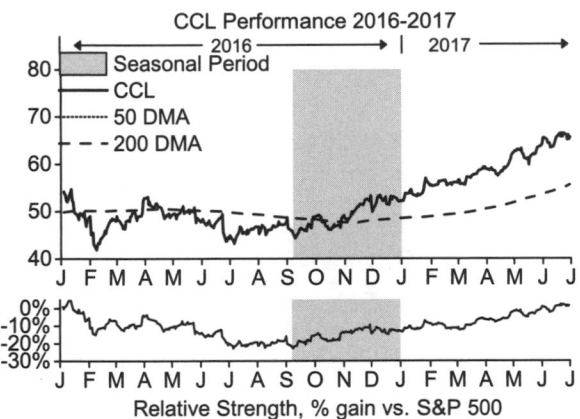

Relative Strength, % gain vs. S&P 500

SEPTEMBER

M	T	W	T	F	S	S
					1	2
3	4	5	6	7	8	9
10	11	12	13	14	15	16
17	18	19	20	21	22	23
24	25	26	27	28	29	30

OCTOBER

M	T	W	T	F	S	S
1	2	3	4	5	6	7
8	9	10	11	12	13	14
15	16	17	18	19	20	21
22	23	24	25	26	27	28
29	30	31				

NOVEMBER

M	T	W	T	F	S	S
			1	2	3	4
5	6	7	8	9	10	11
12	13	14	15	16	17	18
19	20	21	22	23	24	25
26	27	28	29	30		

From 1990 to 2016, the best four contiguous months of the year for Carnival on an average, median and frequency basis were September through December.

From 2012 to 2016, Carnival has followed its general seasonal pattern with the last four months of the year being strong.

In 2016, Carnival started to outperform the S&P 500 at the beginning of its seasonal period and continued its outperformance into the first half of 2017.

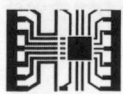

INFORMATION TECHNOLOGY
①Oct9-Dec5 ②Dec15-Jan17

From 1989 to 2016, during its seasonal period of October 9th to December 5th, the information technology sector has produced an average gain of 7.4% and has been positive 71% of the time. From 1989/90 to 2016/17, during the second seasonal period of December 15th to January 17th, the information technology sector has produced an average gain of 3.2% and has been positive 71% of the time. The combined seasonal gains have been 11.2% and has been positive 71% of the time.

11.2% gain

Information technology stocks tend to get bid up at the end of the year for three reasons.

First, a lot of companies operate with year end budgets and if they do not spend the money in their budget, they lose it. In the last few months of the year, whatever money they have, they tend to spend. The number one purchase item for this budget flush is technology equipment. Second, consumers indirectly help push up technology stocks by purchasing electronic items during the holiday season.

Third, the "Conference Effect" helps maintain the momentum of the information technology sector in January. This phenomenon is the result of investors increasing positions in a sector ahead of major conferences in order to benefit from positive announcements. In the case of the information technology sector, investors increase their holdings ahead of the Las Vegas Consumer Electronics Conference that typically occurs in the second week of January.

Info Tech* vs. S&P 500 1989/90 to 2016/17   Positive ☐

Year	Oct 9 to Dec 5 S&P 500	Oct 9 to Dec 5 IT	Dec 15 to Jan 17 S&P 500	Dec 15 to Jan 17 IT	Compound Growth S&P 500	Compound Growth IT
1989/90	-2.6 %	-5.7 %	-3.9 %	3.8 %	-6.3 %	-2.1 %
1990/91	5.2	11.2	0.4	5.5	5.6	17.3
1991/92	-0.9	-1.4	8.9	17.6	8.0	16.0
1992/93	6.0	6.8	1.0	7.4	7.0	14.7
1993/94	1.0	6.9	2.2	8.8	3.2	16.3
1994/95	-0.4	8.5	3.3	9.6	2.9	18.9
1995/96	6.0	3.2	-1.7	-8.0	4.2	-5.1
1996/97	6.2	14.4	6.5	7.3	13.2	22.8
1997/98	1.0	-8.1	0.9	4.0	1.9	-4.4
1998/99	22.7	46.8	8.9	18.7	33.6	74.2
1999/00	7.3	18.7	4.4	9.7	12.0	30.3
2000/01	-2.3	-12.8	-0.9	-3.3	-3.1	-15.7
2001/02	10.2	31.9	1.4	2.3	11.7	34.8
2002/03	13.5	37.2	1.4	-0.6	15.1	36.4
2003/04	2.7	2.3	6.1	11.1	9.0	13.6
2004/05	6.2	11.7	-1.6	-4.1	4.5	7.1
2005/06	5.5	8.4	0.8	1.5	6.4	10.0
2006/07	4.8	6.5	0.4	0.8	5.2	7.4
2007/08	-4.4	-2.6	-9.2	-12.7	-13.1	-14.9
2008/09	-11.1	-14.2	-3.4	-1.9	-14.0	-15.8
2009/10	3.8	6.3	2.0	2.7	5.8	9.2
2010/11	5.1	7.0	4.2	4.9	9.5	12.3
2011/12	8.8	7.6	6.8	4.9	16.1	12.8
2012/13	-3.2	-6.4	4.8	4.0	1.4	-2.6
2013/14	7.8	10.2	3.6	5.5	11.7	16.3
2014/15	5.4	6.8	0.9	-0.7	6.3	6.1
2015/16	3.9	8.2	-7.0	-9.4	-3.4	-1.9
2016/17	2.4	-1.5	0.7	1.5	3.0	0.0
Avg.	4.0 %	7.4 %	1.5 %	3.2 %	5.6 %	11.2 %
Fq > 0	75 %	71 %	75 %	71 %	82 %	71 %

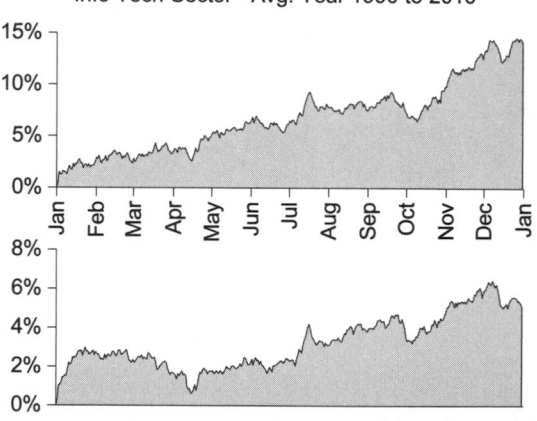

Info Tech Sector - Avg. Year 1990 to 2016

Info Tech / S&P 500 Rel. Strength - Avg Yr. 1990 - 2016

 Alternate Strategy— *Investors can bridge the gap between the two positive seasonal trends for the information technology sector by holding from October 9th to January 17th. Longer term investors may prefer this strategy, shorter term investors can use technical tools to determine the appropriate strategy.*

ⓘ *The SP GICS Information Technology Sector. For more information on the information technology sector, see www.standardandpoors.com*

Canadian Banks Performance

Canadian Banks Monthly Performance (1990-2016)

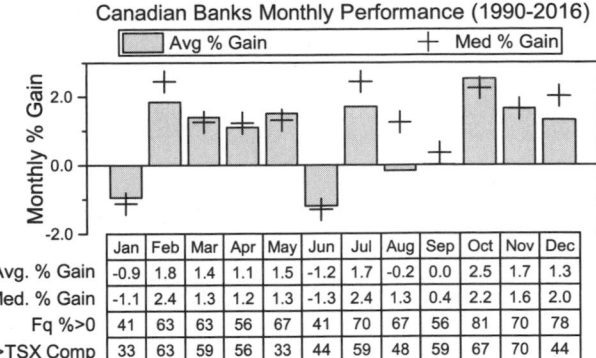

	Jan	Feb	Mar	Apr	May	Jun	Jul	Aug	Sep	Oct	Nov	Dec
Avg. % Gain	-0.9	1.8	1.4	1.1	1.5	-1.2	1.7	-0.2	0.0	2.5	1.7	1.3
Med. % Gain	-1.1	2.4	1.3	1.2	1.3	-1.3	2.4	1.3	0.4	2.2	1.6	2.0
Fq %>0	41	63	63	56	67	41	70	67	56	81	70	78
Fq %>TSX Comp	33	63	59	56	33	44	59	48	59	67	70	44

Canadian Banks 5 Year (2012-2016) % Gain

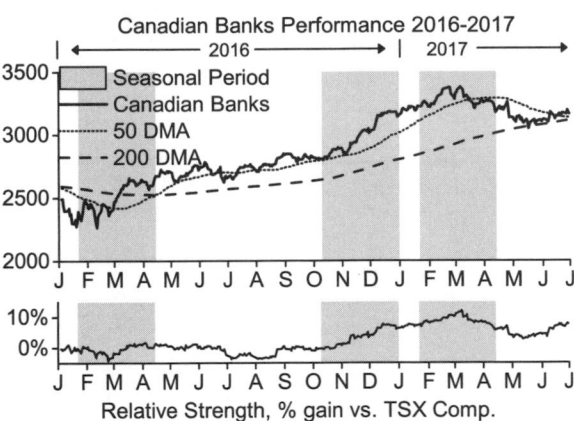

Canadian Banks Performance 2016-2017

Relative Strength, % gain vs. TSX Comp.

SEPTEMBER

M	T	W	T	F	S	S
					1	2
3	4	5	6	7	8	9
10	11	12	13	14	15	16
17	18	19	20	21	22	23
24	25	26	27	28	29	30

OCTOBER

M	T	W	T	F	S	S
1	2	3	4	5	6	7
8	9	10	11	12	13	14
15	16	17	18	19	20	21
22	23	24	25	26	27	28
29	30	31				

NOVEMBER

M	T	W	T	F	S	S
			1	2	3	4
5	6	7	8	9	10	11
12	13	14	15	16	17	18
19	20	21	22	23	24	25
26	27	28	29	30		

From 1990 to 2016, October has been the best month for Canadian banks on an average basis. September has been one of the weaker months of the year. This juxtaposition makes the timing of the transition into the seasonal period, that starts in October, important. The second seasonal period starts in late January. On average, January is a weak month making the timing of the transition critical. Over the last five years, February has been the best month of the year for Canadian banks on a median basis. In the late 2016 seasonal period, Canadian banks outperformed the TSX Composite. It underperformed the TSX Composite in its first 2017 period.

OCTOBER

	MONDAY	TUESDAY	WEDNESDAY
WEEK 40	**1** 30	**2** 29	**3** 28
WEEK 41	**8** 23 USA Bond Market Closed- Columbus Day CAN Market Closed- Thanksgiving Day	**9** 22	**10** 21
WEEK 42	**15** 16	**16** 15	**17** 14
WEEK 43	**22** 9	**23** 8	**24** 7
WEEK 44	**29** 2	**30** 1	**31**

OCTOBER

THURSDAY	FRIDAY
4 27	**5** 26
11 20	**12** 19
18 13	**19** 12
25 6	**26** 5
1	2

NOVEMBER

M	T	W	T	F	S	S
			1	2	3	4
5	6	7	8	9	10	11
12	13	14	15	16	17	18
19	20	21	22	23	24	25
26	27	28	29	30		

DECEMBER

M	T	W	T	F	S	S
					1	2
3	4	5	6	7	8	9
10	11	12	13	14	15	16
17	18	19	20	21	22	23
24	25	26	27	28	29	30
31						

JANUARY

M	T	W	T	F	S	S
	1	2	3	4	5	6
7	8	9	10	11	12	13
14	15	16	17	18	19	20
21	22	23	24	25	26	27
28	29	30	31			

FEBRUARY

M	T	W	T	F	S	S
				1	2	3
4	5	6	7	8	9	10
11	12	13	14	15	16	17
18	19	20	21	22	23	24
25	26	27	28			

OCTOBER
S U M M A R Y

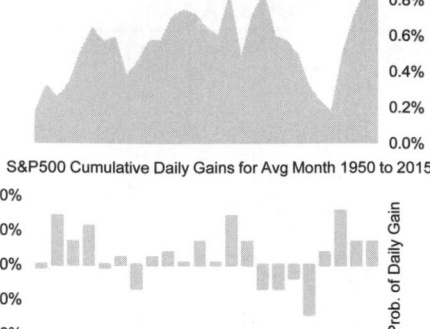

	Dow Jones	S&P 500	Nasdaq	TSX Comp
Month Rank	7	7	6	9
# Up	40	40	25	21
# Down	27	27	20	11
% Pos	60	60	56	66
% Avg. Gain	0.6	0.9	0.8	0.1

Dow & S&P 1950-2016, Nasdaq 1972-2016, TSX 1985-2016

S&P500 Cumulative Daily Gains for Avg Month 1950 to 2015

♦ October, on average, is the most volatile month of the year for the stock market and often provides opportunities for short-term traders. The first half of October tends to be positive. ♦ The second half of the month, leading up to the last four days, tends to be negative, and prone to large drops. ♦ Seasonal opportunities in mid-October include Canadian banks, technology and transportation. ♦ In late October, a lot of sectors start their seasonal period, including the materials, industrials, consumer discretionary and retail sectors.

BEST / WORST OCTOBER BROAD MKTS. 2007-2016

BEST OCTOBER MARKETS
♦ Russell 2000 (2011) 15.0%
♦ Nasdaq (2011) 11.1%
♦ Russell 1000 (2011) 11.1%

WORST OCTOBER MARKETS
♦ Nikkei 225 (2008) -23.8%
♦ Russell 2000 (2008) -20.9%
♦ Nasdaq (2008) -17.7%

Index Values End of Month

	2007	2008	2009	2010	2011	2012	2013	2014	2015	2016
Dow	13,930	9,325	9,713	11,118	11,955	13,096	15,546	17,391	17,664	18,142
S&P 500	1,549	969	1,036	1,183	1,253	1,412	1,757	2,018	2,079	2,126
Nasdaq	2,859	1,721	2,045	2,507	2,684	2,977	3,920	4,631	5,054	5,189
TSX Comp.	14,625	9,763	10,911	12,676	12,252	12,423	13,361	14,613	13,529	14,787
Russell 1000	844	522	567	654	692	779	980	1,122	1,154	1,177
Russell 2000	828	538	563	703	741	819	1,100	1,174	1,162	1,191
FTSE 100	6,722	4,377	5,045	5,675	5,544	5,783	6,731	6,546	6,361	6,954
Nikkei 225	16,738	8,577	10,035	9,202	8,988	8,928	14,328	16,414	19,083	17,425

Percent Gain for October

	2007	2008	2009	2010	2011	2012	2013	2014	2015	2016
Dow	0.2	-14.1	0.0	3.1	9.5	-2.5	2.8	2.0	8.5	-0.9
S&P 500	1.5	-16.9	-2.0	3.7	10.8	-2.0	4.5	2.3	8.3	-1.9
Nasdaq	5.8	-17.7	-3.6	5.9	11.1	-4.5	3.9	3.1	9.4	-2.3
TSX Comp.	3.7	-16.9	-4.2	2.5	5.4	0.9	4.5	-2.3	1.7	0.4
Russell 1000	1.6	-17.5	-2.3	3.8	11.1	-1.8	4.3	2.3	8.0	-2.1
Russell 2000	2.8	-20.9	-6.9	4.0	15.0	-2.2	2.5	6.5	5.6	-4.8
FTSE 100	3.9	-10.7	-1.7	2.3	8.1	0.7	4.2	-1.2	4.9	0.8
Nikkei 225	-0.3	-23.8	-1.0	-1.8	3.3	0.7	-0.9	1.5	9.7	5.9

October Market Avg. Performance 2007 to 2016[1]

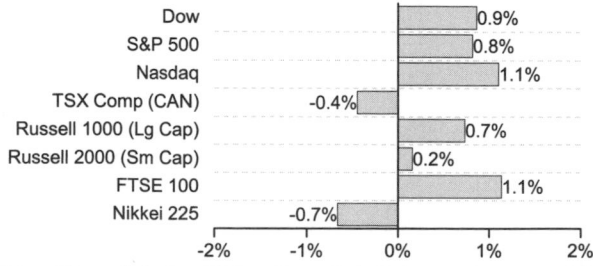

	Dow	0.9%
	S&P 500	0.8%
	Nasdaq	1.1%
	TSX Comp (CAN)	-0.4%
	Russell 1000 (Lg Cap)	0.7%
	Russell 2000 (Sm Cap)	0.2%
	FTSE 100	1.1%
	Nikkei 225	-0.7%

Interest Corner Oct[2]

	Fed Funds % [3]	3 Mo. T-Bill % [4]	10 Yr % [5]	20 Yr % [6]
2016	0.50	0.34	1.84	2.25
2015	0.25	0.08	2.16	2.57
2014	0.25	0.01	2.35	2.81
2013	0.25	0.04	2.57	3.33
2012	0.25	0.11	1.72	2.46

(1) Russell Data provided by Russell (2) Federal Reserve Bank of St. Louis- end of month values (3) Target rate set by FOMC (4)(5)(6) Constant yield maturities.

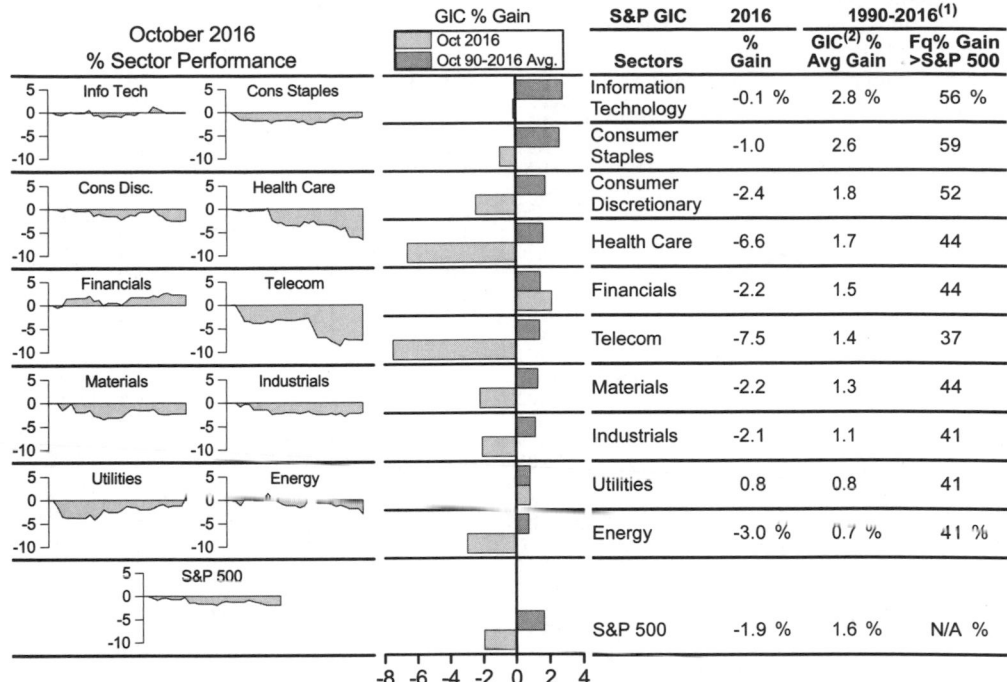

October 2016 % Sector Performance

GIC % Gain — Oct 2016 / Oct 90-2016 Avg.

S&P GIC Sectors	2016 % Gain	1990-2016[1] GIC[2] % Avg Gain	Fq% Gain >S&P 500
Information Technology	-0.1 %	2.8 %	56 %
Consumer Staples	-1.0	2.6	59
Consumer Discretionary	-2.4	1.8	52
Health Care	-6.6	1.7	44
Financials	-2.2	1.5	44
Telecom	-7.5	1.4	37
Materials	-2.2	1.3	44
Industrials	-2.1	1.1	41
Utilities	0.8	0.8	41
Energy	-3.0 %	0.7 %	41 %
S&P 500	-1.9 %	1.6 %	N/A %

Sector Commentary

♦ In October 2016, all of the major sectors of the S&P 500 were negative except the utilities sector. ♦ The consumer staples sector, on average, is one of the top performing sectors of the stock market in October. In 2016, the consumer staples sector outperformed the S&P 500, but was still negative for the month. ♦ The health care sector produced a loss of 6.6% as investors were unsure about possible new health care policies under a new president.

Sub-Sector Commentary

♦ In October 2016, agriculture produced a gain of 3.3%. October is the sweet spot for the agriculture sub-sector. ♦ Banks also performed well as investors increased their speculation that the U.S. Federal Reserve was going to raise its benchmark rate in November. ♦ Gold and silver performed poorly, producing losses of 3.8% and 8.2% respectively. October tends to be a weak time for both gold and silver.

SELECTED SUB-SECTORS[3]

	2016 % Gain	GIC % Avg Gain	Fq% Gain >S&P 500
Agriculture (1994-2016)	3.3 %	6.0 %	78 %
Transportation	-1.1	4.0	74
Railroads	-6.4	3.8	67
Steel	-1.2	2.4	44
Chemicals	-1.9	2.2	56
Pharma	-5.3	2.2	56
SOX (1995-2016)	-1.4	2.1	45
Retail	-2.6	1.9	56
Biotech (1993-2016)	-9.4	1.6	46
Banks	4.7	1.1	37
Homebuilders	-4.2	0.9	37
Automotive & Components	-2.6	0.6	41
Metals & Mining	-2.8	0.3	37
Gold	-3.8	-1.1	22
Silver	-8.2	-1.5	30

MCDONALD'S
①Oct 28-Nov 24 ②Jan 30-Apr 8

McDonald's is part of the consumer discretionary sector, but it has a slightly different seasonal pattern. Investors tend to push up the price of McDonald's stock price in autumn, but then lose interest once the holiday shopping season starts in November.

10.8% gain & 86% of the time positive

From 1989 to 2016, in the period from October 28th to November 24th, McDonald's has produced an average gain of 4.2% and has been positive 86% of the time.

McDonald's tends to underperform the S&P 500 in December and January, but once the holiday season ends and the worst month of the year for retail comes close to finishing (January), investors warm up to the idea of McDonald's once again.

McDonald's tends to perform well from January 30th to April 8th. In this period from 1990 to 2016, McDonald's has produced an average gain of 5.5% and has been positive 68% of the time.

In the summer months, investors lose interest in McDonald's and it tends to underperform the S&P 500. The time period between July 19th to August 31st tends to be very weak for McDonald's. In this time period from 1990 to 2016, McDonald's has produced an average loss of 2.9% and has only been positive 33% of the time.

MCD* vs. S&P 500 - 1989/90 to 2016/17   Positive

Year	Oct 28 to Nov 24 S&P 500	Oct 28 to Nov 24 MCD	Jan 30 to Apr 8 S&P 500	Jan 30 to Apr 8 MCD	Compound Growth S&P 500	Compound Growth MCD
1989/90	2.7 %	6.5 %	4.6 %	0.0 %	7.4 %	6.5 %
1990/91	3.4	12.8	12.8	32.2	16.6	49.2
1991/92	-2.1	-1.5	-3.9	-1.8	-5.9	-3.2
1992/93	2.2	6.8	0.7	3.9	2.9	11.0
1993/94	-0.5	2.9	-6.6	-5.8	-7.0	-3.1
1994/95	-3.4	0.9	7.7	8.1	4.0	9.1
1995/96	3.5	4.8	3.2	-5.0	6.8	-0.4
1996/97	6.8	7.3	-0.8	9.0	5.9	17.0
1997/98	8.0	11.2	11.8	27.2	20.7	41.5
1998/99	11.0	9.7	5.0	19.0	16.6	30.9
1999/00	9.3	14.9	11.5	0.7	21.8	15.7
2000/01	-2.7	13.2	-17.3	-11.1	-19.5	0.7
2001/02	4.1	-4.9	2.2	8.5	6.5	3.1
2002/03	3.7	0.8	1.6	10.2	5.3	11.0
2003/04	2.0	5.7	0.5	12.4	2.5	18.9
2004/05	5.0	4.2	0.8	-2.7	5.9	1.3
2005/06	7.4	6.9	0.9	-0.5	8.3	6.3
2006/07	1.7	1.0	1.6	5.9	3.4	6.9
2007/08	-6.2	-1.3	0.2	10.1	-5.9	8.7
2008/09	0.3	7.2	-2.4	-4.4	-2.0	2.5
2009/10	4.0	8.8	10.5	10.1	14.9	19.8
2010/11	1.3	2.6	4.1	3.8	5.5	6.4
2011/12	-9.6	-1.8	6.2	-0.1	-3.9	-1.8
2012/13	-0.2	0.4	3.7	6.9	3.5	7.3
2013/14	2.6	3.7	4.4	5.3	7.1	9.2
2014/15	5.5	5.6	3.0	3.8	8.7	9.7
2015/16	1.1	2.4	5.5	3.4	6.7	5.8
2016/17	3.4	7.2	2.7	5.8	6.1	13.4
Avg.	2.3 %	4.2 %	2.6 %	5.5 %	5.1 %	10.8 %
Fq>0	75 %	86 %	82 %	68 %	79 %	86 %

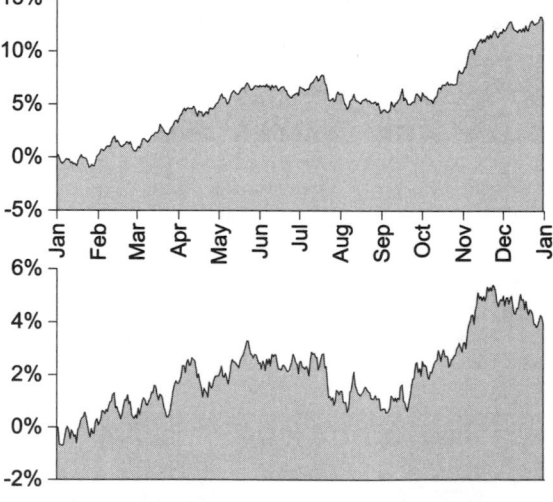

MCD - Avg. Year 1990 to 2016

MCD / S&P 500 Rel. Strength- Avg Yr. 1990-2016

ⓘ *McDonald's Corporation is in the restaurant sector. For more information, see McDonalds.com

McDonald's Performance

MCD Monthly Performance (1990-2016)

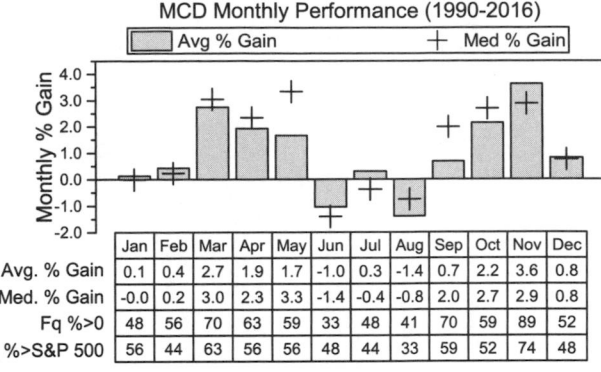

	Jan	Feb	Mar	Apr	May	Jun	Jul	Aug	Sep	Oct	Nov	Dec
Avg. % Gain	0.1	0.4	2.7	1.9	1.7	-1.0	0.3	-1.4	0.7	2.2	3.6	0.8
Med. % Gain	-0.0	0.2	3.0	2.3	3.3	-1.4	-0.4	-0.8	2.0	2.7	2.9	0.8
Fq %>0	48	56	70	63	59	33	48	41	70	59	89	52
Fq %>S&P 500	56	44	63	56	56	48	44	33	59	52	74	48

MCD 5 Year (2012-2016) % Gain

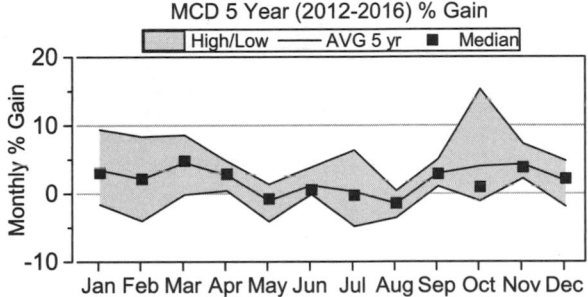

MCD Performance 2016-2017

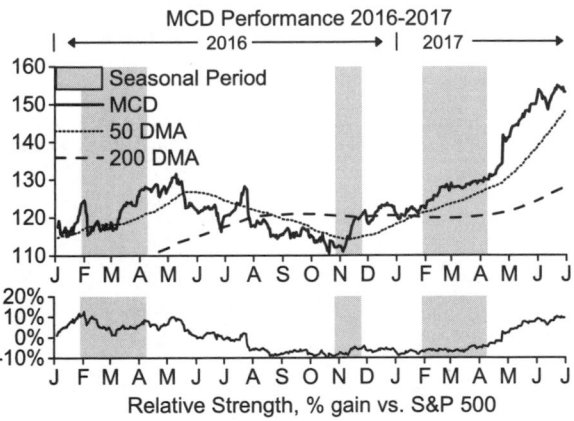

Relative Strength, % gain vs. S&P 500

Market Indices & Rates Weekly Values**

Stock Markets	2015	2016
Dow	16,216	18,242
S&P500	1,912	2,157
Nasdaq	4,603	5,301
TSX	13,186	14,596
FTSE	6,026	7,027
DAX	9,531	10,566
Nikkei	17,482	16,783
Hang Seng	20,970	23,773

Commodities	2015	2016
Oil	45.01	49.52
Gold	1127.4	1275.9

Bond Yields	2015	2016
USA 5 Yr Treasury	1.36	1.24
USA 10 Yr T	2.05	1.70
USA 20 Yr T	2.49	2.10
Moody's Aaa	3.98	3.49
Moody's Baa	5.33	4.34
CAN 5 Yr T	0.79	0.69
CAN 10 Yr T	1.43	1.10

Money Market	2015	2016
USA Fed Funds	0.25	0.50
USA 3 Mo T-B	0.00	0.33
CAN tgt overnight rate	0.50	0.50
CAN 3 Mo T-B	0.44	0.50

Foreign Exchange	2015	2016
EUR/USD	1.12	1.12
GBP/USD	1.52	1.27
USD/CAD	1.33	1.32
USD/JPY	119.88	103.00

OCTOBER

M	T	W	T	F	S	S
1	2	3	4	5	6	7
8	9	10	11	12	13	14
15	16	17	18	19	20	21
22	23	24	25	26	27	28
29	30	31				

NOVEMBER

M	T	W	T	F	S	S
			1	2	3	4
5	6	7	8	9	10	11
12	13	14	15	16	17	18
19	20	21	22	23	24	25
26	27	28	29	30		

DECEMBER

M	T	W	T	F	S	S
					1	2
3	4	5	6	7	8	9
10	11	12	13	14	15	16
17	18	19	20	21	22	23
24	25	26	27	28	29	30
31						

From 1990 to 2016, McDonald's has had two periods of seasonal strength, one in spring and one in autumn.

Over the last five years, from 2012 to 2016, the average and median performance has oscillated in a tight range and has shown a relative seasonal trend.

In its autumn 2016 seasonal period, McDonald's outperformed the S&P 500 in a very positive year for McDonald's. In its 2017 seasonal period, McDonald's slightly outperformed the S&P 500.

HOMEBUILDERS—
TIME TO BREAK & TIME TO BUILD
①SELL SHORT (Apr27-Jun13) ②LONG (Oct28-Feb3)

The homebuilders sector has been in the spotlight for the last few years: first when the mortgage meltdown occurred in 2007 and 2008, and more recently, as the housing market has bounced back giving the homebuilders sector a boost.

20.7% gain & positive 78% of the time

Historically, the best time to be in the homebuilders sector has been from October 28th to February 3rd. In this time period, during the years 1990/91 to 2016/17, the homebuilders sector has produced an average gain of 16.5% and have been positive 89% of the time.

Generally, the time period outside of the strong seasonal period for homebuilders should be avoided by investors, as not only has the average performance relative to the S&P 500 been negative, but the sector has produced both large gains and losses. In other words, the risk is substantially higher that a large drawdown will occur.

This is particularly true for the time period from April 27th to June 13th. In this time period, from 1990 to 2016, the homebuilders sector produced an average loss of 3.5% and was only positive 30% of the time.

Homebuilders (HB)* vs. S&P 500 1990/91 to 2016/17
Negative Short [ ]   Positive Long [ ]

Year	SHORT Apr 27 to Jun 13 S&P 500	HB	LONG Oct 28 to Feb 3 S&P 500	HB	Compound Growth S&P 500	HB
1990/91	9.6 %	7.9 %	12.6 %	58.0 %	1.8 %	45.5 %
1991/92	-0.4	-4.8	6.6	41.2	7.0	48.0
1992/93	0.2	-11.5	6.9	26.7	6.7	41.2
1993/94	3.2	12.6	3.5	8.6	0.2	-5.1
1994/95	1.6	-4.0	2.8	-4.0	1.1	-0.2
1995/96	4.6	11.1	9.7	16.7	4.7	3.7
1996/97	2.2	10.6	12.2	6.3	9.8	-4.9
1997/98	16.7	22.6	14.7	24.8	-4.5	-3.4
1998/99	-0.8	-10.6	19.4	12.4	20.4	24.2
1999/00	-4.9	-7.1	9.9	-3.9	15.3	2.9
2000/01	0.6	-3.8	-2.2	18.6	-2.7	23.1
2001/02	0.6	-17.5	1.6	43.1	1.0	68.1
2002/03	-6.2	-5.3	-4.2	6.7	1.8	12.3
2003/04	10.0	31.5	10.2	7.6	-0.8	-26.3
2004/05	0.1	-2.6	5.7	23.7	5.6	26.9
2005/06	4.3	11.9	7.2	14.8	2.7	1.1
2006/07	-6.3	-27.1	5.2	16.8	11.7	48.4
2007/08	1.4	-7.9	-9.1	8.8	-10.4	17.4
2008/09	-2.7	-25.3	-1.2	27.7	1.4	60.0
2009/10	9.2	-25.1	3.2	15.5	-6.3	44.4
2010/11	-9.9	-22.9	10.5	12.9	21.5	38.7
2011/12	-5.6	-11.2	4.7	35.0	10.6	50.1
2012/13	-6.1	-9.3	7.2	13.7	13.7	24.3
2013/14	3.4	-7.2	-1.0	10.1	-4.4	18.1
2014/15	3.9	4.5	4.5	7.8	0.4	3.0
2015/16	-1.1	-0.8	-7.4	-15.3	-6.4	-14.6
2016/17	-0.6	-2.3	7.7	10.9	8.4	13.5
Avg.	1.0 %	-3.5 %	5.2 %	16.5 %	4.1 %	20.7 %
Fq>0	59 %	30 %	78 %	89 %	74 %	78 %

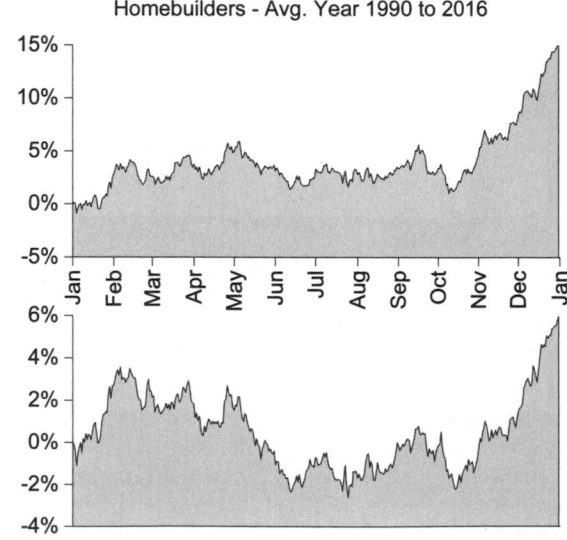

Homebuilders - Avg. Year 1990 to 2016

Homebuilders / S&P 500 Rel. Strength- Avg Yr. 1990-2016

ⓘ *Homebuilders: SP GIC Sector: An index designed to represent a cross section of homebuilding companies. For more information, see www.standardandpoors.com.

- 123 -

Homebuilders Performance

Homebuilders Monthly Performance (1990-2016)

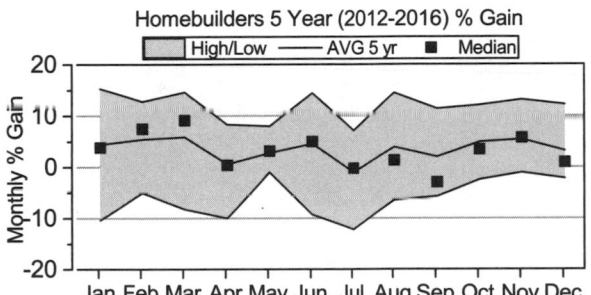

	Jan	Feb	Mar	Apr	May	Jun	Jul	Aug	Sep	Oct	Nov	Dec
Avg. % Gain	2.5	0.2	1.0	1.2	-0.9	-1.2	0.8	0.1	-1.1	0.9	2.7	7.2
Med. % Gain	2.5	1.1	-1.3	-1.4	1.4	-0.3	-0.5	-0.5	0.7	0.8	3.9	5.9
Fq %>0	67	52	48	48	56	48	44	48	56	59	63	74
Fq %>S&P 500	59	59	48	44	48	44	48	56	56	37	52	81

Homebuilders 5 Year (2012-2016) % Gain

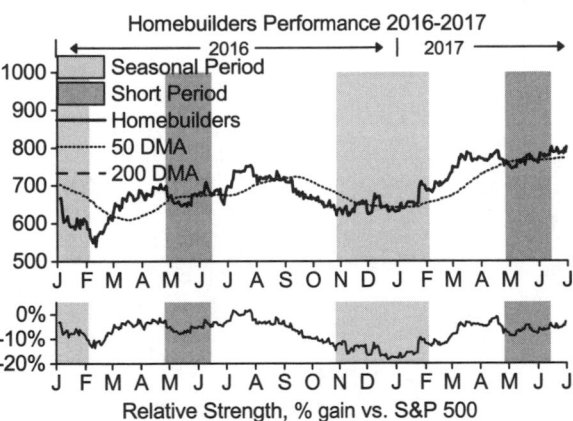

Homebuilders Performance 2016-2017

Relative Strength, % gain vs. S&P 500

WEEK 41

Market Indices & Rates
Weekly Values**

Stock Markets	2015	2016
Dow	16,923	18,168
S&P500	1,998	2,141
Nasdaq	4,792	5,248
TSX	13,802	14,599
FTSE	6,350	7,037
DAX	9,956	10,544
Nikkei	18,219	16,874
Hang Seng	22,203	23,305

Commodities	2015	2016
Oil	48.33	50.62
Gold	1144.7	1256.5

Bond Yields	2015	2016
USA 5 Yr Treasury	1.37	1.29
USA 10 Yr T	2.09	1.78
USA 20 Yr T	2.53	2.18
Moody's Aaa	4.01	3.52
Moody's Baa	5.38	4.38
CAN 5 Yr T	0.82	0.75
CAN 10 Yr T	1.47	1.20

Money Market	2015	2016
USA Fed Funds	0.25	0.50
USA 3 Mo T-B	0.00	0.34
CAN tgt overnight rate	0.50	0.50
CAN 3 Mo T-B	0.41	0.50

Foreign Exchange	2015	2016
EUR/USD	1.13	1.10
GBP/USD	1.53	1.22
USD/CAD	1.30	1.32
USD/JPY	120.18	103.84

OCTOBER

M	T	W	T	F	S	S
1	2	3	4	5	6	7
8	9	10	11	12	13	14
15	16	17	18	19	20	21
22	23	24	25	26	27	28
29	30	31				

NOVEMBER

M	T	W	T	F	S	S
			1	2	3	4
5	6	7	8	9	10	11
12	13	14	15	16	17	18
19	20	21	22	23	24	25
26	27	28	29	30		

DECEMBER

M	T	W	T	F	S	S
					1	2
3	4	5	6	7	8	9
10	11	12	13	14	15	16
17	18	19	20	21	22	23
24	25	26	27	28	29	30
31						

From 1990/91 to 2016/17, the best month of the year for the homebuilders sector has been December on an average, median and frequency basis. May and June on average have produced a loss.

Over the last five years, on average, the homebuilders sector has followed its general seasonal trend.

In 2016/17, the seasonal long position was positive and substantially outperformed the S&P 500. In its 2017 seasonally weak period the homebuilders sector was positive.

UNITED TECHNOLOGIES
①Jan23-May5 ②Oct10-Dec31

United Technologies is a conglomerate industrial company and as such has similar seasonal periods to the industrial sector. The difference is that United Technologies starts one of its seasonal periods earlier in October. The industrial sector starts its seasonal period on October 28th, whereas United Technologies starts its seasonal period on October 10th.

It is worthwhile to consider entering a position in United Technologies before the start of the industrial sector's seasonal period. When United Technologies outperforms in early October, it is often a precursor of what to expect for the broad market.

The combined trade of January 23rd to May 5th and October 10th to December 31st has produced a 19.5% gain and has been successful 96% of the time since 1990.

Investors should note that being positive 96% of the time in the past does not guarantee the success of the trade in the future. Nevertheless, it does indicate the strength of the seasonal trade.

19.5% extra & positive 26 times out of 27

Given that United Technologies produces 6% of its revenues from China (Reuters), investors should be looking to the strength of the Chinese economy in order to help determine the possible strength of the United Technologies seasonal trade.

United Technologies Corporation is a multinational conglomerate in the industrial sector. For more information, see UTC.com

UTX* vs. S&P 500 - 1990 to 2016   Positive

Year	Jan 23 to May 5 S&P 500	Jan 23 to May 5 UTX	Oct 10 to Dec 31 S&P 500	Oct 10 to Dec 31 UTX	Compound Growth S&P 500	Compound Growth UTX
1990	2.4 %	10.2 %	8.2 %	5.2 %	10.8 %	15.9 %
1991	16.0	4.0	10.7	27.3	28.4	32.4
1992	-0.3	-0.9	8.2	4.1	7.9	3.1
1993	1.9	4.7	1.3	8.5	3.3	13.7
1994	-4.9	-0.4	0.9	1.2	-4.0	0.8
1995	11.9	15.0	6.5	12.0	19.2	28.8
1996	4.6	14.1	6.3	7.8	11.2	23.0
1997	5.6	15.9	0.0	-7.5	5.6	7.3
1998	15.8	31.5	24.9	41.7	44.6	86.3
1999	10.0	27.2	10.0	9.7	20.9	39.6
2000	-0.6	7.7	-5.8	12.2	-6.4	20.9
2001	-5.7	9.9	8.6	26.7	2.5	39.2
2002	-4.1	7.6	13.3	25.9	8.6	35.5
2003	5.5	-2.6	7.1	14.7	12.9	11.8
2004	-2.0	-9.6	8.0	11.8	5.9	1.1
2005	0.4	2.3	4.4	11.5	4.8	14.1
2006	5.1	18.0	5.0	-4.1	10.4	13.2
2007	5.8	6.1	-6.2	-5.7	-0.7	0.0
2008	7.4	11.0	-0.7	15.7	6.6	28.4
2009	9.2	5.9	4.1	11.7	13.7	18.2
2010	6.8	6.5	7.9	8.0	15.3	15.0
2011	4.0	10.4	8.8	2.3	13.2	12.9
2012	4.1	3.6	-1.1	6.1	3.0	9.9
2013	8.2	6.5	11.6	10.7	20.7	17.8
2014	2.2	0.6	6.8	15.1	9.1	15.8
2015	1.3	-4.5	1.4	0.7	2.7	-3.8
2016	7.5	16.1	4.0	9.0	11.8	26.6
Avg.	4.4 %	8.0 %	5.7 %	10.4 %	10.4 %	19.5 %
Fq>0	78 %	81 %	81 %	89 %	89 %	96 %

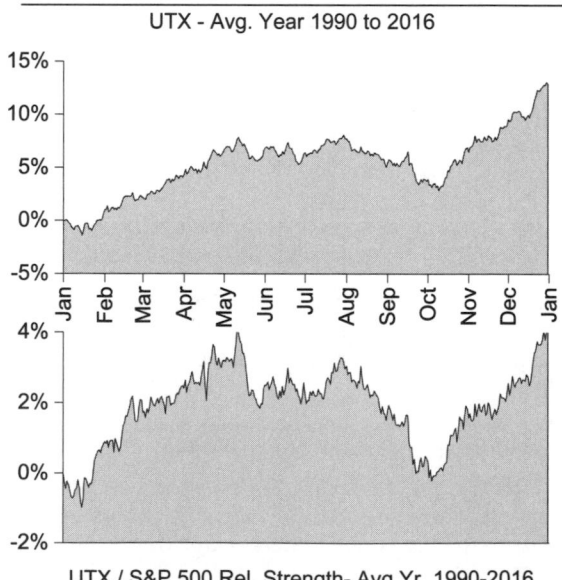

UTX - Avg. Year 1990 to 2016

UTX / S&P 500 Rel. Strength- Avg Yr. 1990-2016

UTX Performance

UTX Monthly Performance (1990-2016)

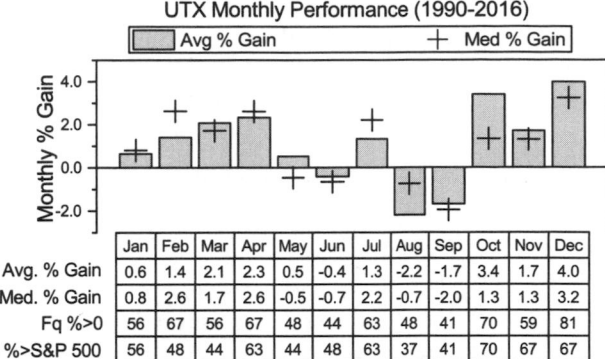

Legend: Avg % Gain | + Med % Gain

	Jan	Feb	Mar	Apr	May	Jun	Jul	Aug	Sep	Oct	Nov	Dec
Avg. % Gain	0.6	1.4	2.1	2.3	0.5	-0.4	1.3	-2.2	-1.7	3.4	1.7	4.0
Med. % Gain	0.8	2.6	1.7	2.6	-0.5	-0.7	2.2	-0.7	-2.0	1.3	1.3	3.2
Fq %>0	56	67	56	67	48	44	63	48	41	70	59	81
Fq %>S&P 500	56	48	44	63	44	48	63	37	41	70	67	67

UTX 5 Year (2012-2016) % Gain

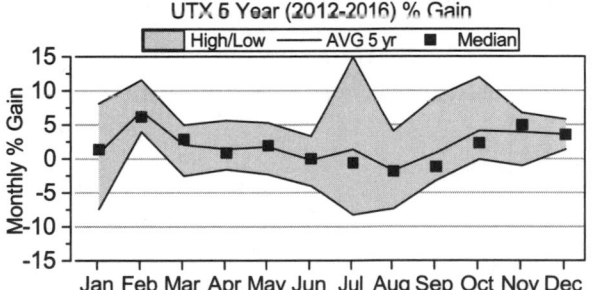

Legend: High/Low | AVG 5 yr | Median

UTX Performance 2016-2017

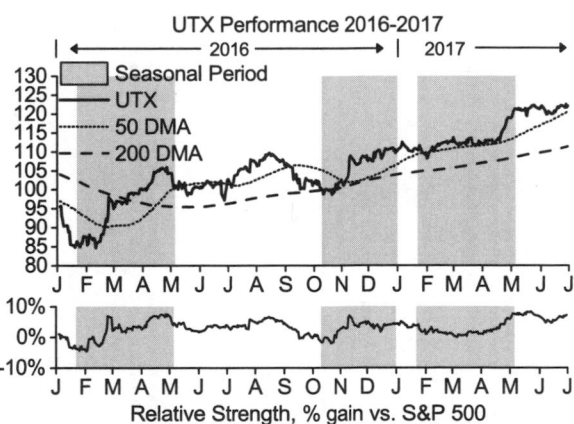

Legend: Seasonal Period | UTX | 50 DMA | 200 DMA

Relative Strength, % gain vs. S&P 500

WEEK 42

Market Indices & Rates
Weekly Values**

Stock Markets	2015	2016
Dow	17,099	18,152
S&P500	2,014	2,139
Nasdaq	4,835	5,238
TSX	13,847	14,795
FTSE	6,340	7,003
DAX	10,048	10,639
Nikkei	18,129	17,057
Hang Seng	22,745	23,278

Commodities	2015	2016
Oil	46.81	50.56
Gold	1173.8	1264.0

Bond Yields	2015	2016
USA 5 Yr Treasury	1.34	1.25
USA 10 Yr T	2.03	1.76
USA 20 Yr T	2.46	2.17
Moody's Aaa	3.92	3.48
Moody's Baa	5.32	4.37
CAN 5 Yr T	0.82	0.70
CAN 10 Yr T	1.45	1.18

Money Market	2015	2016
USA Fed Funds	0.25	0.50
USA 3 Mo T-B	0.01	0.34
CAN tgt overnight rate	0.50	0.50
CAN 3 Mo T-B	0.40	0.49

Foreign Exchange	2015	2016
EUR/USD	1.14	1.10
GBP/USD	1.54	1.23
USD/CAD	1.30	1.32
USD/JPY	119.39	103.79

OCTOBER

M	T	W	T	F	S	S
1	2	3	4	5	6	7
8	9	10	11	12	13	14
15	16	17	18	19	20	21
22	23	24	25	26	27	28
29	30	31				

NOVEMBER

M	T	W	T	F	S	S
			1	2	3	4
5	6	7	8	9	10	11
12	13	14	15	16	17	18
19	20	21	22	23	24	25
26	27	28	29	30		

DECEMBER

M	T	W	T	F	S	S
					1	2
3	4	5	6	7	8	9
10	11	12	13	14	15	16
17	18	19	20	21	22	23
24	25	26	27	28	29	30
31						

From 1990 to 2016, the best month for United Technologies is December on an average, median and frequency basis. December is the last month of the autumn seasonal period and as such, investors should give the stock some leeway to demonstrate its strength at this time. Over the last five years, United Technologies has generally followed its seasonal trend with weaker summer months. The dispersion of returns in the summer months was much larger than at other times, despite the average poor performance at this time. In 2016, United Technologies outperformed the S&P 500 in both seasonal periods and in its 2017 seasonal period.

RETAIL – SHOP EARLY
October 28th to November 29th

The *Retail – Shop Early* strategy is the second retail sector strategy of the year and it occurs before the biggest shopping season of the year – the Christmas holiday season.

2.9% extra & 78% of the time better than S&P 500

The time to go shopping for retail stocks is at the end of October, which is about one month before Thanksgiving. It is the time when two favorable influences happen at the same time.

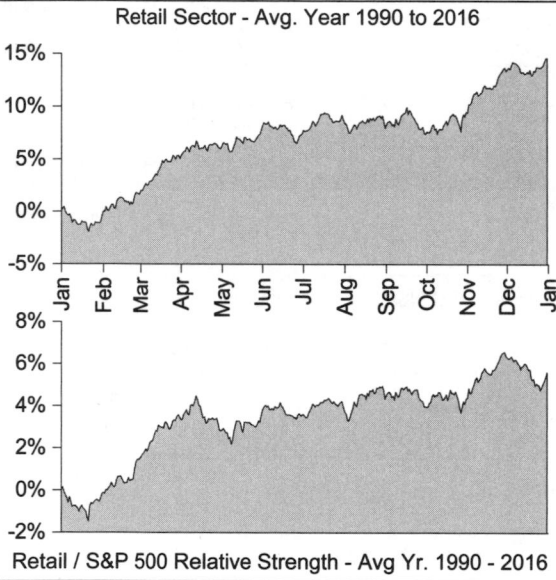

Retail Sector - Avg. Year 1990 to 2016

Retail / S&P 500 Relative Strength - Avg Yr. 1990 - 2016

First, historically, November has been one of the stronger months of the year, which helps support a higher beta sector, such as the retail sector.

Second, investors tend to buy retail stocks in anticipation of a strong holiday sales season. Seasonal investors position themselves ahead of the average investor that typically enters the retail sector in November.

Retail sales tend to be lower in the summer and a lot of investors view investing in retail stocks at this time as dead money. During the summertime, investors prefer not to invest in this sector until it comes back into favor towards the end of October.

The trick to investing is not to be too early, but early.

If an investor gets into a sector too early, they can suffer from the frustration of having dead money– an investment that goes nowhere, while the rest of the market increases.

If an investor moves into a sector too late, there is very little upside potential. In fact, this can be a dangerous strategy because if the sales or earnings numbers disappoint the analysts, the sector can severely correct.

For the *Retail – Shop Early* strategy, the time to enter is approximately one month before Black Friday.

Retail Sector vs. S&P 500 1990 to 2016

Oct 28 to Nov 29	S&P 500	Positive Retail	Diff
1990	3.8 %	9.9 %	6.0 %
1991	-2.3	2.7	5.0
1992	2.8	5.5	2.8
1993	-0.6	6.3	6.9
1994	-2.3	0.4	2.7
1995	4.8	9.5	4.7
1996	8.0	0.4	-7.6
1997	8.9	16.9	7.9
1998	11.9	20.4	8.4
1999	8.6	14.1	5.5
2000	-2.7	9.9	12.6
2001	3.2	7.9	4.7
2002	4.3	-1.7	-6.0
2003	2.6	2.5	-0.1
2004	4.7	7.0	2.3
2005	6.7	9.9	3.2
2006	1.6	0.2	-1.4
2007	-4.3	-7.5	-3.2
2008	5.6	7.5	1.9
2009	2.6	3.6	1.0
2010	0.5	5.2	4.7
2011	-7.0	-4.5	2.5
2012	0.3	5.1	4.8
2013	2.6	5.0	2.4
2014	5.4	8.9	3.5
2015	1.2	3.9	2.7
2016	3.4	2.8	-0.6
Avg.	2.8 %	5.6 %	2.9 %
Fq > 0	78 %	89 %	78 %

Retail SP GIC Sector # 2550:
An index designed to represent a cross section of retail companies
For more information on the retail sector, see www.standardandpoors.com.

Retail Performance

Retail Monthly Performance (1990-2016)

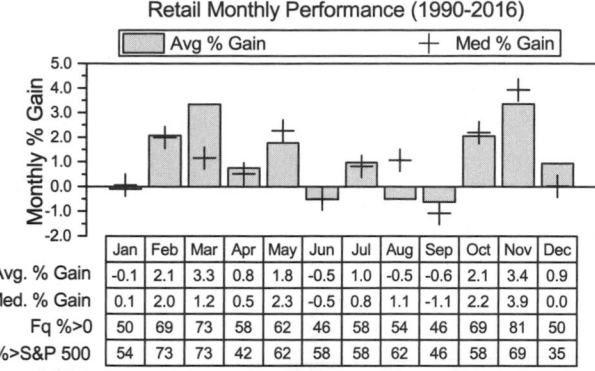

	Jan	Feb	Mar	Apr	May	Jun	Jul	Aug	Sep	Oct	Nov	Dec
Avg. % Gain	-0.1	2.1	3.3	0.8	1.8	-0.5	1.0	-0.5	-0.6	2.1	3.4	0.9
Med. % Gain	0.1	2.0	1.2	0.5	2.3	-0.5	0.8	1.1	-1.1	2.2	3.9	0.0
Fq %>0	50	69	73	58	62	46	58	54	46	69	81	50
Fq %>S&P 500	54	73	73	42	62	58	58	62	46	58	69	35

Retail 5 Year (2012-2016) % Gain

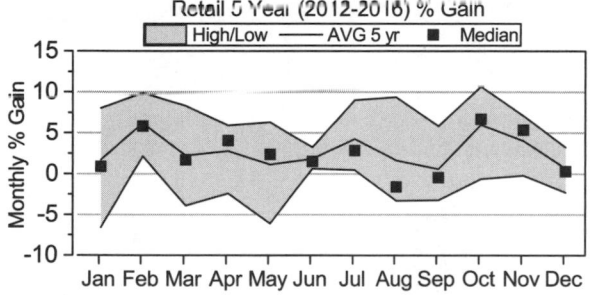

Retail Performance 2016-2017

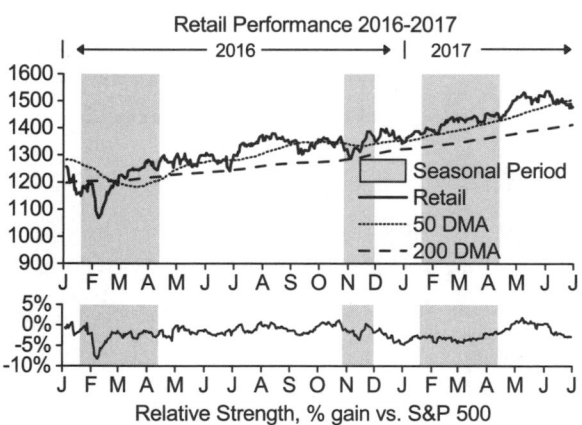

Relative Strength, % gain vs. S&P 500

From 1990 to 2016, March and November were two of the better months of the year on an average basis. November is the core part of the autumn retail seasonal trade and has the highest monthly median performance. Over the last five years, on average, the retail sector has followed its general seasonal pattern.

In 2016, the retail sector underperformed the S&P 500 in its autumn seasonal period, and in 2017 it outperformed in its spring seasonal period.

Market Indices & Rates
Weekly Values**

Stock Markets	2015	2016
Dow	17,350	18,185
S&P500	2,042	2,139
Nasdaq	4,916	5,250
TSX	13,827	14,844
FTSE	6,373	6,989
DAX	10,367	10,728
Nikkei	18,431	17,355
Hang Seng	23,016	23,316

Commodities	2015	2016
Oil	44.91	49.45
Gold	1169.7	1268.9

Bond Yields	2015	2016
USA 5 Yr Treasury	1.38	1.30
USA 10 Yr T	2.06	1.81
USA 20 Yr T	2.50	2.22
Moody's Aaa	3.92	3.54
Moody's Baa	5.33	4.40
CAN 5 Yr T	0.84	0.70
CAN 10 Yr T	1.48	1.19

Money Market	2015	2016
USA Fed Funds	0.25	0.50
USA 3 Mo T-B	0.01	0.32
CAN tgt overnight rate	0.50	0.50
CAN 3 Mo T-B	0.40	0.48

Foreign Exchange	2015	2016
EUR/USD	1.12	1.09
GBP/USD	1.54	1.22
USD/CAD	1.31	1.34
USD/JPY	120.29	104.58

OCTOBER

M	T	W	T	F	S	S
1	2	3	4	5	6	7
8	9	10	11	12	13	14
15	16	17	18	19	20	21
22	23	24	25	26	27	28
29	30	31				

NOVEMBER

M	T	W	T	F	S	S
				1	2	3	4
5	6	7	8	9	10	11
12	13	14	15	16	17	18
19	20	21	22	23	24	25
26	27	28	29	30		

DECEMBER

M	T	W	T	F	S	S
					1	2
3	4	5	6	7	8	9
10	11	12	13	14	15	16
17	18	19	20	21	22	23
24	25	26	27	28	29	30
31						

INDUSTRIAL STRENGTH
①Oct28-Dec31 ②Jan23-May5

The industrial sector's seasonal trends are largely the same as the broad market, such as the S&P 500. Although the trends are similar, there still exists an opportunity to take advantage of the time period when the industrial sector tends to outperform.

12% gain & positive 93% of the time

Industrials tend to outperform in the favorable six months, but there is an opportunity to temporarily get out of the sector to avoid a time period when the sector has on average, decreased before turning positive again.

The overall strategy is to be invested in the industrial sector from October 28th to December 31st, sell at the end of the day on the 31st, and re-enter the sector to be invested from January 23rd to May 5th.

Using the complete *Industrial Strength* strategy from 1989/90 to 2016/17, the industrial sector has produced a total compound average annual gain of 12.0%.

In addition, the industrial sector has been positive 93% of the time and has outperformed the S&P 500, 75% of the time.

During the time period from January 1st to January 22nd, in the yearly period from 1990 to 2017, the industrial sector has on average lost 0.9% and has only been positive 50% of the time.

It should be noted that longer term investors may decide to be invested during the whole time period from October 28th to May 5th. Shorter term investors may decide to use technical analysis to determine, if and when, they should temporarily sell the industrials sector during its weak period from January 1st to January 22nd.

Industrials* vs. S&P 500 1989/90 to 2016/17   Positive ▢

Year	Oct 28 to Dec 31 S&P 500	Oct 28 to Dec 31 Ind.	Jan 23 to May 5 S&P 500	Jan 23 to May 5 Ind.	Compound Growth S&P 500	Compound Growth Ind.
1989/90	5.5 %	6.9 %	2.4 %	5.5 %	8.0 %	12.7 %
1990/91	8.4	10.7	16.0	15.2	25.7	27.5
1991/92	8.6	7.2	-0.3	-1.0	8.2	6.1
1992/93	4.1	6.3	1.9	5.4	6.1	12.0
1993/94	0.4	5.1	-4.9	-6.7	-4.5	-2.0
1994/95	-1.4	-0.5	11.9	12.4	10.3	11.8
1995/96	6.3	10.7	4.6	7.6	11.1	19.1
1996/97	5.7	4.5	5.6	5.2	11.6	9.9
1997/98	10.7	10.5	15.8	11.5	28.2	23.2
1998/99	15.4	10.5	10.0	19.5	26.9	32.1
1999/00	13.3	10.8	-0.6	4.5	12.6	15.8
2000/01	-4.3	1.8	-5.7	4.7	-9.7	6.6
2001/02	3.9	8.1	-4.1	-5.3	-0.3	2.4
2002/03	-2.0	-1.3	5.5	8.6	3.4	7.1
2003/04	7.8	11.6	-2.0	-3.3	5.7	7.9
2004/05	7.7	8.7	0.4	0.2	8.1	8.9
2005/06	5.9	7.6	5.1	14.3	11.3	23.0
2006/07	3.0	3.1	5.8	6.8	9.0	10.1
2007/08	-4.4	-3.4	7.4	9.7	2.7	6.0
2008/09	6.4	7.1	9.2	6.1	16.2	13.7
2009/10	4.9	6.4	6.8	13.4	12.0	20.6
2010/11	6.4	8.1	4.0	4.9	10.6	13.5
2011/12	-2.1	-1.0	4.1	0.3	1.9	-0.7
2012/13	1.0	4.1	8.2	4.9	9.3	9.2
2013/14	5.0	7.3	2.2	1.6	7.3	9.0
2014/15	5.0	5.2	1.3	-1.0	6.3	4.1
2015/16	-1.1	-1.2	7.5	12.8	6.4	11.4
2016/17	5.0	9.7	5.6	5.0	10.9	15.2
Avg.	4.5 %	5.9 %	4.4 %	5.8 %	9.1 %	12.0 %
Fq > 0	79 %	82 %	79 %	82 %	89 %	93 %

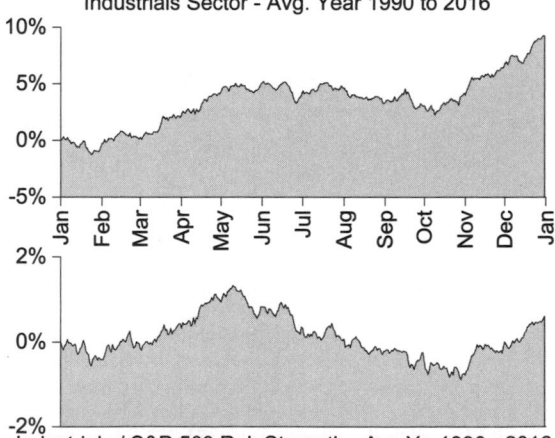

Industrials Sector - Avg. Year 1990 to 2016

Industrials / S&P 500 Rel. Strength - Avg Yr. 1990 - 2016

Ⓨ *Alternate Strategy—*
Investors can bridge the gap between the two positive seasonal trends for the industrials sector by holding from October 28th to May 5th. Longer term investors may prefer this strategy, shorter term investors can use technical tools to determine the appropriate strategy.

ⓘ *The SP GICS Industrial Sector. For more information on the industrials sector, see www.standardandpoors.com*

Industrials Performance

Industrials Monthly Performance (1990-2016)

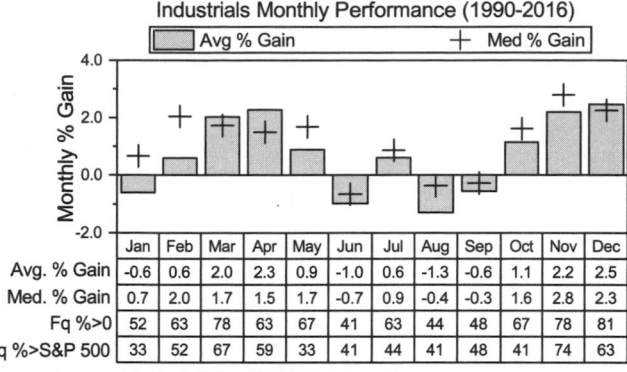

	Jan	Feb	Mar	Apr	May	Jun	Jul	Aug	Sep	Oct	Nov	Dec
Avg. % Gain	-0.6	0.6	2.0	2.3	0.9	-1.0	0.6	-1.3	-0.6	1.1	2.2	2.5
Med. % Gain	0.7	2.0	1.7	1.5	1.7	-0.7	0.9	-0.4	-0.3	1.6	2.8	2.3
Fq %>0	52	63	78	63	67	41	63	44	48	67	78	81
Fq %>S&P 500	33	52	67	59	33	41	44	41	48	41	74	63

Industrials 5 Year (2012-2016) % Gain

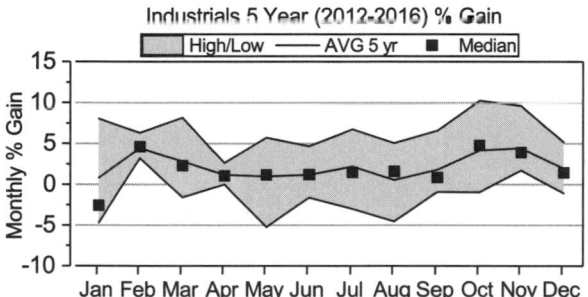

Industrials Performance 2016-2017

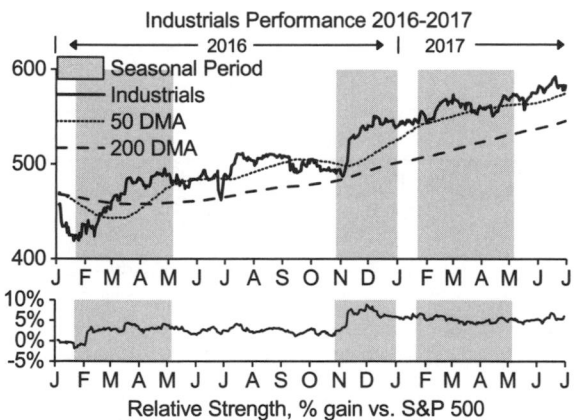

Relative Strength, % gain vs. S&P 500

Market Indices & Rates
Weekly Values**

Stock Markets	2015	2016
Dow	17,681	17,992
S&P500	2,079	2,102
Nasdaq	5,058	5,111
TSX	13,735	14,651
FTSE	6,395	6,840
DAX	10,795	10,429
Nikkei	18,929	17,227
Hang Seng	22,935	22,844

Commodities	2015	2016
Oil	45.15	45.52
Gold	1160.5	1293.6

Bond Yields	2015	2016
USA 5 Yr Treasury	1.46	1.27
USA 10 Yr T	2.11	1.82
USA 20 Yr T	2.53	2.24
Moody's Aaa	3.94	3.62
Moody's Baa	5.00	4.40
CAN 5 Yr T	0.83	0.69
CAN 10 Yr T	1.49	1.19

Money Market	2015	2016
USA Fed Funds	0.25	0.50
USA 3 Mo T-B	0.05	0.36
CAN tgt overnight rate	0.50	0.50
CAN 3 Mo T-B	0.41	0.46

Foreign Exchange	2015	2016
EUR/USD	1.10	1.11
GBP/USD	1.53	1.24
USD/CAD	1.32	1.34
USD/JPY	120.88	103.67

OCTOBER

M	T	W	T	F	S	S
1	2	3	4	5	6	7
8	9	10	11	12	13	14
15	16	17	18	19	20	21
22	23	24	25	26	27	28
29	30	31				

NOVEMBER

M	T	W	T	F	S	S
			1	2	3	4
5	6	7	8	9	10	11
12	13	14	15	16	17	18
19	20	21	22	23	24	25
26	27	28	29	30		

DECEMBER

M	T	W	T	F	S	S
					1	2
3	4	5	6	7	8	9
10	11	12	13	14	15	16
17	18	19	20	21	22	23
24	25	26	27	28	29	30
31						

From 1990 to 2016, the sweet spot for the industrial sector trade, on average, has been November and December. The worst three months have been June, August and September.

Over the last five years, on average, the industrial sector has somewhat followed its seasonal trend, with its poorest performance in the summer months and its better performance in the autumn months.

In 2016, the industrial sector outperformed the S&P 500 in its autumn seasonal period and then nominally underperformed in its 2017 spring seasonal period.

NOVEMBER

	MONDAY	TUESDAY	WEDNESDAY
WEEK 44	29	30	31
WEEK 45	**5** 25	**6** 24	**7** 23
WEEK 46	**12** 18 USA Bond Market Closed- Veterans Day CAD Bond Market Closed- Remembrance Day	**13** 17	**14** 16
WEEK 47	**19** 11	**20** 10	**21** 9
WEEK 48	**26** 4	**27** 3	**28** 2

THURSDAY	FRIDAY
1 29	**2** 28
8 22	**9** 21
15 15	**16** 14
22 8 USA Market Closed- Thanksgiving Day	**23** 7 USA Early Market Close Thanksgiving
29 1	**30**

DECEMBER

M	T	W	T	F	S	S
					1	2
3	4	5	6	7	8	9
10	11	12	13	14	15	16
17	18	19	20	21	22	23
24	25	26	27	28	29	30
31						

JANUARY

M	T	W	T	F	S	S
	1	2	3	4	5	6
7	8	9	10	11	12	13
14	15	16	17	18	19	20
21	22	23	24	25	26	27
28	29	30	31			

FEBRUARY

M	T	W	T	F	S	S
				1	2	3
4	5	6	7	8	9	10
11	12	13	14	15	16	17
18	19	20	21	22	23	24
25	26	27	28			

MARCH

M	T	W	T	F	S	S
				1	2	3
4	5	6	7	8	9	10
11	12	13	14	15	16	17
18	19	20	21	22	23	24
25	26	27	28	29	30	31

NOVEMBER
S U M M A R Y

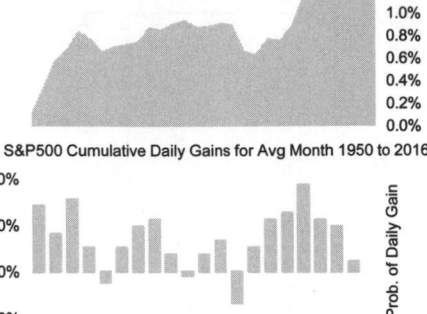

1.6%
1.4%
1.2%
1.0%
0.8%
0.6%
0.4%
0.2%
0.0%

S&P500 Cumulative Daily Gains for Avg Month 1950 to 2016

	Dow Jones	S&P 500	Nasdaq	TSX Comp
Month Rank	3	2	2	8
# Up	46	45	31	19
# Down	21	22	14	13
% Pos	69	67	69	59
% Avg. Gain	1.6	1.5	1.7	0.6

Dow & S&P 1950-2016, Nasdaq 1972-2016, TSX 1985-2016

70%
60%
50%
40%

Prob. of Daily Gain

♦ November, on average, is one of the better months of the year for the S&P 500. From 1950 to 2016, it has produced an average gain of 1.5% and has been positive 67% of the time. ♦ In November, the cyclical sectors tend to start increasing their relative performance to the S&P 500, with the metals and mining sector starting its period of seasonal strength on November 19th. ♦ For investors looking for a short-term investment, the day before and the day after Thanksgiving are on average the two strongest days of the year.

BEST / WORST NOVEMBER BROAD MKTS. 2007-2016

BEST NOVEMBER MARKETS
- ♦ Russell 2000 (2016) 11.0%
- ♦ Nikkei 225 (2013) 9.3%
- ♦ Nikkei 225 (2010) 8.0%

WORST NOVEMBER MARKETS
- ♦ Russell 2000 (2008) -12.0%
- ♦ Nasdaq (2008) -10.8%
- ♦ Russell 1000 (2008) -7.9%

Index Values End of Month

	2007	2008	2009	2010	2011	2012	2013	2014	2015	2016
Dow	13,372	8,829	10,345	11,006	12,046	13,026	16,086	17,828	17,720	19,124
S&P 500	1,481	896	1,096	1,181	1,247	1,416	1,806	2,068	2,080	2,199
Nasdaq	2,661	1,536	2,145	2,498	2,620	3,010	4,060	4,792	5,109	5,324
TSX Comp.	13,689	9,271	11,447	12,953	12,204	12,239	13,395	14,745	13,470	15,083
Russell 1000	806	481	598	654	689	783	1,005	1,149	1,155	1,221
Russell 2000	768	473	580	727	737	822	1,143	1,173	1,198	1,322
FTSE 100	6,433	4,288	5,191	5,528	5,505	5,867	6,651	6,723	6,356	6,784
Nikkei 225	15,681	8,512	9,346	9,937	8,435	9,446	15,662	17,460	19,747	18,308

Percent Gain for November

	2007	2008	2009	2010	2011	2012	2013	2014	2015	2016
Dow	-4.0	-5.3	6.5	-1.0	0.8	-0.5	3.5	2.5	0.3	5.4
S&P 500	-4.4	-7.5	5.7	-0.2	-0.5	0.3	2.8	2.5	0.1	3.4
Nasdaq	-6.9	-10.8	4.9	-0.4	-2.4	1.1	3.6	3.5	1.1	2.6
TSX Comp.	-6.4	-5.0	4.9	2.2	-0.4	-1.5	0.3	0.9	-0.4	2.0
Russell 1000	-4.5	-7.9	5.6	0.1	-0.5	0.5	2.6	2.4	0.1	3.7
Russell 2000	-7.3	-12.0	3.0	3.4	-0.5	0.4	3.9	0.0	3.1	11.0
FTSE 100	-4.3	-2.0	2.9	-2.6	-0.7	1.5	-1.2	2.7	-0.1	-2.5
Nikkei 225	-6.3	-0.8	-6.9	8.0	-6.2	5.8	9.3	6.4	3.5	5.1

November Market Avg. Performance 2007 to 2016[1]

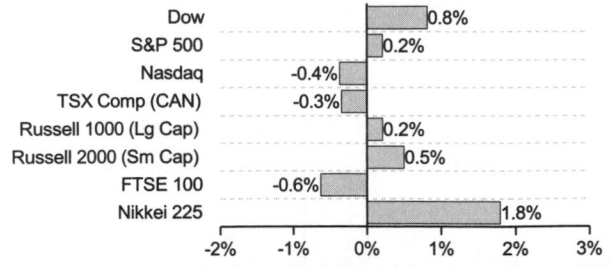

Dow 0.8%
S&P 500 0.2%
Nasdaq -0.4%
TSX Comp (CAN) -0.3%
Russell 1000 (Lg Cap) 0.2%
Russell 2000 (Sm Cap) 0.5%
FTSE 100 -0.6%
Nikkei 225 1.8%

-2%   -1%   0%   1%   2%   3%

Interest Corner Nov[2]

	Fed Funds % [3]	3 Mo. T-Bill % [4]	10 Yr % [5]	20 Yr % [6]
2016	0.50	0.48	2.37	2.73
2015	0.25	0.22	2.21	2.63
2014	0.25	0.02	2.18	2.62
2013	0.25	0.06	2.75	3.54
2012	0.25	0.08	1.62	2.37

(1) Russell Data provided by Russell (2) Federal Reserve Bank of St. Louis- end of month values (3) Target rate set by FOMC (4)(5)(6) Constant yield maturities.

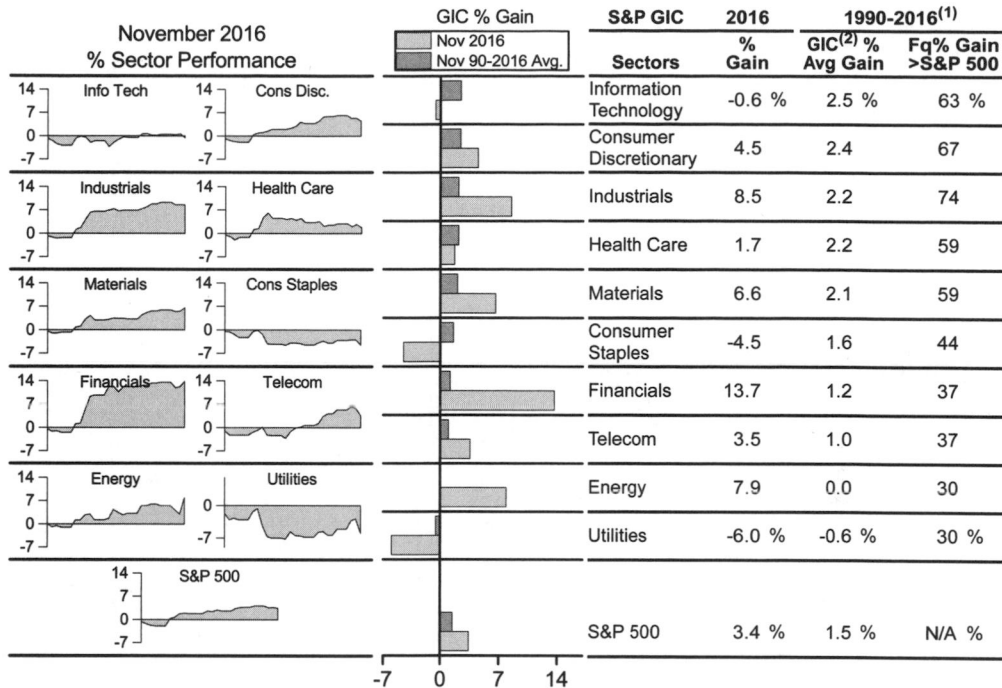

S&P GIC Sectors	2016 % Gain	1990-2016[1] GIC[2] % Avg Gain	1990-2016[1] Fq% Gain >S&P 500
Information Technology	-0.6 %	2.5 %	63 %
Consumer Discretionary	4.5	2.4	67
Industrials	8.5	2.2	74
Health Care	1.7	2.2	59
Materials	6.6	2.1	59
Consumer Staples	-4.5	1.6	44
Financials	13.7	1.2	37
Telecom	3.5	1.0	37
Energy	7.9	0.0	30
Utilities	-6.0 %	-0.6 %	30 %
S&P 500	3.4 %	1.5 %	N/A %

Sector Commentary

♦ In November 2016, the S&P 500 produced a gain of 3.4%. Initially in November, the stock market was declining heading into the presidential election. Once Trump was elected, the stock market rallied and produced a gain for the month. ♦ The financial sector was the top performing sector as investors started to perceive that the sector was going to be one of the main beneficiaries of Trump's possible deregulation policies. ♦ The financial sector ended the month with a gain of 13.7%. ♦ Industrials also had a strong month as the sector benefited from the anticipation of an increasing infrastructure budget.

Sub-Sector Commentary

♦ Banks are not typically one of the better performing sub-sectors, but in November 2016, the sector produced a gain of 17.7%, benefiting from possible deregulation in the financial sector under Trump. ♦ The steel subs-sector produced a gain of 27.3% as investors latched onto the idea that more steel would be required for the Trump infrastructure plan. ♦ Silver and gold were both losers, producing losses of 6.1% and 7.4% respectively.

SELECTED SUB-SECTORS[3]			
Steel	27.3 %	3.7 %	52 %
SOX (1994-2016)	6.8	3.4	59
Retail	2.6	3.3	67
Agriculture (1994-2016)	-0.8	3.0	43
Home-builders	-0.6	2.7	52
Transportation	12.8	2.4	48
Pharma	-0.6	2.0	56
Chemicals	5.7	1.9	52
Biotech (1993-2016)	5.6	1.8	46
Automotive & Components	4.4	1.7	56
Metals & Mining	12.3	1.5	52
Railroads	14.4	1.5	56
Banks	17.7	1.4	48
Gold	-7.4	1.1	52
Silver	-6.1	0.7	48

(1) Sector data provided by Standard and Poors (2) GIC is short form for Global Industry Classification (3) Sub Sector data provided by Standard and Poors, except where marked by symbol.

MATERIAL STOCKS — MATERIAL GAINS
①Oct28-Jan6 ②Jan23-May5

Materials Composition – CAUTION

The U.S. materials sector is substantially different from the Canadian materials sector. The U.S. sector has over a 60% weight in chemical companies, versus the Canadian sector which has over a 60% weight in gold companies.

The materials sector (U.S.) generally does well during the favorable six months of the year, from the end of October to the beginning of May. The sector is economically sensitive and is leveraged to economic forecasts. Generally, if the economy is expected to slow, the materials sector tends to decline and vice versa.

Positive 96% of the time

The materials sector has two seasonal periods. The first period is from October 28th to January 6th and the second period is from January 23rd to May 5th.

In the first seasonal period, the materials sector has produced an average gain of 6.6% in the years from 1990 to 2016 and has been positive 82% of the time.

The second seasonal period from January 23rd to May 5th, has produced an average gain of 7.5% and has been positive 79% of the time.

The time period in between the two seasonal periods, from January 7th to January 22nd, has had an average loss of 2.4% and only been positive 39% of the time (1990 to 2017). Investors may decide to bridge the gap between the two seasonal periods if the materials sector has strong momentum at the beginning of January.

The complete materials strategy is to be invested from October 28th to January 6th, out of the sector from January 7th to the 22nd, and back in from January 23rd to May 5th. This strategy has produced an average gain of 14.6% and has been positive 96% of the time.

Materials* vs. S&P 500 1989/90 to 2016/17   Positive☐

Year	Oct 28 to Jan 6 S&P 500	Oct 28 to Jan 6 Mat.	Jan 23 to May 5 S&P 500	Jan 23 to May 5 Mat.	Compound Growth S&P 500	Compound Growth Mat.
1989/90	5.1 %	9.1 %	2.4 %	-3.1 %	7.7 %	5.7 %
1990/91	5.4	9.2	16.0	15.3	22.2	26.0
1991/92	8.8	1.5	-0.3	5.5	8.5	7.1
1992/93	3.8	5.6	1.9	4.3	5.8	10.2
1993/94	0.5	9.4	-4.9	-5.3	-4.4	3.6
1994/95	-1.1	-3.5	11.9	6.1	10.7	2.4
1995/96	6.4	7.6	4.6	11.1	11.3	19.5
1996/97	6.7	2.3	5.6	2.3	12.6	4.6
1997/98	10.2	1.4	15.8	20.9	27.7	22.6
1998/99	19.4	6.1	10.0	31.5	31.3	39.6
1999/00	8.2	15.7	-0.6	-7.1	7.6	7.5
2000/01	-5.9	19.2	-5.7	15.1	-11.2	37.2
2001/02	6.2	8.5	-4.1	14.9	1.8	24.7
2002/03	3.5	9.2	5.5	2.7	9.2	12.1
2003/04	9.0	16.6	-2.0	-3.0	6.8	13.1
2004/05	5.6	5.4	0.4	0.3	6.0	5.8
2005/06	9.0	16.3	5.1	14.7	14.6	33.5
2006/07	2.4	3.2	5.8	10.7	8.3	14.2
2007/08	-8.1	-5.1	7.4	16.7	-1.2	10.8
2008/09	10.1	12.0	9.2	23.3	20.3	38.1
2009/10	6.9	13.8	6.8	3.0	14.2	17.2
2010/11	7.7	11.7	4.0	4.2	12.1	16.4
2011/12	-0.5	-2.3	4.1	-2.7	3.5	-4.9
2012/13	3.9	7.2	8.2	0.0	12.3	7.2
2013/14	3.8	3.1	2.2	4.3	6.1	7.5
2014/15	2.1	-0.7	1.3	2.9	3.4	2.2
2015/16	-3.7	-6.2	7.5	18.3	3.6	11.0
2016/17	6.8	8.6	5.6	4.5	12.8	13.5
Avg.	4.7 %	6.6 %	4.4 %	7.5 %	9.4 %	14.6 %
Fq > 0	82 %	82 %	79 %	79 %	89 %	96 %

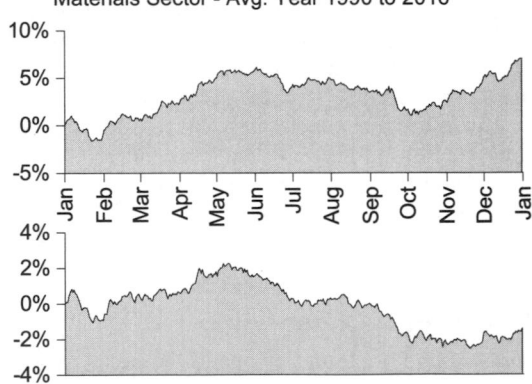

Materials Sector - Avg. Year 1990 to 2016

Materials / S&P 500 Rel. Strength - Avg Yr. 1990 - 2016

Alternate Strategy—
Investors can bridge the gap between the two positive seasonal trends for the materials sector by holding from October 28th to May 5th. Longer term investors may prefer this strategy. Shorter term investors can use technical tools to determine the appropriate strategy.

*The SP GICS Materials Sector encompasses a wide range of materials based companies.
For more information on the materials sector, see www.standardandpoors.com

Materials Performance

Materials Monthly Performance (1990-2016)

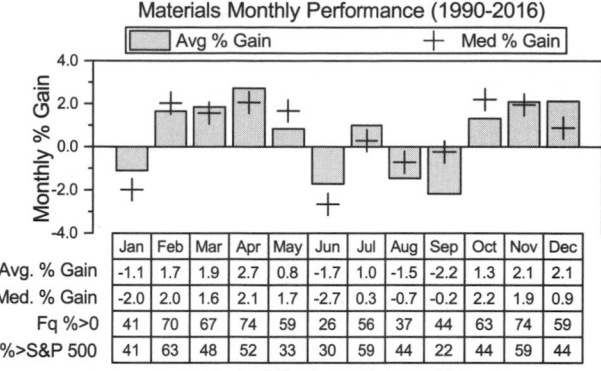

	Jan	Feb	Mar	Apr	May	Jun	Jul	Aug	Sep	Oct	Nov	Dec
Avg. % Gain	-1.1	1.7	1.9	2.7	0.8	-1.7	1.0	-1.5	-2.2	1.3	2.1	2.1
Med. % Gain	-2.0	2.0	1.6	2.1	1.7	-2.7	0.3	-0.7	-0.2	2.2	1.9	0.9
Fq %>0	41	70	67	74	59	26	56	37	44	63	74	59
Fq %>S&P 500	41	63	48	52	33	30	59	44	22	44	59	44

Materials 5 Year (2012-2016) % Gain

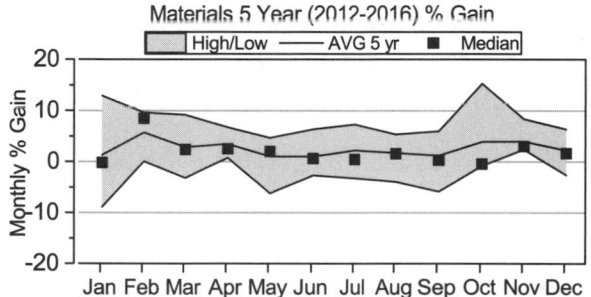

Materials Performance 2016-2017

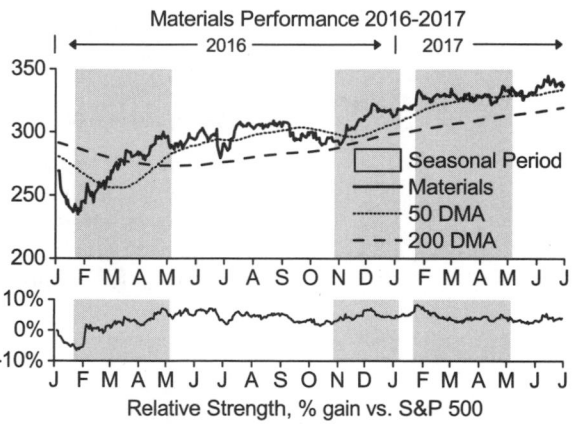

Relative Strength, % gain vs. S&P 500

Market Indices & Rates
Weekly Values*

Stock Markets	2015	2016
Dow	17,878	18,568
S&P500	2,103	2,153
Nasdaq	5,138	5,211
TSX	13,621	14,674
FTSE	6,375	6,824
DAX	10,925	10,577
Nikkei	18,998	17,064
Hang Seng	22,782	22,699

Commodities	2015	2016
Oil	45.97	44.64
Gold	1113.4	1270.2

Bond Yields	2015	2016
USA 5 Yr Treasury	1.64	1.42
USA 10 Yr T	2.26	1.98
USA 20 Yr T	2.67	2.41
Moody's Aaa	4.05	3.77
Moody's Baa	5.43	4.62
CAN 5 Yr T	0.96	0.81
CAN 10 Yr T	1.64	1.34

Money Market	2015	2016
USA Fed Funds	0.25	0.50
USA 3 Mo T-B	0.06	0.44
CAN tgt overnight rate	0.50	0.50
CAN 3 Mo T-B	0.42	0.46

Foreign Exchange	2015	2016
EUR/USD	1.09	1.09
GBP/USD	1.53	1.25
USD/CAD	1.32	1.34
USD/JPY	121.66	105.75

NOVEMBER

M	T	W	T	F	S	S
			1	2	3	4
5	6	7	8	9	10	11
12	13	14	15	16	17	18
19	20	21	22	23	24	25
26	27	28	29	30		

DECEMBER

M	T	W	T	F	S	S
					1	2
3	4	5	6	7	8	9
10	11	12	13	14	15	16
17	18	19	20	21	22	23
24	25	26	27	28	29	30
31						

JANUARY

M	T	W	T	F	S	S
	1	2	3	4	5	6
7	8	9	10	11	12	13
14	15	16	17	18	19	20
21	22	23	24	25	26	27
28	29	30	31			

From 1990 to 2016, on average, the six best months for the materials sector were February, March, April, October, November and December. February, March and April make up the core part of the spring seasonal trade, and October, November and December make up the core part of the winter seasonal trade. Over the last five years, the materials sector has on average, generally followed its seasonal trend with weaker performance in the summer months.

In 2016, the materials sector outperformed the S&P 500 in its winter seasonal period, and then underperformed in its 2017 spring seasonal period.

SUN LIFE FINANCIAL – LET THE SUN SHINE
SLF (NEW) | Oct 10th to Dec 5th

Sun Life Financial not only benefits from a growing economy but also from rising interest rates. Interest rates tend to rise in the last quarter of the year helping to boost insurance companies at this time.

In the fourth quarter of the year, investors and analysts start to ramp up their expectations for next year's economic growth. Generally, sectors of the stock market that are economically sensitive perform well at this time, which benefits insurance companies such as Sun Life Financial.

5.4% gain & positive 81% of the time

From 2001 to 2016, in its strong seasonal period from October 10th to December 5th, Sun Life Financial has produced an average gain of 5.4% and has been positive 81% of the time. It has also outperformed the TSX Composite Index 75% of the time.

SLF* vs. TSX Comp.- 2001 to 2016

Oct 10 to Dec 5	TSX Comp.	SLF	Diff
			Positive
2001	10.9%	10.6%	-0.3%
2002	14.9	15.4	0.5
2003	5.1	5.4	0.3
2004	2.7	5.3	2.6
2005	3.7	10.8	7.1
2006	10.3	8.5	-1.8
2007	-3.7	3.0	6.7
2008	-15.5	-4.9	10.6
2009	0.7	-10.7	-11.4
2010	5.1	10.6	5.4
2011	4.6	-23.2	-27.8
2012	-1.0	15.0	16.0
2013	3.7	11.2	7.5
2014	0.1	9.7	9.6
2015	-4.3	0.1	4.4
2016	3.6	19.6	16.0
Avg	2.6%	5.4%	2.8%
Fq > 0	75%	81%	75%

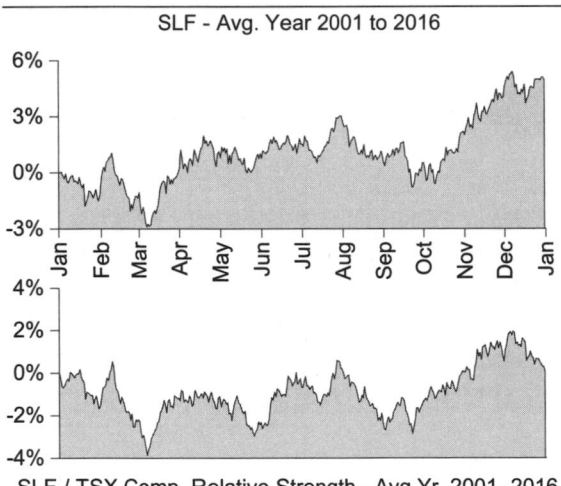

SLF - Avg. Year 2001 to 2016

SLF / TSX Comp. Relative Strength - Avg Yr. 2001- 2016

portfolios used to support insurance payouts.

Nevertheless, insurance companies tend to be bigger benefactors from rising rates. In a rapidly rising rate environment insurance companies will tend to outperform banks, ceteris paribus (everything else equal).

With Sun Life Financial having a similar seasonal period as some of the Canadian bank stocks, investors have the option of adjusting their weighting between the two different investments based upon the expectation of rising rates.

During the seasonal period, if the expectation is low for interest rate increases, banks could be favored. If the expectation for interest rate increases is high, then insurance companies such as Sun Life Financial could be favored.

It is not a coincidence that insurance companies have had their worst monthly performance on average during August, which has on average been a month of falling interest rates.

Sun Life Financial has a seasonal period that is similar to some of the Canadian bank stocks with the period of seasonal strength starting in early to mid-October. Generally, both banks and insurance companies benefit from rising rates. Banks benefit from improving net interest margins and insurance companies from yield exposure in their fixed income

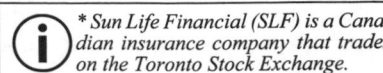

* Sun Life Financial (SLF) is a Canadian insurance company that trades on the Toronto Stock Exchange.

Sun Life Financial Performance

Sun Life Financial Monthly Performance (2001-2016)

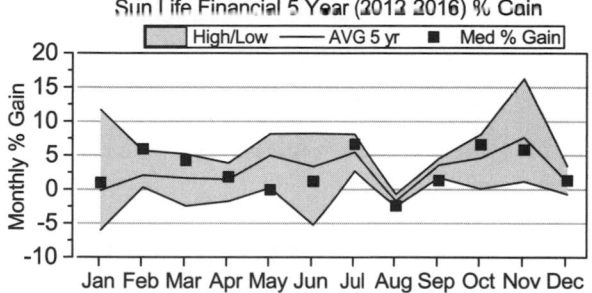

	Jan	Feb	Mar	Apr	May	Jun	Jul	Aug	Sep	Oct	Nov	Dec
Avg. % Gain	-1.2	-0.4	1.5	1.4	0.3	0.5	1.2	-1.9	-0.7	1.2	1.4	1.0
Med. % Gain	1.1	-0.1	1.1	0.8	1.0	1.5	1.9	-0.9	0.6	2.7	2.5	1.6
Fq %>0	50	44	63	56	56	63	56	38	56	75	56	63
Fq %>TSX Comp	50	44	56	50	38	56	50	38	56	63	69	50

Sun Life Financial 5 Year (2012-2016) % Gain

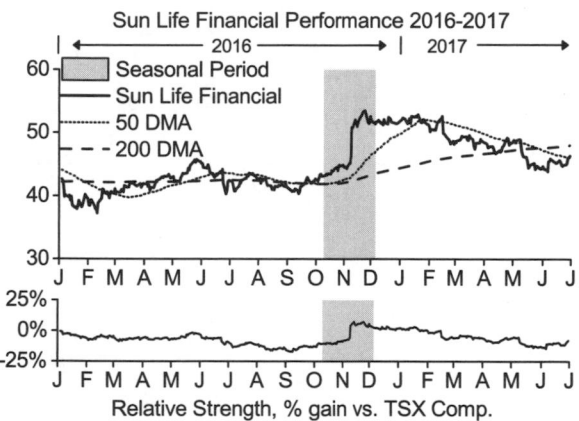

Sun Life Financial Performance 2016-2017

Market Indices & Rates
Weekly Values**

Stock Markets	2015	2016
Dow	17,577	18,886
S&P500	2,061	2,178
Nasdaq	5,036	5,289
TSX	13,288	14,756
FTSE	6,233	6,773
DAX	10,809	10,689
Nikkei	19,660	17,807
Hang Seng	22,553	22,287

Commodities	2015	2016
Oil	42.70	45.16
Gold	1086.3	1221.5

Bond Yields	2015	2016
USA 5 Yr Treasury	1.72	1.71
USA 10 Yr T	2.32	2.26
USA 20 Yr T	2.76	2.66
Moody's Aaa	4.11	3.94
Moody's Baa	5.50	4.82
CAN 5 Yr T	1.00	0.96
CAN 10 Yr T	1.70	1.55

Money Market	2015	2016
USA Fed Funds	0.25	0.50
USA 3 Mo T-B	0.14	0.48
CAN tgt overnight rate	0.50	0.50
CAN 3 Mo T-B	0.44	0.49

Foreign Exchange	2015	2016
EUR/USD	1.08	1.07
GBP/USD	1.52	1.24
USD/CAD	1.33	1.35
USD/JPY	122.88	109.55

Relative Strength, % gain vs. TSX Comp.

NOVEMBER

M	T	W	T	F	S	S
			1	2	3	4
5	6	7	8	9	10	11
12	13	14	15	16	17	18
19	20	21	22	23	24	25
26	27	28	29	30		

DECEMBER

M	T	W	T	F	S	S
					1	2
3	4	5	6	7	8	9
10	11	12	13	14	15	16
17	18	19	20	21	22	23
24	25	26	27	28	29	30
31						

JANUARY

M	T	W	T	F	S	S
	1	2	3	4	5	6
7	8	9	10	11	12	13
14	15	16	17	18	19	20
21	22	23	24	25	26	27
28	29	30	31			

From 2001 to 2016, October and November have been the two best contiguous months of the year on an average and median basis for Sun Life Financial. The medians were higher than the averages which means that a few larger losses pulled the averages down relative to the medians. Over the last five years, October and November have been two of the strongest months of the year for Sun Life Financial. August has also followed its long-term trend over the last five years and has been the worst performing month. In 2016, Sun Life Financial was positive in its seasonal period and outperformed the TSX Composite Index.

METALS AND MINING — STRONG TWO TIMES
①Nov19-Jan 5   ②Jan23-May5

At the macro level, the metals and mining (M&M) sector is driven by future economic growth expectations. When worldwide growth expectations are increasing, there is a greater need for raw materials, and vice versa.

Within the macro trend, the M&M sector has traditionally followed the overall market cycle of performing well from autumn until spring. This is the time of year that investors have a positive outlook on the economy and as a result, the cyclical sectors tend to outperform, including the metals and mining sector.

13.7% gain and positive 82% of the time

The metals and mining sector has two seasonal "sweet spots" – the first from November 19th to January 5th and the second from January 23rd to May 5th.

Investors have the option to hold and "bridge the gap" across the two sweet spots, but over the long-term, nimble traders have been able to capture extra value by being out of the sector from January 6th to the 22nd. During this period, from 1990 to 2017, the metals and mining sector has produced an average loss of 3.2% and has only been positive 50% of the time.

From a portfolio perspective, it is important to consider reducing exposure at the beginning of May. The danger of holding on too long is that the sector tends not to perform well in the late summer, particularly in September.

For more information on the metals and mining sector, see www.standardandpoors.com

Metals & Mining* vs. S&P 500
1989/90 to 2016/17   Positive ☐

| Year | Nov 19 to Jan 5 | | Jan 23 to May 5 | | Compound Growth | |
	S&P 500	M&M	S&P 500	M&M	S&P 500	M&M
1989/90	3.1 %	6.3 %	2.4 %	-4.6 %	5.6 %	1.4 %
1990/91	1.2	6.4	16.0	7.1	17.4	13.9
1991/92	8.9	1.0	-0.3	-1.7	8.5	-0.7
1992/93	2.7	12.5	1.9	3.2	4.7	16.1
1993/94	0.9	9.0	-4.9	-11.1	-4.1	-3.1
1994/95	-0.2	-1.2	11.9	-3.0	11.6	-4.1
1995/96	2.8	8.3	4.6	5.8	7.5	14.6
1996/97	1.5	-1.9	5.6	-1.2	7.2	-3.0
1997/98	4.1	-4.5	15.8	19.3	20.6	13.9
1998/99	8.8	-7.9	10.0	31.0	19.6	20.6
1999/00	-1.6	21.7	-0.6	-10.4	-2.2	9.1
2000/01	-5.1	17.0	-5.7	19.6	-10.5	40.0
2001/02	3.0	5.5	-4.1	12.8	-1.3	19.0
2002/03	0.9	9.3	5.5	3.2	6.4	12.8
2003/04	8.5	18.2	-2.0	-12.1	6.4	3.9
2004/05	0.0	-8.4	0.4	-4.0	0.4	-12.0
2005/06	2.0	17.3	5.1	27.3	7.2	49.4
2006/07	0.6	3.0	5.8	17.2	6.5	20.8
2007/08	-3.2	0.9	7.4	27.4	3.9	28.5
2008/09	8.0	43.8	9.2	30.6	17.9	87.8
2009/10	2.4	6.3	6.8	4.8	9.4	11.3
2010/11	6.7	15.0	4.0	-1.6	11.0	13.1
2011/12	5.4	1.2	4.1	-16.0	9.7	-15.0
2012/13	7.8	3.9	8.2	-16.8	16.6	-13.6
2013/14	2.2	1.2	2.2	2.6	4.4	3.8
2014/15	-1.5	-14.2	1.3	5.3	-0.3	-9.7
2015/16	-3.2	-3.4	7.5	76.3	4.1	70.2
2016/17	4.0	7.2	5.6	-10.8	9.8	-4.4
Avg.	2.5 %	6.2 %	4.4 %	7.1 %	7.1 %	13.7 %
Fq > 0	79 %	75 %	79 %	57 %	68 %	82 %

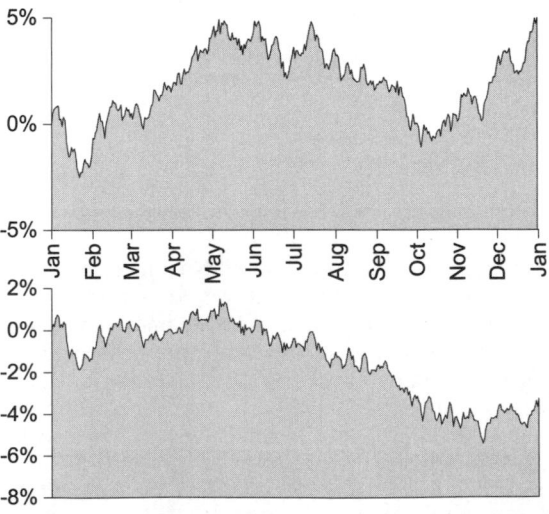

Metals & Mining - Avg. Year 1990 to 2016

Metals & Mining / S&P 500 Rel. Strength- Avg Yr. 1990-2016

Metals & Mining Performance

Metals and Mining Monthly Performance (1990-2016)

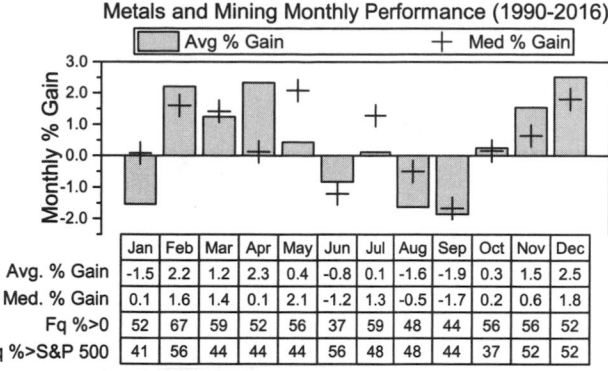

	Jan	Feb	Mar	Apr	May	Jun	Jul	Aug	Sep	Oct	Nov	Dec
Avg. % Gain	-1.5	2.2	1.2	2.3	0.4	-0.8	0.1	-1.6	-1.9	0.3	1.5	2.5
Med. % Gain	0.1	1.6	1.4	0.1	2.1	-1.2	1.3	-0.5	-1.7	0.2	0.6	1.8
Fq %>0	52	67	59	52	56	37	59	48	44	56	56	52
Fq %>S&P 500	41	56	44	44	44	56	48	48	44	37	52	52

Metals and Mining 5 Year (2012-2010) % Gain

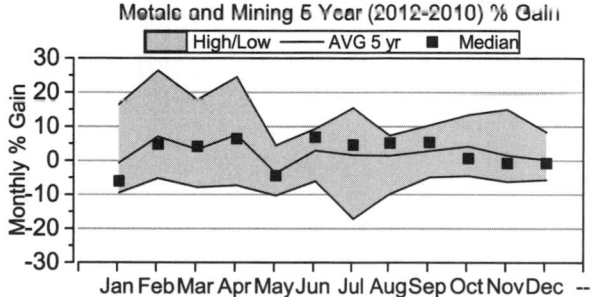

Metals and Mining Performance 2016-2017

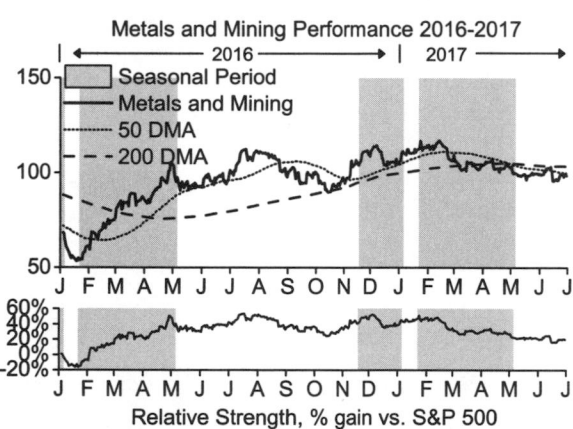

Relative Strength, % gain vs. S&P 500

Market Indices & Rates
Weekly Values**

Stock Markets	2015	2016
Dow	17,653	19,054
S&P500	2,072	2,205
Nasdaq	5,045	5,384
TSX	13,381	15,074
FTSE	6,272	6,817
DAX	10,970	10,690
Nikkei	19,683	18,246
Hang Seng	22,344	22,609

Commodities	2015	2016
Oil	40.82	46.39
Gold	1079.2	1197.1

Bond Yields	2015	2016
USA 5 Yr Treasury	1.68	1.81
USA 10 Yr T	2.26	2.34
USA 20 Yr T	2.69	2.70
Moody's Aaa	4.07	4.01
Moody's Baa	5.47	4.85
CAN 5 Yr T	0.95	0.98
CAN 10 Yr T	1.64	1.56

Money Market	2015	2016
USA Fed Funds	0.25	0.50
USA 3 Mo T-B	0.13	0.49
CAN tgt overnight rate	0.50	0.50
CAN 3 Mo T-B	0.45	0.48

Foreign Exchange	2015	2016
EUR/USD	1.07	1.06
GBP/USD	1.52	1.25
USD/CAD	1.33	1.35
USD/JPY	123.19	112.21

NOVEMBER

M	T	W	T	F	S	S
			1	2	3	4
5	6	7	8	9	10	11
12	13	14	15	16	17	18
19	20	21	22	23	24	25
26	27	28	29	30		

DECEMBER

M	T	W	T	F	S	S
					1	2
3	4	5	6	7	8	9
10	11	12	13	14	15	16
17	18	19	20	21	22	23
24	25	26	27	28	29	30
31						

JANUARY

M	T	W	T	F	S	S
	1	2	3	4	5	6
7	8	9	10	11	12	13
14	15	16	17	18	19	20
21	22	23	24	25	26	27
28	29	30	31			

From 1990 to 2016, the strongest month for the metals and mining sector was December on an average basis. Overall, the metals and mining sector does not have a strong track record of positive performance and outperforming the S&P 500 in any month. Nevertheless, the seasonal trend provides value, particularly in a strong commodity cycle. Over the last five years, on average, the metals and mining sector's monthly performance has somewhat followed its seasonal trend with the first few months of the year performing well (except January). The seasonal period starting in January 2017 underperformed the S&P 500.

UPS — DELIVERING RETURNS
①LONG (Oct10-Dec8)
②SELL SHORT (Dec9-Mar1)

In recent years, Amazon has shown an increasing interest in delivering its own packages, rather than using package delivery companies. Although this trend is expected to continue, consideration should still be given to investing in UPS in its seasonal period before Christmas, as this is when UPS would still be expected to outperform the S&P 500.

Investors look for an activity that could drive a stock price higher. In UPS' case investors typically become more interested in the stock just before the holiday season. The logic is that a busy time of year will help increase earnings, which should raise the stock price.

13.4% growth & positive 94% of the time

The best time to get into UPS is before most investors become excited about the stock. When maximum investor interest for the stock occurs, it has been best to exit.

"Get in before everyone else and exit once everyone is in." In other words, the seasonal trend takes advantage of human behavioral tendencies. From October 10th to December 8th, in the period from 2000 to 2016, UPS has produced an average gain of 7.9% and has been positive 88% of the time. Impressively, UPS has outperformed the S&P 500 during this time period, 88% of time.

Investors typically do not want to invest in UPS at the times of the year when its stock price lacks a near-term catalyst. January and February are low activity months for UPS. As a result, investors tend to reduce their

UPS which trades on the NYSE, adjusted for splits.

UPS* vs. S&P 500 2000/01 to 2016/17

Positive Long ▢   Negative Short ▢

Year	Oct 10 to Dec 8 S&P 500	Oct 10 to Dec 8 UPS	Dec 9 to Mar 1 S&P 500	Dec 9 to Mar 1 UPS	Compound Growth S&P 500	Compound Growth UPS
2000/01	-2.3 %	12.0 %	-9.4 %	-12.1 %	-11.5 %	25.5 %
2001/02	9.6	12.1	-2.3	3.3	7.1	8.5
2002/03	17.4	6.5	-7.8	-10.2	8.3	17.4
2003/04	2.9	11.1	8.1	-4.9	11.3	16.5
2004/05	5.4	14.5	2.3	-11.0	7.9	27.1
2005/06	5.0	9.6	2.8	0.4	8.0	9.2
2006/07	4.4	5.6	-0.5	-10.2	3.9	16.3
2007/08	-3.9	-3.5	-11.6	-5.3	-15.0	1.6
2008/09	0.0	10.6	-19.2	-29.8	-19.2	43.5
2009/10	1.9	3.2	2.2	1.9	4.1	1.2
2010/11	5.4	6.6	6.4	0.5	12.1	6.1
2011/12	6.8	8.7	11.3	6.8	18.9	1.3
2012/13	-1.6	0.2	7.1	13.3	5.3	-13.1
2013/14	9.0	15.5	3.0	-6.5	12.3	23.0
2014/15	6.9	14.2	2.1	-7.7	9.1	22.9
2015/16	2.4	-2.4	-4.1	-2.8	-1.8	0.3
2016/17	4.3	9.4	6.7	-10.2	11.2	20.5
Avg.	4.3 %	7.9 %	-0.2 %	-5.0 %	4.2 %	13.4 %
Fq>0	76 %	88 %	59 %	35 %	76 %	94 %

buying of package delivery companies at the end of the year and into the beginning of March.

From December 9th to March 1st, UPS has on average produced a loss of 5.0% and has only been positive 35% of the time. Collectively, the long and short sell trades have produced an average gain of 13.4% and have been positive 94% of the time.

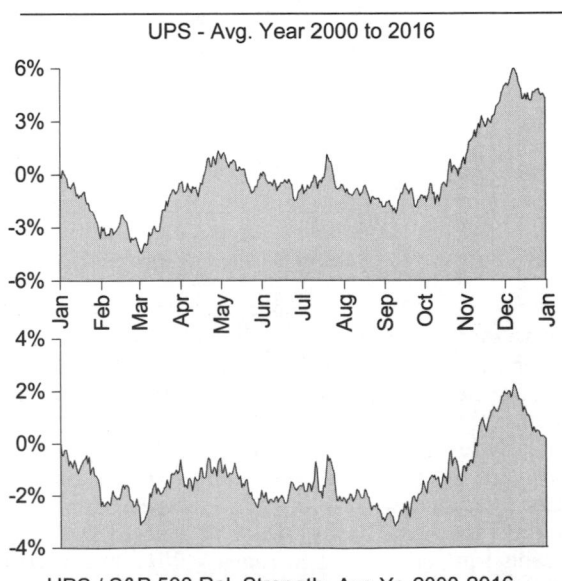

UPS - Avg. Year 2000 to 2016

UPS / S&P 500 Rel. Strength- Avg Yr. 2000-2016

UPS Strategy Performance

UPS Monthly Performance (2000-2016)

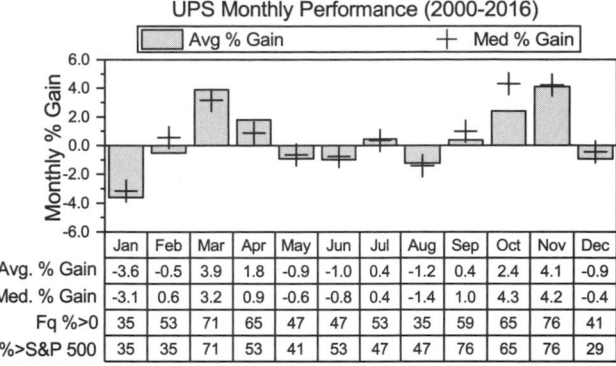

	Jan	Feb	Mar	Apr	May	Jun	Jul	Aug	Sep	Oct	Nov	Dec
Avg. % Gain	-3.6	-0.5	3.9	1.8	-0.9	-1.0	0.4	-1.2	0.4	2.4	4.1	-0.9
Med. % Gain	-3.1	0.6	3.2	0.9	-0.6	-0.8	0.4	-1.4	1.0	4.3	4.2	-0.4
Fq %>0	35	53	71	65	47	47	53	35	59	65	76	41
Fq %>S&P 500	35	35	71	53	41	53	47	47	76	65	76	29

UPS 5 Year (2012-2016) % Gain

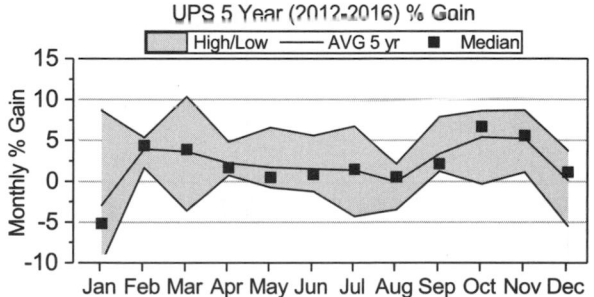

UPS Performance 2016-2017

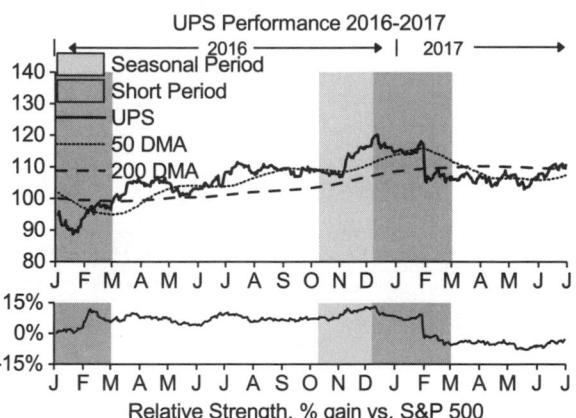

Relative Strength, % gain vs. S&P 500

From 2000 to 2016, October and November have been the strongest months for UPS on a median basis. December has been negative on an average and median basis. The first/second week of December is the pivot point between the long and short sell periods of the trade. January has been the worst month on an average, median and frequency basis.

In the last five years, UPS has generally followed its seasonal trend with October and November being the best months of the year and January the worst month of the year. The long 2016 trade and the short sell 2017 trade, were both successful.

WEEK 48

Market Indices & Rates
Weekly Values**

Stock Markets	2015	2016
Dow	17,804	19,141
S&P500	2,089	2,198
Nasdaq	5,112	5,316
TSX	13,397	15,036
FTSE	6,338	6,768
DAX	11,162	10,578
Nikkei	19,900	18,382
Hang Seng	22,462	22,760

Commodities	2015	2016
Oil	41.21	48.90
Gold	1068.7	1177.4

Bond Yields	2015	2016
USA 5 Yr Treasury	1.67	1.83
USA 10 Yr T	2.24	2.37
USA 20 Yr T	2.65	2.73
Moody's Aaa	4.01	4 01
Moody's Baa	5.44	4.81
CAN 5 Yr T	0.92	1.00
CAN 10 Yr T	1.59	1.58

Money Market	2015	2016
USA Fed Funds	0.25	0.50
USA 3 Mo T-B	0.17	0.48
CAN tgt overnight rate	0.50	0.50
CAN 3 Mo T-B	0.47	0.50

Foreign Exchange	2015	2016
EUR/USD	1.06	1.06
GBP/USD	1.51	1.25
USD/CAD	1.33	1.34
USD/JPY	122.70	113.28

NOVEMBER

M	T	W	T	F	S	S
			1	2	3	4
5	6	7	8	9	10	11
12	13	14	15	16	17	18
19	20	21	22	23	24	25
26	27	28	29	30		

DECEMBER

M	T	W	T	F	S	S
					1	2
3	4	5	6	7	8	9
10	11	12	13	14	15	16
17	18	19	20	21	22	23
24	25	26	27	28	29	30
31						

JANUARY

M	T	W	T	F	S	S
	1	2	3	4	5	6
7	8	9	10	11	12	13
14	15	16	17	18	19	20
21	22	23	24	25	26	27
28	29	30	31			

DECEMBER

	MONDAY	TUESDAY	WEDNESDAY
WEEK 49	**3** 28	**4** 27	**5** 26
WEEK 50	**10** 21	**11** 20	**12** 19
WEEK 51	**17** 14	**18** 13	**19** 12
WEEK 52	**24** 7	**25** 6 CAN Market Closed- Christmas Day USA Market Closed- Christmas Day	**26** 5 CAN Market Closed- Boxing Day
WEEK 53	**31**	1	2

THURSDAY	FRIDAY
6 25	**7** 24
13 18	**14** 17
20 11	**21** 10
27 4	**28** 3
3	4

JANUARY

M	T	W	T	F	S	S
	1	2	3	4	5	6
7	8	9	10	11	12	13
14	15	16	17	18	19	20
21	22	23	24	25	26	27
28	29	30	31			

FEBRUARY

M	T	W	T	F	S	S
				1	2	3
4	5	6	7	8	9	10
11	12	13	14	15	16	17
18	19	20	21	22	23	24
25	26	27	28			

MARCH

M	T	W	T	F	S	S
				1	2	3
4	5	6	7	8	9	10
11	12	13	14	15	16	17
18	19	20	21	22	23	24
25	26	27	28	29	30	31

APRIL

M	T	W	T	F	S	S
1	2	3	4	5	6	7
8	9	10	11	12	13	14
15	16	17	18	19	20	21
22	23	24	25	26	27	28
29	30					

DECEMBER
S U M M A R Y

	Dow Jones	S&P 500	Nasdaq	TSX Comp
Month Rank	2	1	3	1
# Up	47	50	26	27
# Down	20	17	19	5
% Pos	70	75	58	84
% Avg. Gain	1.7	1.6	1.7	2.0

Dow & S&P 1950-2016, Nasdaq 1972-2016 TSX 1985-2016

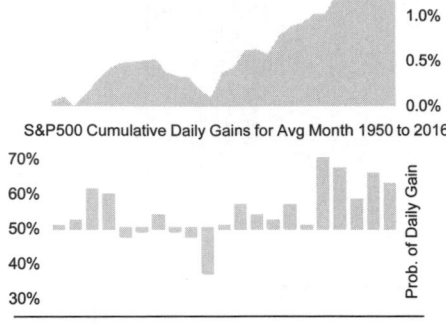

S&P500 Cumulative Daily Gains for Avg Month 1950 to 2016

Prob. of Daily Gain

♦ December is typically one of the strongest months of the year for the S&P 500. From 1950 to 2016, the S&P 500 produced an average gain of 1.6% and was positive 75% of the time. ♦ Most of the gains for the S&P 500 tend to occur in the second half of the month. ♦ The Nasdaq tends to outperform the S&P 500 starting mid-December. ♦ The small cap sector typically starts to outperform the S&P 500 mid-month.

BEST / WORST DECEMBER BROAD MKTS. 2007-2016

BEST DECEMBER MARKETS
♦ Nikkei 225 (2009) 12.8%
♦ Nikkei 225 (2012) 10.0%
♦ Russell 2000 (2009) 7.9%

WORST DECEMBER MARKETS
♦ Russell 2000 (2015) -5.2%
♦ Nikkei 225 (2015) -3.6%
♦ TSX Comp (2015) - 3.4%

Index Values End of Month

	2007	2008	2009	2010	2011	2012	2013	2014	2015	2016
Dow	13,265	8,776	10,428	11,578	12,218	13,104	16,577	17,823	17,425	19,763
S&P 500	1,468	903	1,115	1,258	1,258	1,426	1,848	2,059	2,044	2,239
Nasdaq	2,652	1,577	2,269	2,653	2,605	3,020	4,177	4,736	5,007	5,383
TSX Comp.	13,833	8,988	11,746	13,443	11,955	12,434	13,622	14,632	13,010	15,288
Russell 1000	800	488	612	697	693	790	1,030	1,144	1,132	1,242
Russell 2000	766	499	625	784	741	849	1,164	1,205	1,136	1,357
FTSE 100	6,457	4,434	5,413	5,900	5,572	5,898	6,749	6,566	6,242	7,143
Nikkei 225	15,308	8,860	10,546	10,229	8,455	10,395	16,291	17,451	19,034	19,114

Percent Gain for December

	2007	2008	2009	2010	2011	2012	2013	2014	2015	2016
Dow	-0.8	-0.6	0.8	5.2	1.4	0.6	3.0	0.0	-1.7	3.3
S&P 500	-0.9	0.8	1.8	6.5	0.9	0.7	2.4	-0.4	-1.8	1.8
Nasdaq	-0.3	2.7	5.8	6.2	-0.6	0.3	2.9	-1.2	-2.0	1.1
TSX Comp.	1.1	-3.1	2.6	3.8	-2.0	1.6	1.7	-0.8	-3.4	1.4
Russell 1000	-0.8	1.3	2.3	6.5	0.7	0.8	2.5	-0.4	-2.0	1.7
Russell 2000	-0.2	5.6	7.9	7.8	0.5	3.3	1.8	2.7	-5.2	2.6
FTSE 100	0.4	3.4	4.3	6.7	1.2	0.5	1.5	-2.3	-1.8	5.3
Nikkei 225	-2.4	4.1	12.8	2.9	0.2	10.0	4.0	-0.1	-3.6	4.4

December Market Avg. Performance 2007 to 2016[1]

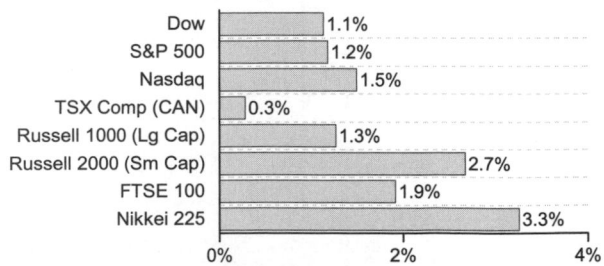

Dow 1.1%
S&P 500 1.2%
Nasdaq 1.5%
TSX Comp (CAN) 0.3%
Russell 1000 (Lg Cap) 1.3%
Russell 2000 (Sm Cap) 2.7%
FTSE 100 1.9%
Nikkei 225 3.3%

Interest Corner Dec[2]

	Fed Funds %[3]	3 Mo. T-Bill %[4]	10 Yr %[5]	20 Yr %[6]
2016	0.75	0.51	2.45	2.79
2015	0.50	0.16	2.27	2.67
2014	0.25	0.04	2.17	2.47
2013	0.25	0.07	3.04	3.72
2012	0.25	0.05	1.78	2.54

(1) Russell Data provided by Russell (2) Federal Reserve Bank of St. Louis- end of month values (3) Target rate set by FOMC (4)(5)(6) Constant yield maturities.

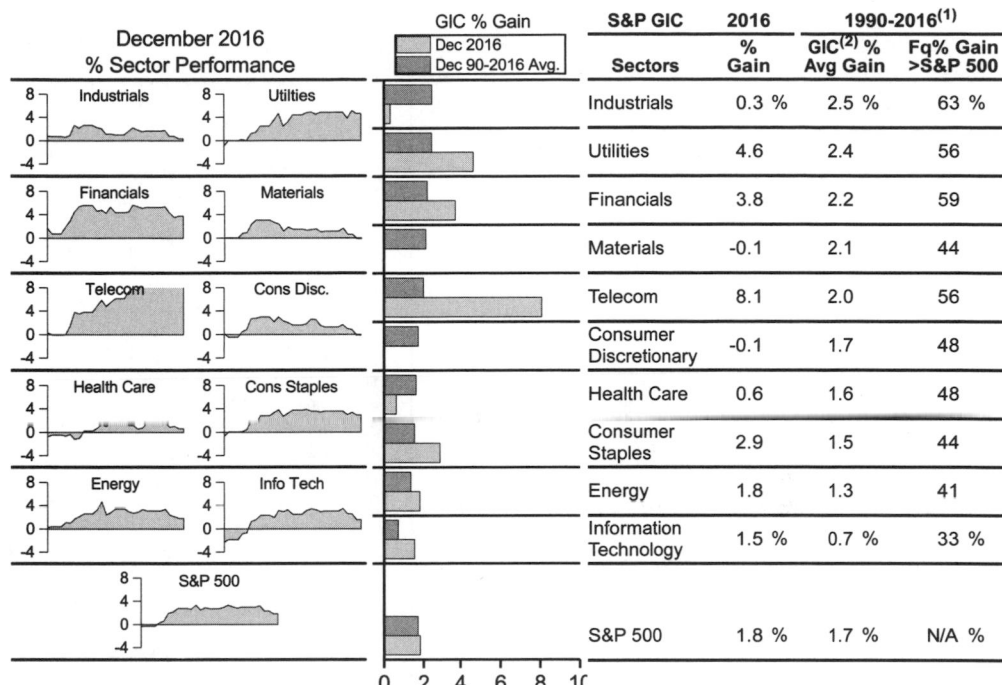

S&P GIC Sectors	2016 % Gain	1990-2016[1]	
		GIC[2] % Avg Gain	Fq% Gain >S&P 500
Industrials	0.3 %	2.5 %	63 %
Utilities	4.6	2.4	56
Financials	3.8	2.2	59
Materials	-0.1	2.1	44
Telecom	8.1	2.0	56
Consumer Discretionary	-0.1	1.7	48
Health Care	0.6	1.6	48
Consumer Staples	2.9	1.5	44
Energy	1.8	1.3	41
Information Technology	1.5 %	0.7 %	33 %
S&P 500	1.8 %	1.7 %	N/A %

Sector Commentary

♦ In December 2016, the S&P 500 produced a gain of 1.8% as investors still expressed hope that Trump would be able to institute pro-business policies to drive growth. ♦ The defensive sectors were generally the top performing sectors, indicating that investors wanted to be invested, but were concerned about the market valuations after the rally over the previous two months. ♦ Telecom was the top performing sector, producing a gain of 8.1%. ♦ The materials and consumer discretionary sectors were the only two major sectors of the S&P 500 that produced losses, with both losing 0.1%.

Sub-Sector Commentary

♦ The homebuilders sub-sector typically performs well in December, but in December 2016, the sub-sector suffered a loss of 0.9%. ♦ Other cyclical sub-sectors also produced a loss, including metals and mining, and steel. ♦ Both gold and silver were negative for the month, with losses of 2.7% and 2.6% respectively.

SELECTED SUB-SECTORS[3]			
Home builders	-0.9 %	7.2 %	81 %
Steel	-4.3	4.5	63
Biotech (1993-2016)	-1.0	4.0	50
Metals & Mining	-4.7	2.5	52
Agriculture (1994-2016)	5.6	2.3	57
Banks	5.5	2.1	59
Chemicals	0.1	1.8	56
Railroads	1.3	1.4	48
Automotive & Components	1.7	1.3	37
Pharma	2.4	1.2	44
SOX (1994-2016)	3.1	1.1	45
Transportation	1.0	1.0	37
Silver	-2.6	1.0	44
Retail	-1.0	0.9	33
Gold	-2.7	-0.2	33

EMERGING MARKETS(USD)– TRUNCATED SIX MONTH SEASONAL
November 24th to April 18th

Emerging markets become popular periodically, mainly after they have had a strong run, or if they have suffered a major correction and investors perceive them as having a lot of value.

Markets around the world tend to have the same broad seasonal trends, including emerging markets. Emerging markets outperform the S&P 500 more often, when the S&P 500 is increasing and underperform when the S&P 500 is decreasing. Given that the S&P 500 has a higher probability of increasing in the favorable six-month period for stocks, from October 27th to May 5th, emerging markets will have a higher probability of outperforming the S&P 500 sometime within the six-month favorable for stocks.

4.7% gain & positive 71% of the time positive

Seasonal investors have benefited from concentrating their emerging market exposure in a truncated, or shorter time period within the favorable six month seasonal period.

Emerging Markets (USD)* vs. S&P 500 1989/90 to 2016/17			
		Positive	
Nov 24 to Apr 18	S&P 500	Em. Mkts.	Diff
1989/90	-0.4%	4.5	4.9%
1990/91	23.8	33.8%	10.5
1991/92	10.6	37.5	26.8
1992/93	5.6	11.8	6.2
1993/94	-4.0	3.7	7.8
1994/95	12.3	-16.4	-28.7
1995/96	7.6	14.7	7.1
1996/97	2.4	7.1	4.7
1997/98	16.6	6.7	-9.9
1998/99	11.0	18.1	7.1
1999/00	2.6	3.5	0.8
2000/01	-6.4	-4.6	1.8
2001/02	-2.3	22.3	24.5
2002/03	-4.0	0.0	4.0
2003/04	9.6	19.5	9.9
2004/05	-2.6	4.3	7.0
2005/06	3.3	24.7	21.4
2006/07	4.7	13.2	8.5
2007/08	-3.5	-0.9	2.6
2008/09	8.7	37.6	28.9
2009/10	7.8	5.6	-2.2
2010/11	10.5	6.6	-3.9
2011/12	19.2	15.6	-3.6
2012/13	9.4	0.1	-9.3
2013/14	3.3	0.3	-3.1
2014/15	0.9	3.8	3.0
2015/16	0.4	0.3	-0.1
2016/17	6.2	11.9	5.7
Avg	5.5%	10.2%	4.7%
Fq > 0	75%	86%	71%

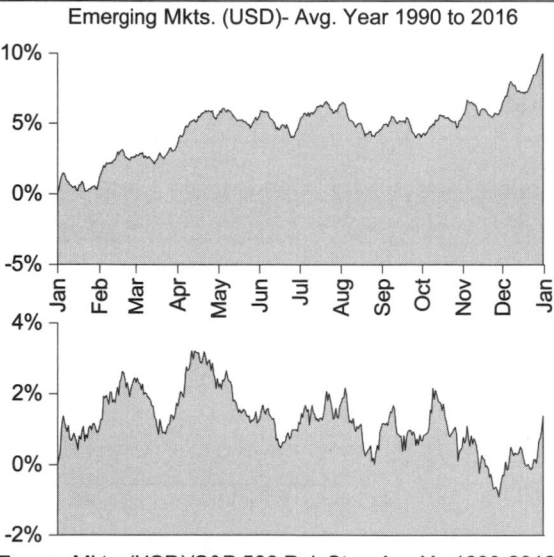

Emerging Mkts. (USD)- Avg. Year 1990 to 2016

Emerg. Mkts. (USD)/S&P 500 Rel. Str. - Avg Yr. 1990-2016

The seasonally strong period for the emerging markets sector is from November 24th to April 18th. In this time period, from 1990/91 to 2015/16, the emerging markets sector (USD) produced an average rate of return of 10.2% and has been positive 86% of the time.

When the world has grappled with the sub-prime crisis and then the EU crisis, investors sought the safety of the U.S. markets and as a result, emerging markets underperformed. In 2017, the trend changed as global growth improved and the U.S. dollar fell relative to worldwide currencies. As a result, emerging markets rallied.

As worldwide economic growth gains traction in the future, seasonal investors should consider adding emerging markets to their portfolio from November 24th to April 18th.

(i) *Emerging Markets (USD)- For more information on the emerging markets, see www.standardandpoors.com*

Emerging Markets Performance

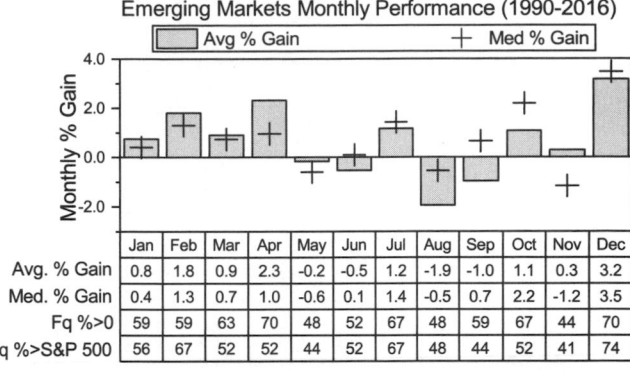

Emerging Markets Monthly Performance (1990-2016)

	Jan	Feb	Mar	Apr	May	Jun	Jul	Aug	Sep	Oct	Nov	Dec
Avg. % Gain	0.8	1.8	0.9	2.3	-0.2	-0.5	1.2	-1.9	-1.0	1.1	0.3	3.2
Med. % Gain	0.4	1.3	0.7	1.0	-0.6	0.1	1.4	-0.5	0.7	2.2	-1.2	3.5
Fq %>0	59	59	63	70	48	52	67	48	59	67	44	70
Fq %>S&P 500	56	67	52	52	44	52	67	48	44	52	41	74

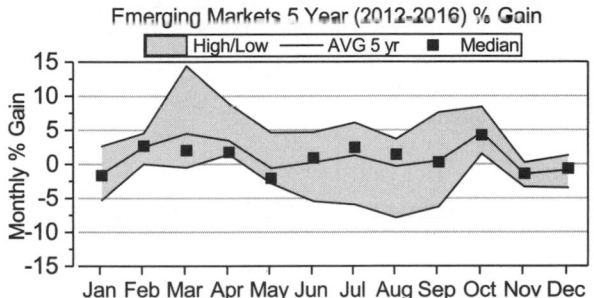

Emerging Markets 5 Year (2012-2016) % Gain

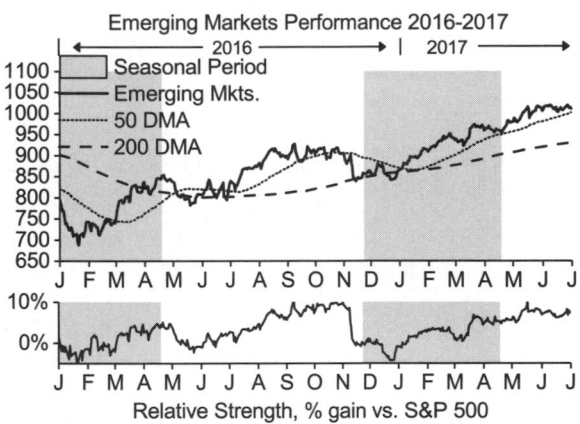

Emerging Markets Performance 2016-2017

Relative Strength, % gain vs. S&P 500

Market Indices & Rates
Weekly Values**

Stock Markets	2015	2016
Dow	17,733	19,478
S&P500	2,081	2,233
Nasdaq	5,114	5,380
TSX	13,451	15,213
FTSE	6,337	6,863
DAX	11,075	10,966
Nikkei	19,828	18,579
Hang Seng	22,302	22,721

Commodities	2015	2016
Oil	40.90	50.97
Gold	1063.5	1169.4

Bond Yields	2015	2016
USA 5 Yr Treasury	1.66	1.84
USA 10 Yr T	2.23	2.40
USA 20 Yr T	2.62	2.79
Moody's Aaa	3.97	4.05
Moody's Baa	5.41	4.83
CAN 5 Yr T	0.91	1.04
CAN 10 Yr T	1.56	1.65

Money Market	2015	2016
USA Fed Funds	0.25	0.50
USA 3 Mo T-B	0.22	0.51
CAN tgt overnight rate	0.50	0.50
CAN 3 Mo T-B	0.48	0.48

Foreign Exchange	2015	2016
EUR/USD	1.07	1.07
GBP/USD	1.51	1.26
USD/CAD	1.34	1.32
USD/JPY	122.99	114.20

DECEMBER

M	T	W	T	F	S	S
					1	2
3	4	5	6	7	8	9
10	11	12	13	14	15	16
17	18	19	20	21	22	23
24	25	26	27	28	29	30
31						

JANUARY

M	T	W	T	F	S	S
	1	2	3	4	5	6
7	8	9	10	11	12	13
14	15	16	17	18	19	20
21	22	23	24	25	26	27
28	29	30	31			

FEBRUARY

M	T	W	T	F	S	S
				1	2	3
4	5	6	7	8	9	10
11	12	13	14	15	16	17
18	19	20	21	22	23	24
25	26	27	28			

From 1990 to 2016, December has been the strongest month of the year for emerging markets on an average, median and frequency basis. Although November tends to have a negative median, the last part of the month tends to be a good launching point into the seasonal period for emerging markets.

Over the last five years, emerging markets performed well in October along with most major global stock markets.

In its 2016/2017 seasonal period, the emerging markets sector was positive and outperformed the S&P 500.

Aerospace & Defense Sector Flying High
December 12th to May 5th

The aerospace and defense sector is highly dependent on government purchases and as a result is subject not only to economic cycles, but also the political environment. Despite the fact that outside variables have a large impact on aerospace and defense orders, the sector has a seasonal trend.

The aerospace and defense sector has a seasonal trend that is similar to the overall broad market's seasonal trend. The big difference is that aerospace and defense has a track record of strongly outperforming the S&P 500 from mid-December until the beginning of May.

9.7% gain & positive 89% of the time

The difference in the sector's seasonal trend compared with the S&P 500's trend is largely the result of the U.S. governments procurement cycle, which has a year-end of September 30th. The first quarter of the government's fiscal year (October, November and December) tends to be the weakest for orders. Government procurement tends to pick up at the start of the new calendar year, helping to boost aerospace and defense stocks up until the beginning of May.

Aerospace & Defense* vs. S&P 500
1989/90 to 2016/17

Dec 12 to May 5	S&P 500	Aero & Def.	Diff (Positive)
1989/90	-2.9%	6.1%	9.0%
1990/91	16.7	11.6	-5.1
1991/92	10.4	10.1	-0.3
1992/93	2.5	14.3	11.9
1993/94	-2.7	2.7	5.4
1994/95	16.4	26.0	9.7
1995/96	3.6	11.6	8.0
1996/97	12.1	8.0	-4.1
1997/98	16.8	11.5	-5.3
1998/99	15.5	29.1	13.6
1999/00	1.1	3.6	2.5
2000/01	-8.2	-0.9	7.4
2001/02	-5.6	23.3	28.9
2002/03	2.4	-7.4	-9.8
2003/04	4.7	5.6	0.9
2004/05	-1.3	4.1	5.4
2005/06	5.3	21.0	15.8
2006/07	6.6	9.0	2.5
2007/08	-4.8	-2.5	2.3
2008/09	3.5	8.5	5.1
2009/10	5.4	12.8	7.4
2010/11	7.6	13.0	5.4
2011/12	9.1	7.4	-1.7
2012/13	13.1	14.7	1.7
2013/14	5.8	8.9	3.1
2014/15	2.7	3.0	0.3
2015/16	1.9	5.5	3.6
2016/17	6.2	10.3	4.1
Avg	5.1%	9.7%	4.6%
Fq > 0	79%	89%	79%

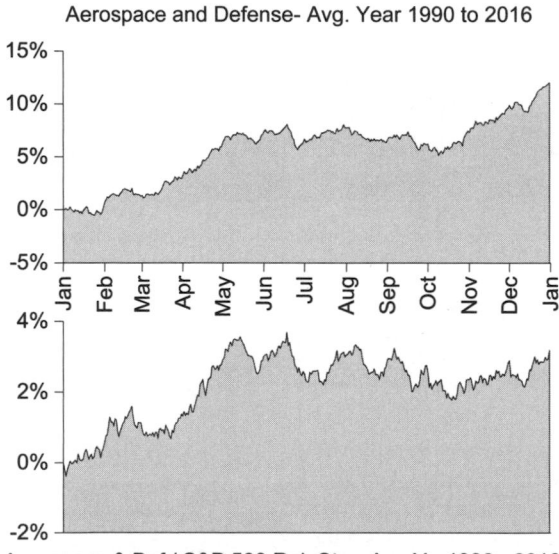

Aerospace and Defense- Avg. Year 1990 to 2016

Aerospace & Def./ S&P 500 Rel. Str. - Avg Yr. 1990 - 2016

From 1989/90 to 2016/17, during its seasonal period, December 12th to May 5th, the aerospace and defense sector has produced an average gain of 9.7% and has been positive 89% of the time. Compared to the S&P 500, it has produced an extra 4.6% and outperformed it 79% of the time.

In the other seven months of the year, from May 6th to December 11th, the aerospace and defense sector has only had an average gain of 2.2% and has only outperformed the S&P 500, 44% of the time. In this unfavorable period, there have been nine years of gains greater than 10% and five years of losses greater than 10%. In other words, the results in the unfavorable period for the sector tend to be volatile and not as strong as the favorable period.

* For more information on the aerospace and defense sector, see www.standardandpoors.com

- 149 -

Aerospace & Defense Performance

Aerospace Monthly Performance (1990-2016)

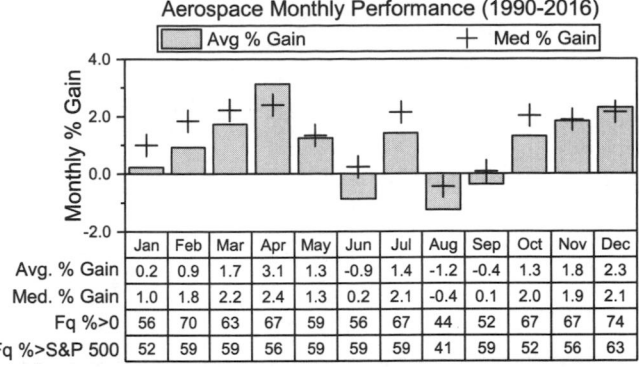

	Jan	Feb	Mar	Apr	May	Jun	Jul	Aug	Sep	Oct	Nov	Dec
Avg. % Gain	0.2	0.9	1.7	3.1	1.3	-0.9	1.4	-1.2	-0.4	1.3	1.8	2.3
Med. % Gain	1.0	1.8	2.2	2.4	1.3	0.2	2.1	-0.4	0.1	2.0	1.9	2.1
Fq %>0	56	70	63	67	59	56	67	44	52	67	67	74
Fq %>S&P 500	52	59	59	56	59	59	59	41	59	52	56	63

Aerospace 5 Year (2012-2016) % Gain

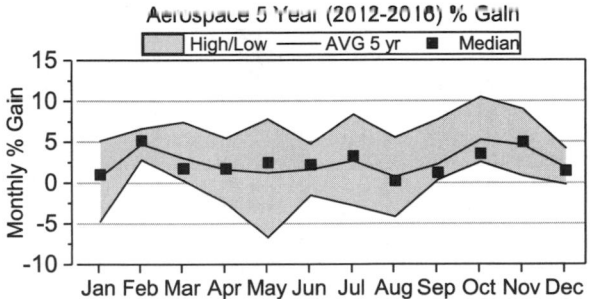

Aerospace Performance 2016-2017

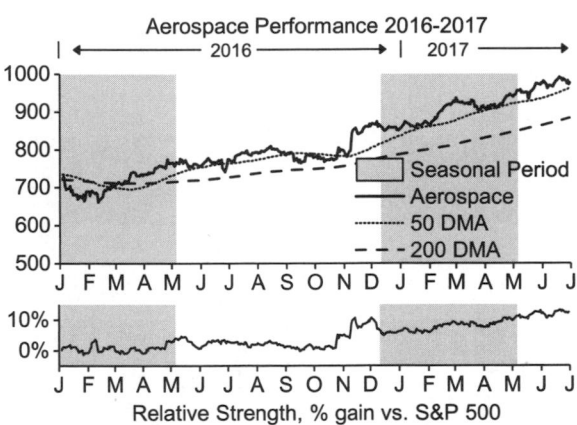

Relative Strength, % gain vs. S&P 500

From 1990 to 2016, the aerospace and defense sector has increased its gains on a monthly basis from January to April, with April being the best month. The summer months have tended to be the weaker months, with August being the weakest.

Over the last five years, on average, the first few months of the year have been stronger than the average month for the rest of the year. August has been the worst month.

In the December 2016 to May 2017 seasonal period, the aerospace and defense sector was positive and outperformed the S&P 500.

Market Indices & Rates
Weekly Values**

Stock Markets	2015	2016
Dow	17,526	19,839
S&P500	2,051	2,260
Nasdaq	5,040	5,441
TSX	12,942	15,268
FTSE	6,105	6,964
DAX	10,618	11,298
Nikkei	19,354	19,267
Hang Seng	21,816	22,283

Commodities	2015	2016
Oil	36.94	51.93
Gold	1074.5	1147.1

Bond Yields	2015	2016
USA 5 Yr Treasury	1.65	2.00
USA 10 Yr T	2.21	2.54
USA 20 Yr T	2.58	2.87
Moody's Aaa	3.95	4.09
Moody's Baa	5.40	4.87
CAN 5 Yr T	0.82	1.17
CAN 10 Yr T	1.48	1.79

Money Market	2015	2016
USA Fed Funds	0.25	0.75
USA 3 Mo T-B	0.26	0.52
CAN tgt overnight rate	0.50	0.50
CAN 3 Mo T-B	0.46	0.48

Foreign Exchange	2015	2016
EUR/USD	1.09	1.05
GBP/USD	1.51	1.26
USD/CAD	1.36	1.32
USD/JPY	122.06	116.67

DECEMBER

M	T	W	T	F	S	S
					1	2
3	4	5	6	7	8	9
10	11	12	13	14	15	16
17	18	19	20	21	22	23
24	25	26	27	28	29	30
31						

JANUARY

M	T	W	T	F	S	S
	1	2	3	4	5	6
7	8	9	10	11	12	13
14	15	16	17	18	19	20
21	22	23	24	25	26	27
28	29	30	31			

FEBRUARY

M	T	W	T	F	S	S
				1	2	3
4	5	6	7	8	9	10
11	12	13	14	15	16	17
18	19	20	21	22	23	24
25	26	27	28			

DO THE "NAZ" WITH SANTA
Nasdaq Gives More at Christmas – Dec 15th to Jan 23rd

One of the best times to invest in the major stock markets is the period around Christmas. The markets are generally positive at this time of the year as investors reposition their portfolios for the start of the new year. A lot of investors are familiar with the *Small Cap Effect* opportunity that starts approximately at this time of the year, where small caps tend to outperform from mid-December until the beginning of March (*see Small Cap Effect*), but few investors know that the last half of December and the first half of January is also a seasonally strong period for the Nasdaq.

80% of time better than S&P 500

The Nasdaq tends to perform well in the last two weeks of December, as investors typically increase their investment allocation to higher beta investments, including the Nasdaq, to finish the year.

In addition, the major sector drivers of the Nasdaq (biotech and technology), tend to perform well in the second half of December and the first half of January. Biotech tends to perform well in the last half of December, and technology tends to perform well in the first half of January. The end result is a Nasdaq Christmas trade that lasts from December 15th to January 23rd. In this time period, for the years 1971/72 to 2016/17, the Nasdaq has outperformed the S&P 500 by an average 2.1% per year. This rate of return is considered to be very high given that the length of the favorable period is just over one month. Even more impressive is the 80% frequency that the Nasdaq outperforms the S&P 500.

Nasdaq vs. S&P 500 Dec 15th to Jan 23rd 1971/72 To 2016/17			
		Positive	
Dec 15 to Jan 23	S&P 500	Nasdaq	Diff
1971/72	6.1 %	7.5 %	1.3 %
1972/73	0.0	-0.7	-0.7
1973/74	4.1	6.8	2.8
1974/75	7.5	8.9	1.4
1975/76	13.0	13.8	0.9
1976/77	-1.7	2.8	4.5
1977/78	-5.1	-3.5	1.6
1978/79	4.7	6.2	1.4
1979/80	4.1	5.6	1.5
1980/81	0.8	3.3	2.5
1981/82	-6.0	-5.0	1.0
1982/83	4.7	5.5	0.8
1983/84	0.9	1.4	0.4
1984/85	9.0	13.3	4.3
1985/86	-2.7	0.8	3.5
1986/87	9.2	10.2	1.0
1987/88	1.8	9.1	7.3
1988/89	3.3	4.6	1.3
1989/90	-5.5	-3.8	1.7
1990/91	1.0	4.1	3.1
1991/92	7.9	15.2	7.2
1992/93	0.8	7.2	6.4
1993/94	2.5	5.7	3.2
1994/95	2.4	4.7	2.3
1995/96	-0.7	-1.0	-0.3
1996/97	6.7	7.3	0.6
1997/98	0.4	2.6	2.1
1998/99	7.4	18.9	11.6
1999/00	2.7	18.6	15.9
2000/01	1.5	4.1	2.6
2001/02	0.5	-1.6	-2.0
2002/03	-0.2	1.9	2.1
2003/04	6.3	9.0	2.7
2004/05	-3.0	-5.8	-2.9
2005/06	-0.7	-0.6	0.1
2006/07	0.2	-0.9	-1.1
2007/08	-8.8	-12.1	-3.3
2008/09	-5.4	-4.1	1.3
2009/10	-2.0	-0.3	1.7
2010/11	3.4	2.4	-1.0
2011/12	8.6	9.6	1.1
2012/13	5.8	6.1	0.4
2013/14	3.0	5.5	2.5
2014/15	2.5	2.2	-0.2
2015/16	-5.7	-7.3	-1.6
2016/17	0.5	2.1	1.6
Avg	1.9 %	3.9 %	2.1 %
Fq > 0	70 %	72 %	80 %

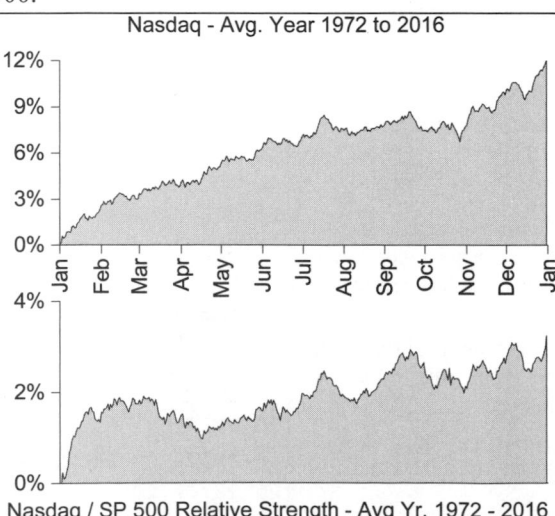

Nasdaq - Avg. Year 1972 to 2016

Nasdaq / SP 500 Relative Strength - Avg Yr. 1972 - 2016

(Y) *Alternate Strategy — For those investors who favor the Nasdaq, an alternative strategy is to invest in the Nasdaq at an earlier date: October 28th. Historically, on average the Nasdaq has started its outperformance at this time. The "Do the Naz with Santa" strategy focuses on the sweet spot of the Nasdaq's outper-*

(i) *Nasdaq is a market that has a focused on biotech and technology and is typically more volatile than the S&P 500.*

Nasdaq Performance

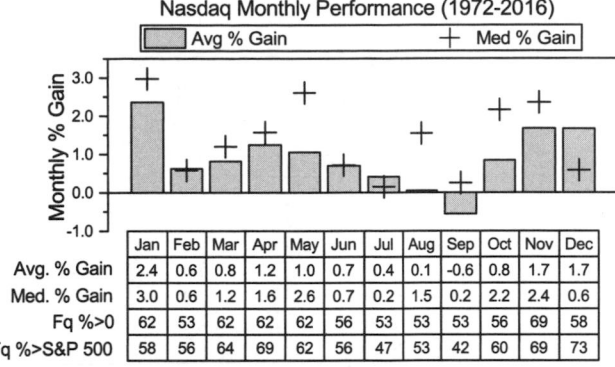

Nasdaq Monthly Performance (1972-2016)

	Jan	Feb	Mar	Apr	May	Jun	Jul	Aug	Sep	Oct	Nov	Dec
Avg. % Gain	2.4	0.6	0.8	1.2	1.0	0.7	0.4	0.1	-0.6	0.8	1.7	1.7
Med. % Gain	3.0	0.6	1.2	1.6	2.6	0.7	0.2	1.5	0.2	2.2	2.4	0.6
Fq %>0	62	53	62	62	62	56	53	53	53	56	69	58
Fq %>S&P 500	58	56	64	69	62	56	47	53	42	60	69	73

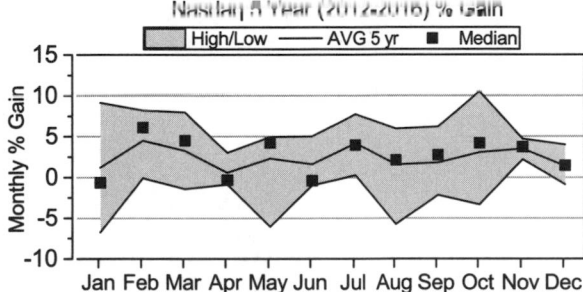

Nasdaq 5 Year (2012-2016) % Gain

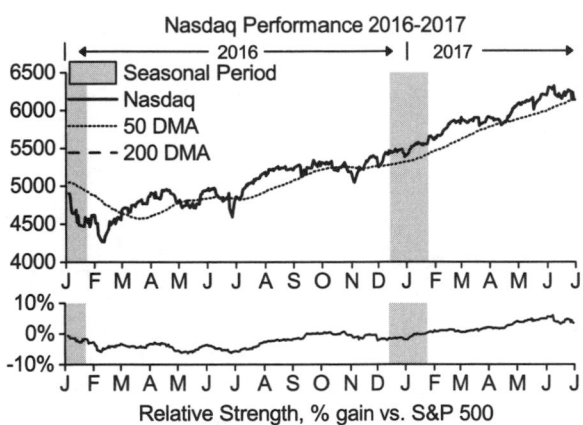

Nasdaq Performance 2016-2017

Relative Strength, % gain vs. S&P 500

Market Indices & Rates
Weekly Values**

Stock Markets	2015	2016
Dow	17,453	19,930
S&P500	2,037	2,265
Nasdaq	4,989	5,465
TSX	12,963	15,306
FTSE	6,022	7,047
DAX	10,481	11,453
Nikkei	18,968	19,440
Hang Seng	21,583	21,717

Commodities	2015	2016
Oil	35.77	51.92
Gold	1063.6	1131.7

Bond Yields	2015	2016
USA 5 Yr Treasury	1.70	2.04
USA 10 Yr T	2.25	2.55
USA 20 Yr T	2.59	2.86
Moody's Aaa	3.97	4.06
Moody's Baa	5.17	4.02
CAN 5 Yr T	0.79	1.20
CAN 10 Yr T	1.46	1.80

Money Market	2015	2016
USA Fed Funds	0.50	0.75
USA 3 Mo T-B	0.23	0.52
CAN tgt overnight rate	0.50	0.50
CAN 3 Mo T-B	0.46	0.47

Foreign Exchange	2015	2016
EUR/USD	1.09	1.04
GBP/USD	1.50	1.23
USD/CAD	1.38	1.34
USD/JPY	121.73	117.47

DECEMBER

M	T	W	T	F	S	S
					1	2
3	4	5	6	7	8	9
10	11	12	13	14	15	16
17	18	19	20	21	22	23
24	25	26	27	28	29	30
31						

JANUARY

M	T	W	T	F	S	S
	1	2	3	4	5	6
7	8	9	10	11	12	13
14	15	16	17	18	19	20
21	22	23	24	25	26	27
28	29	30	31			

FEBRUARY

M	T	W	T	F	S	S
			1	2	3	
4	5	6	7	8	9	10
11	12	13	14	15	16	17
18	19	20	21	22	23	24
25	26	27	28			

From 1972 to 2016, the best month of the year for the Nasdaq has been January on an average and median basis. January is the core part of the Nasdaq trade. December is also a positive month, but on a median basis, it is weaker than most other months. It is the first part of December that tends to be weaker for the Nasdaq, leading to a mid-month entry into the Nasdaq trade. Over the last five years, the strongest month of the year for the Nasdaq has been February.

The 2016/17 Nasdaq trade was positive, but underperformed the S&P 500.

SMALL CAP (SMALL COMPANY) EFFECT
Small Companies Outperform - Dec 19th to Mar 7th

At different stages of the business cycle, small capitalization companies (small caps represented by Russell 2000), perform better than large capitalization companies (large caps represented by Russell 1000).

Evidence shows that the small caps relative outperformance also has a seasonal component as they typically outperform large caps from December 19th to March 7th.

2.8% extra and positive 76% of the time

Russell 2000 - Avg. Year 1979 to 2016

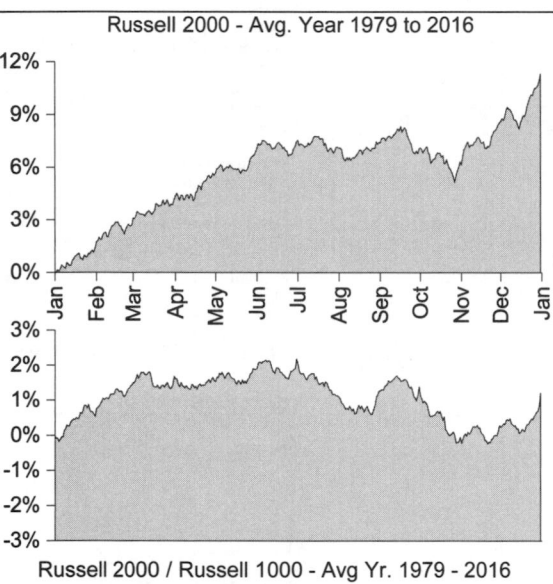

Russell 2000 / Russell 1000 - Avg Yr. 1979 - 2016

Dec 19 - Mar7	Russell 1000	Russell 2000	Diff
1979/80	-1.3 %	-0.4 %	0.9 %
1980/81	-2.8	4.0	6.8
1981/82	-12.4	-12.1	0.3
1982/83	11.8	19.8	8.0
1983/84	-6.4	-7.5	-1.1
1984/85	7.7	17.1	9.4
1985/86	8.2	11.7	3.5
1986/87	17.2	21.3	4.1
1987/88	8.3	16.4	8.0
1988/89	6.9	9.1	2.5
1989/90	-2.0	-1.9	0.2
1990/91	14.6	29.0	14.4
1991/92	6.0	16.8	10.8
1992/93	1.4	5.0	3.5
1993/94	0.5	5.7	5.3
1994/95	5.3	5.5	0.2
1995/96	8.3	7.8	-0.5
1996/97	9.5	3.5	-6.0
1997/98	10.2	10.3	0.1
1998/99	7.3	0.2	-7.2
1999/00	-1.7	27.7	29.4
2000/01	-5.2	4.7	9.8
2001/02	1.6	1.9	0.4
2002/03	-6.7	-7.8	-1.0
2003/04	6.4	9.6	3.3
2004/05	2.8	0.3	-2.5
2005/06	0.8	5.6	4.7
2006/07	-1.6	-0.8	0.9
2007/08	-10.9	-12.5	-1.5
2008/09	-22.2	-26.7	-4.5
2009/10	3.6	9.1	5.5
2010/11	5.5	4.2	-1.3
2011/12	11.3	10.2	-1.1
2012/13	7.1	10.3	3.1
2013/14	4.2	6.1	2.0
2014/15	1.0	2.1	1.1
2015/16	-0.3	-2.4	-2.1
2016/17	4.8	0.8	-4.1
Avg.	2.6 %	5.4 %	2.8 %
Fq > 0	68 %	76 %	66 %

Russell 2000 vs. Russell 1000* % Gains Dec 19th to Mar 7th 1979/80 to 2016/17 Positive

The core part of the small cap seasonal strategy occurs in January and includes what has been described as the January Effect (Wachtel 1942, 184).

This well documented anomaly of superior performance of stocks in the month of January is based upon the tenet that investors sell stocks in December for tax loss reasons, artificially driving down prices, and creating a great opportunity for astute investors.

In recent times, the January Effect start date has shifted to mid-December and is more pronounced for small caps as their prices are more volatile than large caps. At the beginning of the year, small cap stocks benefit from a phenomenon that I have coined, "beta out of the gate, and coast." If small cap stocks are outperforming at the beginning of the year, money managers will gravitate to the sector in order to produce

returns that are above their index benchmark. Once above average returns have been "locked in," the managers then rotate from their small cap overweight positions back to index large cap positions and coast for the rest of the year with above average returns. The overall process boosts small cap stocks at the beginning of the year.

Russell 2000 (small cap index): The 2000 smallest companies in the Russell 3000 stock index (a broad market index). Russell 1000 (large cap index): The 1000 largest companies in the Russell 3000 stock index

For more information on the Russell indexes, see www.Russell.com

Wachtel, S.B. 1942. Certain observations on seasonal movements in stock prices. The Journal of Business and Economics (Winter): 184.

Small Caps Performance

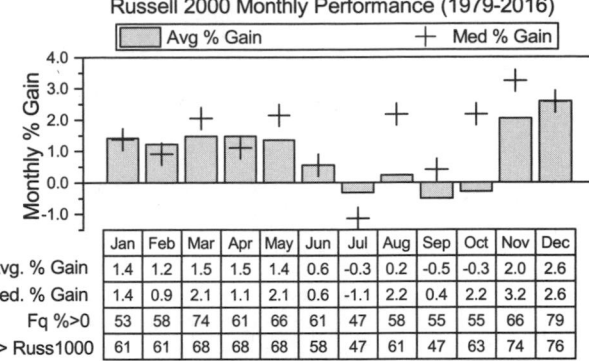

Russell 2000 Monthly Performance (1979-2016)

Legend: Avg % Gain | Med % Gain

	Jan	Feb	Mar	Apr	May	Jun	Jul	Aug	Sep	Oct	Nov	Dec
Avg. % Gain	1.4	1.2	1.5	1.5	1.4	0.6	-0.3	0.2	-0.5	-0.3	2.0	2.6
Med. % Gain	1.4	0.9	2.1	1.1	2.1	0.6	-1.1	2.2	0.4	2.2	3.2	2.6
Fq %>0	53	58	74	61	66	61	47	58	55	55	66	79
Fq %> Russ1000	61	61	68	68	68	58	47	61	47	63	74	76

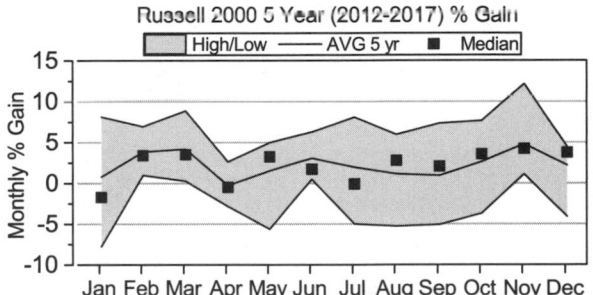

Russell 2000 5 Year (2012-2017) % Gain

Legend: High/Low | AVG 5 yr | Median

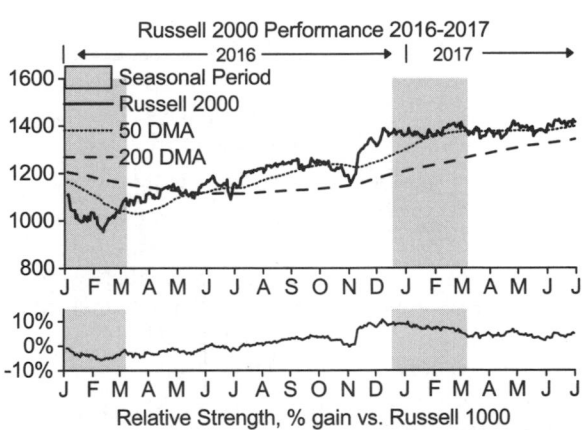

Russell 2000 Performance 2016-2017

Legend: Seasonal Period, Russell 2000, 50 DMA, 200 DMA

Relative Strength, % gain vs. Russell 1000

Market Indices & Rates
Weekly Values**

Stock Markets	2015	2016
Dow	17,456	19,840
S&P500	2,046	2,252
Nasdaq	5,016	5,435
TSX	13,178	15,357
FTSE	6,177	7,123
DAX	10,613	11,470
Nikkei	18,840	19,292
Hang Seng	21,950	21,849

Commodities	2015	2016
Oil	36.38	53.86
Gold	1074.0	1140.3

Bond Yields	2015	2016
USA 5 Yr Treasury	1.71	2.00
USA 10 Yr T	2.24	2.51
USA 20 Yr T	2.60	2.83
Moody's Aaa	3.97	4.02
Moody's Baa	5.49	4.77
CAN 5 Yr T	0.73	1.16
CAN 10 Yr T	1.39	1.75

Money Market	2015	2016
USA Fed Funds	0.50	0.75
USA 3 Mo T-B	0.21	0.51
CAN tgt overnight rate	0.50	0.50
CAN 3 Mo T-B	0.47	0.47

Foreign Exchange	2015	2016
EUR/USD	1.09	1.05
GBP/USD	1.49	1.23
USD/CAD	1.39	1.35
USD/JPY	120.79	117.06

DECEMBER

M	T	W	T	F	S	S
					1	2
3	4	5	6	7	8	9
10	11	12	13	14	15	16
17	18	19	20	21	22	23
24	25	26	27	28	29	30
31						

JANUARY

M	T	W	T	F	S	S
	1	2	3	4	5	6
7	8	9	10	11	12	13
14	15	16	17	18	19	20
21	22	23	24	25	26	27
28	29	30	31			

FEBRUARY

M	T	W	T	F	S	S
				1	2	3
4	5	6	7	8	9	10
11	12	13	14	15	16	17
18	19	20	21	22	23	24
25	26	27	28			

From 1979 to 2016, December through to February have been strong months for small cap stocks. Other months have performed well, but they have not provided the same risk-reward benefits. Over the last five years, the small cap sector has generally followed its seasonal trend with December and February being strong months. January has been the exception, with its poor performance. This data is largely skewed by the dramatic decline in the stock markets in 2016.

In early 2016, the small cap sector underperformed in its seasonal period. In late 2016/17 the small cap sector underperformed the S&P 500.

FINANCIALS (U.S.) YEAR END CLEAN UP
December 15th to April 13th

The U.S. financial sector often starts its strong performance in October, steps up its performance in mid-December and then strongly outperforms the S&P 500 starting in mid-January.

Extra 1.7% &
61% of the time better than the S&P 500

In the 1990s and early 2000s, financial stocks benefited from the tailwind of falling interest rates. During this period, with a few exceptions, this sector has participated in both the rallies and the declines.

Dec 15 to Apr 13	S&P 500	Positive Financials	Diff
1989/90	-1.9 %	-9.9 %	-8.0 %
1990/91	16.4	29.2	12.8
1991/92	5.6	9.2	3.5
1992/93	3.8	17.9	14.1
1993/94	-3.6	-0.4	3.2
1994/95	11.9	14.0	2.1
1995/96	3.2	5.5	2.3
1996/97	1.2	4.7	3.4
19/9798	16.4	19.7	3.3
1998/99	18.3	24.9	6.6
1999/00	2.7	4.0	1.3
2000/01	-11.7	-4.8	6.9
2001/02	-1.1	6.5	7.6
2002/03	-2.4	-1.8	0.6
2003/04	5.2	6.7	1.5
2004/05	-2.5	-6.2	-3.7
2005/06	1.3	1.1	-0.2
2006/07	1.9	-2.2	-4.1
2007/08	-9.2	-14.1	-4.9
2008/09	-2.4	-7.0	-4.6
2009/10	7.5	15.2	7.8
2010/11	5.9	4.6	-1.3
2011/12	13.1	20.7	7.7
2012/13	12.4	16.0	3.6
2013/14	2.3	1.0	-1.3
2014/15	4.5	1.1	-3.4
2015/16	3.0	-2.0	-5.0
2016/17	3.4	-2.0	-5.4
Avg.	3.8 %	5.4 %	1.7 %
Fq > 0	71 %	64 %	61 %

Financials* vs. S&P 500 1989/90 to 2016/17

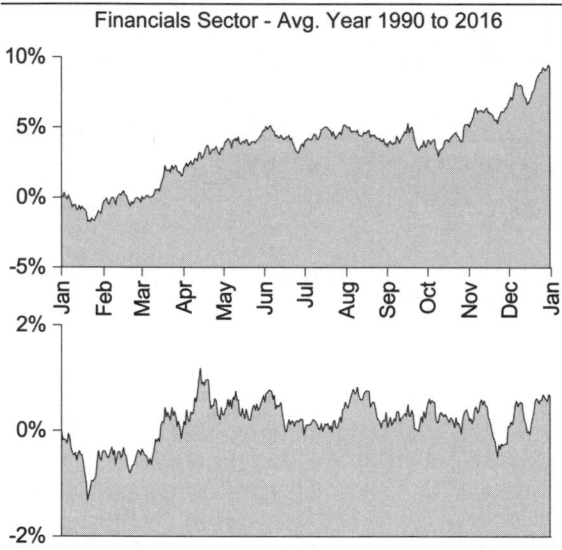

Financials Sector - Avg. Year 1990 to 2016

Financials / S&P 500 Relative Strength - Avg Yr. 1990-2016

The main driver for the strong seasonal performance of the financial sector has been the year-end earnings of the banks that start to report in mid-January. A strong performance from mid-December has been the result of investors getting into the market early to take advantage of positive year-end earnings.

Interest rates, despite recent increases by the Federal Reserve of its benchmark interest rate, continue to be at historic lows. If the Federal Reserve continues to increase its benchmark interest rate, banks should benefit in the short-term as their net interest margin will increase. A large portion of their loans are tied to the Federal Reserve's benchmark rate and with an increase in the rate, the banks will earn more money. Although the interest that they will have to pay out

will also increase, the rate of increase tends to be much lower.

On the other hand, a tighter monetary policy will slow the economy and reduce bank profits. Given this volatile situation, seasonal investors would be wise to concentrate their financial investments during the sector's strong seasonal period.

It should be noted that Canadian banks have their year-ends at the end of October (reporting in November) and as such, their seasonally strong period starts in October.

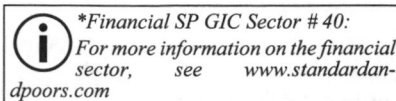

*Financial SP GIC Sector # 40:
For more information on the financial sector, see www.standardandpoors.com

Financials Performance

Financials Monthly Performance (1990-2016)

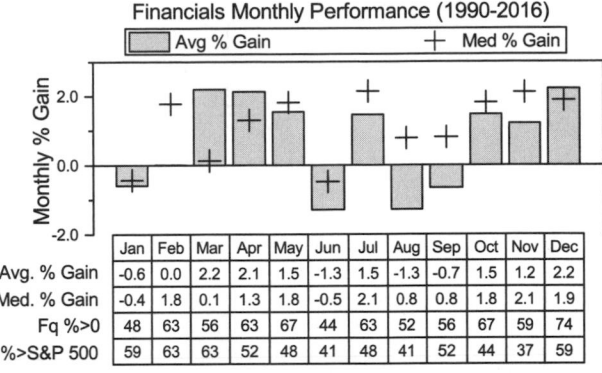

	Jan	Feb	Mar	Apr	May	Jun	Jul	Aug	Sep	Oct	Nov	Dec
Avg. % Gain	-0.6	0.0	2.2	2.1	1.5	-1.3	1.5	-1.3	-0.7	1.5	1.2	2.2
Med. % Gain	-0.4	1.8	0.1	1.3	1.8	-0.5	2.1	0.8	0.8	1.8	2.1	1.9
Fq %>0	48	63	56	63	67	44	63	52	56	67	59	74
Fq %>S&P 500	59	63	63	52	48	41	48	41	52	44	37	59

Financials 5 Year (2012-2016) % Gain

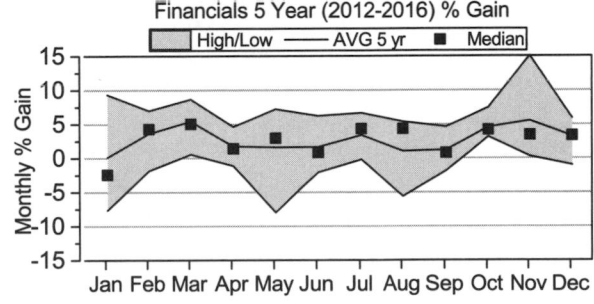

Financials Performance 2016-2017

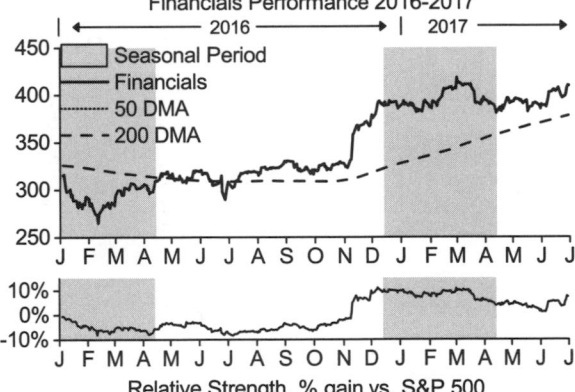

Relative Strength, % gain vs. S&P 500

From 1990 to 2016, the months December through April, the core of the seasonal time period for the financial sector, have been the only months (other than September) that have outperformed the S&P 500 at least half of the time.

Over the last five years, January has been the weakest month of the year on an average and median basis.

In its 2016/17 seasonal period, the financial sector underperformed the S&P 500, after strongly outperforming in November 2016.

JANUARY

M	T	W	T	F	S	S
	1	2	3	4	5	6
7	8	9	10	11	12	13
14	15	16	17	18	19	20
21	22	23	24	25	26	27
28	29	30	31			

FEBRUARY

M	T	W	T	F	S	S
				1	2	3
4	5	6	7	8	9	10
11	12	13	14	15	16	17
18	19	20	21	22	23	24
25	26	27	28			

MARCH

M	T	W	T	F	S	S
				1	2	3
4	5	6	7	8	9	10
11	12	13	14	15	16	17
18	19	20	21	22	23	24
25	26	27	28	29	30	31

APRIL

M	T	W	T	F	S	S
1	2	3	4	5	6	7
8	9	10	11	12	13	14
15	16	17	18	19	20	21
22	23	24	25	26	27	28
29	30					

MAY

M	T	W	T	F	S	S
		1	2	3	4	5
6	7	8	9	10	11	12
13	14	15	16	17	18	19
20	21	22	23	24	25	26
27	28	29	30	31		

JUNE

M	T	W	T	F	S	S
					1	2
3	4	5	6	7	8	9
10	11	12	13	14	15	16
17	18	19	20	21	22	23
24	25	26	27	28	29	30

APPENDIX

STOCK MARKET RETURNS

S&P 500
PERCENT CHANGES

	JAN	FEB	MAR	APR	MAY	JUN
1950	1.5 %	1.0 %	0.4 %	4.5 %	3.9 %	— 5.8 %
1951	6.1	0.6	— 1.8	4.8	— 4.1	— 2.6
1952	1.6	— 3.6	4.8	— 4.3	2.3	4.6
1953	— 0.7	— 1.8	— 2.4	— 2.6	— 0.3	— 1.6
1954	5.1	0.3	3.0	4.9	3.3	0.1
1955	1.8	0.4	— 0.5	3.8	— 0.1	8.2
1956	— 3.6	3.5	6.9	— 0.2	— 6.6	3.9
1957	— 4.2	— 3.3	2.0	3.7	3.7	— 0.1
1958	4.3	2.1	3.1	3.2	1.5	2.6
1959	0.4	— 0.1	0.1	3.9	1.9	— 0.4
1960	— 7.1	0.9	— 1.4	— 1.8	2.7	2.0
1961	6.3	2.7	2.6	0.4	1.9	— 2.9
1962	— 3.8	1.6	— 0.6	— 6.2	— 8.6	— 8.2
1963	4.9	— 2.9	3.5	4.9	1.4	— 2.0
1964	2.7	1.0	1.5	0.6	1.1	1.6
1965	3.3	— 0.1	— 1.5	3.4	— 0.8	— 4.9
1966	0.5	— 1.8	— 2.2	2.1	— 5.4	— 1.6
1967	7.8	0.2	3.9	4.2	— 5.2	1.8
1968	— 4.4	— 3.1	0.9	8.0	1.3	0.9
1969	— 0.8	— 4.7	3.4	2.1	— 0.2	— 5.6
1970	— 7.6	5.3	0.1	— 9.0	— 6.1	— 5.0
1971	4.0	0.9	3.7	3.6	— 4.2	— 0.9
1972	1.8	2.5	0.6	0.4	1.7	— 2.2
1973	— 1.7	— 3.7	— 0.1	— 4.1	— 1.9	— 0.7
1974	— 1.0	— 0.4	— 2.3	— 3.9	— 3.4	— 1.5
1975	12.3	6.0	2.2	4.7	4.4	4.4
1976	11.8	— 1.1	3.1	— 1.1	— 1.4	4.1
1977	— 5.1	— 2.2	— 1.4	0.0	— 2.4	4.5
1978	— 6.2	— 2.5	2.5	8.5	0.4	— 1.8
1979	4.0	— 3.7	5.5	0.2	— 2.6	3.9
1980	5.8	— 0.4	— 10.2	4.1	4.7	2.7
1981	— 4.6	1.3	3.6	— 2.3	— 0.2	— 1.0
1982	— 1.8	— 6.1	— 1.0	4.0	— 3.9	— 2.0
1983	3.3	1.9	3.3	7.5	— 1.2	3.2
1984	— 0.9	— 3.9	1.3	0.5	— 5.9	1.7
1985	7.4	0.9	— 0.3	— 0.5	5.4	1.2
1986	0.2	7.1	5.3	— 1.4	5.0	1.4
1987	13.2	3.7	2.6	— 1.1	0.6	4.8
1988	4.0	4.2	— 3.3	0.9	0.3	4.3
1989	7.1	— 2.9	2.1	5.0	3.5	— 0.8
1990	6.9	0.9	2.4	— 2.7	9.2	— 0.9
1991	4.2	6.7	2.2	0.0	3.9	— 4.8
1992	— 2.0	1.0	— 2.2	2.8	0.1	— 1.7
1993	0.7	1.0	1.9	— 2.5	2.3	0.1
1994	3.3	— 3.0	— 4.6	1.2	1.2	— 2.7
1995	2.4	3.6	2.7	2.8	3.6	2.1
1996	3.3	0.7	0.8	1.3	2.3	0.2
1997	6.1	0.6	— 4.3	5.8	5.9	4.3
1998	1.0	7.0	5.0	0.9	— 1.9	3.9
1999	4.1	— 3.2	3.9	3.8	— 2.5	5.4
2000	— 5.1	— 2.0	9.7	— 3.1	— 2.2	2.4
2001	3.5	— 9.2	— 6.4	7.7	0.5	— 2.5
2002	— 1.6	— 2.1	3.7	— 6.1	— 0.9	— 7.2
2003	— 2.7	— 1.7	0.8	8.1	5.1	1.1
2004	1.7	1.2	— 1.6	— 1.7	1.2	1.8
2005	— 2.5	1.9	— 1.9	— 2.0	3.0	0.0
2006	2.5	0.0	1.1	1.2	— 3.1	0.0
2007	1.4	— 2.2	1.0	4.3	3.3	— 1.8
2008	— 6.1	— 3.5	— 0.6	4.8	1.1	— 8.6
2009	— 8.6	— 11.0	8.5	9.4	5.3	0.0
2010	— 3.7	2.9	5.9	1.5	— 8.2	— 5.4
2011	2.3	3.2	— 0.1	2.8	— 1.4	— 1.8
2012	4.4	4.1	3.1	— 0.7	— 6.3	4.0
2013	5.0	1.1	3.6	1.8	2.1	— 1.5
2014	— 3.6	4.3	0.7	0.6	2.1	1.9
2015	— 3.1	5.5	— 1.7	0.9	1.0	— 2.1
2016	— 5.1	— 0.4	6.6	0.3	1.5	0.1
FQ POS*	40/67	37/67	44/67	46/67	39/67	35/67
% FQ POS*	60 %	55 %	66 %	69 %	58 %	52 %
AVG GAIN*	0.9 %	0.0 %	1.3 %	1.4 %	0.2 %	0.0 %
RANK GAIN*	6	9	4	3	8	10

JUL	AUG	SEP	OCT	NOV	DEC		YEAR
0.8 %	3.3 %	5.6 %	0.4 %	— 0.1 %	4.6 %	**1950**	21.7 %
6.9	3.9	— 0.1	— 1.4	— 0.3	3.9	**1951**	16.5
1.8	— 1.5	— 2.0	— 0.1	4.6	3.5	**1952**	11.8
2.5	— 5.8	0.1	5.1	0.9	0.2	**1953**	— 6.6
5.7	— 3.4	8.3	— 1.9	8.1	5.1	**1954**	45.0
6.1	— 0.8	1.1	— 3.0	7.5	— 0.1	**1955**	26.4
5.2	— 3.8	— 4.5	0.5	— 1.1	3.5	**1956**	2.6
1.1	— 5.6	— 6.2	— 3.2	1.6	— 4.1	**1957**	— 14.3
4.3	1.2	4.8	2.5	2.2	5.2	**1958**	38.1
3.5	— 1.5	— 4.6	1.1	1.3	2.8	**1959**	8.5
— 2.5	2.6	— 6.0	— 0.2	4.0	4.6	**1960**	— 3.0
3.3	2.0	— 2.0	2.8	3.9	0.3	**1961**	23.1
6.4	1.5	— 4.8	0.4	10.2	1.3	**1962**	— 11.8
— 0.3	4.9	— 1.1	3.2	— 1.1	2.4	**1963**	18.9
1.8	— 1.6	2.9	0.8	— 0.5	0.4	**1964**	13.0
1.3	2.3	3.2	2.7	— 0.9	0.9	**1965**	9.1
— 1.3	— 7.8	— 0.7	4.8	0.3	— 0.1	**1966**	— 13.1
4.5	— 1.2	3.3	— 3.5	0.8	2.6	**1967**	20.1
— 1.8	1.1	3.9	0.7	4.8	— 4.2	**1968**	7.7
6.0	4.0	— 2.5	4.3	— 3.4	— 1.9	**1969**	— 11.4
7.3	4.4	3.4	— 1.2	4.7	5.7	**1970**	0.1
— 3.2	3.6	— 0.7	— 4.2	— 0.3	8.6	**1971**	10.8
0.2	3.4	— 0.5	0.9	4.6	1.2	**1972**	15.6
3.8	— 3.7	4.0	— 0.1	— 11.4	1.7	**1973**	— 17.4
— 7.8	— 9.0	— 11.9	16.3	— 5.3	— 2.0	**1974**	— 29.7
— 6.8	— 2.1	— 3.5	6.2	2.5	— 1.2	**1975**	31.5
— 0.8	— 0.5	2.3	— 2.2	— 0.8	5.2	**1976**	19.1
— 1.6	— 2.1	— 0.2	— 4.3	2.7	0.3	**1977**	— 11.5
5.4	2.6	— 0.7	— 9.2	1.7	1.5	**1978**	1.1
0.9	5.3	0.0	— 6.9	4.3	1.7	**1979**	12.3
6.5	0.6	2.5	1.6	10.2	— 3.4	**1980**	25.8
— 0.2	— 6.2	— 5.4	4.9	3.7	— 3.0	**1981**	9.7
— 2.3	11.6	0.8	11.0	3.6	1.5	**1982**	14.8
— 3.0	1.1	1.0	— 1.5	1.7	— 0.9	**1983**	17.3
— 1.6	10.6	— 0.3	0.0	— 1.5	2.2	**1984**	1.4
— 0.5	— 1.2	— 3.5	4.3	6.5	4.5	**1985**	26.3
— 5.9	7.1	— 8.5	5.5	2.1	— 2.8	**1986**	14.6
4.8	3.5	— 2.4	— 21.8	— 8.5	7.3	**1987**	2.0
— 0.5	— 3.9	4.0	2.6	— 1.9	1.5	**1988**	12.4
8.8	1.6	— 0.7	— 2.5	1.7	2.1	**1989**	27.3
— 0.5	— 9.4	— 5.1	— 0.7	6.0	2.5	**1990**	— 6.6
4.5	2.0	— 1.9	1.2	— 4.4	11.2	**1991**	26.3
3.9	— 2.4	0.9	0.2	3.0	1.0	**1992**	4.5
— 0.5	3.4	— 1.0	1.9	— 1.3	1.0	**1993**	7.1
3.1	3.8	— 2.7	2.1	— 4.0	1.2	**1994**	— 1.5
3.2	0.0	4.0	— 0.5	4.1	1.7	**1995**	34.1
— 4.6	1.9	5.4	2.6	7.3	— 2.2	**1996**	20.3
7.8	— 5.7	5.3	— 3.4	4.5	1.6	**1997**	31.0
1.2	— 14.6	6.2	8.0	5.9	5.6	**1998**	26.7
— 3.2	— 0.6	— 2.9	6.3	1.9	5.8	**1999**	19.5
— 1.6	6.1	— 5.3	— 0.5	— 8.0	0.4	**2000**	— 10.1
— 1.1	— 6.4	— 8.2	1.8	7.5	0.8	**2001**	— 13.0
— 7.9	0.5	— 11.0	8.6	5.7	— 6.0	**2002**	— 23.4
1.6	1.8	— 1.2	5.5	0.7	5.1	**2003**	26.4
-3.4	0.2	0.9	1.4	3.9	3.2	**2004**	9.0
3.6	— 1.1	0.7	— 1.8	3.5	— 0.1	**2005**	3.0
0.5	2.1	2.5	3.2	1.6	1.3	**2006**	13.6
— 3.2	1.3	3.6	1.5	— 4.4	— 0.9	**2007**	3.5
— 1.0	1.2	— 9.1	— 16.9	— 7.5	0.8	**2008**	-38.5
7.4	3.4	3.6	— 2.0	5.7	1.8	**2009**	23.5
6.9	— 4.7	8.8	3.7	— 0.2	6.5	**2010**	12.8
— 2.1	— 5.7	— 7.2	10.8	— 0.5	0.9	**2011**	0.0
1.3	2.0	2.4	— 2.0	0.3	0.7	**2012**	13.4
4.9	— 3.1	3.0	4.5	2.8	2.4	**2013**	29.6
— 1.5	3.8	— 1.6	2.3	2.5	— 0.4	**2014**	11.4
2.0	— 6.3	— 2.6	8.3	0.1	— 1.8	**2015**	— 0.7
3.6	— 0.1	— 0.1	— 1.9	3.4	1.8	**2016**	9.5
37/67	36/67	29/67	40/67	45/67	50/67		49/67
55 %	54 %	43 %	60 %	67 %	75 %		73 %
1.0 %	— 0.1 %	— 0.5 %	0.9 %	1.5 %	1.6 %		8.9 %
5	11	12	7	2	1		

S&P 500 MONTH CLOSING VALUES

	JAN	FEB	MAR	APR	MAY	JUN
1950	17	17	17	18	19	18
1951	22	22	21	22	22	21
1952	24	23	24	23	24	25
1953	26	26	25	25	25	24
1954	26	26	27	28	29	29
1955	37	37	37	38	38	41
1956	44	45	48	48	45	47
1957	45	43	44	46	47	47
1958	42	41	42	43	44	45
1959	55	55	55	58	59	58
1960	56	56	55	54	56	57
1961	62	63	65	65	67	65
1962	69	70	70	65	60	55
1963	66	64	67	70	71	69
1964	77	78	79	79	80	82
1965	88	87	86	89	88	84
1966	93	91	89	91	86	85
1967	87	87	90	94	89	91
1968	92	89	90	97	99	100
1969	103	98	102	104	103	98
1970	85	90	90	82	77	73
1971	96	97	100	104	100	99
1972	104	107	107	108	110	107
1973	116	112	112	107	105	104
1974	97	96	94	90	87	86
1975	77	82	83	87	91	95
1976	101	100	103	102	100	104
1977	102	100	98	98	96	100
1978	89	87	89	97	97	96
1979	100	96	102	102	99	103
1980	114	114	102	106	111	114
1981	130	131	136	133	133	131
1982	120	113	112	116	112	110
1983	145	148	153	164	162	168
1984	163	157	159	160	151	153
1985	180	181	181	180	190	192
1986	212	227	239	236	247	251
1987	274	284	292	288	290	304
1988	257	268	259	261	262	274
1989	297	289	295	310	321	318
1990	329	332	340	331	361	358
1991	344	367	375	375	390	371
1992	409	413	404	415	415	408
1993	439	443	452	440	450	451
1994	482	467	446	451	457	444
1995	470	487	501	515	533	545
1996	636	640	646	654	669	671
1997	786	791	757	801	848	885
1998	980	1049	1102	1112	1091	1134
1999	1280	1238	1286	1335	1302	1373
2000	1394	1366	1499	1452	1421	1455
2001	1366	1240	1160	1249	1256	1224
2002	1130	1107	1147	1077	1067	990
2003	856	841	848	917	964	975
2004	1131	1145	1126	1107	1121	1141
2005	1181	1204	1181	1157	1192	1191
2006	1280	1281	1295	1311	1270	1270
2007	1438	1407	1421	1482	1531	1503
2008	1379	1331	1323	1386	1400	1280
2009	826	735	798	873	919	919
2010	1074	1104	1169	1187	1089	1031
2011	1286	1327	1326	1364	1345	1321
2012	1312	1366	1408	1398	1310	1362
2013	1498	1515	1569	1598	1631	1606
2014	1783	1869	1872	1884	1924	1960
2015	1995	2105	2068	2086	2107	2063
2016	1940	1932	2060	2065	2097	2099

S&P 500 MONTH CLOSING VALUES

JUL	AUG	SEP	OCT	NOV	DEC	
18	18	19	20	20	20	1950
22	23	23	23	23	24	1951
25	25	25	25	26	27	1952
25	23	23	25	25	25	1953
31	30	32	32	34	36	1954
44	43	44	42	46	45	1955
49	48	45	46	45	47	1956
48	45	42	41	42	40	1957
47	48	50	51	52	55	1958
61	60	57	58	58	60	1959
56	57	54	53	56	58	1960
67	68	67	69	71	72	1961
58	59	56	57	62	63	1962
69	73	72	74	73	75	1963
83	82	84	85	84	85	1964
85	87	90	92	92	92	1965
84	77	77	80	80	80	1966
95	94	97	93	94	96	1967
98	99	103	103	108	104	1968
92	96	93	97	94	92	1969
78	82	84	83	87	92	1970
96	99	98	94	94	102	1971
107	111	111	112	117	118	1972
108	104	108	108	96	98	1973
79	72	64	74	70	69	1974
89	87	84	89	91	90	1975
103	103	105	103	102	107	1976
99	97	97	92	95	95	1977
101	103	103	93	95	96	1978
104	109	109	102	106	108	1979
122	122	125	127	141	136	1980
131	123	116	122	126	123	1981
107	120	120	134	139	141	1982
163	164	166	164	166	165	1983
151	167	166	166	164	167	1984
191	189	182	190	202	211	1985
236	253	231	244	249	242	1986
319	330	322	252	230	247	1987
272	262	272	279	274	278	1988
346	351	349	340	346	353	1989
356	323	306	304	322	330	1990
388	395	388	392	375	417	1991
424	414	418	419	431	436	1992
448	464	459	468	462	466	1993
458	475	463	472	454	459	1994
562	562	584	582	605	616	1995
640	652	687	705	757	741	1996
954	899	947	915	955	970	1997
1121	957	1017	1099	1164	1229	1998
1329	1320	1283	1363	1389	1469	1999
1431	1518	1437	1429	1315	1320	2000
1211	1134	1041	1060	1139	1148	2001
912	916	815	886	936	880	2002
990	1008	996	1051	1058	1112	2003
1102	1104	1115	1130	1174	1212	2004
1234	1220	1229	1207	1249	1248	2005
1277	1304	1336	1378	1401	1418	2006
1455	1474	1527	1549	1481	1468	2007
1267	1283	1165	969	896	903	2008
987	1021	1057	1036	1096	1115	2009
1102	1049	1141	1183	1181	1258	2010
1292	1219	1131	1253	1247	1258	2011
1379	1407	1441	1412	1416	1426	2012
1686	1633	1682	1757	1806	1848	2013
1931	2003	1972	2018	2068	2059	2014
2104	1972	1920	2079	2080	2044	2015
2174	2171	2168	2126	2199	2239	2016

DOW JONES PERCENT MONTH CHANGES

	JAN	FEB	MAR	APR	MAY	JUN
1950	0.8 %	0.8 %	1.3 %	4.0 %	4.2 %	− 6.4 %
1951	5.7	1.3	− 1.7	4.5	− 3.6	− 2.8
1952	0.6	− 3.9	3.6	− 4.4	2.1	4.3
1953	− 0.7	− 2.0	− 1.5	− 1.8	− 0.9	− 1.5
1954	4.1	0.7	3.1	5.2	2.6	1.8
1955	1.1	0.8	− 0.5	3.9	− 0.2	6.2
1956	− 3.6	2.8	5.8	0.8	− 7.4	3.1
1957	− 4.1	− 3.0	2.2	4.1	2.1	− 0.3
1958	3.3	− 2.2	1.6	2.0	1.5	3.3
1959	1.8	1.6	− 0.3	3.7	3.2	0.0
1960	− 8.4	1.2	− 2.1	− 2.4	4.0	2.4
1961	5.2	2.1	2.2	0.3	2.7	− 1.8
1962	− 4.3	1.2	− 0.2	− 5.9	− 7.8	− 8.5
1963	4.7	− 2.9	3.0	5.2	1.3	− 2.8
1964	2.9	1.9	1.6	− 0.3	1.2	1.3
1965	3.3	0.1	− 1.6	3.7	− 0.5	− 5.4
1966	1.5	− 3.2	− 2.8	1.0	− 5.3	− 1.6
1967	8.2	− 1.2	3.2	3.6	− 5.0	0.9
1968	− 5.5	− 1.8	0.0	8.5	− 1.4	− 0.1
1969	0.2	− 4.3	3.3	1.6	− 1.3	− 6.9
1970	− 7.0	4.5	1.0	− 6.3	− 4.8	− 2.4
1971	3.5	1.2	2.9	4.1	− 3.6	− 1.8
1972	1.3	2.9	1.4	1.4	0.7	− 3.3
1973	− 2.1	− 4.4	− 0.4	3.1	− 2.2	− 1.1
1974	0.6	0.6	− 1.6	− 1.2	− 4.1	0.0
1975	14.2	5.0	3.9	6.9	1.3	5.6
1976	14.4	− 0.3	2.8	− 0.3	− 2.2	2.8
1977	− 5.0	− 1.9	− 1.8	0.8	− 3.0	2.0
1978	− 7.4	− 3.6	2.1	10.5	0.4	− 2.6
1979	4.2	− 3.6	6.6	− 0.8	− 3.8	2.4
1980	4.4	− 1.5	− 9.0	4.0	4.1	2.0
1981	− 1.7	2.9	3.0	− 0.6	− 0.6	− 1.5
1982	− 0.4	− 5.4	− 0.2	3.1	− 3.4	− 0.9
1983	2.8	3.4	1.6	8.5	− 2.1	1.8
1984	− 3.0	− 5.4	0.9	0.5	− 5.6	2.5
1985	6.2	− 0.2	− 1.3	− 0.7	4.6	1.5
1986	1.6	8.8	6.4	− 1.9	5.2	0.9
1987	13.8	3.1	3.6	− 0.8	0.2	5.5
1988	1.0	5.8	− 4.0	2.2	− 0.1	5.4
1989	8.0	− 3.6	1.6	5.5	2.5	− 1.6
1990	− 5.9	1.4	3.0	− 1.9	8.3	0.1
1991	3.9	5.3	1.1	− 0.9	4.8	− 4.0
1992	1.7	1.4	− 1.0	3.8	1.1	− 2.3
1993	0.3	1.8	1.9	− 0.2	2.9	− 0.3
1994	6.0	− 3.7	− 5.1	1.3	2.1	− 3.5
1995	0.2	4.3	3.7	3.9	3.3	2.0
1996	5.4	1.7	1.9	− 0.3	1.3	0.2
1997	5.7	0.9	− 4.3	6.5	4.6	4.7
1998	0.0	8.1	3.0	3.0	− 1.8	0.6
1999	1.9	− 0.6	5.2	10.2	− 2.1	3.9
2000	− 4.5	− 7.4	7.8	− 1.7	− 2.0	− 0.7
2001	0.9	− 3.6	− 5.9	8.7	1.6	− 3.8
2002	− 1.0	1.9	2.9	− 4.4	− 0.2	− 6.9
2003	− 3.5	− 2.0	1.3	6.1	4.4	1.5
2004	0.3	0.9	− 2.1	− 1.3	− 0.4	2.4
2005	− 2.7	2.6	− 2.4	− 3.0	2.7	− 1.8
2006	1.4	1.2	1.1	2.3	− 1.7	− 0.2
2007	1.3	− 2.8	0.7	5.7	4.3	− 1.6
2008	− 4.6	− 3.0	0.0	4.5	− 1.4	− 10.2
2009	− 8.8	− 11.7	7.7	7.3	4.1	− 0.6
2010	− 3.5	2.6	5.1	1.4	− 7.9	− 3.6
2011	2.7	2.8	0.8	4.0	− 1.9	− 1.2
2012	3.4	3.8	2.0	0.0	− 6.2	3.9
2013	5.8	4.8	3.7	1.8	1.9	− 1.4
2014	− 5.3	5.8	0.8	0.7	0.8	0.7
2015	− 3.7	6.8	− 2.0	0.4	1.0	− 2.2
2016	− 5.5	0.3	7.1	0.5	0.1	0.8
FQ POS	42/67	39/67	44/67	45/67	35/67	31/67
% FQ POS	63 %	58 %	66 %	67 %	52 %	46 %
AVG GAIN	0.9 %	0.3 %	1.2 %	1.9 %	0.0 %	− 0.3 %
RANK GAIN	6	8	4	1	9	11

DOW JONES PERCENT MONTH CHANGES   STOCK MKT

JUL	AUG	SEP	OCT	NOV	DEC		YEAR
0.1 %	3.6 %	4.4 %	— 0.6 %	1.2 %	3.4 %	1950	17.6 %
6.3	4.8	0.3	— 3.2	— 0.4	3.0	1951	14.4
1.9	— 1.6	— 1.6	— 0.5	5.4	2.9	1952	8.4
2.6	— 5.2	1.1	4.5	2.0	— 0.2	1953	— 3.8
4.3	— 3.5	7.4	— 2.3	9.9	4.6	1954	44.0
3.2	0.5	— 0.3	— 2.5	6.2	1.1	1955	20.8
5.1	— 3.1	— 5.3	1.0	— 1.5	5.6	1956	2.3
1.0	— 4.7	— 5.8	— 3.4	2.0	— 3.2	1957	— 12.8
5.2	1.1	4.6	2.1	2.6	4.7	1958	34.0
4.9	— 1.6	— 4.9	2.4	1.9	3.1	1959	16.4
— 3.7	1.5	— 7.3	0.1	2.9	3.1	1960	— 9.3
3.1	2.1	— 2.6	0.4	2.5	1.3	1961	18.7
6.5	1.9	— 5.0	1.9	10.1	0.4	1962	— 10.8
— 1.6	4.9	0.5	3.1	— 0.6	1.7	1963	17.0
1.2	— 0.3	4.4	— 0.3	0.3	— 0.1	1964	14.6
1.6	1.3	4.2	3.2	— 1.5	2.4	1965	10.9
— 2.6	— 7.0	— 1.8	4.2	— 1.9	— 0.7	1966	— 18.9
5.1	— 0.3	2.8	— 5.1	— 0.4	3.3	1967	15.2
— 1.6	1.5	4.4	1.8	3.4	— 4.2	1968	4.3
— 6.6	2.6	— 2.8	5.3	— 5.1	— 1.5	1969	— 15.2
7.4	4.2	— 0.5	— 0.7	5.1	5.6	1970	4.8
— 3.7	4.6	— 1.2	— 5.4	— 0.9	7.1	1971	6.1
— 0.5	4.2	— 1.1	0.2	6.6	0.2	1972	14.6
3.9	— 4.2	6.7	1.0	— 14.0	3.5	1973	— 16.6
— 5.6	— 10.4	— 10.4	9.5	— 7.0	— 0.4	1974	— 27.6
— 5.4	0.5	— 5.0	5.3	3.0	— 1.0	1975	38.3
— 1.8	— 1.1	1.7	— 2.6	— 1.8	6.1	1976	17.9
— 2.9	— 3.2	— 1.7	— 3.4	1.4	0.2	1977	— 17.3
5.3	1.7	— 1.3	— 8.5	0.8	0.8	1978	— 3.2
0.5	4.9	— 1.0	— 7.2	0.8	2.0	1979	4.2
7.8	— 0.3	0.0	— 0.8	7.4	— 2.9	1980	14.9
— 2.5	— 7.4	— 3.6	0.3	4.3	— 1.6	1981	9.2
— 0.4	11.5	— 0.6	10.6	4.8	0.7	1982	19.6
— 1.9	1.4	1.4	— 0.6	4.1	— 1.4	1983	20.3
— 1.5	9.8	— 1.4	0.1	— 1.5	1.9	1984	3.7
0.9	— 1.0	— 0.4	3.4	7.1	5.1	1985	27.7
— 6.2	6.9	— 6.9	6.2	1.9	— 1.0	1986	22.6
6.4	3.5	— 2.5	— 23.2	— 8.0	5.7	1987	2.3
— 0.6	— 4.6	4.0	1.7	— 1.6	2.6	1988	11.9
9.0	2.9	— 1.6	— 1.8	2.3	1.7	1989	27.0
0.9	— 10.0	— 6.2	— 0.4	4.8	2.9	1990	— 4.3
4.1	0.6	— 0.9	1.7	— 5.7	9.5	1991	20.3
2.3	— 4.0	0.4	— 1.4	2.4	— 0.1	1992	4.2
0.7	3.2	— 2.6	3.5	0.1	1.9	1993	13.7
3.8	4.0	— 1.8	1.7	— 4.3	2.5	1994	2.1
3.3	— 2.1	3.9	— 0.7	6.7	0.8	1995	33.5
— 2.2	1.6	4.7	2.5	8.2	— 1.1	1996	26.0
7.2	— 7.3	4.2	— 6.3	5.1	1.1	1997	22.6
— 0.8	— 15.1	4.0	9.6	6.1	0.7	1998	16.1
— 2.9	1.6	— 4.5	3.8	1.4	5.3	1999	24.7
0.7	6.6	— 5.0	3.0	— 5.1	3.6	2000	— 5.8
0.2	— 5.4	— 11.1	2.6	8.6	1.7	2001	— 7.1
— 5.5	— 0.8	— 12.4	10.6	5.9	— 6.2	2002	16.8
2.8	2.0	— 1.5	5.7	— 0.2	6.9	2003	25.3
— 2.8	0.3	— 0.9	— 0.5	4.0	3.4	2004	3.1
3.6	— 1.5	0.8	— 1.2	3.5	— 0.8	2005	— 0.6
0.3	1.7	2.6	3.4	1.2	2.0	2006	16.3
1.5	1.1	4.0	0.2	— 4.0	— 0.8	2007	6.4
0.2	1.5	— 6.0	— 14.1	— 5.3	— 0.6	2008	— 33.8
8.6	3.5	2.3	0.0	6.5	0.8	2009	18.8
7.1	— 4.3	7.7	3.1	— 1.0	5.2	2010	11.0
— 2.2	— 4.4	— 6.0	9.5	0.8	1.4	2011	5.5
1.0	0.6	2.6	— 2.5	— 0.5	0.6	2012	7.3
4.0	— 4.4	2.2	2.8	3.5	3.0	2013	26.5
— 1.6	3.2	— 0.3	2.0	2.5	0.0	2014	7.5
0.4	— 6.6	— 1.5	8.5	0.3	— 2.2	2015	— 2.2
2.8	— 0.2	— 0.5	— 0.9	5.4	3.3	2016	13.4
42/67	37/67	26/67	40/67	46/67	47/67		48/67
63 %	55 %	39 %	60 %	69 %	70 %		72 %
1.1 %	— 0.2 %	— 0.8 %	0.6 %	1.6 %	1.7 %		8.3 %
5	10	12	7	3	2		

DOW JONES
MONTH CLOSING VALUES

	JAN	FEB	MAR	APR	MAY	JUN
1950	202	203	206	214	223	209
1951	249	252	248	259	250	243
1952	271	260	270	258	263	274
1953	290	284	280	275	272	268
1954	292	295	304	319	328	334
1955	409	412	410	426	425	451
1956	471	484	512	516	478	493
1957	479	465	475	494	505	503
1958	450	440	447	456	463	478
1959	594	604	602	624	644	644
1960	623	630	617	602	626	641
1961	648	662	677	679	697	684
1962	700	708	707	665	613	561
1963	683	663	683	718	727	707
1964	785	800	813	811	821	832
1965	903	904	889	922	918	868
1966	984	952	925	934	884	870
1967	850	839	866	897	853	860
1968	856	841	841	912	899	898
1969	946	905	936	950	938	873
1970	744	778	786	736	700	684
1971	869	879	904	942	908	891
1972	902	928	941	954	961	929
1973	999	955	951	921	901	892
1974	856	861	847	837	802	802
1975	704	739	768	821	832	879
1976	975	973	1000	997	975	1003
1977	954	936	919	927	899	916
1978	770	742	757	837	841	819
1979	839	809	862	855	822	842
1980	876	863	786	817	851	868
1981	947	975	1004	998	992	977
1982	871	824	823	848	820	812
1983	1076	1113	1130	1226	1200	1222
1984	1221	1155	1165	1171	1105	1132
1985	1287	1284	1267	1258	1315	1336
1986	1571	1709	1819	1784	1877	1893
1987	2158	2224	2305	2286	2292	2419
1988	1958	2072	1988	2032	2031	2142
1989	2342	2258	2294	2419	2480	2440
1990	2591	2627	2707	2657	2877	2881
1991	2736	2882	2914	2888	3028	2907
1992	3223	3268	3236	3359	3397	3319
1993	3310	3371	3435	3428	3527	3516
1994	3978	3832	3636	3682	3758	3625
1995	3844	4011	4158	4321	4465	4556
1996	5395	5486	5587	5569	5643	5655
1997	6813	6878	6584	7009	7331	7673
1998	7907	8546	8800	9063	8900	8952
1999	9359	9307	9786	10789	10560	10971
2000	10941	10128	10922	10734	10522	10448
2001	10887	10495	9879	10735	10912	10502
2002	9920	10106	10404	9946	9925	9243
2003	8054	7891	7992	8480	8850	8985
2004	10488	10584	10358	10226	10188	10435
2005	10490	10766	10504	10193	10467	10275
2006	10865	10993	11109	11367	11168	11150
2007	12622	12269	12354	13063	13628	13409
2008	12650	12266	12263	12820	12638	11350
2009	8001	7063	7609	8168	8500	8447
2010	10067	10325	10857	11009	10137	9774
2011	11892	12226	12320	12811	12570	12414
2012	12633	12952	13212	13214	12393	12880
2013	13861	14054	14579	14840	15116	14910
2014	15699	16322	16458	16581	16717	16827
2015	17165	18133	17776	17841	18011	17620
2016	16466	16517	17685	17774	17787	17930

DOW JONES
MONTH CLOSING VALUES

STOCK MKT

JUL	AUG	SEP	OCT	NOV	DEC	
209	217	226	225	228	235	**1950**
258	270	271	262	261	269	**1951**
280	275	271	269	284	292	**1952**
275	261	264	276	281	281	**1953**
348	336	361	352	387	404	**1954**
466	468	467	455	483	488	**1955**
518	502	475	480	473	500	**1956**
509	484	456	441	450	436	**1957**
503	509	532	543	558	584	**1958**
675	664	632	647	659	679	**1959**
617	626	580	580	597	616	**1960**
705	720	701	704	722	731	**1961**
598	609	579	590	649	652	**1962**
695	729	733	755	751	763	**1963**
841	839	875	873	875	874	**1964**
882	893	931	961	947	969	**1965**
847	788	774	807	792	786	**1966**
904	901	927	880	876	905	**1967**
883	896	936	952	985	944	**1968**
816	837	813	856	812	800	**1969**
734	765	761	756	794	839	**1970**
858	898	887	839	831	890	**1971**
925	964	953	956	1018	1020	**1972**
926	888	947	957	822	851	**1973**
757	679	608	666	619	616	**1974**
832	835	794	836	861	852	**1975**
985	974	990	965	947	1005	**1976**
890	862	847	818	830	831	**1977**
862	877	866	793	799	805	**1978**
846	888	879	816	822	839	**1979**
935	933	932	925	993	964	**1980**
952	882	850	853	889	875	**1981**
809	901	896	992	1039	1047	**1982**
1199	1216	1233	1225	1276	1259	**1983**
1115	1224	1207	1207	1189	1212	**1984**
1348	1334	1329	1374	1472	1547	**1985**
1775	1898	1768	1878	1914	1896	**1986**
2572	2663	2596	1994	1834	1939	**1987**
2129	2032	2113	2149	2115	2169	**1988**
2661	2737	2693	2645	2706	2753	**1989**
2905	2614	2453	2442	2560	2634	**1990**
3025	3044	3017	3069	2895	3169	**1991**
3394	3257	3272	3226	3305	3301	**1992**
3540	3651	3555	3681	3684	3754	**1993**
3765	3913	3843	3908	3739	3834	**1994**
4709	4611	4789	4756	5075	5117	**1995**
5529	5616	5882	6029	6522	6448	**1996**
8223	7622	7945	7442	7823	7908	**1997**
8883	7539	7843	8592	9117	9181	**1998**
10655	10829	10337	10730	10878	11453	**1999**
10522	11215	10651	10971	10415	10788	**2000**
10523	9950	8848	9075	9852	10022	**2001**
8737	8664	7592	8397	8896	8342	**2002**
9234	9416	9275	9801	9782	10454	**2003**
10140	10174	10080	10027	10428	10783	**2004**
10641	10482	10569	10440	10806	10718	**2005**
11186	11381	11679	12801	12222	12463	**2006**
13212	13358	13896	13930	13372	13265	**2007**
11378	11544	10851	9325	8829	8776	**2008**
9172	9496	9712	9713	10345	10428	**2009**
10466	10015	10788	11118	11006	11578	**2010**
12143	11614	10913	11955	12046	12218	**2011**
13009	13091	13437	13096	13026	13104	**2012**
15500	14810	15130	15546	16086	16577	**2013**
16563	17098	17043	17391	17828	17823	**2014**
17690	16528	16285	17664	17720	17425	**2015**
18432	18401	18308	18142	19124	19763	**2016**

NASDAQ PERCENT MONTH CHANGES

	JAN	FEB	MAR	APR	MAY	JUN
1972	4.2	5.5	2.2	2.5	0.9	— 1.8
1973	— 4.0	— 6.2	— 2.4	— 8.2	— 4.8	— 1.6
1974	3.0	— 0.6	— 2.2	— 5.9	— 7.7	— 5.3
1975	16.6	4.6	3.6	3.8	5.8	4.7
1976	12.1	3.7	0.4	— 0.6	— 2.3	2.6
1977	— 2.4	— 1.0	— 0.5	1.4	0.1	4.3
1978	— 4.0	0.6	4.7	8.5	4.4	0.0
1979	6.6	— 2.6	7.5	1.6	— 1.8	5.1
1980	7.0	— 2.3	— 17.1	6.9	7.5	4.9
1981	— 2.2	0.1	6.1	3.1	3.1	— 3.5
1982	— 3.8	— 4.8	— 2.1	5.2	— 3.3	— 4.1
1983	6.9	5.0	3.9	8.2	5.3	3.2
1984	— 3.7	— 5.9	— 0.7	— 1.3	— 5.9	2.9
1985	12.8	2.0	— 1.8	0.5	3.6	1.9
1986	3.4	7.1	4.2	2.3	4.4	1.3
1987	12.4	8.4	1.2	— 2.9	— 0.3	2.0
1988	4.3	6.5	2.1	1.2	— 2.3	6.6
1989	5.2	— 0.4	1.8	5.1	4.3	— 2.4
1990	— 8.6	2.4	2.3	— 3.5	9.3	0.7
1991	10.8	9.4	6.4	0.5	4.4	— 6.0
1992	5.8	2.1	— 4.7	— 4.2	1.1	— 3.7
1993	2.9	— 3.7	2.9	— 4.2	5.9	0.5
1994	3.0	— 1.0	— 6.2	— 1.3	0.2	— 4.0
1995	0.4	5.1	3.0	3.3	2.4	8.0
1996	0.7	3.8	0.1	8.1	4.4	— 4.7
1997	6.9	— 5.1	— 6.7	3.2	11.1	3.0
1998	3.1	9.3	3.7	1.8	— 4.8	6.5
1999	14.3	— 8.7	7.6	3.3	— 2.8	8.7
2000	— 3.2	19.2	— 2.6	— 15.6	— 11.9	16.6
2001	12.2	— 22.4	— 14.5	15.0	— 0.3	2.4
2002	— 0.8	— 10.5	6.6	— 8.5	— 4.3	— 9.4
2003	— 1.1	1.3	0.3	9.2	9.0	1.7
2004	3.1	— 1.8	— 1.8	— 3.7	3.5	3.1
2005	— 5.2	— 0.5	— 2.6	— 3.9	7.6	— 0.5
2006	4.6	— 1.1	2.6	— 0.7	— 6.2	— 0.3
2007	2.0	— 1.9	0.2	4.3	3.1	0.0
2008	— 9.9	— 5.0	0.3	5.9	4.6	— 9.1
2009	— 6.4	— 6.7	10.9	12.3	3.3	3.4
2010	— 5.4	4.2	7.1	2.6	— 8.3	— 6.5
2011	1.8	3.0	0.0	3.3	— 1.3	— 2.2
2012	8.0	5.4	4.2	— 1.5	— 7.2	3.8
2013	4.1	0.6	3.4	1.9	3.8	— 1.5
2014	— 1.7	5.0	— 2.5	— 2.0	3.1	3.9
2015	— 2.1	7.1	— 1.3	0.8	2.6	— 1.6
2016	— 7.9	— 1.2	6.8	— 1.9	3.6	— 2.1
FQ POS	28/45	24/45	28/45	28/45	28/45	25/45
% FQ POS	62 %	53 %	62 %	62 %	62 %	56 %
AVG GAIN	2.4 %	0.6 %	0.8 %	1.2 %	1.0 %	0.7 %
RANK GAIN	1	9	7	4	5	8

JUL	AUG	SEP	OCT	NOV	DEC		YEAR
— 1.8	1.7	— 0.3	0.5	2.1	0.6	1972	17.2
7.6	— 3.5	6.0	— 0.9	— 15.1	— 1.4	1973	— 31.1
— 7.9	— 10.9	— 10.7	17.2	— 3.5	— 5.0	1974	— 35.1
— 4.4	— 5.0	— 5.9	3.6	2.4	— 1.5	1975	29.8
1.1	— 1.7	1.7	— 1.0	0.9	7.4	1976	26.1
0.9	— 0.5	0.7	— 3.3	5.8	1.8	1977	7.3
5.0	6.9	— 1.6	— 16.4	3.2	2.9	1978	12.3
2.3	6.4	— 0.3	— 9.6	6.4	4.8	1979	28.1
8.9	5.7	3.4	2.7	8.0	— 2.8	1980	33.9
— 1.9	— 7.5	— 8.0	8.4	3.1	— 2.7	1981	— 3.2
— 2.3	6.2	5.6	13.3	9.3	0.0	1982	18.7
— 4.6	— 3.8	1.4	— 7.4	4.1	— 2.5	1983	19.9
— 4.2	10.9	— 1.8	— 1.2	1.0	1.9	1984	— 11.3
1.7	— 1.2	— 5.8	4.4	7.4	3.5	1985	31.5
— 8.4	3.1	— 8.4	2.9	— 0.3	— 3.0	1986	7.4
2.4	4.6	— 2.4	— 27.2	— 5.6	8.3	1987	— 5.2
— 1.9	— 2.8	2.9	— 1.3	— 2.9	2.7	1988	15.4
4.2	3.4	0.8	— 3.7	0.1	— 0.3	1989	19.2
— 5.2	— 13.0	— 9.6	— 4.3	8.9	4.1	1990	— 17.8
5.5	4.7	0.2	3.1	— 3.5	11.9	1991	56.9
3.1	— 3.0	3.6	3.8	7.9	3.7	1992	15.5
0.1	5.4	2.7	2.2	— 3.2	3.0	1993	14.7
2.3	6.0	— 0.2	1.7	— 3.5	0.2	1994	— 3.2
7.3	1.9	2.3	— 0.7	2.2	— 0.7	1995	39.9
— 8.8	5.6	7.5	— 0.4	5.8	— 0.1	1996	22.7
10.5	— 0.4	6.2	— -5.5	0.4	— 1.9	1997	21.6
— 1.2	— 19.9	13.0	4.6	10.1	12.5	1998	39.6
— 1.8	3.8	0.2	8.0	12.5	22.0	1999	85.6
— 5.0	11.7	— 12.7	— 8.3	— 22.9	— 4.9	2000	— 39.3
— 6.2	— 10.9	— 17.0	12.8	14.2	1.0	2001	— 21.1
— 9.2	— 1.0	— 10.9	13.5	11.2	— 9.7	2002	— 31.5
6.9	4.3	— 1.3	8.1	1.5	2.2	2003	50.0
— 7.8	— 2.6	3.2	4.1	6.2	3.7	2004	8.6
6.2	— 1.5	0.0	— 1.5	5.3	— 1.2	2005	1.4
— 3.7	4.4	3.4	4.8	2.7	— 0.7	2006	9.5
— 2.2	2.0	4.0	5.8	— 6.9	— 0.3	2007	9.8
1.4	1.8	— 11.6	— 17.7	— 10.8	2.7	2008	— 40.5
7.8	1.5	5.6	— 3.6	4.9	5.8	2009	43.9
6.9	— 6.2	12.0	5.9	— 0.4	6.2	2010	16.9
— 0.6	— 6.4	— 6.4	11.1	— 2.4	— 0.6	2011	— 1.8
0.2	4.3	1.6	— 4.5	1.1	0.3	2012	15.9
6.6	— 1.0	5.1	3.9	3.6	2.9	2013	38.3
— 0.9	4.8	— 1.9	3.1	3.5	— 1.2	2014	13.4
2.8	— 6.9	— 3.3	9.4	1.1	— 2.0	2015	5.7
6.6	1.0	1.9	— 2.3	2.6	1.1	2016	7.5
24/45	24/45	24/45	25/45	31/45	26/45		33/45
53 %	53 %	53 %	56 %	69 %	58 %		73 %
0.4 %	0.1 %	— 0.6 %	0.8 %	1.7 %	1.7 %		12.1 %
10	11	12	6	2	3		

NASDAQ MONTH CLOSING VALUES

	JAN	FEB	MAR	APR	MAY	JUN
1972	119	125	128	131	133	130
1973	128	120	117	108	103	101
1974	95	94	92	87	80	76
1975	70	73	76	79	83	87
1976	87	90	91	90	88	90
1977	96	95	94	95	96	100
1978	101	101	106	115	120	120
1979	126	123	132	134	131	138
1980	162	158	131	140	150	158
1981	198	198	210	217	223	216
1982	188	179	176	185	179	171
1983	248	261	271	293	309	319
1984	268	253	251	247	233	240
1985	279	284	279	281	291	296
1986	336	360	375	383	400	406
1987	392	425	430	418	417	425
1988	345	367	375	379	370	395
1989	401	400	407	428	446	435
1990	416	426	436	420	459	462
1991	414	453	482	485	506	476
1992	620	633	604	579	585	564
1993	696	671	690	661	701	704
1994	800	793	743	734	735	706
1995	755	794	817	844	865	933
1996	1060	1100	1101	1191	1243	1185
1997	1380	1309	1222	1261	1400	1442
1998	1619	1771	1836	1868	1779	1895
1999	2506	2288	2461	2543	2471	2686
2000	3940	4697	4573	3861	3401	3966
2001	2773	2152	1840	2116	2110	2161
2002	1934	1731	1845	1688	1616	1463
2003	1321	1338	1341	1464	1596	1623
2004	2066	2030	1994	1920	1987	2048
2005	2062	2052	1999	1922	2068	2057
2006	2306	2281	2340	2323	2179	2172
2007	2464	2416	2422	2525	2605	2603
2008	2390	2271	2279	2413	2523	2293
2009	1476	1378	1529	1717	1774	1835
2010	2147	2238	2398	2461	2257	2109
2011	2700	2782	2781	2874	2835	2774
2012	2814	2967	3092	3046	2827	2935
2013	3142	3160	3268	3329	3456	3403
2014	4104	4308	4199	4115	4243	4408
2015	4635	4964	4901	4941	5070	4987
2016	4614	4558	4870	4775	4948	4843

NASDAQ MONTH CLOSING VALUES

STOCK MKT

JUL	AUG	SEP	OCT	NOV	DEC	
128	130	130	130	133	134	**1972**
109	105	111	110	94	92	**1973**
70	62	56	65	63	60	**1974**
83	79	74	77	79	78	**1975**
91	90	91	90	91	98	**1976**
101	100	101	98	103	105	**1977**
126	135	133	111	115	118	**1978**
141	150	150	136	144	151	**1979**
172	182	188	193	208	202	**1980**
212	196	180	195	201	196	**1981**
167	178	188	213	232	232	**1982**
304	292	207	275	286	279	**1983**
230	255	250	247	242	247	**1984**
301	298	280	293	314	325	**1985**
371	383	351	361	360	349	**1986**
435	455	444	323	305	331	**1987**
387	377	388	383	372	381	**1988**
454	469	473	456	456	455	**1989**
438	381	345	330	359	374	**1990**
502	526	527	543	524	586	**1991**
581	563	583	605	653	677	**1992**
705	743	763	779	754	777	**1993**
722	766	764	777	750	752	**1994**
1001	1020	1044	1036	1059	1052	**1995**
1081	1142	1227	1222	1293	1291	**1996**
1594	1587	1686	1594	1601	1570	**1997**
1872	1499	1694	1771	1950	2193	**1998**
2638	2739	2746	2966	3336	4069	**1999**
3767	4206	3673	3370	2598	2471	**2000**
2027	1805	1499	1690	1931	1950	**2001**
1328	1315	1172	1330	1479	1336	**2002**
1735	1810	1787	1932	1960	2003	**2003**
1887	1838	1897	1975	2097	2175	**2004**
2185	2152	2152	2120	2233	2205	**2005**
2091	2184	2258	2367	2432	2415	**2006**
2546	2596	2702	2859	2661	2652	**2007**
2326	2368	2092	1721	1536	1577	**2008**
1979	2009	2122	2045	2145	2269	**2009**
2255	2114	2369	2507	2498	2653	**2010**
2756	2579	2415	2684	2620	2605	**2011**
2940	3067	3116	2977	3010	3020	**2012**
3626	3590	3771	3920	4060	4177	**2013**
4370	4580	4493	4631	4792	4736	**2014**
5128	4777	4620	5054	5109	5007	**2015**
5162	5213	5312	5189	5324	5383	**2016**

S&P/TSX MONTH PERCENT CHANGES

	JAN	FEB	MAR	APR	MAY	JUN
1985	8.1	0.0	0.7	0.8	3.8	— 0.8
1986	— 1.7	0.5	6.7	1.1	1.4	— 1.2
1987	9.2	4.5	6.9	— 0.6	— 0.9	1.5
1988	— 3.3	4.8	3.4	0.8	— 2.7	5.9
1989	6.7	— 1.2	0.2	1.4	2.2	1.5
1990	— 6.7	— 0.5	— 1.3	— 8.2	6.7	— 0.6
1991	0.5	5.8	1.0	-0.8	2.2	— 2.3
1992	2.4	— 0.4	— 4.7	— 1.7	1.0	0.0
1993	— 1.3	4.4	4.4	5.2	2.5	2.2
1994	5.4	— 2.9	— 2.1	— 1.4	1.4	— 7.0
1995	— 4.7	2.7	4.6	— -0.8	4.0	1.8
1996	5.4	— 0.7	0.8	3.5	1.9	— 3.9
1997	3.1	0.8	— 5.0	2.2	6.8	0.9
1998	0.0	5.9	6.6	1.4	— 1.0	— 2.9
1999	3.8	— 6.2	4.5	6.3	— 2.5	2.5
2000	0.8	7.6	3.7	— 1.2	— 1.0	10.2
2001	4.3	— 13.3	— 5.8	4.5	2.7	— 5.2
2002	— 0.5	— 0.1	2.8	— 2.4	— 0.1	— 6.7
2003	— 0.7	— 0.2	— 3.2	3.8	4.2	1.8
2004	3.7	3.1	— 2.3	— 4.0	2.1	1.5
2005	— 0.5	5.0	— 0.6	— 3.5	3.6	3.1
2006	6.0	— 2.2	3.6	0.8	— 3.8	— 1.1
2007	1.0	0.1	0.9	1.9	4.8	— 1.1
2008	— 4.9	3.3	— 1.7	4.4	5.6	— 1.7
2009	— 3.3	— 6.6	7.4	6.9	11.2	0.0
2010	— 5.5	4.8	3.5	1.4	— 3.7	— 4.0
2011	0.8	4.3	— 0.1	— 1.2	— 1.0	— 3.6
2012	4.2	1.5	— 2.0	— 0.8	— 6.3	0.7
2013	2.0	1.1	— 0.6	— 2.3	1.6	— 4.1
2014	0.5	3.8	0.9	2.2	— 0.3	3.7
2015	0.3	3.8	— 2.2	2.2	— 1.4	— 3.1
2016	— 1.4	0.3	4.9	3.4	0.8	0.0
FQ POS	20/32	20/32	19/32	19/32	20/32	14/32
% FQ POS	63 %	63 %	59 %	59 %	63 %	44 %
AVG GAIN	1.0 %	1.1 %	1.1 %	0.8 %	1.4 %	-0.4 %
RANK GAIN	5	4	3	7	2	11

S&P/TSX MONTH PERCENT CHANGES 🍁 STOCK MKT

JUL	AUG	SEP	OCT	NOV	DEC		YEAR
2.4	1.5	— 6.7	1.6	6.8	1.3	**1985**	20.5
— 4.9	3.2	— 1.6	1.6	0.7	0.6	**1986**	6.0
7.8	— 0.9	— 2.3	— 22.6	— 1.4	6.1	**1987**	3.1
— 1.9	— 2.7	— 0.1	3.4	— 3.0	2.9	**1988**	7.3
5.6	1.0	— 1.7	— 0.6	0.6	0.7	**1989**	17.1
0.5	— 6.0	— 5.6	— 2.5	2.3	3.4	**1990**	— 18.0
2.1	— 0.6	— 3.7	3.8	— 1.9	1.9	**1991**	7.8
1.6	— 1.2	— 3.1	1.2	— 1.6	2.1	**1992**	— 4.6
0.0	4.3	— 3.6	6.6	— 1.8	3.4	**1993**	29.0
3.8	4.1	0.1	— 1.4	— 4.6	2.9	**1994**	— 2.5
1.9	— 2.1	0.3	— 1.6	4.5	1.1	**1995**	11.9
— 2.3	4.3	2.9	5.8	7.5	— 1.5	**1996**	25.7
6.8	— 3.9	6.5	— 2.8	— 4.8	2.9	**1997**	13.0
— 5.9	— 20.2	1.5	10.6	2.2	2.2	**1998**	— 3.2
1.0	— 1.6	— 0.2	4.3	3.6	11.9	**1999**	29.7
2.1	8.1	— 7.7	— 7.1	— 8.5	1.3	**2000**	6.2
— 0.6	— 3.8	— 7.6	0.7	7.8	3.5	**2001**	— 13.9
— 7.6	0.1	— 6.5	1.1	5.1	0.7	**2002**	— 14.0
3.9	3.6	— 1.3	4.7	1.1	4.6	**2003**	24.3
— 1.0	— 1.0	3.5	2.3	1.8	2.4	**2004**	12.5
5.3	2.4	3.2	— 5.7	4.2	4.1	**2005**	21.9
1.9	2.1	— 2.6	5.0	3.3	1.2	**2006**	14.5
— 0.3	— 1.5	3.2	3.7	— 6.4	1.1	**2007**	7.2
— 6.0	1.3	— 14.7	— 16.9	— 5.0	— 3.1	**2008**	— 35.0
4.0	0.8	4.8	— 4.2	4.9	2.6	**2009**	30.7
3.7	1.7	3.8	2.5	2.2	3.8	**2010**	14.4
— 2.7	— 1.4	— 9.0	5.4	— 0.4	— 2.0	**2011**	— 11.1
0.6	2.4	3.1	0.9	— 1.5	1.6	**2012**	4.0
2.9	1.3	1.1	4.5	0.3	1.7	**2013**	9.6
1.2	1.9	— 4.3	— 2.3	0.9	— 0.8	**2014**	7.4
— 0.6	— 4.2	— 4.0	1.7	— 0.4	— 3.4	**2015**	— 11.1
3.7	0.1	0.9	0.4	2.0	1.4	**2016**	17.5
21/32	18/32	13/32	21/32	19/32	27/32		23/32
66 %	56 %	41 %	66 %	59 %	84 %		72 %
0.9 %	— 0.2 %	— 1.6 %	0.1 %	0.6 %	2.0 %		7.1 %
6	10	12	9	8	1		

S&P/TSX MONTH CLOSING VALUES

	JAN	FEB	MAR	APR	MAY	JUN
1985	2595	2595	2613	2635	2736	2713
1986	2843	2856	3047	3079	3122	3086
1987	3349	3499	3739	3717	3685	3740
1988	3057	3205	3314	3340	3249	3441
1989	3617	3572	3578	3628	3707	3761
1990	3704	3687	3640	3341	3565	3544
1991	3273	3462	3496	3469	3546	3466
1992	3596	3582	3412	3356	3388	3388
1993	3305	3452	3602	3789	3883	3966
1994	4555	4424	4330	4267	4327	4025
1995	4018	4125	4314	4280	4449	4527
1996	4968	4934	4971	5147	5246	5044
1997	6110	6158	5850	5977	6382	6438
1998	6700	7093	7559	7665	7590	7367
1999	6730	6313	6598	7015	6842	7010
2000	8481	9129	9462	9348	9252	10196
2001	9322	8079	7608	7947	8162	7736
2002	7649	7638	7852	7663	7656	7146
2003	6570	6555	6343	6586	6860	6983
2004	8521	8789	8586	8244	8417	8546
2005	9204	9668	9612	9275	9607	9903
2006	11946	11688	12111	12204	11745	11613
2007	13034	13045	13166	13417	14057	13907
2008	13155	13583	13350	13937	14715	14467
2009	8695	8123	8720	9325	10370	10375
2010	11094	11630	12038	12211	11763	11294
2011	13552	14137	14116	13945	13803	13301
2012	12452	12644	12392	12293	11513	11597
2013	12685	12822	12750	12457	12650	12129
2014	13695	14210	14335	14652	14604	15146
2015	14674	15234	14902	15225	15014	14553
2016	12822	12860	13494	13951	14066	14065

S&P/TSX PERCENT CLOSING VALUES

JUL	AUG	SEP	OCT	NOV	DEC	
2779	2820	2632	2675	2857	2893	1985
2935	3028	2979	3027	3047	3066	1986
4030	3994	3902	3019	2978	3160	1987
3377	3286	3284	3396	3295	3390	1988
3971	4010	3943	3919	3943	3970	1989
3561	3346	3159	3081	3151	3257	1990
3540	3518	3388	3516	3449	3512	1991
3443	3403	3298	3336	3283	3350	1992
3967	4138	3991	4256	4180	4321	1993
4179	4350	4354	4292	4093	4214	1994
4615	4517	4530	4459	4661	4714	1995
4929	5143	5291	5599	6017	5927	1996
6878	6612	7040	6842	6513	6699	1997
6931	5531	5614	6208	6344	6486	1998
7081	6971	6958	7256	7520	8414	1999
10406	11248	10378	9640	8820	8934	2000
7690	7399	6839	6886	7426	7688	2001
6605	6612	6180	6249	6570	6615	2002
7258	7517	7421	7773	7859	8221	2003
8458	8377	8668	8871	9030	9247	2004
10423	10669	11012	10383	10824	11272	2005
11831	12074	11761	12345	12752	12908	2006
13869	13660	14099	14625	13689	13833	2007
13593	13771	11753	9763	9271	8988	2008
10787	10868	11935	10911	11447	11746	2009
11713	11914	12369	12676	12953	13443	2010
12946	12769	11624	12252	12204	11955	2011
11665	11949	12317	12423	12239	12434	2012
12487	12654	12787	13361	13395	13622	2013
15331	15626	14961	14613	14745	14632	2014
14468	13859	13307	13529	13470	13010	2015
14583	14598	14726	14787	15083	15288	2016

S&P 500 1950 - 2016
BEST - WORST

10 BEST

YEARS

	Close	Change	Change
1954	36	11 pt	45.0 %
1958	55	15	38.1
1995	616	157	34.1
1975	90	22	31.5
1997	970	230	31.0
2013	1848	422	29.6
1989	353	76	27.3
1998	1229	259	26.7
1955	45	10	26.4
2003	1112	232	26.4

MONTHS

	Close	Change	Change
Oct 1974	74	10 pt	16.3 %
Aug 1982	120	12	11.6
Dec 1991	417	42	11.2
Oct 1982	134	13	11.0
Oct 2011	1253	122	10.8
Aug 1984	167	16	10.6
Nov 1980	141	13	10.2
Nov 1962	62	6	10.2
Mar 2000	1499	132	9.7
Apr 2009	798	75	9.4

DAYS

		Close	Change	Change
Mon	2008 Oct 13	1003	104 pt	11.6 %
Tue	2008 Oct 28	941	92	10.8
Wed	1987 Oct 21	258	22	9.1
Mon	2009 Mar 23	883	54	7.1
Thu	2008 Nov 13	911	59	6.9
Mon	2008 Nov 24	852	52	6.5
Tues	2009 Mar 10	720	43	6.4
Fri	2008 Nov 21	800	48	6.3
Wed	2002 Jul 24	843	46	5.7
Tue	2008 Sep 30	1166	60	5.4

10 WORST

YEARS

	Close	Change	Change
2008	903	– 566 pt	– 38.5 %
1974	69	– 29	– 29.7
2002	880	– 268	– 23.4
1973	98	– 21	– 17.4
1957	40	– 7	– 14.3
1966	80	– 12	– 13.1
2001	1148	– 172	– 13.0
1962	63	– 8	– 11.8
1977	95	– 12	– 11.5
1969	92	– 12	– 11.4

MONTHS

	Close	Change	Change
Oct 1987	252	– 70 pt	– 21.8 %
Oct 2008	969	– 196	– 16.8
Aug 1998	957	– 163	– 14.6
Sep 1974	64	– 9	– 11.9
Nov 1973	96	– 12	– 11.4
Sep 2002	815	– 101	– 11.0
Feb 2009	735	– 91	– 11.0
Mar 1980	102	– 12	– 10.2
Aug 1990	323	– 34	– 9.4
Feb 2001	1240	– 126	– 9.2

DAYS

		Close	Change	Change
Mon	1987 Oct 19	225	– 58 pt	– 20.5 %
Wed	2008 Oct 15	908	– 90	– 9.0
Mon	2008 Dec 01	816	– 80	– 8.9
Mon	2008 Sep 29	1106	– 107	– 8.8
Mon	1987 Oct 26	228	– 21	– 8.3
Thu	2008 Oct 09	910	– 75	– 7.6
Mon	1997 Oct 27	877	– 65	– 6.9
Mon	1998 Aug 31	957	– 70	– 6.8
Fri	1988 Jan 8	243	– 18	– 6.8
Thu	2008 Nov 20	752	– 54	– 6.7

10 BEST

10 WORST

YEARS

	Close	Change	Change
1954	404	124 pt	44.0 %
1975	852	236	38.3
1958	584	148	34.0
1995	5117	1283	33.5
1985	1547	335	27.7
1989	2753	585	27.0
2013	16577	3473	26.5
1996	6448	1331	26.0
2003	10454	2112	25.3
1999	11453	2272	25.2

YEARS

	Close	Change	Change
2008	8776	− 4488 pt	− 33.8 %
1974	616	− 235	− 27.6
1966	786	− 184	− 18.9
1977	831	− 174	− 17.3
2002	8342	− 1680	− 16.8
1973	851	− 169	− 16.6
1969	800	− 143	− 16.2
1957	436	− 64	− 12.8
1962	652	− 79	− 10.8
1960	616	− 64	− 9.3

MONTHS

	Close	Change	Change
Aug 1982	901	93 pt	11.5 %
Oct 1982	992	95	10.6
Oct 2002	8397	805	10.6
Apr 1978	837	80	10.5
Apr 1999	10789	1003	10.2
Nov 1962	649	60	10.1
Nov 1954	387	35	9.9
Aug 1984	1224	109	9.8
Oct 1998	8592	750	9.6
Oct 2011	11955	1042	9.5

MONTHS

	Close	Change	Change
Oct 1987	1994	− 603 pt	− 23.2 %
Aug 1998	7539	− 1344	− 15.1
Oct 2008	9325	− 1526	− 14.1
Nov 1973	822	− 134	− 14.0
Sep 2002	7592	− 1072	− 12.4
Feb 2009	7063	− 938	− 11.7
Sep 2001	8848	− 1102	− 11.1
Sep 1974	608	− 71	− 10.4
Aug 1974	679	− 79	− 10.4
Jun 2008	11350	− 1288	− 10.2

DAYS

		Close	Change	Change
Mon	2008 Oct 13	9388	936 pt	11.1 %
Tue	2008 Oct 28	9065	889	10.9
Wed	1987 Oct 21	2028	187	10.2
Mon	2009 Mar 23	7776	497	6.8
Thu	2008 Nov 13	8835	553	6.7
Fri	2008 Nov 21	8046	494	6.5
Wed	2002 Jul 24	8191	489	6.3
Tue	1987 Oct 20	1841	102	5.9
Tue	2009 Mar 10	6926	379	5.8
Mon	2002 Jul 29	8712	448	5.4

DAYS

		Close	Change	Change
Mon	1987 Oct 19	1739	− 508 pt	− 22.6 %
Mon	1987 Oct 26	1794	− 157	− 8.0
Wed	2008 Oct 15	8578	− 733	− 7.9
Mon	2008 Dec 01	8149	− 680	− 7.7
Thu	2008 Oct 09	8579	− 679	− 7.3
Mon	1997 Oct 27	8366	− 554	− 7.2
Mon	2001 Sep 17	8921	− 685	− 7.1
Mon	2008 Sep 29	10365	− 778	− 7.0
Fri	1989 Oct 13	2569	− 191	− 6.9
Fri	1988 Jan 8	1911	− 141	− 6.9

NASDAQ 1972- 2016
BEST - WORST

10 BEST

10 WORST

YEARS

	Close	Change	Change
1999	4069	1877 pt	85.6 %
1991	586	213	56.9
2003	2003	668	50.0
2009	2269	692	43.9
1995	1052	300	39.9
1998	2193	622	39.6
2013	4161	1157	38.3
1980	202	51	33.9
1985	325	78	31.5
1975	78	18	29.8

YEARS

	Close	Change	Change
2008	1577	– 1075 pt	– 40.5 %
2000	2471	– 1599	– 39.3
1974	60	– 32	– 35.1
2002	1336	– 615	– 31.5
1973	92	– 42	– 31.1
2001	1950	– 520	– 21.1
1990	374	– 81	– 17.8
1984	247	– 32	– 11.3
1987	331	– 18	– 5.2
1981	196	– 7	– 3.2

MONTHS

	Close	Change	Change
Dec 1999	4069	733 pt	22.0 %
Feb 2000	4697	756	19.2
Oct 1974	65	10	17.2
Jun 2000	3966	565	16.6
Apr 2001	2116	276	15.0
Nov 2001	1931	240	14.2
Oct 2002	1330	158	13.5
Oct 1982	1771	25	13.3
Sep 1998	1694	195	13.0
Oct 2001	1690	191	12.8

MONTHS

	Close	Change	Change
Oct 1987	323	– 121 pt	– 27.2 %
Nov 2000	2598	– 772	– 22.9
Feb 2001	2152	– 621	– 22.4
Aug 1998	1499	– 373	– 19.9
Oct 2008	1721	– 371	– 17.7
Mar 1980	131	– 27	– 17.1
Sep 2001	1499	– 307	– 17.0
Oct 1978	111	– 22	– 16.4
Apr 2000	3861	– 712	– 15.6
Nov 1973	94	– 17	– 15.1

DAYS

		Close	Change	Change
Wed	2001 Jan 3	2617	325 pt	14.2 %
Mon	2008 Oct 13	1844	195	11.8
Tue	2000 Dec 5	2890	274	10.5
Tue	2008 Oct 28	1649	144	9.5
Thu	2001 Apr 5	1785	146	8.9
Wed	2001 Apr 18	2079	156	8.1
Tue	2000 May 30	3459	254	7.9
Fri	2000 Oct 13	3317	242	7.9
Thu	2000 Oct 19	3419	247	7.8
Wed	2002 May 8	1696	122	7.8

DAYS

		Close	Change	Change
Mon	1987 Oct 19	360	– 46 pt	– 11.3 %
Fri	2000 Apr 14	3321	– 355	– 9.7
Mon	2008 Sep 29	1984	– 200	– 9.1
Mon	1987 Oct 26	299	– 30	– 9.0
Tue	1987 Oct 20	328	– 32	– 9.0
Mon	2008 Dec 01	1398	– 138	– 9.0
Mon	1998 Aug 31	1499	– 140	– 8.6
Wed	2008 Oct 15	1628	– 151	– 8.5
Mon	2000 Apr 03	4224	– 349	– 7.6
Tue	2001 Jan 02	2292	– 179	– 7.2

S&P /TSX (CANADA) 1985 - 2016
BEST - WORST

10 BEST

10 WORST

YEARS

	Close	Change	Change
2009	8414	2758 pt	30.7 %
1999	4321	1928	29.7
1993	5927	971	29.0
1996	8221	1213	25.7
2003	11272	1606	24.3
2005	2893	2026	21.9
1985	3970	500	20.8
1989	12908	580	17.1
2006	6699	1636	14.5
2010	13433	1697	14.4

YEARS

	Close	Change	Change
2008	8988	– 4845 pt	– 35.0 %
1990	3257	– 713	– 18.0
2002	6615	– 1074	– 14.0
2001	7688	– 1245	– 13.9
2015	13010	– 1622	– 11.9
2011	11955	– 1488	– 11.7
1992	3350	– 102	– 4.6
1998	6486	– 214	– 3.2
1994	4214	– 108	– 2.5
1987	3160	94	3.1

MONTHS

	Close	Change	Change
Dec 1999	8414	891 pt	11.8 %
May 2009	8500	1045	11.2
Oct 1998	6208	594	10.6
Jun 2000	10196	943	10.2
Jan 1985	2595	195	8.1
Aug 2000	11248	842	8.1
Nov 2001	7426	540	7.8
Jul 1987	4030	290	7.8
Feb 2000	9129	648	7.6
Nov 1996	6017	418	7.5

MONTHS

	Close	Change	Change
Oct 1987	3019	– 883 pt	– 22.6 %
Aug 1998	5531	– 1401	– 20.2
Oct 2008	9763	– 1990	– 16.9
Sep 2008	11753	– 2018	– 14.7
Feb 2001	8079	– 1243	– 13.3
Sep 2011	11624	– 1145	– 9.0
Nov 2000	8820	– 820	– 8.5
Apr 1990	3341	– 299	– 8.2
Sep 2000	10378	– 870	– 7.7
Sep 2001	6839	– 561	– 7.6

DAYS

		Close	Change	Change
Tue	2008 Oct 14	9956	891 pt	9.8 %
Wed	1987 Oct 21	3246	269	9.0
Mon	2008 Oct 20	10251	689	7.2
Tue	2008 Oct 28	9152	614	7.2
Fri	2008 Sep 19	12913	848	7.0
Fri	2008 Nov 28	9271	517	5.9
Fri	2008 Nov 21	8155	431	5.6
Mon	2008 Dec 08	8567	450	5.5
Mon	2009 Mar 23	8959	452	5.3
Fri	1987 Oct 30	3019	147	5.1

DAYS

		Close	Change	Change
Mon	1987 Oct 19	3192	– 407 pt	– 11.3 %
Mon	2008 Dec 01	8406	– 864	– 9.3
Thu	2008 Nov 20	7725	– 766	– 9.0
Mon	2008 Oct 27	8537	– 757	– 8.1
Wed	2000 Oct 25	9512	– 840	– 8.1
Mon	1987 Oct 26	2846	– 233	– 7.6
Thu	2008 Oct 02	10901	– 814	– 6.9
Mon	2008 Sep 29	11285	– 841	– 6.9
Tue	1987 Oct 20	2977	– 215	– 6.7
Fri	2001 Feb 16	8393	– 574	– 6.4

BOND YIELDS

BOND YIELDS 10 YEAR TREASURY*

	JAN	FEB	MAR	APR	MAY	JUN
1954	2.48	2.47	2.37	2.29	2.37	2.38
1955	2.61	2.65	2.68	2.75	2.76	2.78
1956	2.9	2.84	2.96	3.18	3.07	3
1957	3.46	3.34	3.41	3.48	3.6	3.8
1958	3.09	3.05	2.98	2.88	2.92	2.97
1959	4.02	3.96	3.99	4.12	4.31	4.34
1960	4.72	4.49	4.25	4.28	4.35	4.15
1961	3.84	3.78	3.74	3.78	3.71	3.88
1962	4.08	4.04	3.93	3.84	3.87	3.91
1963	3.83	3.92	3.93	3.97	3.93	3.99
1964	4.17	4.15	4.22	4.23	4.2	4.17
1965	4.19	4.21	4.21	4.2	4.21	4.21
1966	4.61	4.83	4.87	4.75	4.78	4.81
1967	4.58	4.63	4.54	4.59	4.85	5.02
1968	5.53	5.56	5.74	5.64	5.87	5.72
1969	6.04	6.19	6.3	6.17	6.32	6.57
1970	7.79	7.24	7.07	7.39	7.91	7.84
1971	6.24	6.11	5.7	5.83	6.39	6.52
1972	5.95	6.08	6.07	6.19	6.13	6.11
1973	6.46	6.64	6.71	6.67	6.85	6.9
1974	6.99	6.96	7.21	7.51	7.58	7.54
1975	7.5	7.39	7.73	8.23	8.06	7.86
1976	7.74	7.79	7.73	7.56	7.9	7.86
1977	7.21	7.39	7.46	7.37	7.46	7.28
1978	7.96	8.03	8.04	8.15	8.35	8.46
1979	9.1	9.1	9.12	9.18	9.25	8.91
1980	10.8	12.41	12.75	11.47	10.18	9.78
1981	12.57	13.19	13.12	13.68	14.1	13.47
1982	14.59	14.43	13.86	13.87	13.62	14.3
1983	10.46	10.72	10.51	10.4	10.38	10.85
1984	11.67	11.84	12.32	12.63	13.41	13.56
1985	11.38	11.51	11.86	11.43	10.85	10.16
1986	9.19	8.7	7.78	7.3	7.71	7.8
1987	7.08	7.25	7.25	8.02	8.61	8.4
1988	8.67	8.21	8.37	8.72	9.09	8.92
1989	9.09	9.17	9.36	9.18	8.86	8.28
1990	8.21	8.47	8.59	8.79	8.76	8.48
1991	8.09	7.85	8.11	8.04	8.07	8.28
1992	7.03	7.34	7.54	7.48	7.39	7.26
1993	6.6	6.26	5.98	5.97	6.04	5.96
1994	5.75	5.97	6.48	6.97	7.18	7.1
1995	7.78	7.47	7.2	7.06	6.63	6.17
1996	5.65	5.81	6.27	6.51	6.74	6.91
1997	6.58	6.42	6.69	6.89	6.71	6.49
1998	5.54	5.57	5.65	5.64	5.65	5.5
1999	4.72	5	5.23	5.18	5.54	5.9
2000	6.66	6.52	6.26	5.99	6.44	6.1
2001	5.16	5.1	4.89	5.14	5.39	5.28
2002	5.04	4.91	5.28	5.21	5.16	4.93
2003	4.05	3.9	3.81	3.96	3.57	3.33
2004	4.15	4.08	3.83	4.35	4.72	4.73
2005	4.22	4.17	4.5	4.34	4.14	4.00
2006	4.42	4.57	4.72	4.99	5.11	5.11
2007	4.76	4.72	4.56	4.69	4.75	5.10
2008	3.74	3.74	3.51	3.68	3.88	4.10
2009	2.52	2.87	2.82	2.93	3.29	3.72
2010	3.73	3.69	3.73	3.85	3.42	3.20
2011	3.39	3.58	3.41	3.46	3.17	3.00
2012	1.97	1.97	2.17	2.05	1.80	1.62
2013	1.91	1.98	1.96	1.76	1.93	2.30
2014	2.86	2.71	2.72	2.71	2.56	2.60
2015	1.88	1.98	2.04	1.94	2.20	2.36
2016	2.09	1.78	1.89	1.81	1.81	1.64

* Source: Federal Reserve Bank of St. Louis, monthly data calculated as average of business days

10 YEAR TREASURY  BOND YIELDS

JUL	AUG	SEP	OCT	NOV	DEC	
2.3	2.36	2.38	2.43	2.48	2.51	1954
2.9	2.97	2.97	2.88	2.89	2.96	1955
3.11	3.33	3.38	3.34	3.49	3.59	1956
3.93	3.93	3.92	3.97	3.72	3.21	1957
3.2	3.54	3.76	3.8	3.74	3.86	1958
4.4	4.43	4.68	4.53	4.53	4.69	1959
3.9	3.8	3.8	3.89	3.93	3.84	1960
3.92	4.04	3.98	3.92	3.94	4.06	1961
4.01	3.98	3.98	3.93	3.92	3.86	1962
4.02	4	4.08	4.11	4.12	4.13	1963
4.19	4.19	4.2	4.19	4.15	4.18	1964
4.2	4.25	4.29	4.35	4.45	4.62	1965
5.02	5.22	5.18	5.01	5.16	4.84	1966
5.16	5.28	5.3	5.48	5.75	5.7	1967
5.5	5.42	5.46	5.58	5.7	6.03	1968
6.72	6.69	7.16	7.1	7.14	7.65	1969
7.46	7.53	7.39	7.33	6.84	0.39	1970
6.73	6.68	6.14	5.93	5.81	5.93	1971
6.11	6.21	6.55	6.48	6.28	6.36	1972
7.13	7.4	7.09	6.79	6.73	6.74	1973
7.81	8.04	8.04	7.9	7.68	7.43	1974
8.06	8.4	8.43	8.14	8.05	8	1975
7.83	7.77	7.59	7.41	7.29	6.87	1976
7.33	7.4	7.34	7.52	7.58	7.69	1977
8.64	8.41	8.42	8.64	8.81	9.01	1978
8.95	9.03	9.33	10.3	10.65	10.39	1979
10.25	11.1	11.51	11.75	12.68	12.84	1980
14.28	14.94	15.32	15.15	13.39	13.72	1981
13.95	13.06	12.34	10.91	10.55	10.54	1982
11.38	11.85	11.65	11.54	11.69	11.83	1983
13.36	12.72	12.52	12.16	11.57	11.5	1984
10.31	10.33	10.37	10.24	9.78	9.26	1985
7.3	7.17	7.45	7.43	7.25	7.11	1986
8.45	8.76	9.42	9.52	8.86	8.99	1987
9.06	9.26	8.98	8.8	8.96	9.11	1988
8.02	8.11	8.19	8.01	7.87	7.84	1989
8.47	8.75	8.89	8.72	8.39	8.08	1990
8.27	7.9	7.65	7.53	7.42	7.09	1991
6.84	6.59	6.42	6.59	6.87	6.77	1992
5.81	5.68	5.36	5.33	5.72	5.77	1993
7.3	7.24	7.46	7.74	7.96	7.81	1994
6.28	6.49	6.2	6.04	5.93	5.71	1995
6.87	6.64	6.83	6.53	6.2	6.3	1996
6.22	6.3	6.21	6.03	5.88	5.81	1997
5.46	5.34	4.81	4.53	4.83	4.65	1998
5.79	5.94	5.92	6.11	6.03	6.28	1999
6.05	5.83	5.8	5.74	5.72	5.24	2000
5.24	4.97	4.73	4.57	4.65	5.09	2001
4.65	4.26	3.87	3.94	4.05	4.03	2002
3.98	4.45	4.27	4.29	4.3	4.27	2003
4.5	4.28	4.13	4.1	4.19	4.23	2004
4.18	4.26	4.20	4.46	4.54	4.47	2005
5.09	4.88	4.72	4.73	4.60	4.56	2006
5.00	4.67	4.52	4.53	4.15	4.10	2007
4.01	3.89	3.69	3.81	3.53	2.42	2008
3.56	3.59	3.40	3.39	3.40	3.59	2009
3.01	2.70	2.65	2.54	2.76	3.29	2010
3.00	2.30	1.98	2.15	2.01	1.98	2011
1.53	1.68	1.72	1.75	1.65	1.72	2012
2.58	2.74	2.81	2.62	2.72	2.90	2013
2.54	2.42	2.53	2.30	2.33	2.21	2014
2.32	2.17	2.17	2.07	2.26	2.24	2015
1.50	1.56	1.63	1.76	2.14	2.49	2016

5 YEAR TREASURY*

	JAN	FEB	MAR	APR	MAY	JUN
1954	2.17	2.04	1.93	1.87	1.92	1.92
1955	2.32	2.38	2.48	2.55	2.56	2.59
1956	2.84	2.74	2.93	3.20	3.08	2.97
1957	3.47	3.39	3.46	3.53	3.64	3.83
1958	2.88	2.78	2.64	2.46	2.41	2.46
1959	4.01	3.96	3.99	4.12	4.35	4.50
1960	4.92	4.69	4.31	4.29	4.49	4.12
1961	3.67	3.66	3.60	3.57	3.47	3.81
1962	3.94	3.89	3.68	3.60	3.66	3.64
1963	3.58	3.66	3.68	3.74	3.72	3.81
1964	4.07	4.03	4.14	4.15	4.05	4.02
1965	4.10	4.15	4.15	4.15	4.15	4.15
1966	4.86	4.98	4.92	4.83	4.89	4.97
1967	4.70	4.74	4.54	4.51	4.75	5.01
1968	5.54	5.59	5.76	5.69	6.04	5.85
1969	6.25	6.34	6.41	6.30	6.54	6.75
1970	8.17	7.82	7.21	7.50	7.97	7.85
1971	5.89	5.56	5.00	5.65	6.28	6.53
1972	5.59	5.69	5.87	6.17	5.85	5.91
1973	6.34	6.60	6.80	6.67	6.80	6.69
1974	6.95	6.82	7.31	7.92	8.18	8.10
1975	7.41	7.11	7.30	7.99	7.72	7.51
1976	7.46	7.45	7.49	7.25	7.59	7.61
1977	6.58	6.83	6.93	6.79	6.94	6.76
1978	7.77	7.83	7.86	7.98	8.18	8.36
1979	9.20	9.13	9.20	9.25	9.24	8.85
1980	10.74	12.60	13.47	11.84	9.95	9.21
1981	12.77	13.41	13.41	13.99	14.63	13.95
1982	14.65	14.54	13.98	14.00	13.75	14.43
1983	10.03	10.26	10.08	10.02	10.03	10.63
1984	11.37	11.54	12.02	12.37	13.17	13.48
1985	10.93	11.13	11.52	11.01	10.34	9.60
1986	8.68	8.34	7.46	7.05	7.52	7.64
1987	6.64	6.79	6.79	7.57	8.26	8.02
1988	8.18	7.71	7.83	8.19	8.58	8.49
1989	9.15	9.27	9.51	9.30	8.91	8.29
1990	8.12	8.42	8.60	8.77	8.74	8.43
1991	7.70	7.47	7.77	7.70	7.70	7.94
1992	6.24	6.58	6.95	6.78	6.69	6.48
1993	5.83	5.43	5.19	5.13	5.20	5.22
1994	5.09	5.40	5.94	6.52	6.78	6.70
1995	7.76	7.37	7.05	6.86	6.41	5.93
1996	5.36	5.38	5.97	6.30	6.48	6.69
1997	6.33	6.20	6.54	6.76	6.57	6.38
1998	5.42	5.49	5.61	5.61	5.63	5.52
1999	4.60	4.91	5.14	5.08	5.44	5.81
2000	6.58	6.68	6.50	6.26	6.69	6.30
2001	4.86	4.89	4.64	4.76	4.93	4.81
2002	4.34	4.30	4.74	4.65	4.49	4.19
2003	3.05	2.90	2.78	2.93	2.52	2.27
2004	3.12	3.07	2.79	3.39	3.85	3.93
2005	3.71	3.77	4.17	4.00	3.85	3.77
2006	4.35	4.57	4.72	4.90	5.00	5.07
2007	4.75	4.71	4.48	4.59	4.67	5.03
2008	2.98	2.78	2.48	2.84	3.15	3.49
2009	1.60	1.87	1.82	1.86	2.13	2.71
2010	2.48	2.36	2.43	2.58	2.18	2.00
2011	1.99	2.26	2.11	2.17	1.84	1.58
2012	0.84	0.83	1.02	0.89	0.76	0.71
2013	0.81	0.85	0.82	0.71	0.84	1.20
2014	1.65	1.52	1.64	1.70	1.59	1.68
2015	1.37	1.47	1.52	1.35	1.54	1.68
2016	1.52	1.22	1.38	1.26	1.30	1.17

* Source: Federal Reserve Bank of St. Louis, monthly data calculated as average of business days

5 YEAR TREASURY ≣ BOND YIELDS

JUL	AUG	SEP	OCT	NOV	DEC	
1.85	1.90	1.96	2.02	2.09	2.16	**1954**
2.72	2.86	2.85	2.76	2.81	2.93	**1955**
3.12	3.41	3.47	3.40	3.56	3.70	**1956**
4.00	4.00	4.03	4.08	3.72	3.08	**1957**
2.77	3.29	3.69	3.78	3.70	3.82	**1958**
4.58	4.57	4.90	4.72	4.75	5.01	**1959**
3.79	3.62	3.61	3.76	3.81	3.67	**1960**
3.84	3.96	3.90	3.80	3.82	3.91	**1961**
3.80	3.71	3.70	3.64	3.60	3.56	**1962**
3.89	3.89	3.96	3.97	4.01	4.04	**1963**
4.03	4.05	4.08	4.07	4.04	4.09	**1964**
4.15	4.20	4.25	4.34	4.46	4.72	**1965**
5.17	5.50	5.50	5.27	5.36	5.00	**1966**
5.23	5.31	5.40	5.57	5.78	5.75	**1967**
5.60	5.50	5.48	5.55	5.66	6.12	**1968**
7.01	7.03	7.57	7.51	7.53	7.96	**1969**
7.59	7.57	7.29	7.12	6.47	5.95	**1970**
6.85	6.55	0.14	5.93	5.78	5.69	**1971**
5.97	6.02	6.25	6.18	6.12	6.16	**1972**
7.33	7.63	7.05	6.77	6.92	6.80	**1973**
8.38	8.63	8.37	7.97	7.68	7.31	**1974**
7.92	8.33	8.37	7.97	7.80	7.76	**1975**
7.49	7.31	7.13	6.75	6.52	6.10	**1976**
6.84	7.03	7.04	7.32	7.34	7.48	**1977**
8.54	8.33	8.43	8.61	8.84	9.08	**1978**
8.90	9.06	9.41	10.63	10.93	10.42	**1979**
9.53	10.84	11.62	11.86	12.83	13.25	**1980**
14.79	15.56	15.93	15.41	13.38	13.60	**1981**
14.07	13.00	12.25	10.80	10.38	10.22	**1982**
11.21	11.63	11.43	11.28	11.41	11.54	**1983**
13.27	12.68	12.53	12.06	11.33	11.07	**1984**
9.70	9.81	9.81	9.69	9.28	8.73	**1985**
7.06	6.80	6.92	6.83	6.76	6.67	**1986**
8.01	8.32	8.94	9.08	8.35	8.45	**1987**
8.66	8.94	8.69	8.51	8.79	9.09	**1988**
7.83	8.09	8.17	7.97	7.81	7.75	**1989**
8.33	8.44	8.51	8.33	8.02	7.73	**1990**
7.91	7.43	7.14	6.87	6.62	6.19	**1991**
5.84	5.60	5.38	5.60	6.04	6.08	**1992**
5.09	5.03	4.73	4.71	5.06	5.15	**1993**
6.91	6.88	7.08	7.40	7.72	7.78	**1994**
6.01	6.24	6.00	5.86	5.69	5.51	**1995**
6.64	6.39	6.60	6.27	5.97	6.07	**1996**
6.12	6.16	6.11	5.93	5.80	5.77	**1997**
5.46	5.27	4.62	4.18	4.54	4.45	**1998**
5.68	5.84	5.80	6.03	5.97	6.19	**1999**
6.18	6.06	5.93	5.78	5.70	5.17	**2000**
4.76	4.57	4.12	3.91	3.97	4.39	**2001**
3.81	3.29	2.94	2.95	3.05	3.03	**2002**
2.87	3.37	3.18	3.19	3.29	3.27	**2003**
3.69	3.47	3.36	3.35	3.53	3.60	**2004**
3.98	4.12	4.01	4.33	4.45	4.39	**2005**
5.04	4.82	4.67	4.69	4.58	4.53	**2006**
4.88	4.43	4.20	4.20	3.67	3.49	**2007**
3.30	3.14	2.88	2.73	2.29	1.52	**2008**
2.46	2.57	2.37	2.33	2.23	2.34	**2009**
1.76	1.47	1.41	1.18	1.35	1.93	**2010**
1.54	1.02	0.90	1.06	0.91	0.89	**2011**
0.62	0.71	0.67	0.71	0.67	0.70	**2012**
1.40	1.52	1.60	1.37	1.37	1.58	**2013**
1.70	1.63	1.77	1.55	1.62	1.64	**2014**
1.63	1.54	1.49	1.39	1.67	1.70	**2015**
1.07	1.13	1.18	1.27	1.60	1.96	**2016**

BOND YIELDS 3 MONTH TREASURY

	JAN	FEB	MAR	APR	MAY	JUN
1982	12.92	14.28	13.31	13.34	12.71	13.08
1983	8.12	8.39	8.66	8.51	8.50	9.14
1984	9.26	9.46	9.89	10.07	10.22	10.26
1985	8.02	8.56	8.83	8.22	7.73	7.18
1986	7.30	7.29	6.76	6.24	6.33	6.40
1987	5.58	5.75	5.77	5.82	5.85	5.85
1988	6.00	5.84	5.87	6.08	6.45	6.66
1999	8.56	8.84	9.14	8.96	8.74	8.43
1990	7.90	8.00	8.17	8.04	8.01	7.99
1991	6.41	6.12	6.09	5.83	5.63	5.75
1992	3.91	3.95	4.14	3.84	3.72	3.75
1993	3.07	2.99	3.01	2.93	3.03	3.14
1994	3.04	3.33	3.59	3.78	4.27	4.25
1995	5.90	5.94	5.91	5.84	5.85	5.64
1996	5.15	4.96	5.10	5.09	5.15	5.23
1997	5.17	5.14	5.28	5.30	5.20	5.07
1998	5.18	5.23	5.16	5.08	5.14	5.12
1999	4.45	4.56	4.57	4.41	4.63	4.72
2000	5.50	5.73	5.86	5.82	5.99	5.86
2001	5.29	5.01	4.54	3.97	3.70	3.57
2002	1.68	1.76	1.83	1.75	1.76	1.73
2003	1.19	1.19	1.15	1.15	1.09	0.94
2004	0.90	0.94	0.95	0.96	1.04	1.29
2005	2.37	2.58	2.80	2.84	2.90	3.04
2006	4.34	4.54	4.63	4.72	4.84	4.92
2007	5.11	5.16	5.08	5.01	4.87	4.74
2008	2.82	2.17	1.28	1.31	1.76	1.89
2009	0.13	0.30	0.22	0.16	0.18	0.18
2010	0.06	0.11	0.15	0.16	0.16	0.12
2011	0.15	0.13	0.10	0.06	0.04	0.04
2012	0.03	0.09	0.08	0.08	0.09	0.09
2013	0.07	0.10	0.09	0.06	0.04	0.05
2014	0.04	0.05	0.05	0.03	0.03	0.04
2015	0.03	0.02	0.03	0.02	0.02	0.02
2016	0.26	0.31	0.30	0.23	0.28	0.27

* Source: Federal Reserve Bank of St. Louis, monthly data calculated as average of business days

3 MONTH TREASURY  BOND YIELDS

JUL	AUG	SEP	OCT	NOV	DEC	
11.86	9.00	8.19	7.97	8.35	8.20	**1982**
9.45	9.74	9.36	8.99	9.11	9.36	**1983**
10.53	10.90	10.80	10.12	8.92	8.34	**1984**
7.32	7.37	7.33	7.40	7.48	7.33	**1985**
6.00	5.69	5.35	5.32	5.50	5.68	**1986**
5.88	6.23	6.62	6.35	5.89	5.96	**1987**
6.95	7.30	7.48	7.60	8.03	8.35	**1988**
8.15	8.17	8.01	7.90	7.94	7.88	**1999**
7.87	7.69	7.60	7.40	7.29	6.95	**1990**
5.75	5.50	5.37	5.14	4.69	4.18	**1991**
3.28	3.20	2.97	2.93	3.21	3.29	**1992**
3.11	3.09	3.01	3.09	3.18	3.13	**1993**
4.46	4.61	4.75	5.10	5.45	5.76	**1994**
5.59	5.57	5.43	5.44	5.52	5.29	**1995**
5.30	5.19	5.24	5.12	5.17	5.04	**1996**
5.19	5.28	5.08	5.11	5.28	5.30	**1997**
5.09	5.04	4.74	4.07	4.53	4.50	**1998**
4.69	4.87	4.82	5.02	5.23	5.36	**1999**
6.14	6.28	6.18	6.29	6.36	5.94	**2000**
3.59	3.44	2.69	2.20	1.91	1.72	**2001**
1.71	1.65	1.66	1.61	1.25	1.21	**2002**
0.92	0.97	0.96	0.94	0.95	0.91	**2003**
1.36	1.50	1.68	1.79	2.11	2.22	**2004**
3.29	3.52	3.49	3.79	3.97	3.97	**2005**
5.08	5.09	4.93	5.05	5.07	4.97	**2006**
4.96	4.32	3.99	4.00	3.35	3.07	**2007**
1.66	1.75	1.15	0.69	0.19	0.03	**2008**
0.18	0.17	0.12	0.07	0.05	0.05	**2009**
0.16	0.16	0.15	0.13	0.14	0.14	**2010**
0.04	0.02	0.01	0.02	0.01	0.01	**2011**
0.10	0.10	0.11	0.10	0.09	0.07	**2012**
0.04	0.04	0.02	0.05	0.07	0.07	**2013**
0.03	0.03	0.02	0.02	0.02	0.03	**2014**
0.03	0.07	0.02	0.02	0.13	0.23	**2015**
0.30	0.30	0.29	0.33	0.45	0.51	**2016**

MOODY'S SEASONED CORPORATE Aaa*

	JAN	FEB	MAR	APR	MAY	JUN
1950	2.57	2.58	2.58	2.60	2.61	2.62
1951	2.66	2.66	2.78	2.87	2.89	2.94
1952	2.98	2.93	2.96	2.93	2.93	2.94
1953	3.02	3.07	3.12	3.23	3.34	3.40
1954	3.06	2.95	2.86	2.85	2.88	2.90
1955	2.93	2.93	3.02	3.01	3.04	3.05
1956	3.11	3.08	3.10	3.24	3.28	3.26
1957	3.77	3.67	3.66	3.67	3.74	3.91
1958	3.60	3.59	3.63	3.60	3.57	3.57
1959	4.12	4.14	4.13	4.23	4.37	4.46
1960	4.61	4.56	4.49	4.45	4.46	4.45
1961	4.32	4.27	4.22	4.25	4.27	4.33
1962	4.42	4.42	4.39	4.33	4.28	4.28
1963	4.21	4.19	4.19	4.21	4.22	4.23
1964	4.39	4.36	4.38	4.40	4.41	4.41
1965	4.43	4.41	4.42	4.43	4.44	4.46
1966	4.74	4.78	4.92	4.96	4.98	5.07
1967	5.20	5.03	5.13	5.11	5.24	5.44
1968	6.17	6.10	6.11	6.21	6.27	6.28
1969	6.59	6.66	6.85	6.89	6.79	6.98
1970	7.91	7.93	7.84	7.83	8.11	8.48
1971	7.36	7.08	7.21	7.25	7.53	7.64
1972	7.19	7.27	7.24	7.30	7.30	7.23
1973	7.15	7.22	7.29	7.26	7.29	7.37
1974	7.83	7.85	8.01	8.25	8.37	8.47
1975	8.83	8.62	8.67	8.95	8.90	8.77
1976	8.60	8.55	8.52	8.40	8.58	8.62
1977	7.96	8.04	8.10	8.04	8.05	7.95
1978	8.41	8.47	8.47	8.56	8.69	8.76
1979	9.25	9.26	9.37	9.38	9.50	9.29
1980	11.09	12.38	12.96	12.04	10.99	10.58
1981	12.81	13.35	13.33	13.88	14.32	13.75
1982	15.18	15.27	14.58	14.46	14.26	14.81
1983	11.79	12.01	11.73	11.51	11.46	11.74
1984	12.20	12.08	12.57	12.81	13.28	13.55
1985	12.08	12.13	12.56	12.23	11.72	10.94
1986	10.05	9.67	9.00	8.79	9.09	9.13
1987	8.36	8.38	8.36	8.85	9.33	9.32
1988	9.88	9.40	9.39	9.67	9.90	9.86
1989	9.62	9.64	9.80	9.79	9.57	9.10
1990	8.99	9.22	9.37	9.46	9.47	9.26
1991	9.04	8.83	8.93	8.86	8.86	9.01
1992	8.20	8.29	8.35	8.33	8.28	8.22
1993	7.91	7.71	7.58	7.46	7.43	7.33
1994	6.92	7.08	7.48	7.88	7.99	7.97
1995	8.46	8.26	8.12	8.03	7.65	7.30
1996	6.81	6.99	7.35	7.50	7.62	7.71
1997	7.42	7.31	7.55	7.73	7.58	7.41
1998	6.61	6.67	6.72	6.69	6.69	6.53
1999	6.24	6.40	6.62	6.64	6.93	7.23
2000	7.78	7.68	7.68	7.64	7.99	7.67
2001	7.15	7.10	6.98	7.20	7.29	7.18
2002	6.55	6.51	6.81	6.76	6.75	6.63
2003	6.17	5.95	5.89	5.74	5.22	4.97
2004	5.54	5.50	5.33	5.73	6.04	6.01
2005	5.36	5.20	5.40	5.33	5.15	4.96
2006	5.29	5.35	5.53	5.84	5.95	5.89
2007	5.40	5.39	5.30	5.47	5.47	5.79
2008	5.33	5.53	5.51	5.55	5.57	5.68
2009	5.05	5.27	5.50	5.39	5.54	5.61
2010	5.26	5.35	5.27	5.29	4.96	4.88
2011	5.04	5.22	5.13	5.16	4.96	4.99
2012	3.85	3.85	3.99	3.96	3.80	3.64
2013	3.80	3.90	3.93	3.73	3.89	4.27
2014	4.49	4.45	4.38	4.24	4.16	4.25
2015	3.46	3.61	3.64	3.52	3.98	4.19
2016	4.00	3.96	3.82	3.62	3.65	3.50

* Source: Federal Reserve Bank of St. Louis, monthly data calculated as average of business days

MOODY'S SEASONED CORPORATE Aaa BOND YIELDS

JUL	AUG	SEP	OCT	NOV	DEC	
2.65	2.61	2.64	2.67	2.67	2.67	1950
2.94	2.88	2.84	2.89	2.96	3.01	1951
2.95	2.94	2.95	3.01	2.98	2.97	1952
3.28	3.24	3.29	3.16	3.11	3.13	1953
2.89	2.87	2.89	2.87	2.89	2.90	1954
3.06	3.11	3.13	3.10	3.10	3.15	1955
3.28	3.43	3.56	3.59	3.69	3.75	1956
3.99	4.10	4.12	4.10	4.08	3.81	1957
3.67	3.85	4.09	4.11	4.09	4.08	1958
4.47	4.43	4.52	4.57	4.56	4.58	1959
4.41	4.28	4.25	4.30	4.31	4.35	1960
4.41	4.45	4.45	4.42	4.39	4.42	1961
4.34	4.35	4.32	4.28	4.25	4.24	1962
4.26	4.29	4.31	4.32	4.33	4.35	1963
4.40	4.41	4.42	4.42	4.43	4.44	1964
4.48	4.49	4.52	4.56	4.60	4.68	1965
5.16	5.31	5.49	5.41	5.35	5.39	1966
5.58	5.62	5.65	5.82	6.07	6.19	1967
6.21	0.02	5.97	6.09	6.19	6.45	1968
7.08	6.97	7.14	7.33	7.35	7.72	1969
8.44	8.13	8.09	8.03	8.05	7.64	1970
7.64	7.59	7.44	7.39	7.26	7.25	1971
7.21	7.19	7.22	7.21	7.12	7.08	1972
7.45	7.68	7.63	7.60	7.67	7.68	1973
8.72	9.00	9.24	9.27	8.89	8.89	1974
8.84	8.95	8.95	8.86	8.78	8.79	1975
8.56	8.45	8.38	8.32	8.25	7.98	1976
7.94	7.98	7.92	8.04	8.08	8.19	1977
8.88	8.69	8.69	8.89	9.03	9.16	1978
9.20	9.23	9.44	10.13	10.76	10.74	1979
11.07	11.64	12.02	12.31	12.97	13.21	1980
14.38	14.89	15.49	15.40	14.22	14.23	1981
14.61	13.71	12.94	12.12	11.68	11.83	1982
12.15	12.51	12.37	12.25	12.41	12.57	1983
13.44	12.87	12.66	12.63	12.29	12.13	1984
10.97	11.05	11.07	11.02	10.55	10.16	1985
8.88	8.72	8.89	8.86	8.68	8.49	1986
9.42	9.67	10.18	10.52	10.01	10.11	1987
9.96	10.11	9.82	9.51	9.45	9.57	1988
8.93	8.96	9.01	8.92	8.89	8.86	1989
9.24	9.41	9.56	9.53	9.30	9.05	1990
9.00	8.75	8.61	8.55	8.48	8.31	1991
8.07	7.95	7.92	7.99	8.10	7.98	1992
7.17	6.85	6.66	6.67	6.93	6.93	1993
8.11	8.07	8.34	8.57	8.68	8.46	1994
7.41	7.57	7.32	7.12	7.02	6.82	1995
7.65	7.46	7.66	7.39	7.10	7.20	1996
7.14	7.22	7.15	7.00	6.87	6.76	1997
6.55	6.52	6.40	6.37	6.41	6.22	1998
7.19	7.40	7.39	7.55	7.36	7.55	1999
7.65	7.55	7.62	7.55	7.45	7.21	2000
7.13	7.02	7.17	7.03	6.97	6.77	2001
6.53	6.37	6.15	6.32	6.31	6.21	2002
5.49	5.88	5.72	5.70	5.65	5.62	2003
5.82	5.65	5.46	5.47	5.52	5.47	2004
5.06	5.09	5.13	5.35	5.42	5.37	2005
5.85	5.68	5.51	5.51	5.33	5.32	2006
5.73	5.79	5.74	5.66	5.44	5.49	2007
5.67	5.64	5.65	6.28	6.12	5.05	2008
5.41	5.26	5.13	5.15	5.19	5.26	2009
4.72	4.49	4.53	4.68	4.87	5.02	2010
4.93	4.37	4.09	3.98	3.87	3.93	2011
3.40	3.48	3.49	3.47	3.50	3.65	2012
4.34	4.54	4.64	4.53	4.63	4.62	2013
4.16	4.08	4.11	3.92	3.92	3.79	2014
4.15	4.04	4.07	3.95	4.06	3.97	2015
3.28	3.32	3.41	3.51	3.86	4.06	2016

BOND YIELDS MOODY'S SEASONED CORPORATE Baa*

	JAN	FEB	MAR	APR	MAY	JUN
1950	3.24	3.24	3.24	3.23	3.25	3.28
1951	3.17	3.16	3.23	3.35	3.40	3.49
1952	3.59	3.53	3.51	3.50	3.49	3.50
1953	3.51	3.53	3.57	3.65	3.78	3.86
1954	3.71	3.61	3.51	3.47	3.47	3.49
1955	3.45	3.47	3.48	3.49	3.50	3.51
1956	3.60	3.58	3.60	3.68	3.73	3.76
1957	4.49	4.47	4.43	4.44	4.52	4.63
1958	4.83	4.66	4.68	4.67	4.62	4.55
1959	4.87	4.89	4.85	4.86	4.96	5.04
1960	5.34	5.34	5.25	5.20	5.28	5.26
1961	5.10	5.07	5.02	5.01	5.01	5.03
1962	5.08	5.07	5.04	5.02	5.00	5.02
1963	4.91	4.89	4.88	4.87	4.85	4.84
1964	4.83	4.83	4.83	4.85	4.85	4.85
1965	4.80	4.78	4.78	4.80	4.81	4.85
1966	5.06	5.12	5.32	5.41	5.48	5.58
1967	5.97	5.82	5.85	5.83	5.96	6.15
1968	6.84	6.80	6.85	6.97	7.03	7.07
1969	7.32	7.30	7.51	7.54	7.52	7.70
1970	8.86	8.78	8.63	8.70	8.98	9.25
1971	8.74	8.39	8.46	8.45	8.62	8.75
1972	8.23	8.23	8.24	8.24	8.23	8.20
1973	7.90	7.97	8.03	8.09	8.06	8.13
1974	8.48	8.53	8.62	8.87	9.05	9.27
1975	10.81	10.65	10.48	10.58	10.69	10.62
1976	10.41	10.24	10.12	9.94	9.86	9.89
1977	9.08	9.12	9.12	9.07	9.01	8.91
1978	9.17	9.20	9.22	9.32	9.49	9.60
1979	10.13	10.08	10.26	10.33	10.47	10.38
1980	12.42	13.57	14.45	14.19	13.17	12.71
1981	15.03	15.37	15.34	15.56	15.95	15.80
1982	17.10	17.18	16.82	16.78	16.64	16.92
1983	13.94	13.95	13.61	13.29	13.09	13.37
1984	13.65	13.59	13.99	14.31	14.74	15.05
1985	13.26	13.23	13.69	13.51	13.15	12.40
1986	11.44	11.11	10.50	10.19	10.29	10.34
1987	9.72	9.65	9.61	10.04	10.51	10.52
1988	11.07	10.62	10.57	10.90	11.04	11.00
1989	10.65	10.61	10.67	10.61	10.46	10.03
1990	9.94	10.14	10.21	10.30	10.41	10.22
1991	10.45	10.07	10.09	9.94	9.86	9.96
1992	9.13	9.23	9.25	9.21	9.13	9.05
1993	8.67	8.39	8.15	8.14	8.21	8.07
1994	7.65	7.76	8.13	8.52	8.62	8.65
1995	9.08	8.85	8.70	8.60	8.20	7.90
1996	7.47	7.63	8.03	8.19	8.30	8.40
1997	8.09	7.94	8.18	8.34	8.20	8.02
1998	7.19	7.25	7.32	7.33	7.30	7.13
1999	7.29	7.39	7.53	7.48	7.72	8.02
2000	8.33	8.29	8.37	8.40	8.90	8.48
2001	7.93	7.87	7.84	8.07	8.07	7.97
2002	7.87	7.89	8.11	8.03	8.09	7.95
2003	7.35	7.06	6.95	6.85	6.38	6.19
2004	6.44	6.27	6.11	6.46	6.75	6.78
2005	6.02	5.82	6.06	6.05	6.01	5.86
2006	6.24	6.27	6.41	6.68	6.75	6.78
2007	6.34	6.28	6.27	6.39	6.39	6.70
2008	6.54	6.82	6.89	6.97	6.93	7.07
2009	8.14	8.08	8.42	8.39	8.06	7.50
2010	6.25	6.34	6.27	6.25	6.05	6.23
2011	6.09	6.15	6.03	6.02	5.78	5.75
2012	5.23	5.14	5.23	5.19	5.07	5.02
2013	4.73	4.85	4.85	4.59	4.73	5.19
2014	5.19	5.10	5.06	4.90	4.76	4.80
2015	4.45	4.51	4.54	4.48	4.89	5.13
2016	5.45	5.34	5.13	4.79	4.68	4.53

* Source: Federal Reserve Bank of St. Louis, monthly data calculated as average of business days

MOODY'S SEASONED CORPORATE Baa* BOND YIELDS

JUL	AUG	SEP	OCT	NOV	DEC	
3.32	3.23	3.21	3.22	3.22	3.20	**1950**
3.53	3.50	3.46	3.50	3.56	3.61	**1951**
3.50	3.51	3.52	3.54	3.53	3.51	**1952**
3.86	3.85	3.88	3.82	3.75	3.74	**1953**
3.50	3.49	3.47	3.46	3.45	3.45	**1954**
3.52	3.56	3.59	3.59	3.58	3.62	**1955**
3.80	3.93	4.07	4.17	4.24	4.37	**1956**
4.73	4.82	4.93	4.99	5.09	5.03	**1957**
4.53	4.67	4.87	4.92	4.87	4.85	**1958**
5.08	5.09	5.18	5.28	5.26	5.28	**1959**
5.22	5.08	5.01	5.11	5.08	5.10	**1960**
5.09	5.11	5.12	5.13	5.11	5.10	**1961**
5.05	5.06	5.03	4.99	4.96	4.92	**1962**
4.84	4.83	4.84	4.83	4.84	4.85	**1963**
4.83	4.82	4.82	4.81	4.81	4.81	**1964**
4.88	4.88	4.91	4.93	4.95	5.02	**1965**
5.68	5.83	6.09	6.10	6.13	6.18	**1966**
6.26	6.33	6.40	6.52	6.72	6.93	**1967**
6.98	6.82	6.79	6.84	7.01	7.23	**1968**
7.84	7.86	8.05	8.22	8.25	8.65	**1969**
9.40	9.44	9.39	9.33	9.38	9.12	**1970**
8.76	8.76	8.59	8.48	8.38	8.38	**1971**
8.23	8.19	8.09	8.06	7.99	7.93	**1972**
8.24	8.53	8.63	8.41	8.42	8.48	**1973**
9.48	9.77	10.18	10.48	10.60	10.63	**1974**
10.55	10.59	10.61	10.62	10.56	10.56	**1975**
9.82	9.64	9.40	9.29	9.23	9.12	**1976**
8.87	8.82	8.80	8.89	8.95	8.99	**1977**
9.60	9.48	9.42	9.59	9.83	9.94	**1978**
10.29	10.35	10.54	11.40	11.99	12.06	**1979**
12.65	13.15	13.70	14.23	14.64	15.14	**1980**
16.17	16.34	16.92	17.11	16.39	16.55	**1981**
16.80	16.32	15.63	14.73	14.30	14.14	**1982**
13.39	13.64	13.55	13.46	13.61	13.75	**1983**
15.15	14.63	14.35	13.94	13.48	13.40	**1984**
12.43	12.50	12.48	12.36	11.99	11.58	**1985**
10.16	10.18	10.20	10.24	10.07	9.97	**1986**
10.61	10.80	11.31	11.62	11.23	11.29	**1987**
11.11	11.21	10.90	10.41	10.48	10.65	**1988**
9.87	9.88	9.91	9.81	9.81	9.82	**1989**
10.20	10.41	10.64	10.74	10.62	10.43	**1990**
9.89	9.65	9.51	9.49	9.45	9.26	**1991**
8.84	8.65	8.62	8.84	8.96	8.81	**1992**
7.93	7.60	7.34	7.31	7.66	7.69	**1993**
8.80	8.74	8.98	9.20	9.32	9.10	**1994**
8.04	8.19	7.93	7.75	7.68	7.49	**1995**
8.35	8.18	8.35	8.07	7.79	7.89	**1996**
7.75	7.82	7.70	7.57	7.42	7.32	**1997**
7.15	7.14	7.09	7.18	7.34	7.23	**1998**
7.95	8.15	8.20	8.38	8.15	8.19	**1999**
8.35	8.26	8.35	8.34	8.28	8.02	**2000**
7.97	7.85	8.03	7.91	7.81	8.05	**2001**
7.90	7.58	7.40	7.73	7.62	7.45	**2002**
6.62	7.01	6.79	6.73	6.66	6.60	**2003**
6.62	6.46	6.27	6.21	6.20	6.15	**2004**
5.95	5.96	6.03	6.30	6.39	6.32	**2005**
6.76	6.59	6.43	6.42	6.20	6.22	**2006**
6.65	6.65	6.59	6.48	6.40	6.65	**2007**
7.16	7.15	7.31	8.88	9.21	8.43	**2008**
7.09	6.58	6.31	6.29	6.32	6.37	**2009**
6.01	5.66	5.66	5.72	5.92	6.10	**2010**
5.76	5.36	5.27	5.37	5.14	5.25	**2011**
4.87	4.91	4.84	4.58	4.51	4.63	**2012**
5.32	5.42	5.47	5.31	5.38	5.38	**2013**
4.73	4.69	4.80	4.69	4.79	4.74	**2014**
5.20	5.19	5.34	5.34	5.46	5.46	**2015**
4.22	4.24	4.31	4.38	4.71	4.83	**2016**

COMMODITIES

OIL - WEST TEXAS INTERMEDIATE
CLOSING VALUES $ / bbl

	JAN	FEB	MAR	APR	MAY	JUN
1950	2.6	2.6	2.6	2.6	2.6	2.6
1951	2.6	2.6	2.6	2.6	2.6	2.6
1952	2.6	2.6	2.6	2.6	2.6	2.6
1953	2.6	2.6	2.6	2.6	2.6	2.8
1954	2.8	2.8	2.8	2.8	2.8	2.8
1955	2.8	2.8	2.8	2.8	2.8	2.8
1956	2.8	2.8	2.8	2.8	2.8	2.8
1957	2.8	3.1	3.1	3.1	3.1	3.1
1958	3.1	3.1	3.1	3.1	3.1	3.1
1959	3.0	3.0	3.0	3.0	3.0	3.0
1960	3.0	3.0	3.0	3.0	3.0	3.0
1961	3.0	3.0	3.0	3.0	3.0	3.0
1962	3.0	3.0	3.0	3.0	3.0	3.0
1963	3.0	3.0	3.0	3.0	3.0	3.0
1964	3.0	3.0	3.0	3.0	3.0	3.0
1965	2.9	2.9	2.9	2.9	2.9	2.9
1966	2.9	2.9	2.9	2.9	2.9	2.9
1967	3.0	3.0	3.0	3.0	3.0	3.0
1968	3.1	3.1	3.1	3.1	3.1	3.1
1969	3.1	3.1	3.3	3.4	3.4	3.4
1970	3.4	3.4	3.4	3.4	3.4	3.4
1971	3.6	3.6	3.6	3.6	3.6	3.6
1972	3.6	3.6	3.6	3.6	3.6	3.6
1973	3.6	3.6	3.6	3.6	3.6	3.6
1974	10.1	10.1	10.1	10.1	10.1	10.1
1975	11.2	11.2	11.2	11.2	11.2	11.2
1976	11.2	12.0	12.1	12.2	12.2	12.2
1977	13.9	13.9	13.9	13.9	13.9	13.9
1978	14.9	14.9	14.9	14.9	14.9	14.9
1979	14.9	15.9	15.9	15.9	18.1	19.1
1980	32.5	37.0	38.0	39.5	39.5	39.5
1981	38.0	38.0	38.0	38.0	38.0	36.0
1982	33.9	31.6	28.5	33.5	35.9	35.1
1983	31.2	29.0	28.8	30.6	30.0	31.0
1984	29.7	30.1	30.8	30.6	30.5	30.0
1985	25.6	27.3	28.2	28.8	27.6	27.1
1986	22.9	15.4	12.6	12.8	15.4	13.5
1987	18.7	17.7	18.3	18.6	19.4	20.0
1988	17.2	16.8	16.2	17.9	17.4	16.5
1989	18.0	17.8	19.4	21.0	20.0	20.0
1990	22.6	22.1	20.4	18.6	18.2	16.9
1991	25.0	20.5	19.9	20.8	21.2	20.2
1992	18.8	19.0	18.9	20.2	20.9	22.4
1993	19.1	20.1	20.3	20.3	19.9	19.1
1994	15.0	14.8	14.7	16.4	17.9	19.1
1995	18.0	18.5	18.6	19.9	19.7	18.4
1996	18.9	19.1	21.4	23.6	21.3	20.5
1997	25.2	22.2	21.0	19.7	20.8	19.2
1998	16.7	16.1	15.0	15.4	14.9	13.7
1999	12.5	12.0	14.7	17.3	17.8	17.9
2000	27.2	29.4	29.9	25.7	28.8	31.8
2001	29.6	29.6	27.2	27.4	28.6	27.6
2002	19.7	20.7	24.4	26.3	27.0	25.5
2003	32.9	35.9	33.6	28.3	28.1	30.7
2004	34.3	34.7	36.8	36.7	40.3	38.0
2005	46.8	48.0	54.3	53.0	49.8	56.3
2006	65.5	61.6	62.9	69.7	70.9	71.0
2007	54.6	59.3	60.6	64.0	63.5	67.5
2008	93.0	95.4	105.6	112.6	125.4	133.9
2009	41.7	39.2	48.0	49.8	59.2	69.7
2010	78.2	76.4	81.2	84.5	73.8	75.4
2011	89.4	89.6	102.9	110.0	101.3	96.3
2012	100.3	102.3	106.2	103.3	94.7	82.3
2013	94.8	95.3	92.9	92.0	94.5	95.8
2014	94.6	100.8	100.8	102.1	102.2	105.8
2015	47.2	50.6	47.8	54.5	59.3	59.8
2016	31.7	30.3	37.6	40.8	46.7	48.8

* Source: Federal Reserve

OIL - WEST TEXAS INTERMEDIATE CLOSING VALUES $ / bbl

COMMODITIES

JUL	AUG	SEP	OCT	NOV	DEC	
2.6	2.6	2.6	2.6	2.6	2.6	1950
2.6	2.6	2.6	2.6	2.6	2.6	1951
2.6	2.6	2.6	2.6	2.6	2.6	1952
2.8	2.8	2.8	2.8	2.8	2.8	1953
2.8	2.8	2.8	2.8	2.8	2.8	1954
2.8	2.8	2.8	2.8	2.8	2.8	1955
2.8	2.8	2.8	2.8	2.8	2.8	1956
3.1	3.1	3.1	3.1	3.1	3.0	1957
3.1	3.1	3.1	3.1	3.0	3.0	1958
3.0	3.0	3.0	3.0	3.0	3.0	1959
3.0	3.0	3.0	3.0	3.0	3.0	1960
3.0	3.0	3.0	3.0	3.0	3.0	1961
3.0	3.0	3.0	3.0	3.0	3.0	1962
3.0	3.0	3.0	3.0	3.0	3.0	1963
2.9	2.9	2.9	2.9	2.9	2.9	1964
2.9	2.9	2.9	2.9	2.9	2.9	1965
2.9	2.9	3.0	3.0	3.0	3.0	1966
3.0	3.1	3.1	3.1	3.1	3.1	1967
3.1	3.1	3.1	3.1	3.1	3.1	1968
3.4	3.4	3.4	3.4	3.4	3.4	1969
3.3	3.3	3.3	3.3	3.3	3.6	1970
3.6	3.6	3.6	3.6	3.6	3.6	1971
3.6	3.6	3.6	3.6	3.6	3.6	1972
3.6	4.3	4.3	4.3	4.3	4.3	1973
10.1	10.1	10.1	11.2	11.2	11.2	1974
11.2	11.2	11.2	11.2	11.2	11.2	1975
12.2	12.2	13.9	13.9	13.9	13.9	1976
13.9	14.9	14.9	14.9	14.9	14.9	1977
14.9	14.9	14.9	14.9	14.9	14.9	1978
21.8	26.5	28.5	29.0	31.0	32.5	1979
39.5	38.0	36.0	36.0	36.0	37.0	1980
36.0	36.0	36.0	35.0	36.0	35.0	1981
34.2	34.0	35.6	35.7	34.2	31.7	1982
31.7	31.9	31.1	30.4	29.8	29.2	1983
28.8	29.3	29.3	28.8	28.1	25.4	1984
27.3	27.8	28.3	29.5	30.8	27.2	1985
11.6	15.1	14.9	14.9	15.2	16.1	1986
21.4	20.3	19.5	19.8	18.9	17.2	1987
15.5	15.5	14.5	13.8	14.0	16.3	1988
19.6	18.5	19.6	20.1	19.8	21.1	1989
18.6	27.2	33.7	35.9	32.3	27.3	1990
21.4	21.7	21.9	23.2	22.5	19.5	1991
21.8	21.4	21.9	21.7	20.3	19.4	1992
17.9	18.0	17.5	18.1	16.7	14.5	1993
19.7	18.4	17.5	17.7	18.1	17.2	1994
17.3	18.0	18.2	17.4	18.0	19.0	1995
21.3	22.0	24.0	24.9	23.7	25.4	1996
19.6	19.9	19.8	21.3	20.2	18.3	1997
14.1	13.4	15.0	14.4	12.9	11.3	1998
20.1	21.3	23.9	22.6	25.0	26.1	1999
29.8	31.2	33.9	33.1	34.4	28.5	2000
26.5	27.5	25.9	22.2	19.7	19.3	2001
26.9	28.4	29.7	28.9	26.3	29.4	2002
30.8	31.6	28.3	30.3	31.1	32.2	2003
40.7	44.9	46.0	53.1	48.5	43.3	2004
58.7	65.0	65.6	62.4	58.3	59.4	2005
74.4	73.1	63.9	58.9	59.4	62.0	2006
74.2	72.4	79.9	86.2	94.6	91.7	2007
133.4	116.6	103.9	76.7	57.4	41.0	2008
64.1	71.1	69.5	75.6	78.1	74.3	2009
76.4	76.8	75.3	81.9	84.1	89.0	2010
97.2	86.3	85.6	86.4	97.2	98.6	2011
87.9	94.2	94.7	89.6	86.7	88.3	2012
104.7	106.6	106.3	100.5	93.9	97.6	2013
103.6	96.5	93.2	84.4	75.8	59.3	2014
50.9	42.9	45.5	46.2	42.4	37.2	2015
44.7	44.7	45.2	49.8	45.7	52.0	2016

GOLD $US/OZ LONDON PM MONTH CLOSE

	JAN	FEB	MAR	APR	MAY	JUN
1970	34.9	35.0	35.1	35.6	36.0	35.4
1971	37.9	38.7	38.9	39.0	40.5	40.1
1972	45.8	48.3	48.3	49.0	54.6	62.1
1973	65.1	74.2	84.4	90.5	102.0	120.1
1974	129.2	150.2	168.4	172.2	163.3	154.1
1975	175.8	181.8	178.2	167.0	167.0	166.3
1976	128.2	132.3	129.6	128.4	125.5	123.8
1977	132.3	142.8	148.9	147.3	143.0	143.0
1978	175.8	182.3	181.6	170.9	184.2	183.1
1979	233.7	251.3	240.1	245.3	274.6	277.5
1980	653.0	637.0	494.5	518.0	535.5	653.5
1981	506.5	489.0	513.8	482.8	479.3	426.0
1982	387.0	362.6	320.0	361.3	325.3	317.5
1983	499.5	408.5	414.8	429.3	437.5	416.0
1984	373.8	394.3	388.5	375.8	384.3	373.1
1985	306.7	287.8	329.3	321.4	314.0	317.8
1986	350.5	338.2	344.0	345.8	343.2	345.5
1987	400.5	405.9	405.9	453.3	451.0	447.3
1988	458.0	426.2	457.0	449.0	455.5	436.6
1989	394.0	387.0	383.2	377.6	361.8	373.0
1990	415.1	407.7	368.5	367.8	363.1	352.2
1991	366.0	362.7	355.7	357.8	360.4	368.4
1992	354.1	353.1	341.7	336.4	337.5	343.4
1993	330.5	327.6	337.8	354.3	374.8	378.5
1994	377.9	381.6	389.2	376.5	387.6	388.3
1995	374.9	376.4	392.0	389.8	384.3	387.1
1996	405.6	400.7	396.4	391.3	390.6	382.0
1997	345.5	358.6	348.2	340.2	345.6	334.6
1998	304.9	297.4	301.0	310.7	293.6	296.3
1999	285.4	287.1	279.5	286.6	268.6	261.0
2000	283.3	293.7	276.8	275.1	272.3	288.2
2001	264.5	266.7	257.7	263.2	267.5	270.6
2002	282.3	296.9	301.4	308.2	326.6	318.5
2003	367.5	347.5	334.9	336.8	361.4	346.0
2004	399.8	395.9	423.7	388.5	393.3	395.8
2005	422.2	435.5	427.5	435.7	414.5	437.1
2006	568.8	556.0	582.0	644.0	653.0	613.5
2007	650.5	664.2	661.8	677.0	659.1	650.5
2008	923.3	971.5	933.5	871.0	885.8	930.3
2009	919.5	952.0	916.5	883.3	975.5	934.5
2010	1078.5	1108.3	1115.5	1179.3	1207.5	1244.0
2011	1327.0	1411.0	1439.0	1535.5	1536.5	1505.5
2012	1744.0	1770.0	1662.5	1651.3	1558.0	1598.5
2013	1664.8	1588.5	1598.3	1469.0	1394.5	1192.0
2014	1251.0	1326.5	1291.75	1288.5	1250.5	1315.0
2015	1260.3	1214.0	1187.0	1180.3	1191.4	1171.0
2016	1111.8	1234.9	1237.0	1285.7	1212.1	1320.8

* Source: Bank of England

GOLD $US/OZ LONDON PM MONTH CLOSE

JUL	AUG	SEP	OCT	NOV	DEC	
35.3	35.4	36.2	37.5	37.4	37.4	**1970**
41.0	42.7	42.0	42.5	42.9	43.5	**1971**
65.7	67.0	65.5	64.9	62.9	63.9	**1972**
120.2	106.8	103.0	100.1	94.8	106.7	**1973**
143.0	154.6	151.8	158.8	181.7	183.9	**1974**
166.7	159.8	141.3	142.9	138.2	140.3	**1975**
112.5	104.0	116.0	123.2	130.3	134.5	**1976**
144.1	146.0	154.1	161.5	160.1	165.0	**1977**
200.3	208.7	217.1	242.6	193.4	226.0	**1978**
296.5	315.1	397.3	382.0	415.7	512.0	**1979**
614.3	631.3	666.8	629.0	619.8	589.8	**1980**
406.0	425.5	428.8	427.0	414.5	397.5	**1981**
342.9	411.5	397.0	423.3	436.0	456.9	**1982**
422.0	414.3	405.0	382.0	405.0	382.4	**1983**
342.4	348.3	343.8	333.5	329.0	309.0	**1984**
327.5	333.3	326.5	325.1	325.3	326.8	**1985**
357.5	384.7	423.2	401.0	383.5	388.8	**1986**
462.5	453.4	459.5	468.8	492.5	484.1	**1987**
436.8	427.8	397.7	412.4	422.6	410.3	**1988**
368.3	359.8	366.5	375.3	408.2	398.6	**1989**
372.3	387.8	408.4	379.5	384.9	386.2	**1990**
362.9	347.4	354.9	357.5	366.3	353.2	**1991**
357.9	340.0	349.0	339.3	334.2	332.9	**1992**
401.8	371.6	355.5	369.6	370.9	391.8	**1993**
384.0	385.8	394.9	383.9	383.1	383.3	**1994**
383.4	382.4	384.0	382.7	387.8	387.0	**1995**
385.3	386.5	379.0	379.5	371.3	369.3	**1996**
326.4	325.4	332.1	311.4	296.8	290.2	**1997**
288.9	273.4	293.9	292.3	294.7	287.8	**1998**
255.6	254.8	299.0	299.1	291.4	290.3	**1999**
276.8	277.0	273.7	264.5	269.1	274.5	**2000**
265.9	273.0	293.1	278.8	275.5	276.5	**2001**
304.7	312.8	323.7	316.9	319.1	347.2	**2002**
354.8	375.6	388.0	386.3	398.4	416.3	**2003**
391.4	407.3	415.7	425.6	453.4	435.6	**2004**
429.0	433.3	473.3	470.8	495.7	513.0	**2005**
632.5	623.5	599.3	603.8	646.7	632.0	**2006**
665.5	672.0	743.0	789.5	783.5	833.8	**2007**
918.0	833.0	884.5	730.8	814.5	869.8	**2008**
939.0	955.5	995.8	1040.0	1175.8	1087.5	**2009**
1169.0	1246.0	1307.0	1346.8	1383.5	1405.5	**2010**
1628.5	1813.5	1620.0	1722.0	1746.0	1531.0	**2011**
1622.0	1648.5	1776.0	1719.0	1726.0	1657.5	**2012**
1314.5	1394.8	1326.5	1324.0	1253.0	1204.5	**2013**
1285.3	1285.8	1216.5	1164.8	1282.8	1206.0	**2014**
1098.4	1135.0	1114.0	1142.4	1061.9	1060.0	**2015**
1342.0	1309.3	1322.5	1272.0	1178.1	1145.9	**2016**

FOREIGN EXCHANGE

FOREIGN EXCHANGE — US DOLLAR vs CDN DOLLAR MONTHLY AVG. VALUES*

| | JAN | | FEB | | MAR | | APR | | MAY | | JUN | |
	US / CDN	CDN / US	US / CDN	CDN / US	US / CDN	CDN /US	US / CDN	CDN / US	US / CDN	CDN / US	US / CDN	CDN / US
1971	1.01	0.99	1.01	0.99	1.01	0.99	1.01	0.99	1.01	0.99	1.02	0.98
1972	1.01	0.99	1.00	1.00	1.00	1.00	1.00	1.00	0.99	1.01	0.98	1.02
1973	1.00	1.00	1.00	1.00	1.00	1.00	1.00	1.00	1.00	1.00	1.00	1.00
1974	0.99	1.01	0.98	1.02	0.97	1.03	0.97	1.03	0.96	1.04	0.97	1.03
1975	0.99	1.01	1.00	1.00	1.00	1.00	1.01	0.99	1.03	0.97	1.03	0.97
1976	1.01	0.99	0.99	1.01	0.99	1.01	0.98	1.02	0.98	1.02	0.97	1.03
1977	1.01	0.99	1.03	0.97	1.05	0.95	1.05	0.95	1.05	0.95	1.06	0.95
1978	1.10	0.91	1.11	0.90	1.13	0.89	1.14	0.88	1.12	0.89	1.12	0.89
1979	1.19	0.84	1.20	0.84	1.17	0.85	1.15	0.87	1.16	0.87	1.17	0.85
1980	1.16	0.86	1.16	0.87	1.17	0.85	1.19	0.84	1.17	0.85	1.15	0.87
1981	1.19	0.84	1.20	0.83	1.19	0.84	1.19	0.84	1.20	0.83	1.20	0.83
1982	1.19	0.84	1.21	0.82	1.22	0.82	1.23	0.82	1.23	0.81	1.28	0.78
1983	1.23	0.81	1.23	0.81	1.23	0.82	1.23	0.81	1.23	0.81	1.23	0.81
1984	1.25	0.80	1.25	0.80	1.27	0.79	1.28	0.78	1.29	0.77	1.30	0.77
1985	1.32	0.76	1.35	0.74	1.38	0.72	1.37	0.73	1.38	0.73	1.37	0.73
1986	1.41	0.71	1.40	0.71	1.40	0.71	1.39	0.72	1.38	0.73	1.39	0.72
1987	1.36	0.73	1.33	0.75	1.32	0.76	1.32	0.76	1.34	0.75	1.34	0.75
1988	1.29	0.78	1.27	0.79	1.25	0.80	1.24	0.81	1.24	0.81	1.22	0.82
1989	1.19	0.84	1.19	0.84	1.20	0.84	1.19	0.84	1.19	0.84	1.20	0.83
1990	1.17	0.85	1.20	0.84	1.18	0.85	1.16	0.86	1.17	0.85	1.17	0.85
1991	1.16	0.87	1.15	0.87	1.16	0.86	1.15	0.87	1.15	0.87	1.14	0.87
1992	1.16	0.86	1.18	0.85	1.19	0.84	1.19	0.84	1.20	0.83	1.20	0.84
1993	1.28	0.78	1.26	0.79	1.25	0.80	1.26	0.79	1.27	0.79	1.28	0.78
1994	1.32	0.76	1.34	0.74	1.36	0.73	1.38	0.72	1.38	0.72	1.38	0.72
1995	1.41	0.71	1.40	0.71	1.41	0.71	1.38	0.73	1.36	0.73	1.38	0.73
1996	1.37	0.73	1.38	0.73	1.37	0.73	1.36	0.74	1.37	0.73	1.37	0.73
1997	1.35	0.74	1.36	0.74	1.37	0.73	1.39	0.72	1.38	0.72	1.38	0.72
1998	1.44	0.69	1.43	0.70	1.42	0.71	1.43	0.70	1.45	0.69	1.47	0.68
1999	1.52	0.66	1.50	0.67	1.52	0.66	1.49	0.67	1.46	0.68	1.47	0.68
2000	1.45	0.69	1.45	0.69	1.46	0.68	1.47	0.68	1.50	0.67	1.48	0.68
2001	1.50	0.67	1.52	0.66	1.56	0.64	1.56	0.64	1.54	0.65	1.52	0.66
2002	1.60	0.63	1.60	0.63	1.59	0.63	1.58	0.63	1.55	0.65	1.53	0.65
2003	1.54	0.65	1.51	0.66	1.48	0.68	1.46	0.69	1.38	0.72	1.35	0.74
2004	1.30	0.77	1.33	0.75	1.33	0.75	1.34	0.75	1.38	0.73	1.36	0.74
2005	1.22	0.82	1.24	0.81	1.22	0.82	1.24	0.81	1.26	0.80	1.24	0.81
2006	1.16	0.86	1.15	0.87	1.16	0.86	1.14	0.87	1.11	0.90	1.11	0.90
2007	1.18	0.85	1.17	0.85	1.17	0.86	1.14	0.88	1.10	0.91	1.07	0.94
2008	1.01	0.99	1.00	1.00	1.00	1.00	1.01	0.99	1.00	1.00	1.02	0.98
2009	1.22	0.82	1.25	0.80	1.26	0.79	1.22	0.82	1.15	0.87	1.13	0.89
2010	1.04	0.96	1.06	0.95	1.02	0.98	1.01	0.99	1.04	0.96	1.04	0.96
2011	0.99	1.01	0.99	1.01	0.98	1.02	0.96	1.04	0.97	1.03	0.98	1.02
2012	1.01	0.99	1.00	1.00	0.99	1.01	0.99	1.01	1.01	0.99	1.03	0.97
2013	0.99	1.01	1.01	0.99	1.02	.098	1.02	0.98	1.02	0.98	1.03	0.97
2014	1.09	0.91	1.11	0.90	1.11	0.90	1.10	0.91	1.09	0.92	1.08	0.92
2015	1.21	0.82	1.25	0.80	1.26	0.79	1.23	0.81	1.22	0.82	1.24	0.81
2016	1.42	0.70	1.38	0.72	1.32	0.76	1,28	0.78	1.29	0.77	1.29	0.78

Source: Federal Reserve: Avg of daily rates, noon buying rates in New York City for cable transfers payable in foreign currencies

US DOLLAR vs CDN DOLLAR
MONTHLY AVG. VALUES

JUL US/CDN	JUL CDN/US	AUG US/CDN	AUG CDN/US	SEP US/CDN	SEP CDN/US	OCT US/CDN	OCT CDN/US	NOV US/CDN	NOV CDN/US	DEC US/CDN	DEC CDN/US	Year
1.02	0.98	1.01	0.99	1.01	0.99	1.00	1.00	1.00	1.00	1.00	1.00	1971
0.98	1.02	0.98	1.02	0.98	1.02	0.98	1.02	0.99	1.01	1.00	1.00	1972
1.00	1.00	1.00	1.00	1.01	0.99	1.00	1.00	1.00	1.00	1.00	1.00	1973
0.98	1.02	0.98	1.02	0.99	1.01	0.98	1.02	0.99	1.01	0.99	1.01	1974
1.03	0.97	1.04	0.97	1.03	0.97	1.03	0.98	1.01	0.99	1.01	0.99	1975
0.97	1.03	0.99	1.01	0.98	1.03	0.97	1.03	0.99	1.01	1.02	0.98	1976
1.06	0.94	1.08	0.93	1.07	0.93	1.10	0.91	1.11	0.90	1.10	0.91	1977
1.12	0.89	1.14	0.88	1.17	0.86	1.18	0.85	1.17	0.85	1.18	0.85	1978
1.16	0.86	1.17	0.85	1.17	0.86	1.18	0.85	1.18	0.85	1.17	0.85	1979
1.15	0.87	1.16	0.86	1.16	0.86	1.17	0.86	1.19	0.84	1.20	0.84	1980
1.21	0.83	1.22	0.82	1.20	0.83	1.20	0.83	1.19	0.84	1.19	0.84	1981
1.27	0.79	1.25	0.80	1.23	0.81	1.23	0.81	1.23	0.82	1.24	0.81	1982
1.23	0.81	1.23	0.81	1.23	0.81	1.23	0.81	1.24	0.81	1.25	0.80	1983
1.32	0.76	1.30	0.77	1.31	0.76	1.32	0.76	1.32	0.76	1.32	0.76	1984
1.35	0.74	1.36	0.74	1.37	0.73	1.37	0.73	1.38	0.73	1.40	0.72	1985
1.38	0.72	1.39	0.72	1.39	0.72	1.39	0.72	1.39	0.72	1.38	0.72	1986
1.33	0.75	1.33	0.75	1.32	0.76	1.31	0.76	1.32	0.76	1.31	0.76	1987
1.21	0.83	1.22	0.82	1.23	0.82	1.21	0.83	1.22	0.82	1.20	0.84	1988
1.19	0.84	1.18	0.85	1.18	0.85	1.17	0.85	1.17	0.85	1.16	0.86	1989
1.16	0.86	1.14	0.87	1.16	0.86	1.16	0.86	1.16	0.86	1.16	0.86	1990
1.15	0.87	1.15	0.87	1.14	0.88	1.13	0.89	1.13	0.88	1.15	0.87	1991
1.19	0.84	1.19	0.84	1.22	0.82	1.25	0.80	1.27	0.79	1.27	0.79	1992
1.28	0.78	1.31	0.76	1.32	0.76	1.33	0.75	1.32	0.76	1.33	0.75	1993
1.38	0.72	1.38	0.73	1.35	0.74	1.35	0.74	1.36	0.73	1.39	0.72	1994
1.36	0.73	1.36	0.74	1.35	0.74	1.35	0.74	1.35	0.74	1.37	0.73	1995
1.37	0.73	1.37	0.73	1.37	0.73	1.35	0.74	1.34	0.75	1.36	0.73	1996
1.38	0.73	1.39	0.72	1.39	0.72	1.39	0.72	1.41	0.71	1.43	0.70	1997
1.49	0.67	1.53	0.65	1.52	0.66	1.55	0.65	1.54	0.65	1.54	0.65	1998
1.49	0.67	1.49	0.67	1.48	0.68	1.48	0.68	1.47	0.68	1.47	0.68	1999
1.48	0.68	1.48	0.67	1.49	0.67	1.51	0.66	1.54	0.65	1.52	0.66	2000
1.53	0.65	1.54	0.65	1.57	0.64	1.57	0.64	1.59	0.63	1.58	0.63	2001
1.55	0.65	1.57	0.64	1.58	0.63	1.58	0.63	1.57	0.64	1.56	0.64	2002
1.38	0.72	1.40	0.72	1.36	0.73	1.32	0.76	1.31	0.76	1.31	0.76	2003
1.32	0.76	1.31	0.76	1.29	0.78	1.25	0.80	1.20	0.84	1.22	0.82	2004
1.22	0.82	1.20	0.83	1.18	0.85	1.18	0.85	1.18	0.85	1.16	0.86	2005
1.13	0.89	1.12	0.89	1.12	0.90	1.13	0.89	1.14	0.88	1.15	0.87	2006
1.05	0.95	1.06	0.95	1.03	0.97	0.98	1.03	0.97	1.03	1.00	1.00	2007
1.01	0.99	1.05	0.95	1.06	0.95	1.18	0.84	1.22	0.82	1.23	0.81	2008
1.12	0.89	1.09	0.92	1.08	0.92	1.05	0.95	1.06	0.94	1.05	0.95	2009
1.04	0.96	1.04	0.96	1.03	0.97	1.02	0.98	1.01	0.99	1.01	0.99	2010
0.96	1.05	0.98	1.02	1.00	1.00	1.02	0.98	1.02	0.98	1.02	0.98	2011
1.01	0.99	0.99	1.01	.098	1.02	0.99	1.01	1.00	1.00	0.99	1.01	2012
1.04	0.96	1.04	0.96	1.03	0.97	1.04	0.96	1.05	0.95	1.06	0.94	2013
1.07	0.93	1.09	0.92	1.10	0.91	1.12	0.89	1.13	0.88	1.15	0.87	2014
1.29	0.78	1.31	0.76	1.33	0.75	1.31	0.76	1.33	0.75	1.37	0.73	2015
1.31	0.77	1.30	0.77	1.31	0.76	1.33	0.75	1.34	0.74	1.33	0.75	2016

U.S. DOLLAR vs EURO
MONTHLY AVG. VALUES

	JAN		FEB		MAR		APR		MAY		JUN	
	EUR /US	US / EUR	EUR /US	US / EUR	EUR /US	US / EUR	EUR /US	US / EUR	EUR /US	US / EUR	EUR /US	US / EUR
1999	1.16	0.86	1.12	0.89	1.09	0.92	1.07	0.93	1.06	0.94	1.04	0.96
2000	1.01	0.99	0.98	1.02	0.96	1.04	0.94	1.06	0.91	1.10	0.95	1.05
2001	0.94	1.07	0.92	1.09	0.91	1.10	0.89	1.12	0.88	1.14	0.85	1.17
2002	0.88	1.13	0.87	1.15	0.88	1.14	0.89	1.13	0.92	1.09	0.96	1.05
2003	1.06	0.94	1.08	0.93	1.08	0.93	1.09	0.92	1.16	0.87	1.17	0.86
2004	1.26	0.79	1.26	0.79	1.23	0.82	1.20	0.83	1.20	0.83	1.21	0.82
2005	1.31	0.76	1.30	0.77	1.32	0.76	1.29	0.77	1.27	0.79	1.22	0.82
2006	1.21	0.82	1.19	0.84	1.20	0.83	1.23	0.81	1.28	0.78	1.27	0.79
2007	1.30	0.77	1.31	0.76	1.32	0.75	1.35	0.74	1.35	0.74	1.34	0.75
2008	1.47	0.68	1.48	0.68	1.55	0.64	1.58	0.63	1.56	0.64	1.56	0.64
2009	1.32	0.76	1.28	0.78	1.31	0.77	1.32	0.76	1.36	0.73	1.40	0.71
2010	1.43	0.70	1.37	0.73	1.36	0.74	1.34	0.75	1.26	0.80	1.22	0.82
2011	1.34	0.75	1.37	0.73	1.40	0.71	1.45	0.69	1.43	0.70	1.44	0.69
2012	1.29	0.77	1.32	0.76	1.32	0.76	1.32	0.76	1.28	0.78	1.25	0.80
2013	1.33	0.75	1.33	0.75	1.30	0.77	1.30	0.77	1.30	0.77	1.32	0.76
2014	1.36	0.73	1.37	0.73	1.38	0.72	1.38	0.72	1.37	0.73	1.36	0.74
2015	1.16	0.86	1.14	0.88	1.08	0.92	1.08	0.92	1.12	0.90	1.12	0.89
2016	1.09	0.92	1.11	0.90	1.11	0.90	1.13	0.88	1.13	0.88	1.12	0.89

Source: Federal Reserve: Avg of daily rates, noon buying rates in New York City for cable transfers payable in foreign currencies

US DOLLAR vs EURO
MONTHLY AVG. VALUES

FOREIGN EXCHANGE

JUL		AUG		SEP		OCT		NOV		DEC		
EUR / US	US / EUR	EUR / US	US / EUR	EUR / US	US / EUR	EUR / US	US / EUR	EUR / US	US / EUR	EUR / US	US / EUR	
1.04	0.96	1.06	0.94	1.05	0.95	1.07	0.93	1.03	0.97	1.01	0.99	1999
0.94	1.07	0.90	1.11	0.87	1.15	0.85	1.17	0.86	1.17	0.90	1.11	2000
0.86	1.16	0.90	1.11	0.91	1.10	0.91	1.10	0.89	1.13	0.89	1.12	2001
0.99	1.01	0.08	1.02	0.98	1.02	0.98	1.02	1.00	1.00	1.02	0.98	2002
1.14	0.88	1.12	0.90	1.13	0.89	1.17	0.85	1.17	0.85	1.23	0.81	2003
1.23	0.82	1.22	0.82	1.22	0.82	1.25	0.80	1.30	0.77	1.34	0.75	2004
1.20	0.83	1.23	0.81	1.22	0.82	1.20	0.83	1.18	0.85	1.19	0.84	2005
1.27	0.79	1.28	0.78	1.27	0.79	1.26	0.79	1.29	0.78	1.32	0.76	2006
1.37	0.73	1.36	0.73	1.39	0.72	1.42	0.70	1.47	0.68	1.46	0.69	2007
1.58	0.63	1.50	0.67	1.43	0.70	1.33	0.75	1.27	0.78	1.35	0.74	2008
1.41	0.71	1.43	0.70	1.46	0.69	1.48	0.67	1.49	0.67	1.46	0.69	2009
1.28	0.78	1.29	0.78	1.31	0.76	1.39	0.72	1.37	0.73	1.32	0.76	2010
1.43	0.70	1.43	0.70	1.37	0.73	1.37	0.73	1.36	0.74	1.32	0.76	2011
1.23	0.81	1.24	0.81	1.29	0.78	1.30	0.77	1.28	0.78	1.31	0.76	2012
1.31	0.76	1.33	0.75	1.34	0.75	1.36	0.73	1.35	0.74	1.37	0.73	2013
1.35	0.74	1.33	0.75	1.29	0.78	1.27	0.79	1.25	0.80	1.23	0.81	2014
1.10	0.91	1.11	0.90	1.12	0.89	1.12	0.89	1.07	0.93	1.09	0.92	2015
1.11	0.90	1.12	0.89	1.12	0.89	1.10	0.91	1.08	0.93	1.05	0.95	2016